MAKING SILENCE SPEAK

WOMEN'S VOICES IN GREEK LITERATURE AND SOCIETY

Edited by

André Lardinois and Laura McClure

PRINCETON UNIVERSITY PRESS   PRINCETON AND OXFORD

Library of Congress Cataloging-in-Publication Data

Making silence speak : women's voices in Greek literature and society /
edited by André Lardinois and Laura McClure.
p.   cm.
Includes bibliographical references and index.
ISBN 0-691-00465-X (alk. paper) —
ISBN 0-691-00466-8 (pbk. : alk. paper)
1. Greek literature—History and criticism.   2. Women and
literature—Greece.   3. Greek literature—Women authors—History
and criticism.   4. Women—Greece—Social conditions.
5. Greek language—Spoken Greek.   6. Speech in literature.
7. Women in literature.   I.
Lardinois, A. P. M. H., 1961–   II. McClure, Laura, 1959–
PA3067.M35   2001
88.9′352042—dc21   00-033648

This book has been composed in Janson

The paper used in this publication meets the minimum
requirements of ANSI/NISO
Z39.48-1992 (R 1997) (*Permanence of Paper*)

www.pup.princeton.edu

Printed in the United States of America

1   3   5   7   9   10   8   6   4   2

1   3   5   7   9   10   8   6   4   2

(Pbk.)

For Our Children

παισὶν ἀγαπητοῖς

NINA AND DYLAN

NIKOLAS, JAKOB, AND GABRIEL

Contents

Acknowledgments

THIS BOOK took less time than we anticipated, thanks to the diligence of our contributors, the expertise of the staff at Princeton University Press, the support of colleagues and friends, and the relative patience of our families. First, we would like to thank our contributors for meeting (most of) our deadlines and for putting their faith and work in the hands of two untenured and relatively unknown young classicists. The same can be said for the Classics editors at Princeton, first Brigitta van Rheinberg, whose enthusiasm for the project made the process of submission and revision almost painless, and later Chuck Myers, under whose supervision the book was brought to press. Their editorial assistants, Mark Spencer and Rebecca Myers, provided us with timely responses to our queries and facilitated the editing of the entire manuscript. Our copyeditor, Sherry Wert, helped to catch numerous omissions and inconsistencies, and to refine the style of several of the chapters. Finally, the detailed and sometimes conflicting observations of the two anonymous referees greatly improved individual chapters and the coherence of the book as a whole.

Special thanks go to Froma Zeitlin, who first introduced us to the press and who continued to support the project with her advice. Her work forms the inspiration for many of the chapters in this book. We would also like to thank our departments and home institutions for giving us the space and financial support to complete this project. Generous assistance was provided by the McKnight Landgrant Professorhip Program at the University of Minnesota, and by the Graduate School at the University of Wisconsin at Madison. Our graduate assistants, Michelle Lewis and Matt Semanoff, merit special recognition for helping us prepare the final manuscript.

The jacket illustration shows a red-figure *hydria* by Phintias, c. 520 B.C.E. It depicts two reclining women engaged in a game called *kottabos*. The purpose of this game, which was played at symposia, is to fling some wine from a cup onto a target after dedicating the shot to a loved one (see Lissarrague 1987 [1990]: 80–86). One of the women on the *hydria* addresses the other with the phrase *soi tendi*, "This one is for you." Her words, directed to the other woman but read by the male participants at the drinking parties where this vase was displayed, illustrate the appropriation of a female voice by a male artist for a male audience.

This book has been completed in households far from silent; our children make silence speak every day, and in fact, one of them was born into the din during final preparation of the manuscript. Individually, Laura would like to recognize her husband Richard, and André his wife Cécile, for shielding them from some of this noise and for conversing with them about things other than Euripides or Erinna. Our children, however, have been our greatest distractions, in more sense than one. This book is dedicated to them: may they grow up in a world where all voices can be heard.

List of Illustrations

Note on Abbreviations, Texts, and Translations

Names of ancient authors and titles of texts are abbreviated in accordance with the list in *The Oxford Classical Dictionary*, 3d ed. (1996), xxix–liv. Unless otherwise specified, Greek and Latin authors are quoted from the Oxford Classical Texts, but the early Greek lyric poets are cited from Campbell 1982–93; the early Greek iambic and elegiac poets from West 1989–92; and the poet Pindar according to the text editions of Snell and Maehler 1987 (the *epinicia*) or Maehler 1989 (the fragments). All Greek and Latin are translated, and the translations are the authors' own, unless noted otherwise.

MAKING SILENCE SPEAK

CHAPTER ONE

Introduction

LAURA McCLURE

THE STUDY of status of women and the social construction of gender in the ancient world has had a substantial impact on the field of classical studies since the mid-1970s, although its roots extend back to the late nineteenth century.[1] An increasingly important part of this project has been the study of women's speech and its political and social implications as represented in male-authored texts. Equally critical to the understanding of ancient women has been a new body of work devoted to the question of female subjectivity in both archaic and Hellenistic women poets. While these individual areas have raised the issue of women's speech and its representations, there has been no single sustained study that provides a comprehensive perspective on a variety of sources from diverse historical periods. This collection seeks to fill that gap by offering a wide range of interpretations of women's voices found in both familiar and lesser-known ancient texts. The term "voice" is deliberately broad: it includes not only the few remaining genuine women's voices but also the ways in which male authors render women's speech and the social assumptions such representations reflect and reinforce. This collection, therefore, does not simply attempt to recover the voices of actual ancient women, although that is certainly one of its goals; it also explores how fictional female voices can serve to negotiate complex political, epistemological, and aesthetic issues.[2]

Several ancient Greek sources suggest that men understood women to speak differently. Aristophanes offers two well-known examples in his *Thesmophoriazusae* and *Ecclesiazusae*, two comedies that hinge on scenes of crossdressing and verbal impersonation. In the *Thesmophoriazusae*, a play produced in Athens around 411 B.C.E., the tragic poet Euripides asks his relative, Mnesilochus, to infiltrate the women's celebration of the Thesmophoria and to defend him against charges of slandering women in the

---

[1] Blok 1987.

[2] Literary representations of women may be viewed as male constructs appropriated by men for the purpose of speaking about male concerns rather than as simple reflections of social reality, as Zeitlin, Halperin, and others have argued; see Zeitlin [1985] 1996; Padel 1983; Foley 1988: 1301–2; Halperin 1990b: 298. Most recently, Stehle 1997 discusses how some archaic lyric poetry deploys female voices to convey a male political idea.

theater. The Relative eventually agrees to this scheme, allowing himself to be depilated and dressed as a woman. Once disguised, Euripides enjoins him to speak like a woman (Ar. *Thesm.* 267–68). Presumably he refers not to the pitch of the voice, but to the oaths, case endings, and other linguistic features appropriate to women's speech, an interpretation confirmed by the Relative's impudent reply: "Not by *Apollo*, unless you swear to . . . " (Ar. *Thesm.* 269). In swearing by a male deity, the Relative comically undermines Euripides' injunction.[3] When the tragic poet agrees to rescue him should their plan go awry, the Relative adopts the appropriate markers of female speech, referring to himself with feminine participles (λαβοῦσα, 285; ἔχουσαν, 288). Much of the humor of the play's subsequent scenes derives from the fact that the Relative cannot fully maintain his female persona: his use of scatalogical obscenity and confusion of gender pronouns in the escape scene continually hint at his masculine identity.

Aristophanes' *Ecclesiazusae*, produced at the beginning of the fourth century B.C.E., similarly features a scene of cross-dressing: Athenian matrons disguise themselves as men in order to gain access to a masculine civic space, the Assembly, where they put forward their proposal to take control of the government. In the first part of the play, the women gather in their husbands' clothes to rehearse their parts as rural members of the Assembly. Their leader, Praxagora, guides their rehearsal, exhorting them to speak like men (Ar. *Eccl.* 149–50). She refers not merely to the conventional grammatical markers of male speech such as case endings, forms of address, and oaths, but also to the male declamatory practices of the Assembly that would have accompanied the holding of the staff and the wearing of the speaker's garland.[4] The inaccuracies revealed by the matrons' impersonation of male speech indicate what the Athenian spectators would have considered distinct about women's speech, for example, their lack of familiarity with formal rhetoric, their preoccupation with domestic activities, and their use of feminine oaths (*Eccl.* 155–89). Once they have outfitted themselves and practiced their lines, the women follow the conventions of normal male speech, using the appropriate case endings (291a, 291b, 292a, 292b, 294, 295, 297), addressing themselves as men (ὧνδρες, 285), and calling themselves by common male names (Χαριτιμίδη, Σμίκυθε, Δράκης, 293). While these two scenes from Attic Old Comedy may shed little light on the everyday speech of actual women, they nonetheless illustrate how a comic poet could exploit associations between a speaker's gender and speaking style for humorous effect.[5]

---

[3] Sommerstein 1995: 65; cf. Ar. *Eccl.* 158–60, and the exceptional example, *Lys.* 917.

[4] On the staff, cf. Ar. *Eccl.* 150, 276–77, 546; on the speaker's wreath, cf. 131, 148, 163.

[5] Sources such as Plato and Herodotus suggest that the ancient Greeks considered the speech of women to have been linguistically distinct from that of men. Plato remarks in the *Cratylus* that women's speech tends to be linguistically conservative, retaining the features of

In other texts, the female voice may serve as a vehicle for rendering alterity: thus the nine Muses, as patrons of poetry, are figured as lending their voices to male poets. The Muses embody what Bergren has termed the "double nature of female discourse," since they are represented as capable of two contradictory speaking modes, those of truth and deception.[6] She correlates this ambiguity to women's primary sign-making activity, weaving, an art that serves as a metaphor not only for cunning, trickery, and deception, but also for poetry and poetic narrative. Because of the pervasive association between women and deception, classical writers like Gorgias and Plato assimilate the art of rhetoric to the female through figures such as Helen and courtesans like Aspasia, a tradition that continues through second sophistic literature in works such as the *Dining Sophists* of Athenaeus.[7] The witty and seductive courtesan embodies the strong association between erōs and persuasion in the Greek imagination, as Rosenmeyer will discuss here in her chapter on Alciphron's letter from Phryne. At the same time, a female may tutor or speak through the male, as in the case of the priestess Diotima, who imparts wisdom to Socrates in Plato's *Symposium* just as the Pythia, discussed in this volume by Maurizio, relays the oracle of the male god, Apollo, to his petitioners. Indeed, in tragedy, even song itself has feminine associations.[8]

The ambiguity of women's speech in fifth-century Athenian tragedy and its social and political implications for the male audience have been much discussed in recent years and will receive further consideration with Griffith's chapter in this volume.[9] It is quite remarkable, given the restricted role of women's public speech in classical Athens, that tragedy contains a larger number of speaking female characters than any other Greek literary genre. The plays repeatedly explore, with a mixture of fascination and horror, the catastrophic consequences of women's duplicitous speech. Thus Aeschylus' Clytemnestra persuades Agamemnon to tread the tapestries leading to his death, Medea persuades each of her male interlocutors—Creon, Aegeus, and Jason—to comply with requests that will ultimately destroy them, while Phaedra in Euripides' *Hippolytus* harms her husband's *oikos* ("household, family") by means of a written lie. Tragedy thus frequently involves a

an older, more archaic language (αἱ γυναῖκες . . . μάλιστα τὴν ἀρχαίαν φωνὴν σῴζουσι, 418c). Elsewhere certain forms of address were associated with women; for example, Herodotus, in his description of the Carians, asserts that the wives never address their husbands by name nor share their tables (Hdt. 1.146). For forms of address associated with women in Greek literature, see Skinner 1987; Dickey 1996.

[6] Bergren 1983.

[7] Aspasia, the courtesan who married Pericles, was famous throughout antiquity for her rhetorical ability, a skill linked to her sexual status; see Henry 1995: 35.

[8] Hall 1999.

[9] See Goldhill 1984; Zeitlin [1985] 1996; Goff 1990; Segal 1993; McClure 1999.

discursive dynamic in which outsiders, particularly women and slaves, are represented as skillful at manipulating and even subverting the dominant discourse of husbands and masters.[10]

The focus on male-authored texts has, of late, been balanced by a greater appreciation of women poets in ancient Greece. Some critics have recently suggested that the female poets provide an alternative subjectivity and conceptualize speech differently from their male counterparts, both in their erotic sensibility and in their poetic discourse, a difference that may have in part been influenced by their female audiences.[11] Stehle and Williamson, for example, have argued that Sappho in her poetry presents a more egalitarian and reciprocal form of relationship with her beloved than do her male counterparts.[12] This exciting new area of research receives further consideration in the essays of Lardinois, Stehle, and Skinner included in this collection.

MODELS FOR WOMEN'S SPEECH: SOCIOLINGUISTICS AND DISCOURSE ANALYSIS

Although scholarship on women's voices in ancient Greece has grown in recent years, this type of analysis continues to confront critics with complex and almost insurmountable difficulties. Even authentic women's voices from the classical world, whether represented by the fragments of the women poets, inscriptions, or letters, cannot be definitively construed as "pure" representations of female subjectivity. The extent to which the fragments of Sappho relay autobiographical information about the poet has long been the subject of debate, as have their performative contexts and the social universe they describe. In the case of inscriptions, it is not always clear who actually commissioned them and whether average women could serve as economic agents in such transactions.[13] The status of female subjectivity as

[10] Hall 1997.

[11] Stehle (Stigers [Stehle] 1981; Stehle [1990] 1996: 262–318) argues that Sappho's poetry represents an alternative women's song tradition performed for a speech community separate from men, one consisting of adult women rather than *parthenoi*. Rayor (1993) similarly argues that Corinna reworks traditional male narratives for an audience of women, while Williamson ([1995] 1996) suggests that the poetry of Sappho, which she compares to that of Sappho's male counterpart Anacreon, shows a continual shifting of subject positions in which the boundaries between self and other is "elided" but not dissolved.

[12] Stigers [Stehle] 1981; Williamson [1995] 1996. See further on Sappho: duBois [1978] 1996; Winkler [1981] 1996; Skinner 1993; Greene [1994] 1996; Wilson 1996; Snyder 1997a; and Stehle 1997: 262–311. Rayor (1993) has shown how Corinna retold certain myths in order to emphasize the role female deities played in them, and Skinner (1991a, 1991b) has commented on the women-identified writings of the poet Nossis; on the women poets in general, see Snyder 1989.

[13] Goff 1995.

filtered through the discourses of male authors poses an even larger methodological problem: To what extent are these representations infused with everyday life? What constraints does genre place on rendering women's speech? And although many literary sources portray men's and women's spheres as distinct, current scholarship on women in ancient Greece indicates a strong "behind-the-scenes" involvement in legal and political matters beyond the household, an idea reinforced in this volume by Blok's discussion of women in fifth-century Athens and by Cribiore's work on the letters of women in Roman Egypt.[14]

Another issue confronted by all the authors in this volume is the degree to which ancient sources distinguish women's speech from that of men. The constraints of genre preclude extreme variations of register and style in most ancient literary texts. And although the poetic tradition identifies certain expressions and verbal genres with women, especially ritual forms like lamentation and *aischrologia* (ritual obscenity), they seldom attribute a speech practice exclusively to one gender. Thus Aristophanes could parody feminine speech habits by assigning them to male speakers, or tragic males could be made to lament as a sign of effeminacy, as in the case of the barbarian chorus in Aeschylus' *Persians*. Conversely, poets may render female characters as possessing the rhetorical skills of men, like Clytemnestra in Aeschylus' *Agamemnon* and Medea in Euripides' play of the same name. Both Worman in her chapter on the Homeric Helen and Griffith in his discussion of Attic tragedy explore this issue by showing how female characters may be represented as employing the discursive modes characteristic of men.

The problems inherent in analyzing verbal characteristics of speech as the product of gender differentiation have been well documented by contemporary studies of women's speech in English-speaking countries. By and large, three main methodological approaches have influenced these studies: sociolinguistics, discourse analysis, and comparative ethnographic studies of verbal genres.[15] Robin Lakoff first argued that special vocabularies, such as color terms related to women's social roles ("mauve" instead of "pink"), intensification ("so" and "such"), restriction of negative emotion, avoidance of obscenity, diminutives, tag questions, and hedging, typically characterize women's speech.[16] She speculated that these linguistic features, because they may convey uncertainty and deference, reflect the secondary social status of women in the United States. Other studies have identified women's speech as linguistically conservative, tending toward prestige forms, and

[14] Foxhall 1996.

[15] For sociolinguistic approaches, see Henley and Thorne 1975; Philips, Steele, and Tanz 1987; for women's speech genres in other cultures, see Keenan 1974; Gal 1991; Raheja 1996.

[16] Lakoff 1973 and 1975; see also Coates [1986] 1993: 103–8. It is striking how closely Lakoff's views resemble those of Jesperson (1922: 237–54); see Cameron 1985: 35–44.

have argued that men's speech shows a greater amount of linguistic innovation.[17] Related to the masculine preference for the vernacular is the long-
standing association between male speech and obscenity, a verbal genre not
considered appropriate to women in many cultures.[18]

Although recent research has generally concurred that gender-based linguistic distinctions do exist, the ways in which men's and women's speech
differ and the meaning of these differences have been a continual source of
debate.[19] One theory holds that divergent paths of socialization engender
distinct linguistic styles in men and women; for example, if women exhibit
a more collaborative and cooperative discursive style in the workplace, as
Coates has argued, it might be viewed as resulting from women's socialization within the home.[20] However, discourse analysis, which focuses on discursive strategies and verbal genres in specific social contexts rather than
lexical or morphological features, has revealed the ambiguities and complexities involved in interpreting stylistic elements of conversation. For example, silence may express dominance and disapproval, or it may indicate
submission.[21] Similarly, interruptions can show conversational control, or
the active participation and enthusiasm of the listener.[22]

[17] For a discussion of women's linguistic conservatism, see Barron 1986: 2. In four British
studies discussed by Coates ([1986] 1993: 76–77) working-class women's speech tended to be
hypercorrect, while the men's speech showed a marked divergence from nonstandard forms.
Coates further speculates (94) that women's adherence to more standard linguistic forms is
due to the fact that they are not exposed as frequently to vernacular speech.

[18] Although Jesperson (1922: 245–47) was the first linguist to identify avoidance of obscenity as characteristic of women's speech, Bornstein (1978: 135) has shown that this view can
be traced back to medieval and renaissance courtesy books forbidding women to curse or joke.
Lakoff (1973: 50) describes obscenity as masculine and argues that women tend to use weaker
expletives, such as "oh dear." See also Coates ([1986] 1993: 108–9), and de Klerk (1997: 152),
who associates this verbal genre with a dominating discursive style. She concludes from her
study of obscenity among adolescents in South Africa that "males generally used words which
scored higher in terms of shock value."

[19] Recent debate has centered on whether sociolinguists promulgate a dominance or a difference model; see Johnson and Meinhof 1997: 9–10 for a discussion. The dominance model
views gender-based language differentials as the product of power dynamics, a view supported
by Lakoff 1973; Henley and Thorne 1975; Henley, Kramarae, and Thorne 1983; West and
Zimmerman 1983. The difference model, which attributes the linguistic behavior of women
to divergent paths of language socialization, is represented by Coates [1986] 1993 and Tannen 1996.

[20] Coates 1995: 13; see also [1986] 1993: 11.

[21] Gal 1995: 171 shows how silence can have a range of cultural meanings; see also Tannen
1996: 36–37.

[22] On the ambiguity of linguistic strategies, see Tannen 1996: 20–21; on interruption, 35–
36. Coates ([1986] 1993: 99–100) discusses one study of mixed-group conversation in which
men initiated forty-six out of the forty-eight interruptions. West and Zimmerman (1983: 102–
3) correlate interruptions with a dominant discursive style that sustains status differences; they
cite in support of their position studies of parent-child interaction in which parents are far
more likely to interrupt a child than the other way around.

Classical scholarship on women's speech has largely reflected these trends. The earliest studies of women's speech, most of which focus on comedy, have typically employed a sociolinguistic approach.[23] They have attempted to delineate the linguistic features, such as exclamations, polite modifiers, forms of oaths, imperatives, forms of address, and self-reflexive adjectives, that may have characterized actual women's speech in ancient Greece. Some of these markers, especially those connected with ritual lament, can also be found in the highly formalized language of tragedy, although to a lesser extent than in comedy: the exclamation οἲ γώ, for example, signals lament and is employed only by female speakers in Euripides,[24] whereas female speakers in Aristophanes appear to use primary obscenities far less frequently than their male counterparts do.[25]

COMPARATIVE ANTHROPOLOGY
AND THE ETHNOGRAPHY OF SPEECH

Another strand of classical scholarship has borrowed from contemporary ethnographic research the concept of verbal genres as a means of describing the types of speech associated with women in ancient Greece. Alexiou's research on the form and function of female lamentation, a genre discussed more fully below and in subsequent chapters, from ancient Greece to the modern Greek village represents one of the earliest examples of this work.[26] Contemporary ethnographic studies of linguistic practices in communities showing strong gender segregation have provided an invaluable store of comparative material for classical scholars. Instead of delineating specific morphological and lexical elements of spoken language, features largely inaccessible to classicists, these studies focus more broadly on the verbal genres, the "culturally recognized . . . formalized forms and categories of discourse" that correspond to and accompany everyday activities.[27] Similarly, literary critics such as Bakhtin and Todorov have employed the concept of the speech genre as a means of describing the generic types of speech represented by and in written texts, from the personal letter to the legal brief, from scientific tracts and literary texts to military commands.[28]

---

[23] Gilleland 1980; Bain 1984; Adams 1984; Dickey 1995 and 1996.

[24] McClure 1995.

[25] Sommerstein 1995.

[26] Alexiou 1974. See also Vermeule 1974 and, more recently, Holst-Warhaft 1992; Foley 1993; Sultan 1993; Stears 1998; and Murnaghan 1999.

[27] Sherzer 1987: 98.

[28] Bakhtin 1986: 78; Sherzer (1987: 98) also emphasizes that speech genres are not always formal or literary forms of discourse, but include casual and everyday forms.

Many ethnographic studies indicate that while men and women participate in both public and private spheres, women tend not to use the speech
practices and discourses of public life. Among the Kuna Indians of Central
America, for example, public verbal genres, particularly ritual and traditional forms of speech, are the province of men, while women, who spend
most of their time in the home, are responsible for private genres such as
lullabies.[29] The Araucanians of Chile train boys in the arts of oratory and
conversation, and their speech is viewed as promoting group solidarity; only
they can serve as leaders, public orators, and messengers. In contrast, the
women are expected to remain silent in the presence of men, although they
do participate in ritual, public forms of speech in a type of curing ceremony
and in their role as mourners.[30]

A similar model applies to ancient Greece: women are rarely portrayed
as public speakers in a political context, as orators or messengers, except in
comedy, a genre that frequently inverts gender roles and linguistic genres.
But they did engage in some quasi-public genres, particularly in ritual contexts such as funerals and religious festivals like the Thesmophoria in honor
of Demeter. Ritual lamentation comprises the predominant, although not
exclusive, verbal genre associated with women in both archaic and classical
literature, and is discussed more fully by Lardinois, Blok, and Stehle in this
volume. Socrates in the *Republic* explicitly designates lamentation and the
musical modes associated with it as a feminine discursive practice inappropriate for men: these musical modes are deemed "worthless even for
women, who are to be good, let alone men" (ἄχρηστοι γὰρ καὶ γυναιξὶν
ἃς δεῖ ἐπιεικεῖς εἶναι, μὴ ὅτι ἀνδράσιν, Pl. *Resp.* 398d7–e3). Throughout the Greek tradition, ritual lament remained the province and prerogative of women in whom it was believed there was an innate affinity for weeping and sorrowful songs; thus Medea proclaims that "women by nature are
given to weeping" (γυνὴ δὲ θῆλυ κἀπὶ δακρύοις ἔφυ, Eur. *Med.* 928). In
addition to laments, ancient writers attributed other specific types of song
or musical genre to women, such as the *katabaukalesis* (lullaby), the *ioulos*
(spinning song), the Linus song associated with harvest, and the *hymenaios*
(wedding song). These songs accompanied daily and seasonal domestic
tasks as well as marked major life events.[31]

<hr />

[29] Gal 1991: 182; see also Sherzer 1987: 99.

[30] Sherzer 1987: 101.

[31] On these songs in general, see Ath. 14. 618ff. For the *ioulos*, cf. Apollod. *Hist.* 149J; Er-
atosth. fr. 10. For the Linus song, see Hom. *Il.* 18.570; Pind. fr. 128c.6. On the *hymenaios*,
Hague 1983; Contiades-Tsitsoni 1990; cf. Hom. *Il.* 18.493; Hes. *Sc.* 274; Aesch. *Ag.* 707; Eur.
IA 1036; Pind. *Pyth.* 3.17; Eur. *Alc.* 922; Sappho fr. 111. On lullabies, see Waern 1960; cf. also
Hesychius s.v. βαυκαλᾶν; Theoc. 24.7; Rosenmeyer (1991: 23–24) briefly discusses the lullaby as a speech act in Simonides' Danaë fragment (fr. 543), although she does not identify it
specifically as a feminine verbal genre.

Another verbal genre, *aischrologia* (scurrilous joking), a subject taken up by O'Higgins in this volume, was a notorious feature of women-only festivals in ancient Greece, especially those in honor of Demeter, such as the Stenia, the Haloa, and the Thesmophoria. At the Demetrian festivals, *aischrologia* was closely associated with female sexuality, reproduction, and fertility. Since many of these festivals are shrouded in secrecy, little is known about the content of this speech. All that is known with any certainty is that ritual obscenity involved mocking invective, sexual joking, and the "unspeakable" expressions normally forbidden to women and denoted by the term *arrhēta*.[32] A scholion to Lucian, describing ritual obscenity as practiced by women at the Eleusinian Haloa, suggests that *aischrologia* concerned sexual matters and thus encouraged adultery.[33] Another venue for public performance was the female chorus, composed of girls or married women, that honored female deities. Thus women's voices could be heard on a variety of occasions, both inside and outside the home, as Blok demonstrates in her contribution to the volume.

One of the questions raised by comparative ethnographic studies of women's speech in both contemporary and ancient cultures, and addressed by many of the authors in this volume, is whether women's verbal patterns and expressive genres reinforce or subvert the dominant discourse. In many cultures, including ancient Greece, women's verbal expressions are viewed as potentially dangerous, even when they assume a socially sanctioned ritual form. In her analysis of women's songs and proverbs in rural North India, Raheja remarks that women's ritual speech, while viewed as "auspicious and necessary," is frequently monitored or restricted in some way.[34] Caraveli observes that women's ritual laments in contemporary rural Greece may function as a vehicle for social protest, a strategy applicable to the role of lament and burial in Sophocles' *Antigone*.[35] Even women's silence may denote a form of resistance rather than passive submission: in his study of women and silence in contemporary rural Greek communities, Herzfeld shows how women "perform a submission that ridicules" through their silence.[36]

CONTRIBUTIONS TO THIS VOLUME

The present volume attempts to balance the number of articles devoted to the representation of female speech in male-authored texts with those on

[32] Zeitlin 1982a: 144.
[33] Rabe 1906: 280; for a discussion of this passage, see Winkler 1990b: 195.
[34] Raheja 1996: 151.
[35] Caraveli 1980 and 1986; Foley 1993: 111–13.
[36] Herzfeld 1991: 80.

genuine women's voices. In many instances, these different manifestations of women's voices overlap and inform each other. Thus Martin argues that male poets in the symposium appropriated the enigmatic speech of women, a verbal style also exemplified by the prophetic utterances of the Pythia, a topic examined by Maurizio. Blok and O'Higgins outline the reality of women's voices in the Athenian polis, while Griffith and Gagarin discuss their representation on the tragic stage and in the lawcourts. Skinner argues that the representation of women as art critics in Herodas and Theocritus *Idyll* 15 obliquely criticizes some of the female poets discussed by Lardinois and Stehle. Finally, Rosenmeyer presents us with a fictional letter of Phryne, written by the male author Alciphron, but modeled on such real letters of women as those examined by Cribiore. Although the different contributions complement each other in this way, they do not necessarily adopt the same methodology. Rather, they represent a variety of approaches, historical, philological, anthropological, sociolinguistic, and feminist. The essays are also equally distributed among the three major periods of Greek literary history—archaic, classical, Hellenistic/Roman—and involve a diverse array of speech and literary genres, including divination, prayer, lament, *aischrologia*, epic, lyric, drama, oratory, pastoral, epistolary, and epigraphy.

Part One deals with women's voices in the archaic period. The first three chapters examine a central identification between women and polysemous language in archaic Greek literature and society. In her analysis of Helen in the Homeric poems, Worman elucidates the verbal mutability and versatility of Helen, qualities that contribute to a gap between "meaning and intention": she is not merely a character, but a figure, an enigmatic locus of meanings, who closely resembles Odysseus in her ability to convey the voices of others and to penetrate disguises. Helen is both a perceptive reader of signs as well as an adept conveyer of meanings, the embodiment of the double story. And yet in the *Iliad*, her vocabulary and verbal patterns identify her with the flyting, verbally abusive character of the hero, since she uses a *muthos*, a type of public discourse normally assigned to male speakers, and blame speech, which she turns against herself and others, most notably Paris.

Maurizio also addresses the question of women as interpreters and conveyers of signs in her consideration of the Pythias, the historical priestesses of Apollo who prophesized to male petitioners. She outlines the strategies and contexts that made ambiguity a viable and even desirable mode of speech for the Pythias. Building on the assumption that priestesses composed the oracles later written down by men, she argues that their notorious ambiguity may have been a style developed as a deliberate response to political crises mediated by Delphi in the archaic period. Because the priestesses provide one of the few examples of historical women permitted authoritative, public speech, their presence in the ancient world raises questions also touched upon by the other contributors concerned with the women poets.

Beginning with the passage about the Delian maidens and their mimetic skills in the *Homeric Hymn to Apollo*, Martin explores how male poets and the male poetic traditions shape female personae in Greek lyric poetry. He argues along the lines of the previous two contributors that the female voice is characterized by timeless subject matter and an enigmatic style. These observations serve as the basis for a new reading of a long-standing conundrum in the Theognidean corpus (861–64 West), in which a speaker gendered as feminine poses a sympotic riddle about herself. Martin conjectures a personified *Penia*, "Poverty," as the answer, a type of feminine abstraction later employed by Aristophanes and Plato. Because women may have sounded enigmatic to Greek males, they were reinvested and reinterpreted as mythic abstractions in literary texts.

Turning from representations of women's speech by male authors to a genuine female voice from the same period, Lardinois argues that Sappho closely modeled her poetry on women's public speech genres, including prayers to female goddesses, laments, and praise of young brides. By understanding these verbal genres as aspects of women's experience, he sheds light not only on some key fragments, but also on the performance context of the poems. For example, he observes that frs. 16, 94, and 96 contain elements both of praise and of lament, indicating that they may have been wedding songs. As part of the epithalamium genre, such laments provided a public vehicle for giving voice to the loss and anxiety that girls may have experienced upon marriage.

In Part Two, four contributors address the issue of women's speech and silence in classical Athens. Blok draws on evidence of women's verbal behavior from contemporary rural Greece to show that the social ideology of silence promulgated by literary sources and reflected in contemporary scholarship was not absolute or monolithic. Her essay clarifies the difficulties posed by literary sources for understanding the historical lives of fifth-century Athenian women. Noting that few texts focus on events within the house, where most women's conversations probably occurred, she maps the territory in the city where their voices may have been heard. Blok cites as venues the "semi-public" events such as weddings and funerals and the domestic and religious activities that necessitated women's departure from the house.

As a rich source of representations of women, Athenian tragedy provides perhaps the fullest fictional account of women as speaking subjects, albeit subjects impersonated by male actors before a predominantly, if not exclusively, male audience, an issue Griffith examines in his essay. He argues that tragic drama does not indicate a consistent degree of differentiation in

mode of delivery for male and female characters; rather, female impersonation probably relied more heavily on costume and physical demeanor.
Nonetheless, female patterns of speech frequently consist of lyric expression, prayers, ritual formulations such as prophecies, curses, supplication,
and chants, references to domestic activities, slavery, loss, and motherhood.
But, as Griffith observes, one of the most distinctive markers of women's
speech in tragedy is "a failure to speak at all." Nonetheless, several tragedies
hinge on women who appropriate male speech to commit horrific acts.
Griffith concludes by examining how Sophocles' deploys this diverse array
of female voices in his *Antigone*.

O'Higgins considers one aspect of the public speech ascribed to women
in classical Athens, *aischrologia*, the ritual obscenity and shameful talk that
accompanied their rituals in honor of Demeter at the Thesmophoria and
at women's festivals like the Adonia. Instead of attempting to recover the
words spoken by women at this festival—an impossibility—she examines
the cultural influence of this speech and its meaning for women. In the eyes
of men, such speech challenged the silence and restraint normally imposed
on women while simultaneously threatening to disrupt the normal social
and political order. As a form of *grotesquerie*, ritual obscenity may have provided an opportunity for women to challenge social norms and subvert the
dominant discourses of the polis.

In the final consideration of women's voices in classical Athens, Gagarin
surveys the passages in which the orators quote women's speech and finds
that they do not reliably reflect actual women's voices, but rather represent
rhetorical strategies conducive to forensic success. He notes that the female
speakers quoted in oratory typically employ many rhetorical techniques and
arguments characteristic of the courts, even though actual women would
have had little experience in this type of public speaking. In many cases, the
speaker uses the words of women to introduce a moral standard against
which an action should be judged. Thus in Demosthenes 59, the accuser
Apollodorus invokes the collective voices of Athenian wives as a sort of domestic jury that condemns the putative acquittal of the courtesan Neaera.
Gagarin's essay provides a much-needed corrective to the prevailing view
that fourth-century Athenian oratory offers a more realistic or historically
accurate picture of ancient women than the fictions generated by Attic
tragedy.

Part Three considers the late-classical, Hellenistic, and Roman periods.
The essays of Stehle and Skinner respond directly to one another in their
emphasis on the literary innovations of the later women poets and their use
of female verbal genres. Stehle considers how the late-classical poet Erinna
in her major poem, the *Distaff*, draws on the tradition of women's laments
and funerary epitaphs to address the mother-daughter relationship. Fourth-
century funerary epitaphs convey a new atmosphere in which female do-

mestic virtue becomes an object of public praise, thereby contrasting with the earlier inscriptions and their primary concern with male relationships. Erinna's *Distaff* breaks with the genre of traditional lament and rejects the lessons imparted by the central character's mother, celebrating instead not only friendship between women, but also writing as a means of escaping the social controls placed on women.

In the next chapter, Skinner provides an incisive commentary on the preceding essay by considering how the Hellenistic male poets viewed women's literary activity. Taking as her starting point a scene from Herodas' fourth *Miniamb*, in which a pair of farm wives comment upon the artwork housed in a temple of Asclepius, she argues that such scenes of art appreciation have their roots in fifth-century tragedy. She conjectures that the Hellenistic women poets, beginning with Erinna, moved the place of viewing from the public realm (e.g., exterior temple facades) to the interior, thereby creating an unconventional focalizer in scenes of *ekphrasis*. By parodying a scene from the women poets, Herodas implies that these writers play a far more important role in Hellenistic scholarly and aesthetic exchanges than previously thought.

The last two essays explore both real and fictional letters by women: those written by women living in Roman Egypt, and one fictively composed in the second century C.E. by Phryne, a fourth-century courtesan from Athens, to her artist-lover, Praxiteles. Cribiore brings to light a set of letters written by a circle of women to Apollonios, an upper-class man who served as *stratēgos* in Roman Egypt. These letters, which were part of his archive found around Hermopolis, have received scant attention. They demonstrate that ancient women could be literate, and that some, like the family's oldest child, Heraidous, received education beyond the elementary level. Cribiore's study further shows women commenting on and engaging in the affairs of men, including business transactions, wars, litigation, and financial matters, and thus contravenes the view of seclusion and segregation typically attributed to women in the ancient world.

Turning to the late second century C.E., Rosenmeyer explores another vignette of art appreciation in a fictional correspondence from Phryne to Praxiteles invented by Alciphron, but with an ironic twist: the courtesan confronts her lover in the flesh to commend his creation, a statue of her. Thus she controls what the reader sees and hears in this *ekphrasis*. In "talking back" to her creator, she challenges the viewer's expectations of hierarchy and power relations: copy and original blur as Alciphron portrays the courtesan as slipping back and forth between the voices of woman and statue by an unusually marked use of pronouns. And yet through a form of literary ventriloquism, Alciphron "speaks" through his female creation, transforming Phryne into a vehicle for representing male aesthetic and literary creation.

By publishing these essays, we hope to bring new evidence and interpretations of women's voices to the attention of the scholarly community, and at the same time to stimulate the current debate on female speech in our classical sources by considering a number of questions: How are women in literary texts characterized by their speech? How do we reconstruct the voices of women in religious cult, in the city-state, and in private letters? How do we evaluate male representations and adaptations of female voices and speech genres? What is the relation between female-authored poetry and the traditional female speech genres that were allowed and acknowledged in the wider community? To what extent do the female poets deviate from their male contemporaries, and what was the reaction of the male literary community to these female poetic endeavors? This volume seeks to show that the voices and speech of women played a much more important role in Greek literature and society than previously recognized. Rather than confirming the old model of binary oppositions, in which women's speech was viewed as insignificant and subordinate to male discourse, the sources examined in this volume reveal a dynamic and potentially explosive interrelation between women's speech and the realm of literary production and public discourse.

Part One

THE ARCHAIC PERIOD

CHAPTER TWO

This Voice Which Is Not One

HELEN'S VERBAL GUISES IN HOMERIC EPIC

NANCY WORMAN

THE VOICES of many important female characters in Homeric epic differ from each other in vocabulary choice, tone, and formulaic expression. While occasion dictates these differences to some extent, the style of each female speaker is generally true to her character type. Just as Nestor's measured, honey-sweet tones and use of exempla suit his status as elder statesman, so do Andromache's mournful self-reference and admonishing use of the future tense serve to mark her further as the paradigmatic widow, even when her husband is still alive. If certain characters show a remarkable degree of consistency in their speech types, others speak in a manner that is more changeable, inclusive, and therefore difficult to categorize, the hybrid quality of which arises from their variegated roles in Homeric narrative. Of all the Homeric characters, Odysseus most thoroughly embodies this type of verbal mutability; in this study I focus on the speech patterns of the female figure in Homer who does so—Helen.

It has become standard practice among scholars of gender in Greek literature to emphasize the problem that female characters pose as producers of signs (since they are themselves signs of a sort traded among male agents), and to cite Lévi-Strauss' famous formulation of this conundrum.[1] Helen is in some sense the paradigmatic exchanged sign, in that her figure strikingly encapsulates both the process of objectification inherent in this symbolic exchange and its fundamental problems. Simultaneously the archetypal bride and the most illustrious flouter of the marriage bond, Helen embodies the dangerous potential of all women to be unfaithful to their men. She is also the paradigmatic elusive object of male desire, whose semidivine status underscores the impossibility of complete control over the female as a type, and, on a more abstract level, of all that she might symbolize: the generative forces of both plant life and poetry, the destructive

---

[1] Lévi-Strauss [1958] 1963: 61: "For words do not speak, while women do; as producers of signs, women can never be reduced to the status of symbols or tokens." See, e.g., Bergren 1983; duBois [1978] 1996; Suzuki 1989; Joplin 1991; Katz 1991; Wohl 1990.

powers of both sex and dominion. Helen's cultic associations with the lover Aphrodite and the *parthenos* Artemis indicate her failure to make the transition to a stable marital status, as Claude Calame has argued.[2] She remains in circulation, the glorious bride gone wrong. From the earliest discernible point in the tradition of stories about Helen, she is this multiple, inclusive, and dangerous figure, whose reputation fluctuates repeatedly between praise and blame. Unlike her sister Clytemnestra, she is not only a figure of abuse; unlike Penelope, her predominate story is not that of the faithful wife. Although versions of Clytemnestra's and Penelope's tales suggest the possibility of defending the one and accusing the other, only the figure of Helen comprises both versions of the wife's story poised in tense competition.

Plato relates an episode about the archaic poet Stesichorus that revolves around Helen's praise and blame, in which the poet, struck blind by the angry goddess, is said to have retracted his tale about her journey to Troy.[3] A Hellenistic commentary explains that Stesichorus composed a poem in which a phantasm (εἴδωλον) of Helen went to Troy, while the real Helen was kept safe in Egypt.[4] The episode highlights the dangerous power of Helen's anger and her control of her own reputation, relating it specifically to poetic production.[5] Euripides treats the story of the *eidōlon* in his play *Helen*, where her doubled figure makes manifest the epistemological problem at the heart of theatrical representation. His *Trojan Women*, in some contrast, uses a seductive Helen to suggest the moral threat of the misapplication of praise, especially when couched in a decorative rhetorical style.[6] Archaic and classical writers thus consistently treat Helen as signifying the dangerous aspects not only of women but also of poetic and rhetorical effect. The Homeric poet himself seems to respond to a preexisting tradition of conflicting stories, apparent in the tensions between the more forgiving depiction of Helen that he clearly favors and the darker implications that he allows to intrude. Unlike more narrowly delimited characters in epic, Helen represents a complex of forces in human life and a multitude of stories; her biography constitutes a series of public events, each one a pivotal moment in the lives of many.

So what type of voice does such an inclusive figure have? A voice that is not one, it seems; that is multiple and layered; that includes speech types strongly associated with relatively consistent characters, but transposed

[2] Calame [1977] 1997: 191–93.

[3] Pl. *Phdr.* 243a3–b2.

[4] *P Oxy.* 2506, fr. 26, col. 1.

[5] On Stesichorus and Helen's relationship to the construction of an authoritative tradition, see Bassi 1993; and cf. Nagy 1990: 419–23.

[6] I argue elsewhere (Worman 1997) that this play shares with Gorgias' *Helen* the use of her body to demonstrate the erotic effects of persuasive style.

into other contexts where standard meanings do not necessarily match particular intentions. Helen's special type of verbal mutability arises at least in part from a difference between the formal locutions she employs and the intended impact of her words, so that a gap repeatedly opens up between the usual meanings of familiar formulae and her singular implications. This gap between meaning and intention is not necessarily unique to Helen (again, cf. Odysseus), but it does take a unique form in her usage. Helen is a mimic, as her first husband is quick to point out (*Od.* 4.279); she takes on the voices of others (including both tone and typical phraseology), most often as a means of deflection. In practical terms, she thereby avoids direct blame, but this verbal mutability is also more profoundly related to her as the embodiment of multiple stories.

The Iliadic Helen is the only character in the Homeric poems to engage in self-abuse; no one else turns such barbs against themselves. Nor does any other Homeric character engage in abusing Helen, even though, as Linda Clader has discussed, she arouses in others the shudder that suggests the chilly gusts of Hades or the presence of Nemesis (Indignation, Retribution), whose child she sometimes is.[7] In both the *Iliad* and the *Odyssey* she refers to herself as "dog-faced" (κυνώπιδος), which, especially in the *Iliad*, serves as an important signal of her fateful connections. Dogs are linked to Hades; they attend Hecate, and feed voraciously on human carrion.[8] They are thus bound up with the fated end-point of all human life, which Helen brings about quickly for many Greek heroes. Gregory Nagy has noted the association of blame speech with carrion feeding (specifically the corpses of heroes),[9] while Margaret Graver has argued more recently that Helen's dog insult is evidence of a defaming tradition.[10] Graver's excellent discussion nevertheless overlooks the tension created by Helen's particular use of such insults, in part because she regards Homer's treatment of Helen as unproblematically gentle. But in Homer, the traces of this blame tradition confound any understanding of Helen as simply good or evil—as simply a goddess or a dog. In every scene in which she appears, her speech is edged threateningly with competing implications, with suggestions of precisely the blame that the Homeric poet's dominant images of her repeatedly counter.[11]

[7] *Cypria* fr. 7; see Clader 1976: 18–23, esp. nn. 30 and 31. Her detailed discussion—which predates by fifteen years the more recent flurry of attention around Helen—has served as the basis for many studies, often without sufficient recognition of her work. Vernant ([1985] 1991b: 102–3) similarly associates Helen with *Kēr*, Fate, and the Erinyes. Cf. Vermeule 1979: 159.

[8] See Redfield [1975] 1991: 193–203; also Clader 1976: 18; Graver 1995: 58.

[9] Nagy 1979: 224–31.

[10] Graver 1995: esp. 55–59.

[11] Clader (1976) is not explicit about this alternate tradition, but she does note a number of times the threatening character of Helen's presence in the *Iliad*.

At least in part as a result of this narrative competition, attempts to find consistency of character in the figure of the Homeric Helen impede rather than promote an understanding of how she functions in the poems. In the *Iliad*, Helen's vocabulary and speech patterns seem to echo the mourner's voice[12] and that of some stricken or angry hero, combining the vocabulary of regret with self-abuse and/or abuse of others, in contexts that suggest a covert seduction of her interlocutors. In the *Odyssey*, she speaks in a manner that makes her look like an all-knowing and sympathetic poet-goddess, and she is treated by both the external narrator and her internal audience with such respect that her verbal interactions seem powerful and bewitching. Helen combines the coy perspicacity of the goddesses who host Odysseus in their beds with the commanding tones of both the Muses and the poet, representing her role in Odysseus' adventures as a singular mix of authoritative stances.

Many recent studies have exposed the doubling, fictionalizing aspects of Helen's figure in the *Odyssey*, in some general way supporting the notion that Helen's verbal type is multiple and changeable.[13] But these discussions analyze Helen from outside of her figure, as it were, tending to consider Helen's doubleness as symbolic of the poet's dilemma and not looking in any detail at how Helen's own speech patterns establish her as both a potentially dissembling speaker and one of consummate suitability, a central oratorical criterion for effective speaking.[14] For the purposes of this discussion, I am less interested in the epistemological problems that the figure of Helen poses than in what makes her speeches in the *Odyssey* seem so appropriate and therefore so persuasive. I argue against the grain of recent assumptions about the characterization of Helen in both poems, examining her speaking style in some detail to show how seductively fractious she is in the *Iliad* and how eerily calming she is in the *Odyssey*.

THE VOICE OF NEMESIS

Helen's character in the *Iliad* has usually been taken at face value by scholars: they describe her rueful responses to Priam and Hector and her angry rejection of Paris and Aphrodite as sympathetic depictions, often without analyzing in any detail the ambiguous quality of these verbal exchanges.[15] I suggest, in contrast, that in these exchanges 1) Helen's apparent tone often

---

[12] Martin (1995) has suggested this similarity, and pointed to the use of *ophelon* phrases in Helen's Iliadic speeches. See below.

[13] Zeitlin [1981] 1996; also Bergren 1983; Suzuki 1989; Doherty 1995a.

[14] Arist. *Rh.* 1405a.

[15] See, e.g., Redfield [1975] 1991: 122; Edwards 1987: 195–96; Suzuki 1989; Austin 1994; Graver 1995.

does not match her ultimate intention, and 2) the speech types she uses—which range from the mournful widow's to the flyting warrior's—are transposed from their usual contexts to form locutions unique to her. Helen is also significantly aware of her centrality to the narratives of others, manifesting a concern for reputation (*kleos*) that connects her to the Muses, the Sirens, and ultimately the poet, as a number of scholars have recognized.[16] In the Teichoscopia (*Il.* 3.141–244), for example, when she is asked by Priam to name a warrior, Helen uses her identification of Agamemnon to frame an elegiac look at her own past, thus substituting her story for his. Her reply is not particularly suited to the context. In fact, it somewhat resembles in content Andromache's mournful speech in book 6, when the latter bewails her widow's fate to her living husband. Andromache's voice, however, is consistently grief-stricken, and her use of the mourner's topoi (e.g., lamenting family ties, dilation on the effect the death will have on one's life) coheres with her role as loyal wife.[17] Helen's rueful self-reference instead mingles regret with an emphatic awareness of her own singular status. When Priam asks Helen to name Ajax, her identification moves quickly from his epithets (e.g., ἕρκος Ἀχαιῶν, 3.229) to the Cretan leader Idomeneus, who as a guest-friend of Menelaus reminds her again of her own story, and she remarks on the absence of her brothers from the battlefield (3.234–42). She then conjectures that their absence can be explained by their fears of shame and reproach that are rightfully hers (3.242).

Since she views the actions of others as dependent on her error and rues bitterly this damage to her reputation, Helen assigns herself the crucial role in others' stories, thereby giving voice to the blame tradition that the narrator avoids. Her sense of her public reputation is anomalous among the female figures in Homeric epic; *kleos* is rightfully the concern of the warrior, not of the warrior's prize. Like any good warrior (and unlike her paramour), she fears the insults of others (3.242, 3.412, 24.767–68) and recognizes the vulnerability of her public position. Helen, in contrast to the chaste Andromache, treats her story—in part the battles waged essentially for her that she weaves in her second husband's halls (*Il.* 3.125–28)—as if it were the story most central to every warrior's life. And this in some sense is the case: whereas the mourning wife's story would only be properly told in keening over her husband, Helen's story is on the lips of everyone, since it is relevant to all the warriors. As the catalyzing, fateful figure for these he-

---

[16] See esp. Pucci ([1979] 1998), who associates the Muses' ability with the Sirens, Circe, and Helen; also Crane 1988: 42; Suzuki 1989: 69; Wohl 1993: 33–34; Doherty 1995b, 1995a: 135–38. For broader discussions, see Clader 1976; Bergren 1983; Austin 1975, 1994.

[17] See Alexiou 1974; Holst-Warhaft 1992; and Murnaghan 1999. Andromache repeats nearly the same set of fears and regrets three out of the four times she speaks (6.407–39, 22.450–59, 24.725–45).

roes, her story is their story; her own *kleos* is inevitably bound up with the *kleos* of each.[18]

But the complexity of Helen's figure and voice in this scene does not end there. Before she lapses into self-reflection in response to Priam's first inquiry, she says that he is worthy of veneration (αἰδοῖος) and fearsome (δεινός) in her eyes (3.172), using a show of extreme respect that implies an apologetic attitude consistent with her penchant for self-abuse, the primary stylistic tendency unique to her. Helen then declares, in reference to her coming to Troy, "Would that evil death had pleased me" (ὡς ὄφελεν θάνατός μοι ἀδεῖν κακός, 3.173–74), invoking in a sensuous manner the end point with which she is associated.[19] She makes a similar (though blander) declaration in her mourning speech over the body of Hector in book 24: "Would that I had been destroyed before" (ὡς πρὶν ὤφελον ὀλέσθαι, 764). Andromache uses a related construction when, as Hector is dragged around the city walls, she regrets that Eetion bore her (ὡς μὴ ὤφελλε τεκέσθαι, 22.481).[20] In book 21, fearing an unheroic end to his life, Achilles cries out to Zeus in prayer: "Would that Hector had killed me" (ὥς μ᾽ ὄφελ᾽ Ἕκτωρ κτεῖναι, 279). In the *Odyssey*, the shade of Achilles wishes something similar for Agamemnon: "Would that you had met your death and fate in Troy" (ὡς ὄφελες . . . / δήμῳ ἔνι Τρώων θάνατον καὶ πότμον ἐπισπεῖν, 24.30–31). Most famously, in *Odyssey* 5 Odysseus exclaims as he faces the storm near Scheria, "How I wish I had died and met my fate in Troy" (ὡς δὴ ἐγώ γ᾽ ὄφελον θανέειν καὶ πότμον ἐπισπεῖν, 5.308); he repeats the exclamation in the fictional account of his travails that he gives to Eumaeus (14.274).[21]

The *ophelon* phrase thus seems to be a locution used both by those in mourning and by Homeric heroes caught in threatening or painful situations—or, in the case of Odysseus, when telling about them in guest-friendship situations. The phrase does not, however, only communicate bitter despair (which may be either a *cri du coeur* or a persuasive tactic). When turned on another, it may also be used as an insult in verbal contests, reproaches, and taunts, an important aspect of its usage for analyzing Helen's speeches.[22] In the *Odyssey*, Odysseus most frequently utters the phrase, de-

---

[18] See esp. Clader 1976: 10–12.

[19] Again, see Vernant ([1985] 1991b: 102–3), who argues that *erōs* ("love") and *thanatos* ("death") are strongly linked in the Greek social imagination and calls Helen a "fatal beauty"; cf. Vermeule 1979: 159.

[20] Cf. Priam of Hector in the same scene (*Il.* 22.426); also Thetis when she wishes that Achilles had just stayed by the ships (αἴθ᾽ ὄφελες . . . ἧσθαι, 1.415–16), Achilles when he wishes that his mother had stayed among the sea nymphs (αἴθ᾽ ὄφελες . . . ναίειν, 18.86–87).

[21] Cf. Andromache (*Il.* 6.412) to Hector; and Aeneas in Vergil (*Aen.* 1.94–96). Odysseus also wishes he had remained among the Phaeacians when he lands on his own disguised island (13.204–5).

[22] Cf. *Il.* 11.380–81 (Paris taunts Diomedes); *Il.* 14.84–85 (Odysseus curses Agamemnon);

ploying it twice (of four times in the *Odyssey* and once in the *Iliad*) when he is trying to use a painful situation to gain sympathy, a complex deployment similar to Helen's. In the *Iliad*, it is Helen's favorite locution for expressing both despair and scorn, which she usually does with some other end in mind (of all characters she uses the phrase most often, five times in the *Iliad*). As a stranger in Troy, her usage in the *Iliad* resembles that of Odysseus in the *Odyssey*, who must make clever use of guest-friendship situations to win his way home. Just as Odysseus, when seeking empathy from the Phaeacians (*Od.* 11.547), regrets that he won Achilles' arms instead of Ajax, Helen, when seeking empathy from Priam and Hector (*Il.* 3 and 6), regrets that she followed Paris. Though each time she employs the phrase Helen's aim is slightly different, never is it simply the direct outpouring of emotion that it sounds. Although its repetition links her tone both to mourning diction and to the hero's emotions and concern for *kleos*, her application of this type of phrase is unique. Rather than actually being a widow or a hero in challenging circumstances, Helen echoes their outbursts by employing an emotional appeal that sounds like self-address, a layered locution whose related aims are deflecting blame and cementing allegiances. In her use of the phrase to cast scorn on Paris, for example, once she seems to be teasing him and once to be flattering his brother.

The earlier scene in book 3 involving Paris alone is plotted by Aphrodite, whose machinations irk her protegée and who inspires in her a passion that seems suspended between desire (for the beautiful Paris whom Aphrodite describes, 3.391–94) and anger at the very goddess with whom she is so closely associated.[23] Note that Helen herself calls her painful feelings ἄκριτα (3.412), the most common meaning of which is "confused, indeterminate," a word that thus underscores both the complexity of Helen's passion and (what comes to the same thing) the merging of roles in this scene, so that Helen's abuse of Aphrodite comes close to self-abuse.[24] Helen has been referred to as a "faded Aphrodite";[25] their conversation resembles an internal dialogue—a debate not only between Helen and her *daimōn* but also between two of the facets that make up her many-sided figure, with its multiple motivations and opposing traditions. Moreover, her scornful re-

---

Il. 24.253–54 (Priam curses his living children); *Od.* 2.183–84 (Eurymachos taunts the old seer Halitherses); *Od.* 18.401 (the suitors taunt the beggar Odysseus).

[23] On the extreme proximity of type between Aphrodite and Helen, see Boedeker 1974: 48, 54–55, 61; Clader 1976: 74; also Suter 1987.

[24] See Martin 1989: 111–13 on the interpretation of the epithet ἀκριτόμυθε, which Odysseus uses of Thersites (*Il.* 2.246; cf. Iris regarding the μῦθοι . . . ἄκριτοι of Priam, *Il.* 2.796).

[25] See Friedrich 1978: 46–47. Lyons (1997: 72) notes that the "faded god" theory of such figures is no longer popular among scholars, but cites Clader's 1976 treatment of Helen as a convincing exploration of her close connections to Aphrodite and Artemis. See also Calame [1977] 1997: 191–92.

sponses to her intimates resemble each other: she exhorts both Aphrodite
and Paris with dismissive imperatives (3.406, 432) and pictures each in a
compromised position (3.407–9, 434–36); correlatively, she uses the *ophelon* phrases of both herself and Paris. Her reproach of Aphrodite for using
seductive talk (ἠπεροπεύειν, 3.399) also recalls Hector's insulting of his
brother for being a seducer (ἠπεροπευτά, 3.49). Helen engages in this derogatory language only with those closest to her;[26] a significant variation
on the normal context of such blame speech, her usage parallels as well Hector's treatment of Paris.

The scornful abuse of one so intimate can sound similar to the dueling
speech of warriors (e.g., the use of negative epithets and goading imperatives). Coupled with Helen's self-abusive epithets, this speech and that in
which she reproaches Paris mimic the aggressive challenge of the hero on
the battlefield.[27] When Helen returns to the bedroom as ordered by
Aphrodite, her expression and tone suggest pique,[28] while her taunting
phrases recall the flyting warrior: "Would that you had died there (ὡς
ὤφελες αὐτόθ᾽ ὀλέσθαι)," she says, "subdued by the better man, who was
once my husband" (3.428–29). At the beginning of book 3 Hector similarly
chastises his brother on the battlefield, declaring that he wishes Paris had
never been born or had died unmarried (αἴθ᾽ ὄφελες ἄγονός τ᾽ ἔμεναι
ἄγαμός τ᾽ ἀπολέσθαι, 3.40). In the bedroom Helen changes her tack with
brusque abruptness, first telling Paris to go and challenge Menelaus for a
second time, then remarking that he had better not, since Menelaus would
probably kill him (3.432–36).[29] Compare first Achilles, who goads Aeneas
with a parallel insult in a famous flyting scene, when he urges him to retreat
into the mass of soldiers lest he be harmed (20.197). And compare again
Hector, who challenges his brother in similar terms ("Couldn't you stand

[26] Among female characters, only the confrontational and devious Hera uses such a vitri-
olic response to an intimate, although she fears Zeus when he responds angrily to her (ὡς
ἔφατ᾽, ἔδεισεν δὲ βοῶπις πότνια Ἥρη, 1.568), just as Helen fears Aphrodite (but not Paris;
ὡς ἔφατ᾽, ἔδεισεν δ᾽ Ἑλένη Διὸς ἐκγεγαυῖα, 3.418).

[27] Dog epithets are common flyting tools (Graver 1995: 49); Helen's self-abuse is thus a
technique common in verbal dueling that uniquely boomerangs on the speaker. On the typical contexts of flyting in epic, see Parks 1990. Although he is not sanguine about the transference of flyting patterns to suit amorous or familial conflict, Parks does admit the similarity between these and warrior conflicts (12–13). I am most interested in shared speech patterns,
which Parks does analyze, but not in any great detail and not in relation to what he considers
nondueling verbal exchanges. In contrast, Murnaghan (1999) points out that lament is also an
agonistic genre. On the abuse of Paris in particular, see Suter 1993.

[28] "Averting her eyes, she reproached her husband" (ὄσσε πάλιν κλίνασα, πόσιν δ᾽ ἠνί-
παπε μύθῳ, 3.427).

[29] Attempts have been made to explain Helen's seeming shift of direction and her ultimate
acquiescence to Paris' suggestion as due to her weakness and attraction to him (e.g., Hooker
1979; Edwards 1987:195–96). Kirk (1985: 327), in some contrast, regards the entire speech
as "bitterly sarcastic and hostile."

up to Ares-loving Menelaus?" 3.51), and then predicts that if he did he would end up "mingling with the dust" (μιγείης, 3.55). Both Helen and Hector contrast Paris unfavorably with Menelaus, and point up the superiority of the Greek by giving Paris' defeat sexual overtones (e.g., "mingling" [μιχθείς, μιγείης, 3.48, 55], "subduing" [δαμείς, δαμήης, 3.429, 436]). For Paris the lover, even encounters on the battlefield have a tincture of the bedroom.[30] These two scornful acknowledgments of his unwarlike attitude serve to frame book 3, so that it begins and ends with Paris' sensual presence and the bellicose types who reproach him: Hector and Helen. Helen's use of this stance is not nearly so straightforward as her brother-in-law's, of course. She imports a verbal style that belongs on the battlefield, and that here in the intimate context of the bedroom takes on an additional layer of meaning—offering a sexual as well as a military challenge.

Indeed, Paris (lover that he is) responds to this goading by treating it as a kind of bitter foreplay. And it appears that Helen's amorous husband has interpreted her taunts in some sense rightly, for Helen follows him to bed. By invoking her war-loving first husband in order to prick her bed-loving second, she employs the militaristic attitude of the one in order to denigrate qualities that she herself shares with the other, and her physical acquiescence reiterates her reluctant bond with him. That is, when she turns the emotional phrasing of the angry wish against her too-tender husband, she links herself to him and both of them to Aphrodite (since she and the goddess are the other recipients of such reproach). The hero's despair as well as his scorn thus take on a singular usage in Helen's mouth: in challenging those who share her affinities, she implicates herself in the abuse that she levels at them, while also preempting the criticism of others. In this way she stands poised against the gentle judgments of those who would forgive her, her character operating as a window on this defamatory tradition.

Something similar occurs in book 6, although Helen's tone has changed somewhat since her interaction with Paris in book 3, and now she speaks with a post-coital combination of enticement and gentle abuse. When Hector comes to rouse Paris from his sensuous reverie in the bedroom, Helen tries to get her manly brother-in-law to sit down by scorning her soft and lovely husband.[31] She engages in a delicate seduction of Hector, addressing him with "honey-sweet words" (μύθοισι . . . μειλιχίοισιν, 6.343). Both Nestor and the Sirens also speak in a honeyed manner, so that the term delimits a range of speech types from the authoritatively but gently persuasive to the dangerously seductive,[32] a mesmerizing quality that marks

[30] Cf. Hector's disparaging reference to Paris' "gifts of Aphrodite" (δῶρ' Ἀφροδίτης, 3.54) and Paris' own affirmation of the same (δῶρ' ἐραιὰ . . . χρυσέης Ἀφροδίτης, 3.64).

[31] Mackie (1995: 118–19) remarks that Helen's phrases seem carefully chosen to suit Hector's outlook.

[32] See Dickson 1995: 38.

Helen's speaking style in this passage. When Hector first enters and reproaches his brother, the mild Paris responds that Helen had just been urging him to return to battle with "soft words" (μαλακοῖς ἐπέεσσιν, 6.337)—unusual content for such beguiling tones. The enticing associations that attend *malakos* ("soft") thus contrast strangely with the stringency of her message, while those that attend *meilichios* ("honey-sweet") lend her words a potentially threatening quality. Thus Hector's refusal to sit with her becomes a refusal to play the victim role to her Siren, a role that his brother willingly takes on. While the Homeric poet may counter this ominous seductive quality at the surface level of the scene, it nonetheless resonates there as a disturbing subtext.

From this perspective, it should not be surprising that Helen begins her conversation with Hector by invoking her threatening qualities, but in the self-debasing mode that she employed with his father. She calls herself an "evil-devising, shudder-inspiring dog" (κυνὸς κακομηχάνου ὀκρυοέσσης, 6.344; cf. κυνός, 6.356; κυνώποδος, 3.180). The wish construction that follows (ὥς μ᾽ ὄφελ᾽ . . . οἴχεσθαι) is an elaborate expansion of her earlier use of it. Rather than simply desiring to die, she declares that she wishes that on her day of birth a gust of wind had carried her off to the mountains, or into a wave of the many-voiced sea (6.345–48). Helen purports to desire a type of end that Jean-Pierre Vernant relates to being seized by a god, invoking a connection between erotic love and death that he considers especially relevant to Helen's type.[33] An echo of her wish in book 3 that death had "pleased" her (ἀδεῖν, 3.173), Helen's lyrical desire for rapture here in *Iliad* 6 lends sensuous overtones to her speech. While her words explicitly depict regret, her flowery turns of phrase and sweetened tones suggest an attempt to soften Hector's attitude toward herself if not her husband: she sides with Hector in his chastising of his brother, yearns aloud for divine seizure, and notes ruefully her and Paris' future fame. Recall the similarity of Hector's and Helen's reproaches in book 3; here again she mimics his attitude, this time to his face with the goal of cementing her connection to him. Her maneuver is a delicate one. She must acknowledge her alliance with Paris in order to show her awareness of their shame; but she thereby also isolates herself from him, since he assumes no responsibility for his actions. As in book 3, Helen brackets herself with Paris as objects of abuse, highlighting their status here by using the *ophelon* phrase twice in expressions of heroic bitterness to apply to herself and her husband (6.345, 350). Homer thus has Helen transform the typical intentions of the phrase by using it for this anomalous speech act, layering self-abuse, scorn for an in-

---

[33] Vernant [1985] 1991b: 102–3; cf. above, note 19. Penelope makes a similar despairing wish to be borne away by a gust of wind (*Od.* 20.61–65); see Johnston 1994 for comparable connections to the Erinyes, etc.

timate, and a seductive allegiance of perspective, all of which ultimately aim at softening the heart of her interlocutor. While Hector does not in the end sit down with Helen, neither does he speak roughly to her, instead responding with a respect that resembles his father's treatment of her. By introducing a defamatory tradition that threatens to reveal her infamous side and yet ultimately serves an apotropaic function, Helen succeeds in deflecting blame: again, no one else abuses her as she abuses herself.

At the end of the *Iliad* (24.760–75), Helen has the final mourning speech over Hector's dead body—a surprising status that supports Graver's argument that the Homeric poet is forcefully asserting an alternate tradition that elevates Helen and questions her blame. But if we look more closely at precisely how she mourns Hector, beyond her use of the mourner's topos of bewailing her fate as vulnerable survivor, we can see that her lament in this case focuses entirely on the threat of blame—the threat, that is, of the other story, the tale of bad-dog Helen. This is not to say that other mourners do not fear ill repute: Andromache certainly does, but mostly for her son Astyanax (e.g., *Il.* 22.494–501).[34] Helen's lament, in some contrast, is only about repute; in detailing her fears for the future, she makes no mention of other horrors such as slavery and remarriage, which are often voiced by newly bereft female mourners in both epic and tragedy.[35] After expressing her usual sentiment of regret (24.764), Helen notes that she had never heard a debasing or disrespectful word from her brother-in-law. She adds that if anyone else in his family ever reproached her, Hector would fend them off verbally with his gentle mind and words (24.768–72). She concludes by declaring that everyone else shudders (πεφρίκασιν) in her presence (24.775).

Helen's final word in the *Iliad* resonates with the dread that she might inspire, as the dog-faced daughter of Nemesis whose self-blame in Homer repeatedly suggests this other story. Hector, like the poet, may be gentleminded toward Helen, but her description of his protection reveals how tenuous this praise tradition is; here as elsewhere in the poem her words declare one thing but point to another—this time her dangerous qualities, which cause a sensation in those around her like the chilly hand of Hades. At these moments Helen's figure suggests the deadly side of the female, to which Greek poets often attribute the downfall of men in some profound and sweeping manner. These figures are the embodiment of Fate (Μοῖρα/ Κήρ), the Medusa who freezes the bones, the Nemesis who is the end of the hubristic man, even the Aphrodite who (dog-faced) devours the husband's

---

[34] When alive, Hector seeks to cheer his weeping wife with grim praise for himself (*Il.* 460–61); see above regarding Helen's fear of ill repute, which is a hero's fear rather than a hero's wife's fear.

[35] Holst-Warhatt 1992: 112–13.

energy and wealth alike.[36] The word *nemesis* ("retribution") in fact surfaces repeatedly in Helen's speech and that of those who speak in her presence (e.g., 3.156, 3.410, 6.335–36, 6.351). That is, in the scenes where Helen appears, her presence seems to call forth the *nemesis* that is an essential aspect of her story. And her speeches, in their insistence on her infamous associations, serve as constant reminders of the just indignation and deserved retribution that acts of hubris bring down on the heads of those who commit them.

THE PAINLESS STORY

While Helen is a weaving narrator of her own story in the *Iliad* (3.125–28),[37] in the *Odyssey* the objects that associate her with weaving signal the context of formal ritual conducted by people of high status. In book 4, she descends from her bedroom accompanied by handmaidens and weaving implements that were gifts from Egyptian royalty—her own gifts, as the narrator points out, not those obtained by her husband (4.130). Moreover, she is accompanied by the handmaiden Adraste, a name that Clader notes recalls Adrasteia, a cult title of the goddess Nemesis;[38] the scene of her descent into the *megaron* in its entirety strongly suggests the entrance of a goddess—if a dangerous one. In book 15 she gives to Telemachus a gown of her own fine weaving as a token of guest-friendship, requesting that he accept it as a memory token of herself and that he give it to his future wife (15.124–29). The gesture should possess a disturbing ritual power, since a wedding gown from Helen would symbolize both the marriage bond and its transgression. And yet in both scenes Helen plies, without recoil from others, implements of guest-friendship (the condolence drug and the marriage dress) that not only are profoundly associated with her figure, but also suggest and then eerily suppress the problems that she embodies for storytelling on the one hand and gift-giving on the other.

Helen's speeches, which accompany her handling of these objects, invoke various models of authoritative speech—the Muses, the poet or choral performer, the speaker of prophecy—and demonstrate her sensitivity to the appropriate locution. Helen's first words to her audience draw purposeful attention to her perceptive abilities and narrative control. When she recognizes Telemachus as the son of Odysseus, she asks, "Should I lie or should I speak the truth?" (4.140), recalling the power that the Muses possess.[39] In

[36] See Graver 1995: 51.

[37] Clader 1976: 6–11; Austin 1975: 127–28; 1994: 37–42; Bergren 1980; Zeitlin [1981] 1996: 409–11; Kennedy 1986; Suzuki 1989: 40–43.

[38] Clader 1976: 62.

[39] Hes. *Theog.* 27; Homer's Muses "know all things" (ἴστε τε πάντα, *Il.* 2.485), which implies both truth and lies.

this scene Helen gives shape and purpose to the conversation and saves the dinner party (albeit in questionable fashion) by doling out to her hearers a condolence drug. The narrator terms this substance "no-pain" (νηπενθές, 4.221), while emphasizing the grotesque effects of such emotional benumbing. But the ambiguous and powerful drug, in combination with Helen's words, staunches the flow of tears among the diners, which her husband had tended to augment. The *nēpenthē* thus serves as an essential complement to her control of verbal interaction and storytelling. And although the juxtaposition of Helen's and Menelaus' stories also encourages the audience to question her true inclinations, it similarly promotes her narrative authority. She implicitly associates herself with Zeus, the Muses, and the epic poet, while Menelaus approves her story openly and imitates the structure of her narrative frame.

Most readers have focused on the ominous qualities of both Helen and her drug, and seemed to accept that Menelaus' is the true version of events. But Helen's command of verbal interaction is such that the *Odyssey*, unlike the *Iliad*, almost succeeds in suppressing completely the disturbing implications of her hosting strategies. These surface only briefly and cause little reaction in Helen's interlocutors, leaving behind in the external audience an eerie sense that they have been seduced by a rhetorically agile speaker and that all may not be well in Sparta.[40] As a measure of this near-success, Helen only refers to herself once with the dog epithet (κυνώπιδος, 4.145). That is, her defamatory tradition is not nearly so dominant as it is in the *Iliad*, and even her husband's story avoids blaming her directly for her actions. Although, as a metapoetic figure, Helen does seem in this scene to represent the doubling nature of storytelling,[41] as an adept speaker she calms indecision and effectively overshadows her husband's potentially upsetting tale.

Helen first explains that she will not recount all the feats that Odysseus undertook during the war; rather, she says, she will only describe his achievements within the walls of Troy. The phrase she uses in introducing her narrative resembles her husband's to Peisistratus (4.242, cf. 204–5); later he repeats her phrase almost exactly (4.271).[42] Her usage calls attention to her sensitivity to conversational context: she signals the suitability

---

[40] See Austin 1975: 187–89; he "corrects" his reading in his later analysis of the same scene (1994: 81–82).

[41] Zeitlin ([1981] 1996) has suggested that the scene depicts Helen as the embodiment of the double story and thus of the dissimulating potential of mimesis itself; see also Bergren 1983. Bergren (1981) argues that Helen's use of the drug, in combination with her tale, effects a seduction of her audience that recoils on the epic poet, hinting at his own narrative seduction. (Homer's epithets associate the drug with epic, as a number of scholars have noted.) Cf. Olson 1989; Doherty 1995a: 130 35.

[42] See further discussion below and in note 47.

of her story by sounding like her husband, who has been speaking with great warmth and familiarity about both Odysseus and Nestor. Helen also establishes her status as a narrator by suggesting that, like Telemachus' father, she possesses one of the primary attributes of the authoritative speaker: great perspicuity. Describing Odysseus' appearance in Troy disguised as a slave, she claims that she alone recognized him and taxed him with her knowledge. She emphasizes the extent of his disguise by repeating phrases that mark his likeness to a man of low status, a rhetorical strategy that underscores both his cleverness at deception and hers at detection (4.244–51). Odysseus, having beaten himself with blows that are unbefitting (ἀεικελί-ῃσι, 4.244) of the hero, is so unlike himself—so like a household slave or a beggar (οἰκῆ ἐοικώς, ἤισκε / δέκτῃ . . . τῷ ἴκελος, 4.245, 247–49)—that he slips into Troy (κατέδυ πόλιν, 4.246, 249) unnoticed, except by Helen herself. Odysseus counters her probing eye by refusing to confirm her identification until she has bathed and anointed him, dressed him well, and sworn a great oath of secrecy to him—that is, until she has treated him as do those other dread goddesses Calypso and Circe, from the care of the hero's body to the swearing of an oath not to harm him.[43]

Helen then explicitly claims that, after she played the role of ministering goddess, Odysseus told her the "whole plot" (πάντα νόον, 4.256) of the Greeks. Once again she emphasizes her omniscience, or at least the vast extent of her knowledge, leaving open the possibility that she may have even been told then about the Trojan horse (the device that would end the war)—as her probing response to it in Menelaus' story suggests. Helen also describes her heart's rejoicing amid the wail of the Trojan women at Odysseus' subsequent killing of Trojans (4.259–60), which (as she implies) she made possible by being loyal to those with whom she now dines.[44] Sitting once again with her first husband, she ends her story by implicitly comparing Menelaus favorably to Paris, calling the former "my husband" ([ἐμόν] πόσιν, 4.263), who, she declares, is not inferior to "anyone" (τευ, 4.264). Helen's self-portrait is carefully calibrated both to support her claims to narrative authority and to gratify her audience; it could not be more delicately balanced or more suitably told.

This elegant story is thrown into some question by Menelaus' depiction of Helen's loyalties in the war (4.265–89), although how well he succeeds in doing so or even how much he desires to has, I think, been exaggerated by recent readers of the scene. He initially responds to his wife's tale by remarking that she has told everything "in a fitting fashion" (κατὰ μοῖραν, 4.266), an interesting characterization for a speech whose pivotal sympathies he seems himself to refute. In rhetorical terms, phrases such as *kata moiran* do not assess the truth of the speech, but rather whether the speaker

[43] Cf. *Od.* 5.177–79, 5.263–64, 10.342–44, 358–65.
[44] Zeitlin [1981] 1996; Bergren 1983; Suzuki 1989: 42–43.

is behaving appropriately with her words. Gregory Nagy has argued convincingly that in Homer the phrases *kata moiran* and *kata aisan* indicate conformity to epic diction in particular.[45] Helen's speech would then meet the criteria not only of dinner-table etiquette but also of the poet's genre, further supporting her status both as an authoritative speaker and as a metarhetorical figure whose implications for speech-making help delineate the boundaries of the genre itself.

Menelaus thus implicitly approves Helen's ability to tell a story that highlights Odysseus' ingenuity and his military prowess and that thereby flatters and gratifies his son. He then reaffirms the aptness of her speech by using a similar frame for his own tale. Helen's first words had paid homage to Zeus, father of the Muses and of Helen herself, so that she established her unparalleled authority as a knower and a speaker by implied association with both (a connection aided by the repetition of "all" [ἅπαντα . . . πάντα, 4.237, 240])—in effect collapsing the roles of the Muses and the poet.[46] And perhaps most important, by underscoring her role as a knowing storyteller, she allied herself with Odysseus. In his introduction Menelaus echoes one phrase of Helen's exactly (4.242 and 4.271); he also employs a similar introductory strategy, pointing up his own status and exclaiming over the endurance of Odysseus in the service of the Achaeans (4.267–73).[47] Most

---

[45] Nagy 1979: 40 and n. 2, 82n., 134; cf. the related phrase "beyond measure" (ὑπὲρ μόρον, ὑπὲρ αἶσαν), which denotes the opposite—that is, a hubristic inattention to fitting measure, an excess that is anathema to epic.

[46] Cf. *Il.* 2.484–93 (Catalogue of Ships), and see Ford 1992: 72–74 (*Il.* 2.488 = *Od.* 4.240); on this collapse of roles by Hesiod, see Lardinois 1995: 201. Helen's use of the phrase makes it sound as if she might be able to tell all, while the poet emphasizes his incapability (*Il.* 2.489–90). See note 47 below for details.

[47] Helen:

ἀτὰρ θεὸς ἄλλοτε ἄλλῳ
Ζεὺς ἀγαθόν τε κακόν τε διδοῖ· δύναται γὰρ <u>ἅπαντα</u>·	} narrator's status
ἦ τοι νῦν δαίνυσθε καθήμενοι ἐν μεγάροισι	↓
καὶ μύθοις τέρπεσθε· ἐοικότα γαρ καταλέξω.	↓
<u>πάντα</u> μὲν οὐκ ἂν ἐγὼ μυθήσομαι οὐδ' ὀνομήνω	} narrator's status (cf. *Il.* 2.488)
<u>ὅσσοι Ὀδυσσῆος ταλασίφρονος</u> εἰσιν ἄεθλοι.	} subject + epithet
<u>ἀλλ' οἶον τόδ' ἔρεξε καὶ ἔτλη καρτερὸς ἀνὴρ</u>	} deed + subject
<u>δήμῳ ἔνι Τρώων,</u> ὅθι πάσχετε πήματ' Ἀχαιοί.	} site of deed; reference to pain (Trojan → Greek) (4.242–43)

Menelaus:

ἤδη μὲν πολέων ἐδάην βουλήν τε νόον τε	} narrator's status
ἀνδρῶν ἡρώων, πολλὴν δ' ἐπελήλυθα γαῖαν·	} (cf. *Od.* 1.3)
ἀλλ' οὔ πω τοιοῦτον ἐγὼν ἴδον ὀφθαλμοῖσιν	
<u>οἶον Ὀδυσσῆος ταλασίφρονος</u> ἔσκε φίλον κῆρ·	} subject + epithet
<u>οἶον καὶ τόδ' ἔρεξε καὶ ἔτλη καρτερὸς ἀνὴρ</u>	} deed + subject
<u>ἵππῳ ἔνι ξεστῷ,</u> ἵν' ἐνήμεθα πάντες ἄριστοι	} site of deed;
Ἀργείων Τρώεσσι φόνον καὶ κῆρα φέροντες.	} reference to pain (Trojan → Greek) (4.242–73)

pointedly, he declares that, although he has encountered the strategies and mental types of many men and traveled far (like Odysseus), he has never seen such a one as Odysseus. Both introductory strategies seek to control the reception of the tale by pointing (either implicitly or explicitly) to the wisdom and experience of the tellers, thereby grounding the authority of both as narrators in their known characters and their fortuitous resemblance to the authoritative type whose story they tell (i.e., Menelaus is a hero-traveler, Helen is an associate of the Muses). In affirming the appropriateness of his wife's speech and echoing her verbal strategy, Menelaus effectively weakens the negative impact of his own story.

This potential conflict is further mitigated by the fact that Menelaus blames his wife's actions on Aphrodite, who intended that Helen be driven to bring ruin to the Trojans (4.274–75). In the end, Odysseus' protector Athena leads Helen away from the horse, so that in Menelaus' story, goddesses compel both her arrival on the scene and her leave-taking. The only event not motivated by the goddesses—and for which Helen may thus be held responsible—is her imitation of the voices of the warriors' wives. In this she is met and matched by Odysseus. As in her own story, here in her husband's Helen and Odysseus are paired as singularly clever, especially in relation to verbal manipulation. If Helen can don multiple verbal disguises (something the hero does elsewhere in the *Odyssey*), Odysseus can effectively see through her disguise (as she alone saw through his).

Thus while Odysseus sits inside the Trojan horse, alone in his recognition of Helen, she—still a sharp-eyed detector—literally probes its significance, fondling its sides as if touching all the Greek husbands and mouthing the voices of their wives (4.277–79). This mimetic ability matches that which the female chorus is said to have (to its great glory) in the *Hymn to Delian Apollo* (162–64).[48] Like the Muses, Helen can tell the truth or not; like the rhapsode or choral performer, she can imitate the voices of others to the delight and/or danger of her audience. And although as an object of narrative she does signal the doubling, dissimulating nature of mimesis, as a speaking subject she exhibits a formidable facility to detect the identities of others, to assume the roles of various authoritative types, and to suit her tale to the context of its utterance. Helen herself merely claims before she tells her story that she will speak "suitable things" (ἐοικότα, 4.239)—things that, if they are not true, ought to be, by virtue of the extent to which they fit the context in which they are told. *Eoikota* are ethically "true"; they suit character and situation and are thus the mainstay of the rhetorically adept speaker.

---

[48] In the *Hymn. Hom. Ap.*, the poet calls this feat a "wondrous thing" (θαῦμα, 156), and his praise of the Delian maidens is covert praise for himself, just as Helen's narrative seduction suggests the poet's own. See further on this passage in the *Hymn. Hom. Ap.* in Richard Martin's contribution to this volume.

Compare the scene in book 15, where Helen's extraordinary control of signifying objects (e.g., the gown, but also the eagle and the goose in the omen that she deciphers) effects a near-complete suppression of the troubling aspects of her figure, to the extent that she is able to hand over an item that she explicitly labels as a marriage gift without any negative reaction on the part of its recipient. When Helen gives Telemachus the robe, she calls it "a memory token from the hands of Helen for the much-desired wedding time" (15.126), precisely the ritual whose luxurious trappings and illicit transgression she symbolizes. This scene echoes one in *Iliad* 6 where Hecuba chooses a gown to dedicate to Athena, but with emphatically different effect. There the poet states explicitly that Paris took these gowns from Sidon on his way home with Helen (6.289–92), so that Hecuba's offering—which she makes when the Greeks are effectively at the door—is a precisely matched payment for Helen's having been brought to Troy with these same items. In this scene Helen's figure surfaces as a reminder of Paris' transgression, as another ruinous object, whose return may not bring about the gods' protection (as the dedication of the gown does not, 6.311). When Helen gives the marriage dress to Telemachus in *Odyssey* 15, it is of her own making (i.e., she is associated with it as a craftsman, rather than as a fellow object). She is its author, in effect, and she assigns to it the label and type of narrative that she desires for it.[49] While the object, in its connection to marriage and gift-giving, may still resonate with negative connotations for the external audience, Helen exercises impressive control over its signification for the internal audience, transforming it from a would-be ruinous object into one with happy associations.

This scene also adds another model of authoritative speech to Helen's repertoire. Her agile reading of the omen that marks the departure of Telemachus and Peisistratus from Sparta (15.160–78) precisely forecasts Odysseus' interpretation of Penelope's dream (*Od.* 19.555–58), thereby linking Helen both to the seer's role and, once again, to Odysseus himself. Helen's prophecy foreshadows Odysseus', and like a good seer she foretells what does come to pass. Most interestingly, she relates with striking brevity the plot and conclusion of the *Odyssey* ("Thus Odysseus having suffered many evils and wandered much, will return home and exact retribution"),[50] again collapsing the roles that mark a special authority: the omniscience of the Muses and the narrative compass of the poet. Compare especially the opening of the *Odyssey* (1.1–5), with its similar repetition of "many/much" (πολλά), its juxtaposition of wandering and suffering, and its reference to

---

[49] Note that Helen uses the word μνῆμα, a word that designates some sort of ritual marker—like a monument, or tombstone—something often *inscribed*, which is analogous to what Helen effects with her speech.

[50] ὣς Ὀδυσεὺς κακὰ <u>πολλὰ παθὼν</u> καὶ <u>πόλλ' ἐπαληθεὶς</u> / οἴκαδε <u>νοστήσει</u> καὶ τίσεται, 15.176–77.

nostos, Odysseus' primary goal.[51] Where the Homeric poet holds off the end of the story, Helen includes it, spanning the entire narrative in a single sentence.[52]

In *Odyssey* 15, then, Helen seems in possession of an inhuman knowledge, and as usual Menelaus is greatly overshadowed by his more mentally and rhetorically agile wife. Here he "ponders how he might express his thoughts judiciously" (κατὰ μοῖραν, 15.169–70), while his wife prophesies with startling alacrity. Note that Menelaus is unsure how to speak in a context that requires a suitable response, precisely the kind of response that Helen is capable of, as her husband himself had acknowledged earlier (κατὰ μοῖραν, 4.266). Helen's mantic capabilities elicit an avowal from Telemachus that he will worship her as a goddess in his own land, pledging the establishment of a cult in Ithaca like that which did exist in the archaic period in Sparta and perhaps elsewhere.[53] Thus the scene's final words on Helen acknowledge her status not merely as prophet or poet but also as herself divine—as one, that is, who might know more than the average human, not just about the details of the story but also about how to tell it in a deeply appropriate manner. In the *Odyssey,* Helen is persuasive enough that she nearly manages to circumvent entirely the obvious problem with her voice in the first place: that it is changeable and multiple, just as her figure is symbolic of the multiplicity of stories to be told.

Both the *Iliad* and the *Odyssey* depict Helen as a subtly appropriate and appropriative speaker. She echoes the typical phrases of the mournful wife and the challenged hero in a unique form of self-abuse, often deploying this emotional tone to draw her audience into sympathy with her. Or she speaks like a divinely persuasive narrator, while the self-image she projects invokes the inevitable suitability of her words. The changeable quality of Helen's voice reflects her indeterminate and yet authoritative status in Homeric epic: she is half god, half mortal, a forbidding presence even among aristocratic men; she is the wife of too many men, and so the contested possession of everyone and no one; her speaking style is similarly that of everyone and no one. In the *Iliad* Helen's voice is not openly authoritative, but she succeeds in using her despairing, self-abusive tone to maintain a covert control of verbal exchanges. The *Odyssey* represents Helen as being in easy command of the conversation; her voice is authoritative and deeply suitable

---

[51]   Ἄνδρα μοι ἔννεπε Μοῦσα, πολύτροπον, <u>ὃς μάλα πολλὰ</u>
        <u>πλάγχθη,</u> ἐπεὶ Τροίης ἱερὸν πτολίεθρον ἔπερσε·
        <u>πολλῶν</u> ἀνθρώπων ἴδεν ἄστεα καὶ νόον ἔγνω
        <u>πολλὰ</u> δ᾽ ὅ γ᾽ ἐν πόντῳ <u>πάθεν ἄλγεα</u> ὃν κατὰ θύμον,
        ἀρνύμενος ἥν τε ψυχὴν καὶ <u>νόστον</u> ἑταιρῶν.

[52] Contrast Helen's imperfect knowledge of events in the Teichoscopia (Lynn-George 1988: 33).

[53] See Clader 1976: 63–64, 69, 72–78; Skutsch 1987: 189, 190–91.

in manner, if often ambiguous or possibly deceptive in content. In her verbal guises of the mournful wife, the despairing or scornful warrior, the perspicacious poet-goddess, or the gracious host, she shows herself capable of the mimesis with which Menelaus charges her—with all the subtle enticement and potential danger that implies. Helen's variegated speaking style and striking narrative control signal her encompassing role in the Homeric poems as the embodiment of Nemesis. She is the beginning and end of the Trojan War story for both the Greeks and the Trojans, and the figure whose conflicting characterizations and multiple voices repeatedly raise the specter of fateful competition, be it military or poetic.

CHAPTER THREE

The Voice at the Center of the World

THE PYTHIAS' AMBIGUITY AND AUTHORITY

LISA MAURIZIO

THE TITLE of this volume, "Making Silence Speak," indicates a goal of many historical enterprises, namely, how do we make long silent empirical evidence speak to us about the experiences, practices, and events of those who have come before us? New trends such as cultural studies and postmodernism, not to mention the behemoth relativism,[1] have challenged rudimentary notions about the relationship between evidence and past reality, creating a crisis in the discipline of history.[2] Such trends pose particular difficulties for any history of ancient women because, although ever-present in artistic representations, ancient women have left few artistic works of their own to posterity. Silent objects in most ancient sources, they often understandably become silent objects in scholarship, which focuses on male representations of and attitudes toward the female. Perhaps this tendency explains why Apollo's inspired priestesses at Delphi are judged, if not silent, then incoherent babblers or mere mouthpieces of Delphic priests, and not the composers of Delphic oracles. Every ancient source without exception speaks of the Pythias (or Apollo) delivering oracles, and the Pythias, not priests, are accused in cases of blackmail.[3] Routinized or perhaps wishful thinking,[4] not evidence, has created an enduring orthodoxy about Delphi

---

[1] On historical studies and relativism, see Appleby, Hunt, and Jacob 1994: 271–309.

[2] Useful overviews of the crises in historical studies may be found in Appleby, Hunt, and Jacob 1994; Bunzl 1997; Jenkins 1997; and N. J. Wilson 1999, to name but a few.

[3] Pleistonax and his brother bribe the prophetess at Delphi (Thuc. 5.16); Cleisthenes bribes the Pythia with money (Hdt. 5.63, 5.66, and 6.123), and Cobon bribes a Pythia named Perialla, who is then deprived of her office (Hdt. 6.66 and 6.75). See Roux 1976: 163.

[4] E.g., Amandry 1950: 168: "If one believes that a supernatural intervention occurs at the moment of revelation, the primacy of the Pythia can be maintained. If not, it would be difficult to admit that an illiterate woman, without any of the gifts of a Cassandra, chosen only for her moral virtue, could annnounce the response instantaneously, formulated in prose, let alone in hexameters. . . . But one can scarcely believe that, for a political affair such as a treaty of alliance, the response was not dictated to the Pythia . . . the questions were presented in writing, a certain delay was necessary for the elaboration of a response, which was officially carried by the Pythia to the consultants" (my translation). Amandry's hypotheticals illustrate the

that only recently has been corrected.[5] Simply put, the Pythias did compose and deliver Delphic oracles. The Pythias did speak. There is no evidence to the contrary. Apart from this fact, we know virtually nothing about the women who filled this post.[6] How to interpret Delphic oracles as women's speech nonetheless poses many difficulties because the Pythias were interrogated by exclusively male clients,[7] and their oracles were transmitted orally and then recorded in writing by men.[8]

The ancients were sanguine about the possibility of interpreting the Pythias' language. Often Delphic tales reveal how clients misinterpreted oracles. Similarly, in Aeschylus' *Agamemnon*, the male chorus cannot understand the seemingly unambiguous prophecy, "I say that you shall look upon Agamemnon's end," uttered by Cassandra, a prophetess inspired by Apollo (*Ag.* 1246).[9] The interpretative failure of the chorus and of many of the Pythias' clients—whether willful or inevitable—presents the possibility that ancient reflections on interpreting the Pythias' and Cassandra's prophecies may provide clues for our historical inquiries. In particular, both address the relationship between ambiguity and authority in female prophetic speech.

In the *Agamemnon*, we can ascribe the chorus' obtuseness to Apollo's curse: because Cassandra deceived Apollo, he has granted her prophetic visions, but not authority, the ability to persuade her audience of her dire predictions. On the other hand, Aeschylus' attention to interpreting words and signs[10] and his adoption of metaphoric expression, typical of Delphic

---

fanciful reasoning that flies in the face of all evidence, evidence soberly reviewed by Fontenrose (1978: 196–232), who argues that the Pythia did indeed give oracles. One should note, however, that Fontenrose dismisses most oracles as *post eventum* creations and imagines a very limited role for the Pythias.

[5] Fontenrose 1978: 196–232; Price 1985; Maurizio 1995.

[6] A late Delphic inscription implies that they were selected from the local population of Delphians (Fontenrose 1978: 211). They were perhaps young women who were later replaced by old women dressed as young women (Diod. Sic. 16.26, with Sissa [1987] 1990: 36).

[7] Plutarch (*Mor.* 385c) records a law forbidding women from approaching the temple, on which see Fontenrose 1978: 217.

[8] Oracular texts reflect an oral tradition in which the effect of male transmission is problematic if not impossible to evaluate. No oracles, because of their oral transmission and reformulation in writing, represent the exact words of any one Pythia. Nonetheless, they are reflections of the types of oracle the Pythias issued at Delphi, just as our text of the *Iliad* is a representative rendition of the type of song early oral poets sang. Thus the focus of this project is not "Are oracles the *ipsissima verba* of the Pythias in light of male oral and written transmission?" This question would be impossible to answer, and finally unnecessary for a consideration of Delphic oracles as evidence of the female voice in archaic Greece. See Maurizio 1997 on oracles as an oral tradition.

[9] All translations of Aeschylus' *Oresteia* are from Lloyd-Jones 1979.

[10] See, for example, Goldhill (1984 and 1986), who has written extensively on how the *Oresteia* addresses questions of interpretation.

speech, suggest that this scene is a meditation upon ambiguous speech and the dynamics of communal interpretation of a female voice. Ambiguity, Aeschylus suggests, appears necessary for prophetic authority because when Cassandra speaks most clearly, the chorus most adamantly rejects her words. Thus, Cassandra's sometimes ambiguous speech and failed prophetic authority is the inverse of the Pythias' frequently ambiguous oracles and unquestioned authority. In Delphic tales, the responsibility for falsehood inherent in ambiguous oracles is displaced onto male clients, who often misinterpret oracles. This repeating motif protects the Pythias' speech from accusations of deception and safeguards their authority as Apollo's mediums.

Many historians have interpreted Delphic ambiguity as a feature typical of prophetic language (like the chorus when confronted by Cassandra [Aesch. *Ag.* 1255]), as a poetic elaboration of those who recorded oracles,[11] or as a strategy of Delphic priests to ensure that Delphic oracles would always seem true.[12] Other scholars, examining mythological figures such as the Muses or Pandora as well as metaphors of weaving and seduction for poetic composition, have noted a persistent link between ambiguous language and the female in the Greek male imagination.[13] These studies suggest why a Greek male might have accepted ambiguous oracles from a prophetess and remain relevant in a consideration of the female authorship of ambiguous Delphic oracles. Yet we can pursue other analyses of Delphic ambiguity and of female prophetic authority, to which it is linked.[14]

In Michel de Certeau's treatment of mystics and demoniacs ("possessed women"), he draws parallels between the nature of their language, its in-

[11] Crahay 1956: 72 and 343–46.

[12] Parke and Wormell 1956, 1: 94.

[13] Bergren (1983: 71) argues that the Greek male attributes a special knowledge to the female "that results in a capacity for double speech, for both truth and the imitation of truth, a paradoxical speech hopelessly ambiguous to anyone whose knowledge is less than the speaker's." She lists the Pythias as females who fall on the positive end of this imagined spectrum because they possess "voices of truth." Detienne ([1967] 1996: 79) summarizes "ambivalent speech is a woman . . . " and captures the persistent association between femaleness and ambiguity. The recent study of Scheid and Svenbro ([1994] 1996) on weaving as a metaphor for speech complements Bergren.

[14] Not all oracles are ambiguous. Of the roughly six hundred oracles attributed to Delphi whose style and content vary greatly—some contain straightforward instructions about ritual matters in simple prose, others are in hexameters—one-third can be labeled ambiguous. This variety of styles does not require us (*pace* Fontenrose) to cull "authentic" oracles from forgeries. First, the ancients accepted all of these oracles as authentic. Second, in a cogent analysis of Delphi's oracular style (*De Pyth. or.*), Plutarch explains that the generic features of ambiguity and verse, while typical of the early Pythias' oracular style, evolved into less poetic and more prosaic responses. Delphic oracles have been collected by Parke and Wormell (1956) and Fontenrose (1978). Andersen (1987) has collected the oracles in hexameter. For a catalogue of ambiguous oracles, see Maurizio 1993: Appendix I. Hereafter all oracles will be designated "PW" with the number indicating their place in Parke and Wormell's collection (1956: vol. 2).

terpretation, and our own historical projects. Mystical writings, he argues, "display a passion for what *is*, for the world as it 'exists,' for the thing itself" and entice the scholar to question what referent, what thing, makes a text properly "mystical."[15] De Certeau defers this question in favor of asking how the social conditions of sixteenth- and seventeenth-century Europe shaped the formal dimensions of mystical writings. I likewise propose to ask: "What social and cultural trends in archaic Greece made ambiguity a viable and even desirable mode of speech for the Pythias?" and conversely: "How did Delphic ritual authorize and validate the Pythias' ambiguous oracles?" I will not define Delphic oracles, nor distinguish them from other prophetic speech or Delphic ambiguity from other forms of ambiguity in favor of considering how Delphic ambiguity functioned in archaic Greece.[16]

In his essay on demoniacs, de Certeau argues that inquisitors' spiritual beliefs and social aspirations shaped the questions they asked female demoniacs, which in turn dictated the answers they accepted and recorded.[17] In this way, the voice of demoniacs is doubly other—a demon's and then an inquisitor's. This voice entices one to search for its identity or subjectivity, a search de Certeau dismisses in favor of analyzing the contours of these texts' "I." Similarly, I shall ask: "How does ambiguity trace, if not wholly define, the paradox of the Pythias' experiences as women with authoritative voices, whose speech followed cultural stereotypes and was accepted insofar as it was believed to be Apollo's and not their own?" I eschew the question of finding the real and true subject of the Pythias, and instead suggest that we can find traces of that subject in the complex web of their ambiguity, which enshrined the possible though limited ways in which women could speak in archaic Greece.

AMBIGUITY: "THE POWER TO INDUCE A DEPARTURE"

Delphi's rise to prominence in archaic Greece is contemporaneous and inextricably linked with colonization, tyranny, and political reforms, beyond

[15] De Certeau [1986] 1993: 81.

[16] The topic of ambiguity in language and even in prophecy, on which the locus classicus is Stanford 1939, is beyond the scope of this chapter. See also the brief and insightful essay on rationality and oracular ambiguity by Vernant ([1974] 1991: 303–17). Roth (1982) surveys Greek prophets and prophetesses and argues that ecstatic or intuitive prophecy, that is, prophecy that involves inspiration and not the reading of entrails, beans, etc., is almost exclusively female. Ambiguity is also associated with certain male figures, such as Teiresias, Proteus, and Odysseus, who have features linked with the female, and is not exclusively the language of females, real or imagined. The fact that some males speak ambiguously does not affect my discussion, which does not depend on an exclusive association, whether for cultural or essentialist reasons, of the female with ambiguity in Greek thought and practice.

[17] De Certeau [1975] 1988.

the functionalist notion that Delphi sanctioned these new ventures.[18] Without being able to ascertain causality in any precise fashion, we can observe that Delphi's renowned ambiguity evolved in response to the spiritual, practical, and conceptual needs of oikists ("colonial founders"), tyrants, and their respective constituents as articulated in the divinatory ritual.[19] Both sets of clients were involved in the creation of a new social and political reality and required a new source of authoritative wisdom to forge ahead. Exiled from the past, whether from mother city or from former modes of governance and social structure, and in need of an imaginable future, colonizers and tyrants traveled to Delphi, which proved itself necessary and vital by providing both a past and a future. Its consequent prominence and the language it adapted to suit its clients' needs, then, was inevitably shaped by both tyranny and colonization, the two movements I will explore.[20]

The Pythias responded to colonists' needs by mirroring them: the Pythias developed a "style," ambiguity,[21] that traced the colonists' desire to make the unknown readable by replicating it in language. They translated clients' confusion about a necessary exploration of unknown land to the exploration of an unknown voice, simultaneously female and divine. Ambiguous oracles and foreign soil became loci for the recognition of uncertainty in changing times. The Pythias' ambiguous style, however, was not merely a representational strategy.[22] Rather, ambiguous oracles sanctioned the attempt to move beyond the known world by advising clients to seek

[18] Malkin (1989) outlines the various ways in which Delphi developed alongside colonization, tyranny, and political reforms and assesses whether Delphi had a consistent policy with respect to such social and political upheaval. While I disagree with his founding assumption that the "men of Delphoi" directed its policy (131), I have benefited greatly from and agree in large measure with his emphasis on Delphi's role as an innovator of change and not a proponent of the status quo (152). I examine the impact of Delphi's beginning on the type of language its Pythias used as well as on a slightly different set of causal factors that facilitated Delphi becoming a progressive rather than a conservative institution.

[19] The voluminous literature on colonization is reviewed by (with useful summaries and bibliographies of earlier work therein) Cawkwell (1992) and Tandy (1997: esp. 75–76). See also Snodgrass 1980; Murray 1980; Malkin 1987 and 1989; and Morgan 1990. On tyranny, see Andrewes 1956; Berve 1967; Mosse 1969; Pleket 1969; with McGlew (1993: 1–13), who overviews various scholarly approaches to tyranny.

[20] Malkin (1989: 135) writes, "Forrest [1957] seems to be right in saying that colonization contributed more to Delphoi's rise than *vice versa.*"

[21] De Certeau [1986] 1993: 81.

[22] Dougherty (1993) focuses on how ambiguous oracles presented colonists as wise interpreters, capable of establishing cities abroad, and provided a rhetorical structure that mimicked and represented colonization in *post eventum* colonial narratives. Much of my study is consonant with and has benefited from her work. However, I would emphasize how colonization influenced Delphi to adopt ambiguity as a "style," which in turn responded to the social rift that leave-taking entailed, and not how narratives of Delphic oracles provided useful rhetorical strategies for justifying the Greek usurpation of foreign lands after the fact (Dougherty 1993: 54).

seemingly impossible objects, landscapes, or animals (*adunata*). Colonists, for example, were told to find where "a wooden dog bites" (PW 323) or "rain falls from a clear sky" (PW 525) or "fish and deer graze in the same field" (PW 497–98).[23] To seek a wooden dog that bites is to search simultaneously for a new understanding of the world embodied in the ambiguous command, and for god, the ultimate referent, the ground, the source of being. In this way, the Pythias forged a way to view the world that responded to social upheavals by the adoption and elevation of an ambiguous style. Conversely, colonists' impending exploration of an unknown land encouraged the development and widespread acceptance of a female voice that was unknowable, yet existentially secured as true.

While colonists were spatially exiled to an unknown land, tyrants and their subjects were chronologically exiled. To tyrants, who often lacked an aristocratic genealogy to justify their rise to power, to those who had a genealogy that no longer guaranteed their place in a social order, and to the societies where social unrest led to tyranny, the past was politically dead because it no longer justified the tyrant's impending redistribution of power and wealth, while the future was uncertain. Just as the Pythias' ambiguous oracles were analogous to foreign soil (both were unknown and had to be explored in order to provide a foundation, both literal and political, for a new society), tyrannical oracles were analogous to the tyrant himself. Both were unknown and had to be "discovered" to provide a political ground for a new social order. Thus tyrants' oracles describe their ancestors, their birth, or their identity in seemingly impossible ways. The Corinthians are told about their future tyrant Kypselus that "an eagle gives birth among the rocks and will bear a strong flesh-eating lion" (PW 7). Kypselus is also described as a "rock" in an oracle given to his father, Aetion (PW 6). Orthagoras is described as a scourge to the Sicyonians (PW 23). Here, too, ambiguity mirrored the tyrant and his society's predicament: it described their genealogies in impossible ways and thereby established their birth as the guarantor and spiritual anchor for the future.

The Pythias adopted ambiguity because it not only accommodated their clients' predicaments but also bolstered Delphi's position as a source of wisdom in archaic Greece. They deployed hexameter and some traditional hexametric formulae, but they neither replicated Homeric or Hesiodic poetry in a sustained way nor contradicted or violated its conventions.[24] More important than the formal similarities and differences between Delphic oracles and Homer and Hesiod are their social roles in archaic Greece.

[23] For a complete list of colonization oracles, see Fontenrose 1978: 439. On oracles with *adunata*, see ibid.: 70–72, 79–83; and Dougherty 1993: ch. 3.

[24] The relationship betweeen hexametric oracles and Hesiodic and Homeric verse is treated extensively by Fernández Delgado (1986) and Fontenrose (1978: ch. 6). For treatments of individual hexametric oracles and traditional poetry, see, for example, McLeod 1961 and Dobson 1979.

Homer and Hesiod provided traditional knowledge that could be used analogously to address social problems and were "ethical and legal exemplars."[25] There were, however, no compelling parallels in such poetry that could palliate, explain, or justify the risks of colonization or radical changes in governance on behalf of a group of citizens who had to create a political identity sundered from their city of birth or their past.[26] Delphic oracles enabled such departures, yet they did not simply replace Homer and Hesiod because they never constituted a formal body of knowledge, but merely responded to particular crises.[27]

Ambiguous oracles, rather, demanded interpretation, which in turn allowed for the reevaluation of traditional poetry by pointing to a general linguistic indeterminacy. To search for a wooden dog that bites or a rock who will rule is to recognize that reality and language are not commensurate or transparent. Ambiguous oracles inculcated a questioning of the world as their interpreters knew it. They freed their clients from tradition, from oral stories celebrating heroes' virtues heard and digested, and modeled ways of reinterpreting both the known and the unknown. Since ambiguous oracles suggested that all language was unstable and in need of interpretation, even perhaps of rejection, the Pythias were able to dislodge Homer and Hesiod's authority as sources of wisdom.[28] Thus ambiguity served Delphi by indirectly weakening the importance of Homer and Hesiod. Delphi's own authority and importance could only grow proportionally.

Ambiguity also served the clients outside of the divinatory ritual and thereby increased Delphi's success. The Pythias did not provide obvious answers to clients' dilemmas, but instead issued ambiguous oracles full of promises that the clients could create, yet believe that they had discovered. In this way, the Pythias removed themselves from the oracle's reception, interpretation, and use. The emphasis of most oracular tales is on the client's ability to interpret his oracle and thereby communicate with Apollo. The Pythias were simply faithful translators of Apollo who enabled a conversation, if not a contest, between male clients and a male god, best illustrated in Sophocles' *Oedipus Rex*,[29] or in Herodotus' tale of the impending Persian invasion of Athens. When the Athenians were told to put their trust in a "wooden wall," they debated its meaning in an Assembly (Hdt. 7.141–43). This tale shows how oracular interpretation became pivotal in a commu-

[25] Robb 1994: 61–62, 83. Robb argues more comprehensively throughout his book how Homer and Hesiod were used in archaic Greece.

[26] One possible exception may be Homer's description of how the Phaeacians established Scheria (*Od.* 6.9–10), with Tandy 1997: 81.

[27] De Certeau [1986] 1993: 88–90. De Certeau's ideas about mystical writings have greatly influenced my thinking about oracular language here and throughout this chapter.

[28] The competitive nature of Greek society is well documented. On the Seven Sages and the Pre-Socratics, two groups of Delphi's competitors for authoritative knowledge in the archaic arena, see Martin 1993 and Spariosu 1991: 57–98, respectively.

[29] On the relationship of gender, translation, and Oedipal contests, see Chamberlain 1988.

nity's acceptance of an oracle and replaced the hidden divinatory enunciation at Delphi with open exegesis that forged an exclusive bond between community and Apollo. In colonial tales, the irrelevance of the Pythias in the fulfillment of their oracles is registered in the geographic distance between Delphi and the new colony, in tyrannical tales merely by the power and success of the tyrant. Yet, herein lies an irony: if Delphic ambiguity is attributed to the Pythias at a particular historical moment, this ambiguity nonetheless had the effect of erasing the Pythias' importance as the human and female voices of Apollo. Likewise, oracles erased themselves once fulfilled and dissolved into their referents. Thus the Pythias and their oracles were powerful and authoritative, but only for a fleeting moment.

Despite their transitory power, ambiguous oracles had an undeniable materiality. For ambiguous oracles almost paradoxically asserted that they had a fixed referent, namely a future site or tyrant, an assertion for which the Pythias' divine voice became the epistemic foundation (it predicts and hence guarantees the future).[30] Oracles induced an attention to language and interpretation but equally displayed a passion for things, for the world as it exists, "a passion for what is its own authority and depends on no outside guarantee."[31] To find a colony or forge a new polity is to enter a brave new world that would no longer need any justification or raison d'être. It was. It was as the oracle said it would be. The Pythias' oracles were ambiguous, but simultaneously definitive, powerful, and complete in themselves, without need of confirmation, because pregnant with reference. Once that reference was apparent, the oracle, however ambiguous or potent, dissolved and expended itself in that explosive moment. In colonial tales, an oikist, often serendipitously, finds the sign an oracle predicted and there builds his colony. His discovery is simultaneously irrefutable proof of the Pythias' oracles and the birth of a new society.[32] The reality of Apollo's word, like a seed, marks and germinates the colonists' soil and blossoms into a city, so that the new social order appears to be born from the oracle itself.[33]

Similarly in tyrants' tales, the oracle seems not simply to forecast his rule, but to engender it, for the tyrant's birth is often emphasized in these tales, making Apollo appear to be his progenitor. In the story of Orthagoras, for example, a Sikyonian embassy at Delphi is told that Sikyon needs a scourge and that whoever upon returning to Sikyon first hears that a son has been born to him will be father of Sikyon's next ruler. Because Andreas, a cook of the embassy, hears first that his son has been born, his son Orthagoras becomes tyrant or scourge of Sikyon (Diod. Sic. 8.24).[34] Within the logic

---

[30] De Certeau [1986] 1993: 81.
[31] Ibid.
[32] Maurizio 1993: ch. 4.
[33] Bloch 1983: 37.
[34] PW 23. On Sikyon, see Griffin 1982.

of this story, when the embassy returns to Sikyon, a new social order will arise. At that originary moment, the first male born will be Sikyon's oldest son, who will rule. The oracle's emphasis on the birth of the tyrant seemingly from the country itself and a human father makes Orthagoras' rule as just and inevitable as birth itself. The repetition of prophetic words in this story in the form of an inadvertent "birth announcement" replaces the act of procreation itself with prophetic words and emphasizes how prophetic language reproduces itself in the world. Just as the oracle must come true, must give birth to the future, the first birth announcement the embassy hears must announce Sikyon's next tyrant because saying makes it so. Orthagoras must rule, and harshly. The birth of Orthagoras and the new social order he will impose is seemingly a result of the father's reception of the divine word.[35] Thus, colonial and tyrannical oracles acquire a materiality not only because or when they are fulfilled, but also because social production is analogized to human reproduction with the divine word as the seed. Moreover, the image of human reproduction and birth is dominant in ideas about the Pythias' inspiration at Delphi.

DELPHI AS *OMPHALOS:* LEGITIMATE PROPHETIC OFFSPRING

At Delphi, the divinatory ritual was figured as an impregnation of the Pythias by Apollo.[36] Apollo's temple at Delphi, more than any other temple, is called a house (*domos*) and a recess or woman's quarters (*muchos*), a word also used to describe its inner shrine.[37] *Domos* suggests that Apollo's temple is his house wherein the Pythias are his wives, who appropriately remain indoors and manage the household goods, exchanging gifts received for oracles. *Muchos* is more specific. Apollo's oracles issue from the Pythia, who is stationed in the woman's quarters understood as a dark recess—the appropriate place from which prophetic knowledge as well as poetic production arise in terms of Greek notions about inner recesses, whether of

[35] Once again, no female appears in this story about birth, and in this sense the story replays the logic of most oracular tales: the Pythias disappear as the male client interprets an oracle and thereby creates a future with Apollo's assistance.

[36] This formulation of the union of Pythia and Apollo is discussed extensively by Sissa ([1987] 1990) and is reinforced by evidence from other Apolline temples in which his visitations to his female prophetesses are explicitly figured as sexual, on which see Latte 1940.

[37] The use of *domos* for Apollo's temple is especially pronounced in the opening scene of Aeschylus' *Eumenides,* when the Pythia and Apollo confront the Furies at Delphi (*Eum.* 35, 60, 179, 185, 207, and 577). This term and the united front they present to the Furies emphasize that Apollo's temple has been assimilated to harmonious domestic space invaded from the outside and contrasts with the house of Agamemnon, where threats to the house come from an unruly woman within the house. *Muchos* for temple: *Eum.* 180, *Cho.* 954; for inner shrine: *Eum.* 39, 170. Cf. Padel 1992: 72 n. 85.

bodies, earth, or temples.[38] *Splanchna*, or internal organs, a dark and obscure place whence prophecy and poetry were believed to come, are described as active agents that bubble and ooze forth and as receptacles for liquids and airs that enter from the outside. When imagined as passive recipients of outside substances that embody daimonic forces, especially liquids and winds, *splanchna* are often sexualized insofar as they are assimilated to the womb.[39] Indeed, *splanchna* can refer to the womb as well as to internal organs,[40] and Greek often makes no distinction between stomach and womb, calling both *gastēr*.[41] For these reasons, the action of outside daimonic forces on *splanchna* was often understood as impregnation and fertilization. Pindar calls his poetry "a gift of the Muses" (*Moisan dosin*) and "a sweet fruit of his mind" (*glukon karpon phrenos*), suggesting that his poetic production is simultaneously a result of a gift from the outside, of fertilization, and of his own efforts (Pind. *Ol.* 1.110.).

The Pythias' *muchos* recalls this vast network of imagery, often sexualized, about the exchange between outside forces and human innards. The famed vapors at Delphi, which enter the Pythias on their tripod (Fig. 1) from below, first mentioned by Diodorus Siculus, are an attempt to realize this earlier constellation of ideas about Apollo and the Pythias' interaction—the action of outside winds upon the human *splanchna*—that was implicit and that explained human and divine interaction as impregnation. The delivery of oracles from the Pythias' mouth is simply a displacement upward; *stoma* is used to describe both the mouth and the female pudendum.[42] The ancients then understood Apollo's possession as an impregnation of the Pythias. If this dynamic event had various and even conflicting nuances,[43]

---

[38] Padel 1992: 110 n. 5.

[39] Ibid.: 109–11; 111: "The sexualization of the innards is stronger in the passive than in the active model [of the mind]. Mind or soul can be imaged as vessel, as a female organ, more concretely than mind as agent, as male organ."

[40] Aesch. *Sept.* 1031; Pind. *Ol.* 6.43; Pind. *Nem.* 1.35; cf. Padel 1992: 99 n. 2.

[41] Sissa [1987] 1990: 63–80.

[42] Ibid.: 53 n. 1.

[43] Murray 1981; Tigerstedt 1970. Poetry was not the result of the poet's submission to divine influence, often embodied in an outside wind, despite the ideas of Plato, who was anxious to displace poetry's esteemed position in classical Greece in favor of his own brand of knowledge available only to those who engage in dialectic. If in his *Ion*, Plato envisages poets as wholly passive and ignorant of their poems' meaning, he simply promotes a view of poetic production that captures only one aspect of other contemporary and more complicated ideas that saw poetic and prophetic production as a result of a more nebulous interaction between a poet and the divine, an interaction not unlike the commingling of male and female that was variously understood in models of human reproduction. One ancient notion, that the female contributes little to her offspring and is a mere incubator of male semen (Aesch. *Eum.* 659 and Arist. *Gen. an.* 738, with Zeitlin [1978] 1996: 107), is countered by Democritus and Empedocles, who argued that the female can and does contribute to her offspring (Arist. *Gen. an.* 764a6, 722b, with Padel 1992: 109). These conflicting notions about female contribution to offspring intersected and reinforced equally conflicting notions about the *splanchna*'s activity in the production of both prophecy and poetry.

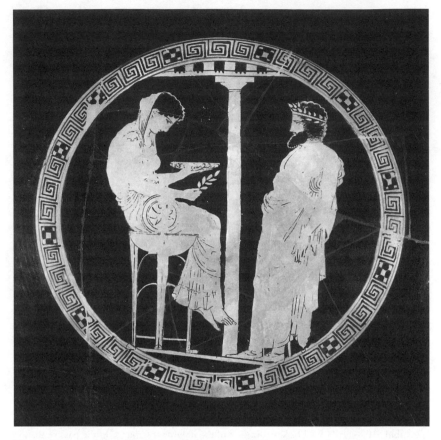

Fig. 1. The tondo of this Attic red-figure cup (440–430 B.C.E.) represents Aegeus, king of Athens, seeking an oracular response from a Pythia, who is identified on the cup as Themis. The central Doric column and hints of entablature above indicate that we are looking within the temple of Apollo at Delphi. Ancient writers insisted that the Pythia adopted this uncomfortable position atop the tripod (Eur. *Ion* 91–93; Strabo 9.3.5; Diod. Sic. 16.26), but this scene is mythic rather than historical, and it is unclear how helpful it can be in reconstructing the actual process of consultation: see Sellew, forthcoming.

it nonetheless was the mechanism that figured the Pythias' oracles as the legitimate offspring of their sexual union with Apollo. Thus child-birthing imagery made ambiguity a sign of linguistic abundance or fecundity, and emphasized the potency of Delphic oracles as divine speech that can call the world into being.

A carved stone at Delphi marks the site as the center or navel (*omphalos*) of the world. While the *omphalos* marks the place where two of Zeus' eagles meet at the world's center in some myths (Plut. *Mor.* 409e),[44] the *omphalos* also underscores that Delphi will give birth to the world through its establishment of new social orders, such as colonies or tyrannies, because it is frequently associated with Zeus' own birth. Hesiod reports that the stone that Cronus swallowed in place of Zeus, his last-born son, and then gave birth to first when he disgorged all his ingested children, is at Delphi (Hes. *Th.* 496–500). A "visible emblem" of Zeus' double birth that "ratifies the principle of substitution in the form of a material sign,"[45] this stone, according to Mezzadri, "realizes temporally what the voyage of the eagles accomplish spatially" and is commensurate with the *omphalos.*[46] Both conjoin opposites, beginnings and endings or poles of the world, and hence allude to Delphic oracles, which must stage a beginning or past in the present to establish the future. For an oracle, like Cronus' stone, is a second birth leading to a future that must replace the original "birth" of a society, individual, ritual, or law, which has led to the current crisis and dead end. It is also a sign of Zeus' control of the principle of substitution and signification,[47] and suggests that oracles signify and substitute for the future until they are realized. Thus Cronus' stone and its correlative, the *omphalos,* underscore the analogy between linguistic production and reproduction at Delphi, as well as the logic of oracular fulfillment.

Not surprisingly, birthing imagery erupts in the content of oracles. Colonial and tyrannical oracles deploy images of birthing and bring to the surface this dominant metaphor in the divinatory ritual and in oracular pronouncements. Several clients who visited Delphi because of infertility were told to find a colony.[48] Countless colonization oracles deploy metaphors of marriage, rape, intercourse, and birth and figure colonization as any or all of these.[49] Tyrannical oracles often address the tyrant's birth.[50] Birth announcements, umbilical cords between, from, among male and female, divine and mortal, the immateriality of oracular language and its concrete fulfillment, the stones at Delphi proclaim Zeus in Apollo and the Pythias' divine coupling and prophetic offspring as the source of being, and make Delphi the *omphalos* or navel of the world. This site, marked by Zeus, and

---

[44] PW 14. See also Roscher 1913.

[45] Zeitlin 1996: 81.

[46] Mezzadri 1987: 217.

[47] Bergren 1983: 75, quoted and discussed in Zeitlin 1995b: 68.

[48] See Fontenrose 1978: 443, for a list of all oracles concerning infertility. On childlessness leading to colonization, see PW 43 and perhaps the collection of oracles concerning Battos (PW 37–42), the founder of Cyrene, if we accept Cosi's interpretation of Battos' stutter as a sign of infertility (Cosi 1987: 115–45).

[49] Dougherty (1993: ch. 3) thoroughly examines the metaphors of rape and marriage in colonial oracles.

[50] See Kypselus (PW 6–9), Orthagoras (PW 23).

the means of oracular production to which Zeus' stones allude, not the content of oracles themselves, authorized the Pythias' voice.

UNAMBIGUOUS AND ILLEGITIMATE: CASSANDRA'S VIOLATIONS

Cassandra's relationship with Apollo, unlike the Pythias', does not legitimate her communication with others. When Cassandra explains in Aeschylus' *Agamemnon* that her gift of prophecy comes from Apollo, the chorus asks: "Did you come to the act of getting children, as is the way?" Cassandra replies: "I played Loxias false," and "I could make none believe me, once I committed this offense" (Aesch. *Ag.* 1207–13). Cassandra's words appear as sterile as her encounter with Apollo. She remains trapped in the knowledge Apollo gives her, unable to convey that knowledge to others and hence outside of any interpretative community of believers. Cassandra's speech makes present an absence, an absence of a god who does not authorize her words and make them a believable part of any linguistic exchange. Yet, her offense, her refusal of the Pythias' position as fecund wife, does not fully explain Cassandra's curse, her lack of prophetic authority.

This is evident in the last moments of the Cassandra scene in the *Agamemnon*, when Cassandra predicts in clear and unadorned language: "I say that you shall look on Agamemnon's end," to which the chorus responds: "Lull your voice to utter no ill-omened word," praying that her prediction will not happen and wondering who might accomplish this scheme (*Ag.* 1246–47). Here the chorus seems not to be perturbed, but to resent the intrusion Cassandra's prediction makes on their world. Cassandra's clear statement of Agamemnon's death should force the chorus to confront the political coup d'état about to occur. It does not. Instead the chorus pushes Cassandra out of their circle of communication and thereby restores the difference between their false notion of a well-governed Argos and a state in the throes of revolution.

Cassandra prefaces her revolutionary statement ("You shall look upon Agamemnon's end") with the following remarks: "Now shall my oracle be no longer one that looks forth from a veil, like a newly wedded bride, but as a bright, clear wind it shall rush toward the sunrise, so that like a wave there shall surge toward the light a woe far greater than this; no more in riddles shall I instruct you" (*Ag.* 1178–83). The image of the unveiled bride to describe her lucid prediction not only alludes to the discretion of the Pythia, who, veiled, if you will, encounters Apollo in the privacy of his temple, but also links Apollo's relationship with Cassandra, indiscreet and on public streets, or unveiled, with her manner of speech in the line, "You shall look upon Agamemnon's end" (*Ag.* 1246). Indeed, this line stands in great contrast to most of Cassandra's prophecies, which up until this point have been metaphoric, enigmatic, and similar to Delphic oracles, as the chorus makes clear (*Ag.* 1254–55).[51] Cassandra's prediction, "You will see Agamemnon's end," by contrast, is direct, purged of metaphor and poetic devices, and easy to understand. Moreover, it demands a response, for it is nothing less than a prescription for political action. Thus, Cassandra's violation of Delphic ritual norms, evident in her betrayal of Apollo, is matched by her violation of Delphic linguistic norms.[52]

Perhaps the Cassandra scene is a cautionary tale. Insofar as Cassandra appears to "speak her own mind," to bemoan her own fate, she does not speak for a male, Apollo or the chorus, and thus suffers an incomprehensible isolation that prefigures her death. Perhaps Aeschylus provides us an anatomy of communal (male) acceptance or rejection of female authoritative speech. If female speech "fits" the male imaginary and is ambiguous, thereby facilitating interpretation and appropriation, and if it is inscribed and contained by an institution that defines it as Apollo's, then it will be granted authority. Perhaps the moment the Pythias spoke, chose to speak ambiguously in Apollo's temple, the dominant male discourse about the female erased her voice so that we can only say that women did not and could not speak or that female authority and power is visible only when compliant with dominant male ideologies. However, such recourse to what Greek males may have thought about female speech leads to a closure of analysis and creates a condition of "definitional unknowability"[53] for the Pythias as historical figures, and by extension for all Greek women, and further paves the way for analyzing Greece as a society of male agents and historical subjects and of females, who are available for study only as objects of male thought. Without conjuring up an ideal authenticity or subject, free from social constraints, can we read the Pythias' authority and ambiguity otherwise? Can we recover some glimpses of a female point of view in Delphic oracles, despite male interpretation, oral transmission, and written records, all of which would seem to undermine this possibility?

In Aeschylus' *Agamemnon*, the Watchman provides a most useful comparandum to Cassandra and the Pythia for addressing these questions. The

---

[51] When Cassandra says, "Ah, ah. Alas, alas. What is this that comes into view? Indeed it is some net of Hades. But it is the net that shares his bed, that shares the guilt of murder" (*Ag.* 1114–18), she uses the metaphor of a hunting net to describe the garment that Clytemnestra will throw around Agamemnon when she kills him. Cassandra again employs metaphors to describe Agamemnon's murder in "Keep away the bull from the cow! In the robe she has caught him with the contrivance of her black horn, and she strikes; and he falls in the vessel of water" (*Ag.* 1125–27).

[52] Most ambiguous oracles use metaphors, their kindred cousins, synecdoches and metonyms, or homonyms, on which see Maurizio 1993: Appendix I.

[53] Loomba 1993: 220.

Watchman's speech is filled with intimations about Clytemnestra's impending murder of Agamemnon, the plight of the soldiers at Troy, the fall of the house of Atreus, the question of justice, and the diseased state of Atreus' house, which needs a drastic cure. The Watchman conveys this information through his use of metaphor (stars are dynasties that rise and fall; his song that keeps him awake is a "cure") and other oblique expressions (for example, he sits on the roof in the "manner" [*dikēn, Ag.* 3] of a dog—*dikē* is also the Greek word for justice; his nightly duty is as baleful as the soldiers' at Troy). The Watchman's proclamation about his and the house's true state is also a concealment of those very things as well as of his sense of impending events. The Watchman's last remark—he speaks to those who know, while to others he is silent (*Ag.* 38)—indicates that he is aware that his speech has multiple meanings and hence will have multiple receptions.

To an uninformed audience, the Watchman's speech will say no more than its strictly literal meaning. His observation that stars rise and fall like dynasties will remain an astronomical calculation and not a comment on the house of Atreus. Robbed of exegetes, the Watchman's speech will remain one-dimensional, and a simple economy of one meaning per one word will prevail. Only those who refuse to accept that language works this way will observe not only the true state of affairs in Argos (at least from the Watchman's point of view) but also the Watchman's wavering subjectivity, his desire to express his knowledge and experience wherein resides his identity, a desire that he appears to believe is inappropriate. Nonetheless, his desire is proclaimed and concealed in the space between his words and their possible interpretations, though it exists only insofar as someone finds it there. Thus the Watchman writes himself into the play by refusing a straightforward economy of meaning and elevates that which escapes signification. Importantly, his choice of ambiguous and multivalent words betrays his awareness of how identities are constructed in speech and its communal reception.

Cassandra's speech is no different than the Watchman's, with one important exception: Cassandra has an internal audience in the play, the chorus. In her scene, Aeschylus gives the house of Atreus a voice, as he does the Watchman. However, with Cassandra, Aeschylus emphasizes that a community that does not, cannot, or refuses to "read between the lines" of a speech that does not conform to acceptable norms of speaking, because of either ambiguity or clarity, in effect kills that speech by rendering it meaningless, and hence kills its speaker.[54] Cassandra already "dies" before she

---

[54] Consider the Sirens and the Sphinx, mythological cousins of the Pythias and Cassandra. When their songs have the capacity to seduce or confound their (male) listeners, persuade them into listening to their meanings, their listeners die. When their songs are unheeded or resisted, they themselves die.

enters Agamemnon's house, and herein lies the poignancy of this scene—we watch her painful and increasing social and existential isolation and thereby glimpse her impending death, which literalizes her "murder" at the chorus' hands. Cassandra, though speaking, is silent or silenced. While we, modern readers or ancient viewers, may comprise the audience Cassandra needs to "live," we watch how communities dissolve and form around shared interpretations and how individual subjecthood is not only shaped by but also depends on communal acceptance.

The Pythia's monologue that begins the *Eumenides* succeeds where Cassandra and even the Watchman failed. She unambiguously proclaims Delphi's genealogy, its peaceful transference from Titan to Olympian and female to male. Delphi's history, here revised by Aeschylus and in sharp contrast to, for example, its portrayal in the *Homeric Hymn to Apollo*, models a peaceful succession and transfer of powers between generations and genders for the whole of the *Oresteia*.[55] Conforming with the play's discourse about the rightful relationship between male and female, the Pythia's speech iterates the play's dominant values in a clear and concise fashion and replaces Cassandra and the Watchman's poetic and ambiguous speeches, which betrayed their vacillating sense of self. Thus Cassandra, the Watchman, and the Pythia demonstrate a range of possible outcomes for the project of coordinating language, authority, and identity within a community. Nonetheless, the Cassandra scene and the Watchman's monologue provide more useful insights for understanding how and why the historical Pythias developed ambiguity as a style than does the Pythia of Aeschylus' *Eumenides*.

The historical Pythias, I have argued, adopted and embellished an ambiguous style of oracular pronouncement in order to address the spiritual and social needs that their earliest clients, colonists and tyrants, brought to the divinatory session. This style distinguished their hexameters from those of traditional poetry and indirectly suggested that all language is ambiguous and open to multiple interpretations. Thus the Pythias instituted the practice of interpretation and made Delphi an *omphalos*, a place for interpreting, that is, giving birth to a new vision of the world. While ambiguity allowed the Pythias to disappear in their oracles' interpretation and fulfillment, a residue of indeterminacy remains about their words because the course of time may prove any interpretation false. In this residue, I suggest, there remains the Pythias' sense of selfhood or subjectivity.

Like the Watchman, the Pythias wrote themselves into their oracles by refusing a masculine economy of one meaning per word—an economy that male interpreters insist upon in their treatment of oracles and in their telling of oracular tales. The Pythias elevated that which escapes signification, the inchoate, incoherent, ill-defined yet possible worlds that ambigu-

[55] Zeitlin [1978] 1996: 101–2.

ity makes possible. This ambiguity represents the paradox of an authoritative and truthful female subject speaking in a world where the dominant discourse figures the female as primarily deceptive. In pronouncing the future and accepting their institutional authority, the Pythias both proclaimed and concealed themselves in that space between the world as it is and the world as it might be.

The Pythias' male interpreters believed that they could close off that space, circumvent the female and linguistic ambiguity, interpret and speak directly to Apollo. Most modern scholars have done the same insofar as they read Delphic ambiguity as a manipulative strategy that served the shrine or treat ambiguity as a product of the male imaginary. I have tried to recognize the functional uses of ambiguity at Delphi and the effects of male imagination and male dominance on the Pythias, but to not concede that either influence determined or erased the Pythias. Ambiguity is the place where the Pythias negotiated social expectations and their sense of themselves as Apollo's mediums. Perhaps all interpretations of Delphic ambiguity must remain provisional by virtue of the fact that ambiguity is open to multiple interpretations. But that stance would ultimately close off analysis and relegate historical interpretation to "definitional unknowability."

I prefer to imagine that Aeschylus' gloss on ambiguity is more apt for understanding the Pythias and our own historical projects. The self lives and speaks only within a community of interpreters that in turn constrains, but never fully erases, that which is said. The Pythias did not die when they spoke, however much their speech may seem to conform to the dominant ideology of their society, unless we, like the chorus of the *Agamemnon*, refuse to hear them. Rather, the Pythias tethered their mantic authority to their mantic ambiguity and forged a way to accommodate their male clients, Apollo and themselves. I leave it to the reader to interpret whether their accommodating voice is typically feminine, as long as the reader entertains the notion that the Pythias themselves created and chose the tactic and style of ambiguity and thereby rendered their own subjectivity.

CHAPTER FOUR.

Just Like a Woman

ENIGMAS OF THE LYRIC VOICE

RICHARD P. MARTIN

THE FEW but significant passages in which Greek male lyric poets represent the voice of women must be heard in dialogue with a number of other ancient mimetic practices, both social and poetic. They are related to an entire range of "sociopoetic" acts that includes dressing up at drinking parties, competing in state-sponsored theatrical events, and passing the time in talk.[1] Instead of attempting to touch on all the segments within this broad band of activities that can be said to signify something about status and attitude, I will work outward, in several directions, from one small point: elegiac verse of the sixth century B.C.E., within the highly stylized setting of the aristocratic symposium. Even this starting-point requires some preliminary widening of the spectrum, as it is hardly possible to discuss ancient Greek lyric poetry apart from epic—not because the former imitated or adapted the latter, as earlier generations of critics would have it, but because comparative evidence regarding diction, meter, and performance has made it clear that the two poetic modes must have had a symbiotic relationship in archaic times.[2] This cross-genre sharing of poetic strategies can be seen in such features as the treatment of mythic narrative, the framing of speeches, and the creation of personae, both male and—my concern here—female.

The *Iliad* and the *Odyssey* contain many convincing dramatic imitations of the speech of women. The attention paid to emotional detail in representing such figures as Andromache, Helen, Penelope, and Nausicaa argues for a deep sympathy between male singers—whether the "Homer" to whom these creations are attributed, or the generations of rhapsodes who

---

[1] For analysis of "sociopoetic" aspects of Greek culture, see Herzfeld 1991 and Martin 1989.

[2] For the evidence on lyric meters as predecessor forms for hexameter, see especially Nagy 1990: 414–64. On the interaction of lyric diction and meter with Hesiodic poetry, see Martin 1992. For comparative evidence on interactions between lyric and epic genres, see Martin 1997.

continued to shape their characterization—and female subjects.[3] Epic convention never lets us see how these women are staged; unlike Aristophanic comedy, which puts on view its own procedures and motivations for the representation of women, earlier Greek poetry generally remains reticent about its own devices.[4] Of course, ancient audiences experiencing Homeric poetry could themselves see and hear the performers shift into female roles; consequently, what dramatic illusion may have existed bore a closer resemblance to that of comic portrayal, the successive acts of mimesis by the performer being in this case (unlike comedy) intermittently broken by diegetic passages.

If we think of the Homeric poetic performer as a man with many voices, some of them female, the epic interest in certain scenes of polyphony becomes all the more relevant for a study of the genre's poetics. Helen, as depicted in a pointed story by her husband ten years after Troy fell (*Od.* 4.266– 89), nearly enticed to their deaths the Achaean heroes hidden in the wooden horse through her ability to imitate the voice of each one's wife. [5] This image of multivocal ability may strike us as an ironically negative counterpart to the epic singer's own art. It is midway between the fearsome polyphony of the Hesiodic Typhōeus (*Theog.* 829–35), whose many heads emitted a range of human and animal sounds, and the most positive representation of mimetic ability in Greek poetry, that in a passage from the *Homeric Hymn to Apollo* concerning the Delian Maidens (*Hymn. Hom. Ap.* 156–64):

πρὸς δὲ τόδε μέγα θαῦμα, ὅου κλέος οὔποτ᾽ ὀλεῖται,
κοῦραι Δηλιάδες Ἑκατηβελέταο θεράπναι·
αἵ τ᾽ ἐπεὶ ἂρ πρῶτον μὲν Ἀπόλλων᾽ ὑμνήσωσιν,
αὖτις δ᾽ αὖ Λητώ τε καὶ Ἄρτεμιν ἰοχέαιραν,
μνησάμεναι ἀνδρῶν τε παλαιῶν ἠδὲ γυναικῶν   160
ὕμνον ἀείδουσιν, θέλγουσι δὲ φῦλ᾽ ἀνθρώπων.
πάντων δ᾽ ἀνθρώπων φωνὰς καὶ κρεμβαλιαστὺν

---

[3] On the habit, starting in antiquity, of attributing some Homeric composition to women poets, see Martino 1991a: 46–48. Perhaps the sympathy lay in the sense of marginality and dependency shared by singers and women, such as can be seen in contemporary Egyptian poets' communities: Reynolds 1995: 64–71. Plato (*Ion* 535b–c) presents the rhapsode as feeling a certain pride in his ability to experience the emotions of female as well as male characters. Good recent work on representation of women in the *Odyssey* includes Papadopoulou-Belmehdi 1994; Felson-Rubin 1994; Doherty 1995a; and Cohen 1995. For Iliadic women, see Martin 1989; Lohmann 1988; and Murnaghan 1999.

[4] On Aristophanic unmasking of device and questions of representing women onstage, see Zeitlin [1981] 1996.

[5] In a forthcoming study, I compare Helen's polyphonic ability with that of traditional Greek choral performers (ancient and modern) of lament; cf. Martin 1995. See also Nancy Worman's contribution to this volume.

μιμεῖσθ᾽ ἴσασιν· φαίη δέ κεν αὐτὸς ἕκαστος
φθέγγεσθ᾽· οὕτω σφιν καλὴ συνάρηρεν ἀοιδή.

And there is this great marvel—its fame will never die:
The young women of Delos, the Far Darter's servants,
who praise Apollo first, then Leto and Artemis, who rains arrows,
and recalling men of old, and women, sing a *hymnos*
charming the human race. All peoples' voices and motions
they know to imitate. Each would say that he himself
was giving voice, so finely does their song fit.[6]

This artful description, which has been termed "parabatic" on the basis of its resemblance to the personal poetic statements of comic poets, presents us with the clearest and earliest image of a male poet actually putting words into the mouths of women performers.[7] "Homer"—for this is the persona the performer of the hymn would like to project—rehearses a chorus of young women performers who themselves are renowned for impersonating voices of others.[8] Like the figure of Alcman preserved by the choral poetry that the poet is said to have written for Laconian women in the seventh century B.C.E., "Homer" in the *Hymn to Apollo* acts as chorus-trainer, projecting his own voice onto that of women.[9] In this case, however, the composer of the hymn goes further by depicting the *process* of instruction. In a contractual arrangement, "Homer" promises to spread the Delian maidens' fame in return for their future attestations about his own fame (*Hymn. Hom. Ap.* 166–75):

χαίρετε δ᾽ ὑμεῖς πᾶσαι· ἐμεῖο δὲ καὶ μετόπισθε
μνήσασθ᾽, ὁππότε κέν τις ἐπιχθονίων ἀνθρώπων
ἐνθάδ᾽ ἀνείρηται ξεῖνος ταλαπείριος ἐλθών·
ὦ κοῦραι, τίς δ᾽ ὕμμιν ἀνὴρ ἥδιστος ἀοιδῶν
ἐνθάδε πωλεῖται, καὶ τέῳ τέρπεσθε μάλιστα;   170
ὑμεῖς δ᾽ εὖ μάλα πᾶσαι ὑποκρίνασθαι ἀφήμως·
τυφλὸς ἀνήρ, οἰκεῖ δὲ Χίῳ ἔνι παιπαλοέσσῃ,
τοῦ πᾶσαι μετόπισθεν ἀριστεύουσιν ἀοιδαί.
ἡμεῖς δ᾽ ὑμέτερον κλέος οἴσομεν ὅσσον ἐπ᾽ αἶαν
ἀνθρώπων στρεφόμεσθα πόλεις εὖ ναιεταώσας·
οἱ δ᾽ ἐπὶ δὴ πείσονται, ἐπεὶ καὶ ἐτήτυμόν ἐστιν.

---

[6] All translations are mine unless otherwise identified.

[7] The term is from the discussion by Martino (1982: 74, 91).

[8] There is still debate on exactly what their imitation comprises: they might, as in the poetry of Stesichorus, imitate by taking on the personae of mythic speakers within a choral-lyric context: see Burkert 1987.

[9] On the resemblance between "Homer" in the *Hymn to Apollo* and Alcman, see the forthcoming monograph by A.-E. Peponi. On the figure of Alcman as a function of the poetry attributed to him, see Nagy 1990: 370–71.

Farewell, all. Remember me hereafter, too,
when some man of the earth, a stranger who has endured,
comes and asks, "Girls, who is the sweetest singer hereabouts?
Who delights you most?' All of you, answer well:
"A blind man, he lives in rocky Chios; it's his
songs, all of them, that are best later on."
And we will bring *your* fame as far on earth
as the cities on our circuit, the well-inhabited,
and they will believe it, because it's true.

Coaching them in their reply to the "stranger," the hymn performer manages to create a neat self-advertisement (of practical importance if this hymn in fact represents a contest piece).[10] But the "reply" that the poet commends is far from being straightforward. First, scholarly opinion has long been divided on whether the reference to the "blind man of Chios" actually denotes Homer at all; some have seen it as alluding to a different, otherwise unknown singer. The expression leaves open either option.[11] And the force of the adverb *aphēmōs*, "without naming," is equally puzzling: if this is the correct reading (rather than *saphēnōs*: "clearly," *euphēmōs*: "with good report," or *amph'hēmeōn*: "about us"), what does it mean in this context?[12]

I suggest that the performer of the *Hymn to Apollo* is pretending to be Homer; moreover, in asserting that the Delian chorus must describe him in the future "without naming" (*aphēmōs*), he is making an even greater claim to fame—all audiences will know him, even *without* his being named (just as "the King" in a rock-and-roll context needs no other identification). And, of course, the composer of this hymn—surely not in fact the same as the famed composer of the epics—in this way creates a mask for the *next* performer of the same hymn. That is to say, precisely through his self-projective device, the fame of the "blind man" will indeed survive.

Yet another feature of the passage, thus far unnoticed, can bring us to the heart of the question: how do male poets or male poetic traditions shape female personae within Greek lyric poetry? Clearly, this particular male poet—the poet in the text as well as the performer outside it—felt it appropriate for a female chorus to speak allusively; the uncertainties we have

[10] As I have argued in Martin forthcoming.

[11] On the problem, see Dyer 1975; Burkert 1979: 57; and Janko 1982: 114–15.

[12] I print here line 171 as found in most manuscripts of Thucydides 3.104.5; the direct tradition of the *Hymn* does not include this adverb, but offers the nonsensical variants *aph'hēmon/humon* (see Càssola 1975: ad loc.). Allen (Allen et al. 1936: 226) adopts Marx's emendation *amph'hēmeōn*: "about us." Burkert (1979: 61) argues for *aphēmōs* as meaning "without mentioning the name"; cf. Wilamowitz 1916: 454–55 and Snell and Mette 1955: cols. 1703–4 s.v. for arguments against this reading. *Saphēnōs* is the prosaic emendation of Carey 1980.

noon in the lines that he scripts for the Delian maidens are less a function of his voice than a reflection of his desire to represent others' voices in the way he imagines (or has experienced) women's stylized poetic speech. It is worth recalling that the poetic speech thus envisioned is essentially *lyric*, a choral event, although the medium that describes it is rhapsodic hexameter.[13] In this connection, two aspects of the scripted female utterance in the *Hymn to Apollo* will turn out to be emblematic, as we shall see, for other lyric female personae: the subject foregrounds a phenomenon that is markedly timeless (i.e., the ever-recurrent fame of the performer "Homer"), and the style is enigmatic.

If the *Hymn to Apollo* reached its present form in the second half of the sixth century, as seems probable, then its composition would have overlapped that of the *Theognidea*, a body of elegiac couplets preserved through successive anthologies and attributed to the sixth-century Megarian poet Theognis. Only some of the 1,400 or so verses that have come down to us under this name form complete poems; many, it is clear, are quotable excerpts on ethics, politics, and love that may have been "fragmented" by the ancient educational and rhetorical tradition, rather than by accidental loss and partial recovery, as was the case with most Greek lyric.[14] One passage from this corpus (which I shall refer to as "Theognis" for convenience) has been uppermost in histories of Greek poetry: lines 19–26, the so-called *sphragis* or seal of Theognis, an apparent assertion of authorship that has often been compared to the "blind man's" boast of *Hymn to Apollo* 171–73.[15] But I wish to turn to a less-studied poem within the corpus, lines in which the hints about female speech given by the *Homeric Hymn to Apollo* can help us resolve a long-standing conundrum, as well as see further into lyric strategies for projecting women's voices. Lines 861–64 run as follows in the editions of West and Young:[16]

οἵ με φίλοι προδιδοῦσι καὶ οὐκ ἐθέλουσί τι δοῦναι
ἀνδρῶν φαινομένων· ἀλλ᾽ ἐγὼ αὐτομάτη

[13] On its choral nature, see Lonsdale 1995; Calame [1977] 1997: 107–10; and Nagy 1990: 376.

[14] On the date of the *Hymn to Apollo*, see most recently Aloni 1989. On the formation of the *Theognidea*, see Nagy 1985 and Bowie 1997. It should be stressed, in contrast to Bowie's view, that, from the standpoint of performer-audience interaction, there is nothing "fragmentary" about Theognis: singing even a few couplets, in context, can be as fully performative as the creative application of a proverb or apophthegm in the right social context.

[15] On previous views about the meaning of the seal, see now Edmunds (1997), who argues convincingly that the assertion of "authority" rather than authorship in this way allows us to view the *Theognidea* as "from its origin a miscellaneous collection of gnomic lore for sympotic and didactic purposes" (43). In addition, Edmunds' analysis of the doubly framed pragmatics of lines 19–26 could also be applied to *Hymn. Hom. Ap.* 171–73.

[16] West 1989–92, 1: 214–15; Young 1971: 53; see also Ferrari 1989: 216–17; and Gerber 1999: 298.

ἑσπερίη τ' ἔξειμι καὶ ὀρθρίη αὖθις ἔσειμι,
ἦμος ἀλεκτρυόνων φθόγγος ἐγειρομένων.

The friends betray me and do not want to give
anything when men appear. But I, of my own accord,
will go out at evening and at dawn come back in,
with the sound of roosters waking.

The adjectives (αὐτομάτη, ἑσπερίη, ὀρθρίη) highlight the feminine gender of the speaker. The unsolved question centers on her identity. Commentators since the sixteenth century have puzzled over the lines, suggesting various more or less probable speakers, based on the few details we are given. A domestic animal, says Harrison; Labarbe, the most recent exegete, prefers an owl.[17] A *hetaira*, say Camerarius, Geyso, and many others.[18] The redoubtable Edmonds in his antiquated Loeb neatly if redundantly packages these solutions, suggesting that the speaker is a courtesan's cat. The moon (or sun, or night) has been suggested.[19] Like a cat, heavenly phenomena go "in" and "out," but we still do not get a snug fit: what friends betray any of these, and why? Bergk proposes that the speaker is a woman deprived of dowry although suitors are available; Ferrari envisions the same situation, with the additional twist that the woman in question has decided to become a courtesan.[20] Young's note in the Teubner edition presents a typically minority opinion, suggesting that this is a riddle about the perpetual flame of a stone lamp decorated with the image of a girl. Without seeing any further argumentation, it is not easy to be persuaded, since perpetual flames do not go out.[21]

By far the most popular solution to this puzzle is that the speaker is a courtesan (*hetaira*). At one level of metaphor, this is appealing, as I shall show below, but if we take it as the ultimate answer, the interpretive contortions to which this leads are still too numerous. The hilarious three-and-a-half pages devoted to the problem by van Groningen show most of the variations and the dead-ends they encounter.[22] The most difficult challenge is to explain why a *hetaira* would leave (assuming *exeimi* means that) just when men are arriving for the night. Perhaps, suggests van Groningen, it

[17] Harrison (1902: 203), who takes the phrase "give anything" to mean "feed"; Labarbe 1992.

[18] For earlier bibliography, see Garzya (1958: 251), who himself adheres to this view. Apparently first made by Joachim Camerarius (the elder) in his *Libellus scholasticus utilis et valde bonus, quo continentur Theognidis praecepta* (Basel, 1550), the suggestion was cited and rejected by Welcker (1826: 134), and revived by Diehl and Crusius (see Labarbe 1992: 238 n. 4).

[19] Cat: Edmonds 1931: 331; moon: Carrière 1975: 178.

[20] Ferrari 1989: 216–17; with earlier bibliography; Bergk 1915: 193.

[21] Young 1971: 53.

[22] Groningen 1966: 328–31. Stehle (1997: 221) thinks it may be a courtesan speaking, but calls the riddle "unsolvable."

is because her so-called friends betrayed her by not paying her on some occasions and so this is her way to get back at them; actually, maybe she is not a real *hetaira* (something between a higher-class call girl and a geisha) but a sort of freelance prostitute who goes on strike, he suggests. The procedure, he concedes, would appear to be bad business for a lady of the night. More drastic solutions emend away the men altogether in this scenario. Hermann sees stars (*astrōn*) as making better sense than *andrōn*, while Ahrens calls for torches (*daidōn*).[23]

Despite his confusion about the status of various female sex workers in Megara, van Groningen seems to favor the complicated courtesan solution but feels sufficiently unsure that he ventures another solution as well: that this is the speech of a sorceress, who practices her métier by night. His interpretation of *andrōn phainomenōn* ("with men coming into view") presses the genitive absolute for all it is worth by turning it into a concessive. He then reads the lines to mean, in effect: "People don't pay me for my professional services even though I can make *phasmata* (ghosts) appear." I am afraid this desperate gambit does not deserve serious consideration.[24]

It should be clear by now that answering such a riddle, and reading further the implications for the female voicing of lyric verses, brings into play an implicit hermeneutic, one it would repay us to uncover. Finding a solution involves our notions about the acceptable parameters for riddle solutions; but there is no reason to assume that the poetics of *our* "genre of discourse," the riddle, match at all those of archaic and classical Greeks.[25] Even the etymology of the modern English term, after all, reveals a mindset quite different from that behind the contemporary treatment of this genre as a sort of logical puzzle-solving. For the word "riddle" and its Germanic cognates can be derived from a suffixed form of the Indo-European root *rē- (cf. Latin *reri*) related to giving advice (cf. English *rede*).[26] Embedded in the semantics of our term are social habits that employed these verbal game-pieces for larger educative functions.[27] Another sign that we cannot map a contemporary understanding of riddles directly onto Greek notions emerges from the ancient scholarship on this form, especially the

[23] See Garzya 1958: 251 for details.

[24] The problems come with the meaning of the verb (it does not immediately evoke the derived form *phantasma*) and with the limitations of a genitive construction unaccompanied by adverbial marking to show concession, on which see Schwyzer-Debrunner 1950: 398.

[25] On riddles as a genre of discourse, see Todorov 1978: 223–45.

[26] Watkins 1985: 3, s.v. *ar-* III.2. German *Rat*.

[27] Other lines of Theognis, generally taken as *hypothēkai*, are actually referred to as riddles by Athenaeus (10.457a–b). We might say that the indirection and demand for interpretation posed by riddles are simply more stylized versions of the underlying stance taken by didactic poetry as a whole toward its addressee. The relationship is clear from the etymological links among *ainos*, "ambiguous story; riddle"; *epainos*, "praise"; *parainesis*, "advice"; and *ainigma*, "riddle, obscure saying." See the concise formulation in Edmunds 1985: 105–8.

fragmentary comments of the Peripatetic investigator Clearchus, preserved in Athenaeus 10.448b–459.[28] Reading these examples, we find that a number of verbal games that modern Western critics might define separately fall under the ancient scholar's definition of a riddle; according to Athenaeus (10.448c), Clearchus had defined *griphos* as a problem for enjoyment (*problēma . . . paistikon*) set so as to make the mind search for what was propounded, for a reward or penalty. The term apparently covered arithmetical problems, enigmatic expressions, puns and puzzles requiring one to provide words with or without certain letters or syllables, poetic kennings, contests in which the symposiasts find Homeric lines that represent various phonetic symmetries, and even comic skits with funny punchlines.[29] A full social history and poetics of Greek riddling remains to be written. But it is clear that the ancient deployment of this genre was both more restricted and at the same time more widely functional within social life. Although not hedged about by taboos as to when and where it might be performed, nevertheless riddling seems to have been a marked feature of some rituals, and, most important for this argument, a conventional component of that key male institution, the symposium.[30]

Aristophanes' *Wasps* (lines 20–23), Plutarch's *Symposium of the Seven Sages*, and the fragments of New Comedy quoted by Athenaeus provide indirect and stylized evidence of this performance context. Especially interesting, among the latter, is a passage from Antiphanes *Knoithideus* or *Gastrōn* (122 Kassel-Austin), as it coincides with the conclusions of folklorists regarding the potential for the occasion-specific reperformance of riddles and related forms.[31] In the comedy, a party-goer says he used to consider nonsense the requirement of telling riddles at symposia, such things as "what did somebody bring that he did not bring." Yet now he finds this paradoxical description fits him and his fellow revelers, who appear to be evaders of contributions. In other words, the traditional riddle can be interpreted by the teller and the audience in specific terms relevant to the very

---

[28] See collected fragments of this scholar's *Peri griphōn* with commentary in Wehrli 1969: 31–36.

[29] Clearchus is said to have classified seven types of riddle, of which three are illustrated in Athenaeus.

[30] On restrictions regarding the times and places for riddles, see Potter [1949] 1984: 940; and Burns 1976: 143–47. On riddles and rituals, see, e.g., the depiction by Diphilos (49 Kassel-Austin) of women telling obscene riddles at the Samian Adonia (apud Ath. 10.451b). On the centrality of the symposium, see Murray 1990; Lissarrague [1987] 1990. On the role of poetry, especially *skolia* ("drinking songs"), at symposia: Fabbro 1995: vii–xxxiv. What must have been a regular association between riddling and symposium makes it probable that the otherwise unknown Symphosius, to whom is attributed a collection of riddles within the *Anthologia Latina*, is actually a ghost author, the result of scribal misunderstanding of the work's title, *aenigmata symp(h)osii*: see Jiménez 1987; and Murru 1980.

[31] See Briggs 1988: esp. 122–35, with further bibliography.

symposium in which they find themselves. In this connection, it is significant that several of the riddles transmitted to us as being recited at symposia in fact allude to the equipment, guests, or conditions at the drinking-party. For example, the clever young woman Cleobulina, daughter of a sage, poses the following riddle to the other sages (Plut. *Conv. sept. sap.* 150e): "A dead donkey struck me on the ear with a horn-bearing shin." The answer—the flute (*aulos*)—fits the description (as it is made from bone); but the subject also fits the symposium, the primary site for *aulos*-playing; in fact, the riddle arises from a discussion at this particular party about the presence of the *aulos*.[32] Later in the party, Cleobulina's riddle concerning a cupping glass is posed to one of the guests, the physician Cleodorus—precisely the one who uses the instrument. Apart from these "staged" examples, a number of riddles that reach us context-free, as those in book 14 of the *Greek Anthology*, bear solutions relevant to sympotic occasions: the *aulos* again (*Anth. Pal.* 14.14), pickled fish (nos. 23, 36), a linen hand-towel (no. 26), and wine itself (no. 52).

To sum up at this juncture: the Delian maidens' choral lyric utterance is rendered as enigmatic, with reference to an enduring phenomenon; actual enigmas in sympotic poetry (Theognis) or depictions of the symposia (Plutarch) have an association with female speakers, and often objects that relate to the symposium itself. Extrapolating from the first point, we might try to explain the particular riddle at Theognis 861–64 by imagining something enduring that is at the same time related to the symposium. There is an answer fitting both categories: the personified abstraction *Penia*, "Poverty." It is true that most of the preserved ancient Greek riddles have concrete solutions (pickled fish and so on). But there are some attestations of abstract solutions. Particularly germane is the example recorded by Aristotle's nephew Callisthenes (apud Ath. 10.452a): Hippodamus, a Spartan inside the besieged town of Krōmnos, transmits a message concerning the dire situation to a Spartan herald by telling him that "the woman bound in Apollo's shrine" must be loosed within ten days. This performance of wit (*gnōmē*) was interpreted correctly by his countrymen, who came to the rescue, because they knew that Famine (*Limos*) was painted in a woman's form next to Apollo's seat in their temple.[33] In the thought and diction of Hes-

[32] It is relevant, too, that *hetairai* are the usual players of the *aulos* at these events: for an intriguing illustration of such accompaniment, see Peschel 1987: 32–33. On Cleobulina and her art in the context of Indo-European comparative traditions of poetic riddles, see Bader 1989: 24, 145–49. A comedy of Cratinus may be the source for the figure of this female riddler, but the remains of his *Kleouboulinai* do not allow us to reconstruct much: cf. Kassel and Austin 1983–96, 4: fr. 92–101. Even if the fiction begins in the fourth century B.C.E., it is important that this role is allotted to a woman; on Sappho as riddler in comedy, see below.

[33] For other personifications of famine, see West 1966: 231. On the *gnōmē* as part of the performance of wisdom, see Martin 1993: 117–19.

iodic poetry, Limos and Penia are homologous. Perses must work, says the poet to his brother, so that Limos will hate him; she is always the *sumphoros* ("companion") of the unemployed (*Op.* 300–302); if one does work, the shiftless man envies him as he grows wealthy (*plouteonta: Op.* 312–13). By this logic, Penia and Limos are equally threatening, equally opposed to work and wealth. In the Hesiodic *Theogony's* extended meditation regarding marriage, work, and sacrifice, the invention of Pandora leads to the creation of the race of women, who in turn are "not companions of destructive Penia, but of Fullness (*Koros*)": that is, women require men to work.[34] We should note that both feminine personifications, Famine and Poverty, are potential "companions" (*sumphoroi*).[35]

If a personified Penia, of this Hesiodic type, is the answer to the riddle in question, then Theognis 861–64 embody an inventive twist on a number of conventional tropes that apply to the symposium—the very occasion at which verses such as this might have been performed and reperformed. It is a common feature of symposiastic elegy and iambos to describe the performance event itself (e.g., Xenophanes fr. 1; Ion of Chios frs. 26 and 32). The symposium is the place for delight (*terpsis*), for good feeling (*euphrosunē*), for banishing cares (*merimnai*).[36] Given this attitude, the highest praise one could give the symposium would be to say that the evening event makes you forget your troubles completely. Poverty—that is, thinking about Penia—simply goes away by itself (*automatē*) when the symposiasts appear.[37] The two phenomena, symposium and Penia, are mutually repellent. In the Theognis riddle, "my friends betray me" would then mean that the people whom Penia usually makes her companions—poorer folks—forget about her. And they fail to give to her because by definition Poverty does not give to them.[38] The trope is related to the long-lived convention, poetic and social, of drinking to forget, as is clearest perhaps in lines 1129–30: "I will drink up, not caring about soul-killing *penia* nor enemies, who speak ill of me."[39]

---

[34] On the intricacies of the passage, see Vernant [1977] 1981; and Zeitlin 1995a.

[35] On the notion that Poverty and Wealth enter a man's house to live, see the citations in West 1966: 331.

[36] See Anacreon fr. 2; Archilochus fr. 13; Theognis 765–68.

[37] Being *automatē*, she resembles the diseases that escape from Pandora's jar as described in Hes. *Op.* 102–4. For further association of wealth, the presence of friends, and the symposiastic context, see Pind. *Ol.* 7.1–6.

[38] Hesiod renders the underlying idea here more explicit at *Op.* 354: "Give to one who gives, do not give to one who doesn't." The ideology of *xenia* ("guest-friendship") requires reciprocity, which poverty is seen as short-circuiting. Cf. Eur. *El.* 1131: πένητας οὐδεὶς βούλεται κτᾶσθαι φίλους ("Nobody wishes to make friends with paupers").

[39] Cf. Frank Sinatra's "One More for the Road"; within the conventions of this trope, it is equally important that Poverty is a *woman* one wants to forget.

The picture that I am sketching can be filled out with evidence from the Theognidean corpus, as well as from the works of Hesiod, Pindar, Aristophanes, and Plato. It will be seen that Theognis in particular uses the same tropes as found in Pindaric and Hesiodic personification and that the tropes found in all these authors form a coherent, consistent system. They are, in effect, deep cultural metaphors energized by performance.[40] Knowledge of one part of the tropological system—the Greek audience's cultural competence—clarifies other parts, even though the works in which the tropes appear may be diachronically separated.

The female "voicing" that I am proposing for Penia can also be paralleled in Hesiod's *Works and Days*, a treasury of personified abstractions, particularly those representing social phenomena (e.g., "Giving" and "Snatching" at *Op.* 356; Eris, 11–26; Elpis, 96, etc.). In the case of Justice (*Dikē*) the poet spends more effort stylizing the abstract notion as a *parthenos* (*Op.* 256–62):

ἡ δέ τε παρθένος ἐστὶ Δίκη, Διὸς ἐκγεγαυῖα,
κυδρή τ᾽ αἰδοίη τε θεοῖς οἳ Ὄλυμπον ἔχουσιν,
καὶ ῥ᾽ ὁπότ᾽ ἄν τίς μιν βλάπτῃ σκολιῶς ὀνοτάζων,
αὐτίκα πὰρ Διὶ πατρὶ καθεζομένη Κρονίωνι
γηρύετ᾽ ἀνθρώπων ἀδίκων νόον, ὄφρ᾽ ἀποτείσῃ
δῆμος ἀτασθαλίας βασιλέων οἳ λυγρὰ νοεῦντες
ἄλλῃ παρκλίνωσι δίκας σκολιῶς ἐνέποντες.

Dikē is a maiden, Zeus' child,
honorable and revered by the gods who own Olympus.
And when someone harms her, scorning her, crookedly,
right away, sitting down with Zeus, Cronus' son,
she gives voice about men's unjust mind, until
the *dēmos* pays for the recklessness of evil-minded kings
who bend their decisions (*dikas*), speaking crookedly.

Significantly, Dikē's voice of complaint to Zeus is described with a verb (*gēruet'*) used in the *Theogony* proem (line 28) to describe the truth-telling of the Muses and by Pindar (*Ol.* 1.3) to denote his own act of poetic praise. Thus, the personified feminine abstraction can be said to have a poet's voice, although the poet Hesiod overrides her and, unlike Homer with Aphrodite in a similar type-scene of parental consolation (*Il.* 5.370–80), does not reproduce the substance of her indictment. Of course, Hesiod's own complaint (*Op.* 35–39) matches that of his personified Justice, so we do not need a direct-speech account of her truth-telling. The other voice of Dikē is de-

---

[40] On the role of such metaphors in creating cultural movement, see Fernandez 1986: 3–27.

scribed slightly before this passage in the same poem of Hesiod. The clamor (*rothos*, *Op.* 200) that arises when she is assaulted by the unjust, and her weeping (222), might be heard as sharing the tone of another typically female genre, lament. At any rate, this full-voiced abstraction turns into a vengeful, invisible spirit, one whom her enemies (the unjust) drive away from their homes (*exelasousi*, 224).

The voice and movement of Dikē, then, offer a paradigm for personification of the type that I claim for Penia. Turning now to concentrate on the recurrent Theognidean discourse about Penia, we find the concept denoted fourteen times by this noun in the corpus, often in terms of personification. Penia is, in the words of lines 267, "known although she is a stranger (*allotriē*), nor does she ever come to the *agora* or to law-cases (*dikas*)"; along with being scoffed at (*epimuktos*, 269) she is hated wherever she might be (270). The picture resembles that of the scorned Hesiodic Justice. In another passage (173–82), it is the potential victim of Penia who is in constant movement, fleeing her even if it comes to hurling himself into the sea, since being oppressed with Poverty means even the loss of speaking ability (γλῶσα δέ οἱ δέδεται, 178).[41] Although less overtly personified, Penia here pursues her prey not unlike an Aeschylean Erinys. Lines 352–55 offer a clearer image of Penia, through direct address.[42] "Vile Poverty, why do you stay, and fail to go to some other man? Don't be loving (*philei*) someone who doesn't want it. Go on now, visit another house, and don't share with us, always, this wretched life." Notice especially in these lines the verb *philei* (352): Penia, in this trope, can be the "near and dear one" (*philos*) of her victim. Assuming that the reciprocal applies, we have yet another piece of the Theognidean riddle, for Poverty, in this view, can complain about her "friends" (*philoi*, 861) and mean those with whom she stays—unwilling though they may be. In yet another passage (383–87), the personification is further joined with an ironic, Hesiodic mention of justice. Those who love just dealings (τὰ δίκαια φιλεῦντες) obtain, for all their good intentions, Penia, the "mother of Helplessness."[43] We see further in the lines on Penia at 1114a–b that *Amēkhania* ("Helplessness") is implicitly connected with poverty, as if the kinship is assumed even when no personification

---

[41] Cf. Hesiod *Op.* 104 on the diseases that Zeus has made silent. Paradoxically, the "woman" who paralyzes men's speech (because those men are excluded from the in-group of aristocrats) can in another view be voiceless herself (and thus impossible to deal with rationally). On the further thematic connections relating this passage to Herodotean portraits of involuntary speechlessness and loss of power, see Edmunds 1987.

[42] In tone, the direct address to the unwanted companion resembles similar evocations by traditional singers in another popular, epichoric art form, the blues, the genre named after what it wants to escape.

[43] This Hesiodic attitude clarifies line 268, where it must be implied that only the wealthy succeed in legal dealings.

seems to be apparent: "I am swirled about by helplessness, sick at heart, because we did not outrun the beginning (*arkhēn*) of Penia"—could also be read "its beginning, consisting of Penia" since Penia is mother of Amēkhania. As in Hesiod, once more, connections are made at the level of mythic genealogy.[44]

If Poverty is the problem that haunts the male aristocrats of Theognis' symposia, how can we say that the party itself is the solution? Continuing along the chain of association by dictional elements, we can find clarification by means of lines 1133–34, which feature another key thematic formula, familiar from its prominent use in *Il.* 11.604, the "beginning of evil" (pointed up by the narrator when Patroclus answers the summons that will lead to his death). It appears here in the same metrical positions (at trochaic caesura and line-final), and in a similar thematic context. Achilles had summoned Patroclus to find out about the wounding that would bring an end to his absence from battle; as it turns out, Patroclus himself is the substitute (*therapōn*) who will provide therapy for the Achaeans' trouble.[45] In Theognis, the metaphor of curing a wound, and the pragmatics of an older adviser figure speaking to a younger addressee, resemble the combination that underlies the Iliadic scene. The elegiac speaker proposes: "Cyrnus, let us put a stop to the beginning of evil (*kakou . . . arkhēn*) for our friends being present; let us seek cures for the growing wound." Within the sphere of sympotic poetry, this language, in turn, should remind us of Archilochus fr. 13. In that poem, an Odyssean endurance (*tlēmosunē*, 6) is recommended as the *pharmakon* for a bloody wound (*haimatoen . . . helkos*, 8), namely the grief caused by the drowning of friends.[46] Endurance is juxtaposed with "feminine grief" (*gunaikeion penthos*), which is to be rejected (line 10). It seems that proper sympotic behavior is meant to be a model for emotional reaction that extends beyond the confines of the party; it is therefore interesting that the reaction is constructed around a gendered response, itself iconic: endurance (keeping it all in) is male (like the male in-group), whereas grief (the typical outburst of lament) is female, and must be kept out.[47] I return soon to this image of distinguishing male from female space. For now, it is important to see that not only is symposiastic self-control a *pharmakon*; so is the symposium itself, in the form of its metonym, wine. The metaphor is explicit, for example, in lines from Alcaeus (fr. 335) that recommend drinking in place of grief. In Campbell's translation: "We should not surrender our hearts to our troubles, for we shall make no head-

---

[44] On the epic and lyric topos of *amēkhania*, see Martin 1983.

[45] On the interwoven themes of helplessness, battle, and healing in the poem, see Martin 1983.

[46] On the Odyssean quality of *tlēmosunē*, see Pucci 1987: 46–53.

[47] On the "gendering of grief" in the poem, see Stehle 1997: 278–79.

way by grieving, Bycchis: the best of remedies (*pharmakōn*) is to bring wine and get drunk."[48]

Since, as we saw above, Poverty, too, is an evil—the mother of helplessness, speechlessness, and incapacity—we can extrapolate slightly to make conceptual links here. Theognis 1133–34 is then restating, nonmetaphorically, the theme of the Theognis riddle I began by examining.[49] At line 1133, the dative phrase *parousi philoisi* sets the social scenario. If dative of advantage, the *pharmakon* that the speaker urges his hearer to find is then to be a cure "*for* friends who are present." But I believe we might get a sharper picture by taking this as an instrumental dative, in which case *parousi philoisi* means *by the presence of friends*. In other words, the relief for ills (poverty included) *will consist of* the sympotic gathering itself.[50] The instrumental phrase here would then function in the same way as the genitive absolute in the riddle, line 862, "when friends are present."[51]

Penia and Ploutos, then, are a Theognidean obsession, and can be addressed by the poet directly as personifications. My solution to the riddle of lines 861–64 simply elevates a personification to the slightly higher narrative node of persona: if Theognis can speak *to* Penia, Penia, too, can get a voice—necessarily, a woman's voice, since she, like most abstract nouns in Greek, is feminine. Given twice as much space, I might extend the discussion to the social reasons for the Theognidean obsession with Penia and Ploutos. Clearly, there are wide implications in this symbiosis of persona and personification for our reading of other texts structured around similar abstracts (e.g., the *Peace* of Aristophanes, or the *Agamemnon* of Aeschylus with its focus on Dikē). It is not surprising that Penia, in particular, would be endowed with a voice, since her opposite number, Ploutos, Wealth, is the most important conditioning factor for the very existence of the symposium at which we can picture this poetry performed, as we hear expressed in lines 885–86: "May peace and wealth hold the city, so that with others I might celebrate a *kōmos*. I don't love evil war."

---

[48] Campbell [1982] 1990: 373.

[49] The diction makes this a tighter link: cf. *arkhēn peniēs* at line 1114b and *kakou . . . arkhēn* at 1133. Poverty can itself be the "beginning of evil."

[50] On such causal instrumental datives, see Schwyzer-Debrunner 1950: 167; and for a similar use in the same context and diction, cf. *Od.* 15.335, where *toi . . . pareonti* means "because you are here." For "friends being present" as a synonym for the symposium, see Pind. *Ol.* 7.1–6.

[51] Meanwhile, it is worth noting something commentators have missed: that the verb in the latter phrase is nearly a formulaic expression used to describe social encounters (rather than simply meaning "appear" in a broader sense). See the evidence of fourth-century Athenian practice, in Pl. *Prt.* 309a and Xen. *Mem.* 2.8.1, from which it is clear that *phainomai* used absolutely has a built-in connotation close to the English "show up" (at meetings, appointments, etc.).

Penia, as the cause of speechlessness, is also implicitly the enemy of poetic performance at the symposium, so that poetically personifying her
makes for a clever paradox. Both the sociopolitical and the poetic aspects of
Ploutos and Penia are always underlying the poetry of the Theognidean
corpus; a performative link binds them: in effect, one must have money to
hold symposia, must have peace to have money (as lines 885–86 say), and
must, by adhering to the proper decorum, show that one can handle Ploutos
well, with neither excess or stinginess. The theme is deeply embedded in
poetry from the *Odyssey*, through Xenophanes, to Ion of Chios and the
Wasps of Aristophanes.[52] The highly politicized poetry of Pindar and Alcaeus, both of which have roots in the symposiastic setting, revolves around
the same topoi of wealth and its evil opposite, and can be used to illuminate
further the female riddling voice in Theognis. Alcaeus, for example, gives
us an alternate family relationship of Penia (364), whereby she is sister of
Amēkhania and an "ungovernable evil" that can destroy a great people. And
Pindar, in two passages, continues the kinship tropes in describing Peace as
the dispenser of Ploutos (*Ol.* 13.7; cf. Theognis 885–86 above), and Stasis
as the giver of Poverty (fr. 109). Such examples could be multiplied. My
point is that it would not be implausible for an in-group such as that of the
symposium, a group that is alternately audience and performer, to think of
such an abstraction as Penia, relevant as it is to the sympotic occasion, as
the solution to our riddle.

Another fragment of Pindaric poetry, from the encomium to Thrasyboulos (fr. 124 a–b), provides the clearest parallel to the thought behind the
Theognidean riddle:

ὦ Θρασύβουλ᾽ ἐρατᾶν ὄχημ᾽ ἀοιδᾶν
τοῦτο ⟨τοι⟩ πέμπω μεταδόρπιον. ἐν ξυνῷ κεν εἴη
συμπόταισίν τε γλυκερὸν καὶ Διωνύσοιο καρπῷ
καὶ κυλίκεσσιν Ἀθαναίαισι κέντρον·
ἁνίκ᾽ ἀνθρώπων καματώδεες οἴχονται μέριμναι
στηθέων ἔξω· πελάγει δ᾽ ἐν πολυχρύσοιο πλούτου
πάντες ἴσᾳ νέομεν ψευδῆ πρὸς ἀκτάν·
ὃς μὲν ἀχρήμων, ἀφνεὸς τότε.

Thrasyboulos, I am sending you for after dinner
this wagonload of lovely songs. May it be a sweet goad
in common for fellow-drinkers, Dionysos' fruit,
and Athenian cups, when the wearisome cares of men leave their breasts,
and in a sea of full-golden wealth, we all swim alike to a false shore:
whoever is without money, is rich, then.

---

[52] Bielohlawek 1940. On poverty as a theme in Alcaeus, see Bernardini 1984

The sympotic setting is clear, as is the idea that this time is precisely when men's cares go away (*oikhontai*, 5). The entire force of the rhetoric of the lines is carried by the adverb "then" (*tote*). That is, the one who is without money is rich when the alcohol-induced fog of the symposium brings fantasies of wealth and erases thoughts of Penia. Cares are "outside" (*exō*). Of course, through the magic of Pindaric rhetoric, "then" happens to equal the sympotic "now" of the *hic et nunc* performance.[53]

If, as seems likely, the early development of comedy took place within the institution of the men's *kōmos*, it may not be so surprising that the dramatic genre often features personified abstractions. As Ralph Rosen has recently shown, choruses representing abstractions (demes, city-states) were a staple of non-Aristophanic comedy; furthermore, they required comic poets to think through a series of associations put into play by the preexisting gender of the abstract noun: that is, cities (*poleis*) had to be portrayed as women, with all the consequent sexual-political ramifications.[54] Although nothing quite like this survives in the fragments of Aristophanes, a similar process underlies his nonchoral personifications of abstracts: for example, Peace, Sovereignty, Poetry.[55] Aristophanes' explicit dramatic personification of Poverty in the *Ploutos* (426ff.) plays on several ambiguities: she is unknown (unlike Poverty in Theognis 267), yet in the paratragic recognition-scene, she identifies herself as one who has lived with Chremylus and Blepsidemus many a year (437). Poverty literally moves in if you are poor (cf. Theognis 352–55 above). Again, she is apparently austere and threatening, mistaken by the two men as some Erinys from a tragedy (423), but also capable of being taken for a bean-meal seller, barmaid, or innkeeper.[56] Penia accuses the comic heroes of trying to throw her out of every land, to destroy her (430, 434). This appears to be a dramatic blunder (no one in the play has

---

[53] On the fragment, see Groningen 1960: 84–103, esp. 92. As happens often, popular productive song traditions prove to contain closer analogues than "literary" examples (perhaps naturally, as what we call Greek "literature" is more often than not oral-traditional performance material). Cf. the point of view of the suffering "I" represented in the Judds' country ballad "Mr Pain." The (unnamed) lyricist may have intended an allusion to Billie Holiday's "Good Morning Heartache."

[54] Rosen 1997.

[55] On the fragmentary *Poiesis*, in which apparently men must search for the missing woman/art, see Stephens 1981.

[56] *Pandokeutria*, the last term, may connote "whore" (literally, "all-receiver"; cf. Ar. *Wasps* 35, where it is adjectival and means "voracious"). If so, this suggests that the Theognis riddle might have intended *hetaira* as a *false* answer, in the manner of double-entendre riddles (cf. the Old English "dough" riddle in the *Exeter Book*), just as the *pandokeutria* proves to be a false (but metaphorically appropriate) identity for Penia in the comedy. On the metatheatrical meaning of Penia here, see Fernández 1997: 132–33; and on the paratragic aspect, Sfyroeras 1995: 242. A further encouragment to hear a *hetaira*'s voice in riddling speech might arise if there is any truth to the custom mentioned in Anaxilas 22.22–30 Kessel-Austin (apud Ath. 10.13.558a) that *pornai* ("prostitutes") spoke their enticements to men via riddles (e.g., "Let's do the three-foot," etc.).

mentioned banishing her), but can be understood if we read Penia's rhetoric with *sympotic* discourse in mind: it is naturally assumed that men want to distance themselves from her.[57] In sum, the picture of Poverty in Aristophanes' treatment, that of the unwanted female companion, dovetails with the answer proposed for the Theognis riddle.

This dossier would not be complete without another fourth-century use of the Penia personification, that in Plato's *Symposium* (203b–c). Instead of the banishment of an unwanted permanent houseguest, we get the opposite scenario. Socrates' party-story—significantly, told to *him* by a woman (Diotima)—has the gods finishing their meal (i.e., ready for a symposium) when Penia appears in order to beg a handout, and stays outside (*ēn peri tas thuras*).[58] The drunken Poros only meets her when he emerges from the banquet room. Because Penia is helpless, subject to *aporia*, she must plot an ingenious impregnation, the result being Eros.[59] Plato's Penia has more in common with the sage riddling woman Cleobulina (whose original name, Plutarch says, was *Eumetis*, or "Good at cunning intelligence"); although Poros is the son of *Mētis* ("Cunning Intelligence"), in Plato's version, it is his lover Penia who uses her wit to get a son. If Penia is the speaker of Theognis 861–64, as I have been suggesting, she resembles not only the woman whom men want to eject (the Aristophanic image), but also this more positive Platonic image, exactly because she *can* speak and riddle.

It is time to expand outward from the densely packed riddle to other lyric enigmas. What does it mean to talk, in lyric, just like a woman? A number of issues cluster around this problem, even if we confine discussion, as I do here, to symposiastic performance events.[60] It is not probable, despite Plutarch's imaginings, that women actually performed verbally at symposia, with witty repartee, riddles, or stories.[61] But their voices were still heard. In addition to the Theognis lines just examined, there are two other fairly

---

[57] Rogers (1907: 48–49) noticed the apparent slip and suggested that it anticipates the plot, since ultimate success in the plan to cure Ploutos would result in Penia's exile.

[58] She thus paradoxically resembles one of the uninvited entertainers, the *aklētoi*, a common feature at symposia: see Fehr 1990.

[59] Plato has already set us up to see Socrates himself as Penia. Socrates, after all, is the one who conspicuously hangs around outside at the very start of the symposium (174d) and immediately talks, on entering, about his own deficiency (175d). Sfyroeras (1995: 246) sees Socrates as embodying both Ploutos and Penia.

[60] I realize that Alcman's *Partheneia*, the Lille papyrus of Stesichorus, and Simonides fr. 543 Page offer similar problems, which cannot be touched on here. They are different inasmuch as they offer named, nonabstract female speakers (the Laconian maidens, Epikaste, Danae). For an intriguing suggestion concerning a possible female speaker of the "new" Simonides fr. 22, see now Yatromanolakis 1998.

[61] I owe to Elizabeth Greene the observation that female *vocal* performance of songs, as we see it in vase-paintings, is not attested for human symposium scenes, despite the frequence of *aulos*-players. *A fortiori*, verbal performance seems unlikely. The image we get from Plutarch of Aspasia, Cleobulina, and others is of course colored by his own historical circumstances much later: see Nikolaidis 1997. On women's performance spaces, see Stehle 1997: 72–73.

enigmatic passages marked for feminine gender. Lines 257–60 enact the voice of a mare ("I am a beautiful prize-winning horse . . . ") that complains of a bad (male) rider. The image can be taken as either an allegory for political expression or a traditional woman's invective against an unworthy husband. A similar complaint on the part of the woman comes in the unusual paired couplets (one voiced as male, one female) in 579–82. We should not imagine, however, that men spoke in feminine gender only to mime complaints. What of the symposiasts who reperformed Sappho? Surely a fuller range of emotion and oppression was opened for them by the experience.[62] Nor was this an accidental effect of casual reperformance, for it seems from some scraps of Alcaeus that this male poet composed verses offering a mimesis of women. Fragment 10B is unusual because it presents in verses unframed by a diegetic introduction, a lamenting woman, in a mood as dramatic as Sapphic verse: "Me a woman pitiable, me who am spared no misery . . . for upon me comes grievous injury . . . the belling of the deer grows . . . in the timid heart . . . maddened . . . infatuations."[63] Fragment 439 captures the simple declaration of a woman: "I am Pitana." The forthright statement might have come at the end of a dramatic monologue, perhaps even in a lament. But what we know of Pitana (probably the Aeolic polis, named after an Amazon, in Asia Minor, in a locale where bricks were said to float on water) does not pave the way to reconstruction.[64] Rather than feminizing the male speaker, these voices would offer the performer the opportunity to express and define himself in affiliation with and opposition to certain known types. He could take on the voice of a lamenter, like the unnamed figures in Archilochus fr. 13 (above), immersed in "womanly grief." Such a performance of the female genre par excellence would then offer a foil or lead-in to a counter-poem of the refusal-to-mourn type. Or he might fashion himself as spokesperson for a polis, literally the "voice" of, say, Pitana. The ethos of the oligarchically equal sympotic group might never allow a man to do such a thing as an individual *male* performer using his own voice, so threatening is the prospect.[65]

Another distancing effect of assuming the female voice parallels that of masking: a persona is useful *because* it can be put off, torn aside to reinforce and reinvigorate the viewers' sense of the "real" man behind the mask. A complex set of moves, therefore, would have surrounded a male's performance of the Penia riddle, for it is highly meta-performative. Failing to solve a riddle was itself a form of *aporia*, punishable by enforced drinking of

[62] For evidence of reperformance of lyric in Athenian settings, see Nagy 1990: 106–8; and Stehle 1997: 65–67.

[63] Translation and interpretation according to Page 1955: 291–94.

[64] See Strabo 13.1.67; Diod. Sic. 3.55.6.

[65] For the polis as a pregnant woman, who may give birth to an unwanted tyrant, see Theognis 39–40, and on the later tradition, Rosen 1997, regarding Eupolis *Poleis*.

a whole cup of wine, or even brine.[66] So "Penia," conceived as poverty of thought, being "at a loss," is in the context of sympotic gaming just as much to be avoided as the real thing, taking an economic loss. Of course, in Greek terms, inability to think on one's feet, failure to heed the wisdom of a wise adviser or of the group, sowing or sailing or begetting at the wrong time, means real loss as well as symbolic failure.[67] Furthermore, the institution itself of the aristocratic men's group required its members to understand how to evaluate and maintain wealth while not allowing any one member to flaunt an excess of it, which would produce (in the terms of elegiac poetry) satiety and resultant hubris. In brief, the ability to answer "Penia" to this Theognidean riddle would, first, articulate all that the symposiast sought to avoid, and at the same time prove that, by knowing the rules (the tropes of this discourse), the symposiast really belonged in the symposium set; being able to appreciate the "riddle" (*ainos*) makes and marks one as one of the "wise" (*sophoi*).[68]

Women's voices in lyric, and more generally in Greek literature, are a hybrid of stylizations—the genres women actually practiced (such as lament) and an equally old tradition of what men *thought* women sounded like. To Greek male performers, I suggest, and perhaps to Greek males generally, women sounded enigmatic. Because an accident of historical morphology —that abstract nouns so often coincided with feminine gender—was reinvested and reinterpreted as a mythopoeic reality, Penia, Themis, Atē, and a host of other concepts very hard to understand and deal with must necessarily, when they do take a voice, talk like a woman. When they speak, they riddle, because they *are* riddles themselves. The Hesiodic Muses, the Delphic Pythia, and the ultimate mythic riddle-singer, the Sphinx, are paradigms of this behavior.[69] On the mortal level, the paradigm of a woman's voice, the poetess Sappho, could also be dramatized, at least in Antiphanes' comedy, as a riddle-teller (apud Ath. 10.450e). Men fail to solve her *griphos*, which is itself about a feminine being (*phusis thēleia*) that has silent, crying children who talk to people not present. The failure is instructive; in the play, a clueless male character interprets the feminine subject of the riddle as the polis, and her children as the demagogic orators. This male herme-

---

[66] Athenaeus 10.458f–459b.

[67] Hesiod's *Works and Days* is the prime example; later stories about the wit of sages and failures by their advisees continue this topos: see Martin 1993, with further bibliography. That Penia is a good teacher of philosophy, the "gymnasium of the soul," mother of invention, and so on is an equally old topos, on which material is conveniently collected already by Stobaeus: see Gaisford 1822: 249–55 under the heads *penias epainos*, *penias psogos*, and *sunkrisis penias kai ploutou*.

[68] On *ainos* and *sophia*, see Nagy 1979: 239–42.

[69] On the complex relationships among authoritative wisdom, women's voices, the Sphinx, and Delphi, see Maurizio in this volume.

neutic, typically symposiastic in its own topoi, reads the female riddle as public, political, a product of the symposiastic group. Sappho's answer is none of the above: the *phusis* she alludes to is a letter, whose child-letters (*grammata*) only talk to those they want to, and even nearness (the proximity of the symposium, we might say) cannot crack the private world of the script. It circumvents the in-group by going out to the world—perhaps why Sappho herself, in the *testimonia* lore, is a kind of Socrates, short and deficient (like Penia) in many ways. Deficient, we might say, but all the more powerful. The creation of intimacy, the power to communicate, and the ability to extend words throughout all the world are things that Sappho's letter, feminine abstract concepts, and women's voices all share. As we know from much Greek poetry, starting with Homer, these are values men prize. Theognis, for instance, gives Cyrnus wings to gain fame, but wants intimacy in return (lines 23–54). In this and many other regards, we can see why Greek men want to dress up, and talk, sometimes, just like a woman.[70]

[70] On Greek men dressing up at symposia and *kōmos*, see Lissarrague 1992: 221–22, with illustration from a Louvre cup. If men in fact mimed women in dress at such events, why not in speech as well?

CHAPTER FIVE

Keening Sappho

FEMALE SPEECH GENRES IN SAPPHO'S POETRY

ANDRÉ LARDINOIS

ONE OF the greatest obstacles to our understanding of Sappho's poetry is the lack of similar material to which to compare her work. The work of no other archaic Greek female poet has survived, and that of her male counterparts is of limited value for this purpose, differing from hers both in subject matter and in perspective.[1] There is, however, one relevant body of material that so far has been largely neglected in the study of Sappho's poetry: that of ordinary female speech genres. In a celebrated essay, Tzvetan Todorov has suggested that all literary genres derive from ordinary speech genres.[2] This seems to hold true in particular for ancient Greece, where the two are sometimes hard to distinguish: one may think, for example, of the *Homeric Hymns*, which are both invocations of the gods and narrative extensions of ordinary prayers.

I argue in this chapter that the poetry of Sappho was closely modeled on the public speech genres of women in ancient Greece. Her poetry is an important testimony to these female speech genres, of which otherwise very little survives, while our understanding of these speech genres can, in turn, help elucidate Sappho's poetry. I examine Sappho's use of three speech genres in particular, which are already represented in the Homeric epics as typically female: prayers to female goddesses, laments, and the praise of young brides. The first of these genres explains Sappho's hymns to the gods; the other two, I argue, are incorporated in Sappho's wedding songs. A recognition of Sappho's use of these speech genres will throw a new light on her poetry, in particular fragments 1, 2, 16, 31, 94, and 96.[3]

---

[1] See, for example, Stigers [Stehle] 1981 and Williamson [1995] 1996.

[2] Todorov [1975] 1990.

[3] All fragments and testimonia of Sappho, Corinna, Telesilla, Praxilla, and the other lyric poets are cited from Campbell's edition in the Loeb Classical Library (1982–93), unless noted otherwise. The epigrams of Anyte, Erinna, Moiro, and Nossis are cited from Page 1975, the *Distaff* of Erinna and Melinno's "Roma" from Lloyd Jones and Parsons 1983. Translations are based loosely on those of Campbell (1982–93) and Rayor (1991).

PRAYERS TO FEMALE DEITIES

In Homer's *Iliad*, Hecuba leads the old women of Troy in a procession to the temple of Athena, where they offer the goddess a woven *peplos* ("robe") and pray for the safety of the city. In a more private ritual, Penelope in the *Odyssey* sacrifices to Athena on behalf of her son, and, when all seems to be lost, prays to Artemis to make an end to her life.[4] Greek women seem to have venerated the female gods in particular. They played an important role in the public worship of these goddesses and were encouraged to see their own lives reflected in their different manifestations. A Greek woman's life could be described as a transition from the state of Artemis (*parthenos* or girl) to Aphrodite (*numphē* or marriageable young woman) to Hera (*gunē* or wife) and Demeter (*mētēr* or mother).[5] The same gender identification is reflected in the different swearing formulas for men and women: Greek men usually swore by male gods, while Greek women invoked various female deities, such as "the Two" (Demeter and Persephone).[6]

Among the fragments attributed to the women poets are several hymns and prayers addressed, with very few exceptions, to female goddesses. There are hymns and prayers to Aphrodite (Sappho frs. 1, 2, 15, 33, 86, 134), including songs about Adonis (Sappho frs. 140a, 168; Praxilla fr. 747), to Aphrodite and the Nereids (Sappho fr. 5), to Artemis (Telesilla fr. 717; Nossis 12; cf. Sappho test. 21 and 47), to Hera (Sappho fr. 17), to the Graces (Sappho fr. 53), to the Muses (Sappho frs. 124, 127), to the Graces and the Muses (Sappho frs. 103.8, 128), and to Roma (Melinno fr. 541). In addition there are a number of dedicatory poems for female deities among the epigrams of Anyte, Nossis, and Moiro (Anyte 1–3; Nossis 3–6; Moiro 1 and 2).

There are exceptions: the fragments of Sappho and Telesilla include traces of hymns to Apollo (Sappho frs. 99, 208?; Telesilla frs. 718 and 719), and Alcman's *partheneia* show that it was possible for male poets to compose hymns to goddesses for performances by female voices as well. Still, the many fragments of the women poets addressed to goddesses suggest that the women poets were largely restricted, or restricted themselves, to hymns that commemorated these deities. In the following paragraphs I examine some of the hymns by Sappho and try to determine if they reveal the same

---

[4] *Il.* 6.286–311; *Od.* 4.759–67, 18.201–5. For these and other religious activities of women in the Homeric epics, see Wickert-Micknat 1982: 22–38.

[5] For the worship of female deities by Greek women and the life stages they represent, see, among others, Calame [1977] 1997: 91–141; Bremmer 1994: 69–83; and Josine Blok's contribution to this volume. On Demeter as a prototypical mother figure, see also Foley 1994: 79–137.

[6] Bain 1984: 39–42; Sommerstein 1995: 64–68; see also Laura McClure's introduction and Josine Blok's contribution to this volume.

relationship between the goddesses and ordinary women as suggested by the Homeric epics, the public worship of female deities, or the Greek swearing formulas.

As the list above shows, there are a great number of hymns to female goddesses among the fragments of Sappho. First of all, there are the remnants of a song about Adonis (frs. 140a, 168), which seems to have been part of a public celebration of the Adonia, a typical women's festival.[7] According to the Hellenistic poet Dioscorides (*Anth. Pal.* 7.407 = Sappho test. 58), Sappho could be heard "lamenting with Aphrodite" as she mourned the young Adonis. This situation is exactly what we find in fragment 140a, except that it is not Sappho herself but a chorus of young women that laments with the goddess. The first line of the fragment is apparently spoken by a group of girls, to whom someone impersonating the goddess responds in the following line:

—κατθνάσκει, Κυθέρη᾿, ἄβρος Ἄδωνις· τί κε θεῖμεν;
—καττύπτεσθε, κόραι, καὶ κατερείκεσθε κίθωνας.

"Delicate Adonis is dying, Cytherea, what are we to do?"
"Beat your breasts, girls, and tear your clothes."

Beating one's breasts and tearing one's clothes were typical gestures of lament in ancient Greece.[8] In fragment 168 the mournful address of Adonis is preserved: ὦ τὸν Ἄδωνιν ("o that Adonis"). What is interesting about these fragments is the close connection between the young women and the goddess: they engage in dialogue, and in their grief over Adonis the young women identify with the goddess, who herself displays a mortal weakness in her mourning for the dead.[9]

In another poem (fr. 2), Sappho summons Aphrodite to her temple in a grove of apple trees. In this shrine the goddess is asked to "pour gracefully into golden cups nectar that is mingled with the festivities" (fr. 2.14–16), to which Athenaeus adds, in a likely imitation of Sappho's next line, which is missing, "for my companions (ἑταίροις) and yours."[10] If such words were part of Sappho's poem, the hymn was probably sung by a chorus of young

---

[7] Versnel 1990: 103–5, with earlier bibliography; Winkler 1990b; Bremmer 1994: 80; Simms 1998.

[8] Alexiou 1974: 8. See also Figure 3 in this volume (p. 105). A group of young women (κόραι) is similarly addressed in a fragment of Telesilla (fr. 717), which may have been part of a hymn to Artemis.

[9] Compare Helene Foley's remarks about Demeter's grief in the *Hymn to Demeter* (Foley 1994: 88–91), and contrast, for example, Artemis' reaction to the death of Hippolytus in Eur. *Hipp.* 1397 and 1437–39.

[10] Athenaeus 11.463c, also quoted by Campbell ([1982] 1990: 58). Athenaeus' words were identified as a possible imitation of Sappho by West (1970: 317 n. 25).

women, who would have referred to each other as *hetairai*.[11] What is remarkable is the claim of these young women also to be the "companions" of Aphrodite and the degree of intimacy suggested by the goddess pouring nectar for them. This gesture brings Aphrodite close to the mortals she serves, while elevating the celebrants to the status of gods who feast on nectar.[12] Both this hymn to Aphrodite and the previous song for Adonis suggest an intimate relationship between the goddess of love and young women, who were probably meant to adopt her as a model for their own budding sexuality.[13]

Sappho claims some of the same intimacy with Aphrodite in her "personal" poetry. I put quotation marks around the word "personal" because, like all archaic Greek poetry, these songs were probably composed for public performances. The most famous example of Sappho's "personal" poetry is fragment 1. The speaker in this poem is Sappho herself, whose name is mentioned in line 20. She prays to Aphrodite to help her with a young woman who spurns her love.[14] What is remarkable about this poem is Sappho's assertion that the goddess previously had appeared to her face-to-face. She even quotes the words Aphrodite spoke to her (fr. 1.18–24) and thus, in performance, Sappho's voice would blend with that of the goddess. Sappho's claim of a face-to-face meeting with the goddess may well be a purely literary assertion, but it suggests the same intimate relationship between the goddess and ordinary women as shown in her song for Adonis or fragment 2.[15]

We may compare Sappho fragment 1 to a similar poem by Anacreon (fr. 357). Anacreon prays to the god Dionysos to come and persuade a young

[11] On female chorus members referring to themselves as *hetairai* ("companions"), see Calame [1977] 1997: 33–34 and [1992] 1999: 98–99 (on Sappho's circle); cf. Sappho fr. 160, which I believe to be a choral fragment as well. On Sappho fr. 2 as probably choral, see Williamson 1995: 140; Lardinois 1996: 165; Aloni 1997: li; and Stehle 1997: 287.

[12] One may again compare the figure of Demeter, who in the *Hymn to Demeter* serves as a nurse to the mortal child Demophoön. Foley (1994: 88) observes that this humanizes the goddess and prepares for her role in the Mysteries.

[13] Aphrodite was particularly associated with rituals for older girls and young brides: Calame [1977] 1997: 123–28, 141; cf. Sappho fr. 112. It is further worth noting that in Athens and Ephesus a cult has been attested for Aphrodite Hetaira, who was said to bring groups of male and female companions (*hetairai*) together: see Lanata [1966] 1996: 15, and Calame 1989: 109 n. 6 for the evidence.

[14] I assume that the woman is young because young women are the subjects of most of Sappho's songs: see Lardinois 1994. In fact, the sex of Sappho's beloved in this poem is not entirely certain and rests upon the questionable reading of a single manuscript in line 24; see Most [1995] 1996: 33.

[15] There is some evidence that Sappho fr. 1 is not meant entirely seriously: Page 1955: 12–18; Stanley 1976; cf. Wilson 1996: 29: "This song is an artistic production, not a true confession." Sappho apparently made the same claim of speaking to the goddess elsewhere in her poetry: frs. 65? (with Campbell's note, 1982–93: ad loc.), 133b?, 134, 159.

man named Cleobulus to accept him as his lover. While Sappho turns to Aphrodite, Anacreon chooses a male god for his prayer. His choice is undoubtedly influenced by the performance setting of the poem, which was in all likelihood a symposium. Another reason for his choice of Dionysos is that the male poets liked to suggest an affinity between their beloved boys and the gods they invoked.[16] However, as Lyn Heatherly Wilson points out, only in Sappho's poem is the invoked deity said to have appeared in person before the speaker.[17] Sappho may have found the model for such an intimate, personal relationship with the goddess in women's festivals like the Adonia or in her own ritual hymns performed by young women.

Sappho's invocation of predominantly female deities is matched by her choice of myths. Eva Stehle has examined some of the mythological stories Sappho treated in her poetry, and she concludes that they often focus on relationships between a strong female goddess and a weaker mortal man, such as the relationship between Eos and Tithonus, Selene and Endymion, Aphrodite and Adonis, or Aphrodite and Phaon.[18] She argues that these stories allowed Sappho to explore a different kind of sexuality than the one advanced by the dominant culture, in which men dominated and women were supposed to be passive. Her reading shows that, just as in the case of the ritual hymns, the women who sang about these relationships or listened to the songs were encouraged to identify themselves with the goddesses.

Goddesses and heroines also figure prominently in the remainder of Sappho's mythological fragments, which provide more evidence of identification between ordinary women and divine female figures: just as men were compared to male gods and heroes, for example in Sappho's own wedding songs,[19] the speakers in these fragments compare themselves or other women to goddesses and heroines. In fragment 16, the speaker adduces Helen of Troy as example both for herself and for a woman named Anactoria, and in fragment 23 another addressee is compared to Helen.[20] In fragment 96, a woman in Lydia is said to be like Selene, and in fragment 142 Leto and Niobe are held up as examples of "dear companions" (φίλαι . . . ἔταιραι), perhaps for the young women in Sappho's choruses who were supposed to establish similar bonds with each other (see above). More speculatively, the wedding of Hector and Andromache in fragment 44 may have

[16] Lardinois 1998b.

[17] Wilson 1996: 32.

[18] Stehle [1990] 1996. See, for example, frs. 58, 199, and 211a–c.

[19] Sappho frs. 105b and 111; see below. There are many more examples in Pindar's *epinikia*.

[20] On the dual identification of Helen with the speaker and the laudanda in fr. 16, see Lardinois 1994: 69 n. 48, with earlier bibliography. Add Saake 1972: 72–73; Calame 1987: 218–21; and Segal 1998: 77.

served as a mythological paradigm for a real marriage ceremony, and in fragment 44A the maidenhood for which Artemis prays may reflect the age of the young women who made up Sappho's choruses.[21]

Other mythological figures mentioned in Sappho's poetry are Leda, who is said to have found an egg (fr. 166), Medea (nothing more than her name is preseved in fr. 186), Peitho, whom Sappho identified as the daughter of Aphrodite (fr. 200), and Pandora, whose story Sappho apparently treated as well (fr. 207). It is admittedly hard to see how some of these figures could have served as role models for Sappho's speakers or their addressees, but then we probably would have said the same about Helen of Troy if we did not have the positive identifications with her figure in Sappho fragments 16 and 23. The goddess Aphrodite is, for that matter, not an unproblematic example either: one need only think of her depiction as an adulteress in *Odyssey* 8. I agree with Stehle (above) that Sappho's religious hymns and mythological stories allowed women to explore aspects of their lives and sexuality that were largely ignored in the dominant culture, including male poetry, primarily by identifying them with strong female goddesses and heroines. However, I do not agree that such poetry necessarily would have been considered "subversive."[22] The identification of ordinary women with powerful goddesses and heroines may be typical of Sappho's poetry, but it was also part of Greek religion, and most of Sappho's songs that compare ordinary women with goddesses or heroines appear to have been composed for public performances, either by Sappho herself (Fig. 2) or by choruses of young women.[23]

LAMENTS

Another important and much-studied speech genre of women in ancient Greece was the lament.[24] The most famous example of this speech genre

---

[21] Sappho fr. 44 has been identified as a wedding song by Merkelbach 1957: 17; Fränkel [1962] 1973: 174; Rösler 1975; Lasserre 1989: 81–106; and Contiades-Tsitsoni 1990: 102–8; Wilson (1996: 87–94) points out that the emphasis on Artemis' virginity is very strong in fr. 44A and suggests that this virginity may reflect that of the women in Sappho's circle. She, however, seems to follow Holt Parker's suggestion (1993) that Sappho's circle was primarily made up of adult women. For my arguments against this view, see Lardinois 1994.

[22] Stehle [1990] 1996: 225.

[23] Lardinois 1996. I argue below that frs. 16 and 96, in which two women are compared to Helen of Troy and Selene, respectively, were composed for wedding ceremonies, while Sappho's hymn to Aphrodite (fr. 2) and the song for Adonis (fr. 140a) were probably composed for public celebrations as well (Page 1955: 42 and 119; Lardinois 1996: 165).

[24] See, among others, Reiner 1938; Alexiou 1974; Wickert-Micknat 1982: 18–22; Holst-Warhaft 1992; Foley 1993; Seaford 1994: 74–92; Stears 1998; McClure 1999: 40–47; and Murnaghan 1999.

Fig. 2. The earliest portrait of Sappho, c. 510–500 B.C.E., in a drawing that slightly improves on the original vase-painting. Sappho is shown alone playing a long-armed type of lyre known as a *barbitos*. She is depicted on several Attic vases from the late sixth and fifth centuries B.C.E., demonstrating the widespread popularity of her poetry in this period, but the relevance of these representations for our reconstruction of the "real" Sappho is probably very limited: see Snyder 1997b.

in the women poets is the so-called *Distaff* of Erinna,[25] but there are also traces of lament in Sappho's song for Adonis (fr. 140a, quoted above) and in some of her wedding songs. In fragment 114, a bride addresses her maidenhood in a dialogue reminiscent of Sappho's song for Adonis:

—παρθενία, παρθενία, ποῖ με λίποισ᾽ ἀποίχῃ;
—† οὐκέτι ἥξω πρὸς σέ, οὐκέτι ἥξω †

[25] Fr. 401 Lloyd-Jones and Parsons (1983) See Eva Stehle's contribution to this volume. For more examples, see the epigrams of Anyte discussed in Greene 2000.

"Maidenhood, maidenhood, where have you gone, deserting me?"

"Never again shall I come to you, never again shall I come"

The direct address of the "deceased" and the accusation that he or she "left" or "deserted" the speaker are typical of laments.[26] Demetrius, who quotes the two lines, identifies the two speakers as a bride and her maidenhood, and there is more evidence that brides at their wedding could perform laments for themselves.[27] Such a custom is not so surprising, since young Greek women were often imagined as "dying" the death of a young girl before being reborn as women (and mothers) in marriage.[28]

At modern Greek weddings, family and friends of the bride also can sing a lament for the bride.[29] An ancient example may be found in one of the stanzas of Catullus 62, an imitation of a Greek wedding song that appears to have been, at least in part, modeled on Sappho's wedding songs.[30] In this poem, a chorus of unmarried young women (*innuptae*) and a chorus of young men (*iuvenes*) engage each other in a dialogue about the married couple, and at one point the maiden chorus sings:

> Evening Star, what more cruel fire than you moves in the sky?
> For you can endure to tear the daughter from her mother's embrace,
> from her mother's embrace to tear the close-clinging daughter,
> and give the chaste maiden to the burning youth.
> What more cruel than this do enemies when a city falls?[31]

---

[26] Compare Andromache's lament for Hector in *Il.* 24.725–26: ἄνερ . . . κὰδ δέ με χήρην / λείπεις ἐν μεγάροισι ("Husband, . . . you leave me behind a widow in your halls"), or Theseus' lament for Phaedra (ἔλιπες, ἔλιπες, ὦ φίλα, "You left me, you left me, dear one," Eur. *Hipp.* 848). Alexiou (1974: 121) cites two modern Greek wedding laments in which a mother addresses her daughter and bemoans that she is "leaving" her.

[27] Demetr. *Eloc.* 140, quoted by Campbell (1982–93: ad loc.). Seaford (1987: 113–14) cites the other evidence. For a modern Greek example, see Alexiou 1974: 121. Bowra (1961: 222) compares Sappho fr. 114 to a Moravian marriage song, in which the bride laments the loss of her "green crown."

[28] Lada-Richards 1999: 57, with earlier bibliography. Add Redfield 1982: 188–91; Foley 1985: 85–89, and 1994: 104; Dowden 1989: esp. 35–37, 47; and Johnston 1999: 218. Redfield (1982: 188–89, 190), Seaford (1987: 107), and Rehm (1994: 29) detail the many similarities between ancient Greek marriage and death rituals: for example, a bride will offer a lock of hair before her marriage, just as mourners do when visiting a grave, and, like a corpse, she is ritually bathed, "covered" or veiled, and driven in a cart to her new home in a procession that includes torchbearers, family, and friends; cf. Danforth (1982: 79) on the similarities between modern Greek wedding and death rituals.

[29] Alexiou and Dronke 1971: 848–50; Alexiou 1974: 120–21; Danforth 1982: 74–79; Holst-Warhaft 1992: 41.

[30] Bowra 1961: 219–21.

[31] Catull. 62.20–24. Text and translation after Goold 1988. Seaford (1987: 110–19) argues that Aeschylus' *Suppliants* dramatizes, in extreme form, the negative attitude of the bride and her female companions toward marriage. The protagonists in this play are also presented as lamenting (Aesch. *Supp.* 69–76, 112–16).

At the beginning of the next stanza, in line 32, the young women complain that "the Evening Star has taken one of us away" (*Hesperus e nobis, aequales, abstulit unam*).[32] The two forms of wedding lament, by the bride and by her friends, can also be combined, as may be the case in Sappho fragment 114 (quoted above). If the second line of this fragment was sung by female friends of the bride, they would be bidding her farewell at the same time as she laments the loss of her youth.

John Rauk has compared Erinna's *Distaff*, in which she mourns the death of a female friend, to fragments 16, 94, and 96 of Sappho, which he has labeled "farewell addresses," but which others have identified as "consolation songs" or "poems of separation and memory."[33] I will argue that these fragments in fact represent laments that Sappho herself or young friends of the bride performed at weddings.

Fragment 16 is dedicated to Anacatoria, who has been identified as a young woman. Ovid (*Her.* 15.15–17 = test. 19) lists her among the *puellae* ("girls") of Sappho, and Maximus of Tyre 18.9 (= test. 20) compares her relationship with Sappho to that of Alcibiades, Charmides, or Phaedrus with Socrates.[34] Recently, Christopher Brown has argued that Anactoria must have been of marriageable age, because of the "sparkle" (ἀμάρυχμα, 18) in her face, which is paralleled by similar descriptions of young, marriageable women in Hesiod's *Catalogue of Women*.[35] The fragment takes the form of a public praise poem,[36] but it also contains elements of lament. It was probably performed by a chorus, which, if my identification of the poem as a

---

[32] This line may contain an allusion to Sappho fr. 104a, especially if the last line of this fragment is read as saying that the Evening Star "leads away the child from its mother": see Griffith 1989: 56 n. 11, with earlier bibliography. Add Hague 1984: 34.

[33] Rauk 1989; Merkelbach 1957: 12–16; Aloni 1997: lii; see also Burnett 1979 and 1983: 277–313. Merkelbach (1957: 12–13) refers to these poems as *Trostgedichte* (consolation poems) or *Trostlieder* (consolation songs)—"ähnlich wie wir auch heute noch Leidtragende nach einem Todesfall zu trösten . . . suchen" (similar to the way we still try today to console the conflicted after a death). Stehle (Stigers [Stehle] 1981: 55–56) says that they "mourn" the elusiveness of happiness and take as their subject "the loss of the beloved by parting," comparing them to fr. 140a (the song for Adonis). Rauk (1989: 110) actually refers to fr. 94 as a "lament."

[34] The Suda Σ 107 (test. 2) lists an Anagora, which is probably a corruption of Anactoria's name (Page 1955: 135 n. 1; Lefkowitz 1981: 64), among the pupils (μαθήτριαι) of Sappho. For the misidentification of Sappho's young addressees as pupils by later Hellenistic and Roman scholars, see Lardinois 1994: 63–64.

[35] Brown 1989. Stehle (1997: 270) objects that Sappho may have used the word differently from the male Greek poets, but this would have to be proven rather than assumed. The erotic vocabulary of Sappho is generally very close to that of her male counterparts: see Lanata [1966] 1996; Carson [1980] 1996; Cavallini 1986; and Calame [1992] 1999: 13–38.

[36] For a detailed comparison between Sappho fr. 16 and Pindar's *epinikia*, see Howie 1977: esp. 209–14. The similarity was already noted by Fränkel ([1924] 1968: 90–93), and by Bundy ([1962] 1986: 5–6).

wedding song is correct, most likely would have been made up of female friends of the bride.[37]

In the poem, Anactoria is compared to Helen of Troy, a comparison that may seem surprising to us, but that was in fact not uncommon in ancient Greek wedding songs. Lucian (*Symp.* 41) in a mock wedding song likens his bride to Helen, and Sappho fragment 23, in which another woman is compared to Helen, is probably derived from a wedding song as well.[38] Despite, or perhaps because of, her many marriages, Helen was often portrayed as the prototypical bride: she is the bride in Theocritus *Idyll* 18 ("Helen's Epithalamium") and was regularly depicted as such on Greek wedding vases.[39] Helen was also closely associated with death, and her abduction by Paris could be imagined as a descent into the underworld, for example in Euripides' *Helen*.[40] This association makes her presence in a mixed wedding/ lament song all the more appropriate.

In Sappho fragment 16, Helen is said to have "left" or "deserted" (καλλίποισ᾿, 9) her "most valiant husband" (τὸν ἄνδρα / τὸν πανάριστον, 7–8) in order to follow her heart and sail to Troy.[41] The implication is that Anactoria has done the same to the speaker. She can now only conjure up a memory of Anactoria, "who is not here" (με νῦν Ἀνακτορίας ὀνέμναι[σ᾿ / οὐ] παρεοίσας, 15–16). The word καλλίποισ᾿, which is used to describe the "desertion" of Helen, is reminiscent of the participle used by the bride

---

[37] For another wedding song, in the same meter, sung by female friends of the bride, see Sappho fr. 30, with the comments of Contiades-Tsitsoni (1990: 100–101). For more evidence that Sappho fr. 16 was part of a choral song, see Lardinois 1996: 166–67, with earlier references.

[38] McEvilley 1978: 15 n. 41; Hague 1983: 133.

[39] Oakley and Sinos 1993: 13 and 132 n. 16. Charles Segal (1998: 65) remarks concerning her position in *Iliad* book 3: "Helen's conflicts here approximate (*mutatis mutandis*) those of the bride generally in virilocal marriage, as she experiences the pull between her new household and the house of origin she has left behind." On Helen's varied reputation in antiquity, see Nancy Worman's contribution to this volume. For her association with female rites of passage, see Calame [1977] 1997: 191–202; and Zweig 1999.

[40] On Helen's association with death, see Vernant [1985] 1991b: 102; Martin 1995; and Worman in this volume. For the death imagery in Euripides' *Helen*, see Rehm 1994: 121–27, with earlier bibliography.

[41] I translate τὸν ἄνδρα / τὸν πανάριστον in lines 7–8 as "the most valiant husband," because I believe that it belongs to the "love versus war" theme that runs through the poem. Helen rejects τὸν ἄνδρα / τὸν πανάριστον for Paris, just as the speaker chooses whom she loves over cavalry, infantry, or ships (1–4). In *Iliad* 3.19, Paris challenges "all the best" (πάντας ἀρίστους) of the Achaeans to fight with him. Menelaus, "dear to Ares" (ἀρηΐφιλος, 3.21, etc.), accepts the challenge and, of course, beats him in the duel, but it is Paris who gets the girl, because Aphrodite "leads" Helen (ἦρχε δὲ δαίμων, 3.420; cf. ἄξεις, 3.401) to his bedroom, just as she appears to be doing in Sappho fr. 16.11–12. It was Aphrodite's characteristic role at Greek weddings to persuade the bride and lead her to the groom (Seaford 1987: 117).

ω address her lost maidenhood (λίποισ', fr. 114), and also of Andromache's lament for Hector in *Iliad* 24.725–26 (κὰδ δέ με χήρην / λείπεις). Allusions to memory occur frequently in laments,[42] as does the affirmation that the deceased is no longer here.[43] The speaker in fragment 16 mourns the loss of a dear friend, while at the same time acknowledging that she is following her heart.

Fragment 94 reports a dialogue between Sappho and a woman who left her reluctantly (ἄ με ψισδομένα κατελίμπανεν, 2; cf. ἀέκοισ' ἀπυλιμπάνω, 5). Sappho is the speaker of the poem, although the first-person plural in line 8 ("we cared for you" [πεδήπομεν]) suggests that she is not just speaking for herself.[44] It has been suggested that this woman was a girl who recently had left Sappho's circle in order to get married.[45] This proposition is quite plausible. As I have argued elsewhere, most of Sappho's songs speak about young women, and the activities of which Sappho reminds the woman in the second half of this poem are compatible with those of a chorus, the most likely organizational form of Sappho's so-called circle.[46] I would like to add that the poem was probably performed at the young woman's wedding.

There are again traces of lament in this song. Fragment 94 opens with a statement that is common in laments: "Honestly, I wish I were dead."[47] Scholars are divided as to whether this line is spoken by the girl or by Sappho, and given the fact that both the bride and her former friends could lament at the wedding, both options are possible.[48] I prefer to give the line

---

[42] E.g., *Il.* 24.745 (Andromache's final lament for Hector); cf. Theoc. *Id.* 18.41 ("Helen's Epithalamium"), with Gow's comments ad loc. (Gow 1952, 2: 358). For the role of memory in Greek laments, see Reiner (1938: 12, 16), who cites many examples from Greek tragedy, Skinner (1982: 266), and Holst-Warhaft (1992: 35–37).

[43] E.g., *Il.* 24.725 (Andromache's final lament for Hector): ἀπ' αἰῶνος νέος ὤλεο; Eur. *Alc.* 394–95: μαῖα δὴ κάτω βέβακεν, οὐκέτ' ἔστιν (Eumelus' lament for his dead mother); Eur. *Hipp.* 828, *Hec.* 513, *Supp.* 1138 and 1163.

[44] See Page 1955: 78; du Bois 1995: 140; Lardinois 1996: 163; and Aloni 1997: liv.

[45] E.g., Merkelbach 1957: 12–13; Rauk 1989: 110; Foley 1994: 135.

[46] Lardinois 1994: esp. 70–71. On Sappho's circle as made up of choruses of young women, see also Merkelbach 1957; Calame [1977] 1997: 210–14; and Calame 1996.

[47] Compare *Il.* 22.481 (Andromache's first lament for Hector), 24.764 (Helen's lament for Hector), with Worman's contribution to this volume; Aesch. *Pers.* 915–17; Soph. *El.* 1131, *OC* 1689–90; Eur. *Med.* 1210, *Hipp.* 836–37, *Suppl.* 796. In a lament, this phrase expresses the desire of the mourner to be one with the deceased and the recognition that life without him or her is not worth living. In Sappho fr. 95 we find a more elaborate formulation of this wish, perhaps spoken to Hermes as guide of the souls (Campbell 1982 [1990]: ad loc.).

[48] Gomme (1957: 255–56), Burnett (1983: 292), Snyder (1989: 26), and Greene ([1994] 1996: 239) assume that the girl speaks the first line, contra Wilamowitz (1913: 50), Page (1955: 82), McEvilly (1971: 4), Saake (1971: 189), Campbell (1983: 226), Rauk (1989: 107), Robbins (1990), and Stehle (1997: 307), who opt for Sappho.

to Sappho. In this case, she would lament the departure of the young woman from her company right before the girl is said to have "left" her (κατελίμπανεν, 2).[49] This initial lament is followed by another, short lament of the young woman (4–5), and a longer passage (7ff.) in which Sappho reminds her audience how she tried to console the girl (and herself?) at the moment of departure. She asks the girl to remember her (κἄμεθεν / μέμναισ', 7–8), and then reminds her (ὄμναισαι, 10) of all the beautiful things they did together.[50] There is thus a double moment of remembrance in the poem: first of the conversation Sappho had with the girl when she left, and subsequently of all the pleasant things they did together on previous occasions, like stringing flower-wreaths (12–14), putting on garlands (15–17), wearing perfumes (18–20), and going to holy places (25, 27).[51] As in fragment 16 and in laments in general, memory is what keeps the bond alive between the mourner and the departed.[52] The whole fragment therefore appears to adopt the form of a lament, although it may well be celebrating at the same time the girl's imminent marriage.

Fragment 96 could have been considered a real lament for a dead woman, if the reading κ[ᾶ]ρ[ι σᾶι] ("because of your *kēr*") in line 17 were correct.[53] A *kēr* is the bringer of an evil fate, and "almost invariably in fact that of death."[54] It is, however, more likely that the letter traces hide an adjective that describes the "desire" (ἰμέρῳ) by which a woman in Lydia is consumed when remembering gentle Atthis.[55] But even if the fragment therefore does

---

[49] The verb καταλιμπάνειν is an alternative present stem of καταλείπειν ("to leave" or "to desert"), which is the verb used of Helen in Sappho fr. 16.9 and of Hector in Andromache's lament in *Iliad* 24.725–26.

[50] Sappho fr. 94.9–11. Slings (1994) reconstructs the stanza as follows: αἰ δὲ μή, ἀλλά σ' ἔγω θέλω / ὄμναισαι, [σὺ δὲ] δ[ὴ φρ]άσαι, / ὄσ[σ' ἴμερτά τε]καὶ κάλ' ἐπάσχομεν ("If not, then I want to remind you, and you consider all the lovely and beautiful things we experienced").

[51] In the middle of all this we read that "on soft beds, tender . . . you would satisfy your longing" (καὶ στρώμν[αν ἐ]πὶ μολθάκαν / ἀπάλαν πα .[ ] . . . ων / ἐξίης πόθο[ν] . νίδων, fr. 94.21–23). This passage has been widely interpreted as referring to sexual gratification, but it is just as likely that the girl took a nap: Lardinois 1996: 164 n. 70, with earlier references. Add to the evidence collected there that the young women's chorus in Alcman fr. 3.6–8 says that it scatters sweet sleep from its eyes before going to the gathering place to participate in the dancing.

[52] Rauk (1989: 110–14) compares Sappho's insistence on remembering in this poem to Erinna's remark in the *Distaff* that Baucis "in her marriage" "forgot everything" that she had learned from her mother (lines 28–30), and to Helen, who in Sappho fr. 16 "forgot" her dear ones when she ran off with Paris. He also notes the similarity with the language of laments.

[53] This reading was first proposed by Page (1955: 92) and is printed by Campbell ([1982] 1990: 120).

[54] Parker 1996b: 806. Alcaeus fr. 38A.7 also uses the word in this sense.

[55] E.g., κ[α]ρ[τερ]ω‹ι›, which Kamerbeek (1956: 101) proposes, or κ[α]ρ[χάρ]ω‹ι›, suggested by Bonanno (1973–74: 114); cf. Degani and Burzacchini 1977: 169 (I owe this reference to Albert Henrichs). Following Kamerbeek's suggestion, the stanza would read: πόλλα

not constitute an actual lament for the dead, it contains elements of this speech genre. The woman's remembrance (ἐπιμνάσθεισ', 16–17) of gentle Atthis, who is far away, is reminiscent of Sappho fragments 16 and 94 and of the language of laments. Alexander Turyn has compared the woman's "wandering to and fro" (ζαφοίταισ', 15), perhaps along the seashore if the reading δι' ἄλον in line 20 is correct, to that of other grieving figures in Greek literature,[56] and the nocturnal imagery surrounding the woman also carries connotations of death.

Most of the fragment is taken up by a description of the woman in Lydia, who is likened to the moon goddess.[57] This woman is said to remember Atthis, who is the likely addressee of the poem and a young woman.[58] The persistent use of the first-person plural for the speaker in the poem suggests that it was sung by a chorus, which was probably made up of Atthis' (former?) companions.[59] The Lydian woman may function as an example to them, just as Helen of Troy functions as paradigm for the speaker in fragment 16. Her desire is emblematic of the desire they themselves feel for Atthis, just as her mourning matches theirs. In lines 4–5, they repeat the claim of the Lydian woman that Atthis is like a goddess manifest, thus effectively adopting her voice. Thomas McEvilley saw in this comparison of Atthis to a goddess an allusion to the hymeneal convention of the *makarismos* (on which, see below), but he confuses *laudator* and *laudanda* when he concludes that "Atthis and the departed girl are seen for the moment as potential bride and groom."[60] The Lydian woman is in the same position as the chorus: she praises the (future) bride.

Since the woman in Lydia left Atthis (rather than the other way around), she can only try to remember her, just as the chorus in the second, much damaged part of the fragment seems to be engaged in recalling events of

---

δὲ ζαφοίταισ', ἀγάνας ἐπι- / μνάσθεισ' Ἄτθιδος ἰμέρῳ / λέπταν ποι φρένα καρτέρῳ βόρηται ("Often wandering to and fro, remembering gentle Atthis, she is devoured in her tender heart by strong desire [for Atthis]," 15–17). (The genitive Ἄτθιδος is so placed that it can be taken both with ἐπιμνάσθεισ' and with ἰμέρῳ·) An adjective like κάρτερος ("strong") would nicely balance the "tenderness" of the woman's heart, as Kamerbeek noted, and together with ἰμέρῳ it would surround λέπταν ποι φρένα ("her tender heart") and iconically suggest the very act of devouring. Cavallini (1994) also argues in favor of taking ἰμέρῳ with βόρηται.

[56] Turyn 1929: 59–60, quoted by McEvilley (1973: 276).

[57] Schubart's emendation σέλαννα in line 8 for the unmetrical μήνα of the papyrus is supported by Janko (1982b), who also defends Lobel's suggestion that Selanna represents the personal name of the goddess; cf. McEvilley 1973: 262, contra Page 1955: 90.

[58] Atthis is, just like Anactoria (above), listed by Ovid among the *puellae* of Sappho (test. 19), and her relationship with Sappho is compared to that of Socrates and his pupils (test. 20). On Atthis as the likely addressee of the poem, see Page 1955: 92; Campbell [1982] 1990: 123 n. 1; Burnett 1983: 302–3; Lasserre 1989: 144–45; and Aloni 1997: xvii.

[59] Lardinois 1996: 161–63.

[60] McEvilley 1973: 262.

the past, including one time when Aphrodite poured nectar from a golden (pitcher?).[61] This event is very similar to the ritual described in Sappho fragment 2 (above), and it is not unlikely that the second half of this poem, like fragment 94, contained a series of events that the speaker remembered experiencing with Atthis in the past.[62] Like Helen in fragment 16, the Lydian woman probably plays a dual role in the poem: besides functioning as an example to the speaker of the poem, she also functions as comparison for the addressee, Atthis. Like the Lydian woman, Atthis is compared to a goddess (4), and together the two of them are distinct from the chorus, which says that it cannot rival goddesses in loveliness of figure (21–22). If my interpretation of the poem as a wedding song is correct, Atthis is no longer a girl, but, like the Lydian woman, she "now stands out among women" (6–7). The poem thus celebrates the newly found status of Atthis, while at the same time mourning the loss of the friends of her youth.

I have taken a detailed look at fragments 16, 94, and 96 of Sappho. By comparing these fragments to lament speeches and the information we possess about performances of laments at Greek weddings, I have identified them as wedding songs, which were performed either by Sappho herself (fr. 94) or by female friends of the bride (frs. 16 and 96). It has been argued that the speech genre of lament allowed women, both in ancient and in modern Greece, to voice a degree of "social protest."[63] They could express in laments their displeasure with their own lot as well as with the lot of their relatives who were taken away from them by war or disease. One may find traces of this function in these wedding songs as well. Although the "protest" here is highly stylized and was probably expected as part of the wedding ceremony, the language of lament embedded in these wedding songs provided the female performers with a vehicle for voicing, in public, something of their sense of loss and anxiety about the marriage. One may compare John Campbell's observation of the sisters of the bride at a modern Greek wedding: "The unmarried sisters whom the bride leaves behind display a grief which in its public aspect is certainly conventionally expected, but for some days after the wedding they seem even in the privacy of the family hut to be stunned by the loss of their sister's accustomed presence. Sisters sense the dread and apprehension which the bride herself feels when she leaves the protective circle of her family to be given into the care of strangers."[64]

---

[61] Ἀφροδίτα κα[   ] νέκταρ ἔχευ' ἀπὺ / χρυσίας, fr. 96.26–28. Zuntz (1939: 107) suggests reading κἄμμι κάλπιδος or κάλπιδος ἄμμι in the lacuna, which would translate: "and she poured for us nectar from a golden pitcher." Some scholars believe that a new poem begins after line 20, but this is unlikely: see Saake 1971: 174; Carey 1978: 368; Burnett 1983: 311; and Lardinois 1996: 161–62.

[62] Carey 1978: 368.

[63] Caraveli 1986; cf. Holst-Warhaft 1992; Foley 1993.

[64] Campbell 1964: 173, partially quoted by Jenkins (1983: 145 n. 50).

THE PRAISE OF BRIDES

Sappho was perhaps most famous in antiquity for her wedding songs. At least one book, probably the ninth, in the Alexandrian edition of her poetry consisted wholly of wedding songs, while other marriage songs were included among the other eight books, which were organized according to meter.[65] Young women again played a prominent role in the performance of such songs. Sappho herself describes the wedding procession for Hector and Andromache, in which "maidens (*parthenoi*) sang clearly a holy song," and Pindar imagines a wedding feast, where one could hear "the sound of full-voiced wedding songs (*hymenaioi*), such as young women (*parthenoi*), who are companions (*hetairai*) and age-mates (*halikes*) of the bride, are wont to utter seductively in evening songs." [66]

As we have seen in the previous section, part of the function of Greek wedding songs was to lament and console the bride over the loss of her youth. Another function was to praise the groom. One greeted the groom with a traditional blessing (*makarismos*), in which he was compared to a god or famous hero.[67] Traces of this practice can be found in Sappho fragments 105b, 111, and perhaps 31 (see below). But the singers seem to have reserved most of their attention for the bride. She was described in highly erotic terms, as is clear from Sappho fragment 112: after the groom is hailed as being "blessed" (ὄλβιε), the speaker of this fragment turns to the bride and tells her: "Your form is graceful, your eyes . . . honey-sweet, and *erōs* streams over your desirable face. . . . Aphrodite has honored you outstandingly."[68]

When the speaker in this fragment says that *erōs* streams over the desirable face of the bride, it is by no means clear that this is supposed to have an effect on her husband only. There is some evidence to suggest that a bride was expected to be the object of widespread erotic admiration at ancient Greek weddings.[69] In fragment 16, which I discussed above, the chorus expresses its desire for Anactoria, when they recall her "lovely step" (ἔρατόν τε βᾶμα, 17) and adduce her as an example of the thing they love (ἔραται, 4). Similarly, the chorus in fragment 96 recalls the desire for Atthis (Ἄτθιδος ἰμέρῳ, 16), by which the tender heart of a woman in Lydia is con-

[65] Page 1955: 125; Contiades-Tsitsoni 1990: 71.

[66] Sappho fr. 44.25–26; Pind. *Pyth.* 3.16–19. See also Figure 4 in this volume (p. 108). On ancient Greek wedding songs in general, see Mangelsdorff 1913; Maas 1914; Muth 1954; Hague 1983; Contiades-Tsitsoni 1990; and Lyghounis 1991.

[67] Hague 1983: 134–35; Lyghounis 1991: 185.

[68] σοὶ χάριεν μὲν εἶδος, ὄππατα δ'. . . / μέλλιχ', ἔρος δ' ἐπ' ἰμέρτωι κέχυται προσώπωι, fr. 112.3–4. The context in Choricius (*Oratio nuptialis in Zachariam* 19), who quotes part of the fragment, makes it clear that these words are addressed to the bride.

[69] Seaford 1994: 36 n. 25 cites the evidence.

sumed. I believe that these fragments demonstrate the erotic appeal that the bride was supposed to hold for the choruses who sing these songs as well as for the audience at large.

The strongest expression of desire for another woman occurs in Sappho fragment 31. This fragment describes a series of emotions that the speaker feels when she sees a woman laughing and talking to a man. Her heart misses a beat, her ears ring, she cannot speak, and sweat pours down her face. She enumerates ten of these afflictions in all before concluding that "all can be endured" (17). The speaker in the fragment is not identified, and most interpreters assume that she is Sappho, but she could just as well represent a chorus of young women.[70] Scholars at the beginning of the twentieth century believed that this poem represented a wedding song.[71] The opening line, in which the man is compared to a god, recalls the traditional *makarismos* of the groom, and the position of the man and woman, sitting opposite one another, is paralleled by the depiction of other married couples in Greek literature and art.[72] Most recent interpreters, starting with Denys Page, have rejected this view.[73] Page objects that it would be inappropriate for Sappho (or, presumably, any other speaker) to speak about the intensity of her passions for a bride on her wedding day, but we have seen that such declarations of desire were indeed not out of place in Greek wedding songs. Jane Snyder objects that "a wedding song must have chiefly to do with the bride and the groom, not with the speaker's passion for one of them," but as Glenn Most remarks: "It is in fact the beauty of the unnamed girl that is the burden of the poem and the justification for its composition and performance: every detail Sappho provides is designed to testify, not to the poet's susceptibility, but to the girl's seductiveness."[74]

The *partheneia* or "maiden songs" of Alcman provide a close parallel for the erotic praise of a young woman by a female chorus. The term *partheneion* is Hellenistic, and the two main fragments (frs. 1 and 3) appear to be reli-

---

[70] Lardinois 1996: esp. 167–69.

[71] Welcker [1857] 1861: 89–90; Wilamowitz 1913: 58; and Snell [1931] 1966: 82. More recently: Schadewaldt 1950: 98; Merkelbach 1957: 6; Fränkel [1962] 1973: 176; Lasserre 1974: 22; and Rissman 1983: 103–4.

[72] Snell [1931] 1966: 82–83; Rissman 1983: 90–93. See also McEvilley (1978: 6–8) and Latacz (1985: 86–87), who, on the basis of the diction, conclude that ἄνηρ, ὄττις ἐνάντιός τοι / ἰσδάνει must refer to a husband. McEvilley further cites as evidence a likely allusion to Sappho's opening stanza in *Anth. Pal.* 5.94, and Seaford (1994: 36) adduces a vase (*ARV*² 1017.44) depicting a bride and groom who sit opposite one another. This vase is reproduced in Oakley and Sinos 1993: 83, figs. 60 and 61.

[73] Page 1955: 30–33; cf. Lanata [1966] 1996: 22; Saake 1971: 36–37; Kirkwood 1974: 121–22; Snyder 1989: 19–20 and 1991: 12–13.

[74] Snyder 1991: 13; Most 1982: 97.

gious hymns designed to be sung by choruses of young women.[75] In Alcman fragment 3, the chorus describes a young woman named Astymeloisa, who is probably their chorus leader, in highly erotic terms. They say that she causes "longing that loosens the limbs," and that "she casts glances that are more melting than sleep or death; not in vain is she sweet."[76] Maurice Bowra says about the girl: "We are left with the impression that the whole company is in love with her . . . ," but later he adds: "The aim of the song is the celebration of a girl's beauty and charm which everyone is intended to feel."[77] The homoerotic feelings that the chorus expresses for Astymeloisa in this poem, and similar sentiments detectable in Alcman fragment 1, therefore appear to be intended as public praise rather than as personal declarations of love.[78] I would argue that the same holds true for the erotic appeal that Sappho and her choruses attribute to young brides.

Eva Stehle has explained the use of young women's choruses to praise the sexual attractiveness of other women by pointing out that "Greek culture generally insisted on a construction of the socially acceptable female body as sexually passive. One consequence is that women could praise other women sexually without compromising men's appropriation of those women."[79] I would add that the relationship between homo- and heterosexuality was also viewed differently from modern times, and that the ancient Greeks commonly assumed that if a young person was erotically appealing to the one sex, he or she would also be attractive for the other.[80] Still, it is significant that women were called upon to praise other women at all, given how seldom they were allowed to express their views in public. It is also noteworthy that they were allowed to describe their female companions in such erotic terms. As Stehle further remarks: "Since women were called on to praise other women in public, the idea of desire between women was not repressed."[81]

---

[75] See Calame 1977 on Alcman frs. 1 and 3 and the origin of the term *partheneion*. Griffiths (1972) has argued that Alcman fr. 1 actually constitutes a marriage song. This interpretation has to be rejected, but it is instructive that such a reading could even be considered, and some of the parallels Griffiths draws between Alcman's *partheneia* and ancient Greek wedding songs are certainly valid.

[76] Alcman fr. 3.61–63: λυσιμελεῖ τε πόσωι, τακερώτερα / δ' ὕπνω και σανάτω ποτιδέρκεται / οὐδέ τι μαψιδίως γλυκ[ῆα κ]ήνα.

[77] Bowra 1961: 177 and 213. The celebrated girl is said to be running among a large crowd in lines 73–74.

[78] It has been argued by Calame and others that these young women were involved in actual homoerotic relationships with each other, but the evidence is not very strong: see Lardinois 1998a: 122–24.

[79] Stehle 1997: 78.

[80] Dover 1978: 1, 65–67; Lardinois 1989: 24; Halperin 1990a: 33–35; and Calame [1992] 1999: 54–55.

[81] Stehle 1997: 93.

SOMETHING OF THE VOICES OF YOUNG WOMEN

In the previous paragraphs, I have tried to use our fragmentary knowledge of ancient Greek female speech genres to explain some of the fragmentary remains of Sappho's songs. These songs in turn can tell us something about these speech genres and are important witnesses to them. We have seen how in the religious hymns of Sappho, young women were allowed to experience a close relationship with a powerful goddess such as Aphrodite. Through the myths they told they could further liken themselves, and their addressees, to famous mythological figures such as Helen of Troy, Eos, Selene, Leto, and Niobe. In laments incorporated into wedding songs, the young women could voice something of their bitterness in losing their family or friends, and in the same wedding songs as well as in some religious hymns, they could reveal something of their erotic passion for other women. It is true that none of these songs represent genuine outpourings of personal emotions. They are all scripted by poets such as Sappho or Alcman and must have been experienced as conventional by the audiences that first listened to them. Still, the young women presented these songs in their own voices and probably could relate some of the lyrics to their own experiences.

The very formality of the occasion on which the young women performed these songs signifies another restriction placed on their voices. Brides may have been allowed to lament the loss of their virginity on their wedding day, but they were not expected to repeat the performance every night in the bedroom. Similarly, women may have been able to identify themselves with powerful goddesses during religious rituals, as long as they were willing to assume a subservient role to their husbands and fathers once they returned home. These performances are part of rituals of controlled ambiguity, in which the rules of ordinary society are temporarily suspended in order to expose the underlying tensions on which it is founded.[82] Yet, for the duration of the rituals, such tensions are recognized as real, and the original audiences could have heard in these songs, however faintly, through the ritual and authorial filters placed on them, something of the hopes and anxieties of young women. So can we.

[82] For the concept of rituals of controlled ambiguity, see Oudemans and Lardinois 1987: esp. 56–57. This chapter was composed with the generous support of the University of Minnesota Faculty Summer Research Program and the McKnight Summer Fellowship Program (1998). An oral version was delivered at the University of Minnesota and the University of Wisconsin at Madison. I would like to thank the different audiences, my coeditor Laura McClure, and Michelle Lewis for their valuable suggestions and comments.

Part Two

THE CLASSICAL PERIOD

CHAPTER SIX

Virtual Voices

TOWARD A CHOREOGRAPHY OF WOMEN'S SPEECH IN CLASSICAL ATHENS

JOSINE H. BLOK

AN ATHENIAN housewife's intermittent balancing of speech against silence, of deference toward her husband against the need to act on behalf of her own responsibilities, is voiced by the heroine of Aristophanes' comedy *Lysistrata*. Explaining why the women, tired of the devastating war, have gathered on the Akropolis, she tells the magistrate who has been sent to check them:

> All this while, ever since the beginning of the war until now, we have borne through our self-restraint with whatever you men choose to do—you did not allow us to utter a syllable, did you?—but all the same we did not agree with you at all. But well we knew all this time of your doings; and often, when keeping inside our homes, we heard of yet another absurd instance of your mismanagement. And while inwardly grieving but with a smile on our face, we would ask you again and again, "What did you decide to write further about the Treaty on the stone in the Assembly today?" But the husband would say: "What is that of your business? Keep your mouth shut!" and so I did keep it. [The magistrate says that she otherwise would have been beaten.] Therefore certainly I held my tongue. Soon we would hear again of another, even more damaging endeavor of yours; and we would ask: "Husband dear, how could you take such foolish decisions?"[1]

When Lysistrata reveals that the women have decided to swap roles with the men, she explains how this principle is to be realized: the men, as women, must be silent and obedient, the women, as men, will assume control in order to restore peace (*Lys.* 527–28).

The presentation and representation of gender roles in this scene, as in the whole of *Lysistrata*, are extremely complex, the more so because the role

---

[1] Ar. *Lys.* 507–18 (ed Henderson 1987). I thank S.L. Radt for discussing the translations in this chapter with me; all remaining errors are mine.

of the heroine was played by a male actor.[2] Since in this play the women have left their private existence to occupy public space, the traditional order of life has become confused: the women have acquired a certain masculinity by leaving their homes, raising their voices, and taking charge of the city, while the public area of the Akropolis and neighboring spaces to some extent have been made feminine and private by the presence of so many women. An even more complicated question is how to evaluate the representation of daily life—the so-called historical reality of the average citizen in the audience—within the context of the comic theater. Against the background of a daily life structured by the distinction between public/politics/male and private/home/female, how is the inverted world of *Lysistrata*, and of the other "women's plays" by Aristophanes, to be judged? Is the very idea of women taking over the management of the city so radically absurd in the eyes of the audience that everything said or done within the context of the play could only be seen as part of a topsy-turvy world?

Obviously the play could have its intended impact only because many elements were familiar. The make-believe was effective because it resembled the real.[3] The man in the Athenian street was both the implied subject of Aristophanic comedy and its object; he could identify with the main tenets of the play solely if he could somehow see and hear his own world onstage. He probably would have recognized in Lysistrata's role-playing words his own wife might have spoken. In the lawsuit against the fraudulent courtesan Neaera, the accuser played upon the jurors' anxiety by evoking similar discussions. What would they say, when they returned home after the trial and were questioned by their wives on their verdict?[4] In this context, so different from that of the *Lysistrata*, the speaker supposed the husbands to be ashamed upon questioning instead of beating their wives to silence, because such a supposition would contradict his speech, which hinged on the unique value of the Athenian citizen wife.

But not only words in the strict sense convey meaning. In the attempt to perceive significant patterns of behavior and intention, evidence from contemporary rural Greece and occasionally from other Mediterranean countries proves to be valuable, not as a litmus test for historical truth, nor as seismograph of historical continuity, but as a comparative model providing an indispensable context for ancient material.[5] The way Lysistrata covers

---

[2] On the multilayered representation of gender in the *Lysistrata*, cf. Foley 1982; Saïd 1987; Høibye 1995; Zeitlin [1981] 1996, though mainly dealing with the *Thesmophoriazusae*, is also relevant to *Lysistrata;* on the effects of role-swapping in speech, Sommerstein 1995; on male actors playing female roles, Taaffe 1993: 49–51, and Griffith's contribution to this volume.

[3] Zeitlin ([1985] 1996: 361), who deals foremost with tragedy, but in her discussion of mimesis deals also with drama in general.

[4] [Dem.] 59 (*Against Neaera*) 110–11.

[5] For a methodological validation of this approach, which elicits much debate, see Versnel

her feelings with irony, outwardly complying with male authority but inside deeply critical of, indeed angry about, the men's pretentions and actions, resembles the way women in Greek rural villages nowadays can express their resentment.[6] A woman will never overtly hold up her husband or male kin for ridicule, but she can verbalize her point of view through barely veiled mockery. Though a husband may ultimately beat his wife to silence, a threat about which the magistrate also hints in Lysistrata's speech, he has actually lost some ground if the woman's critique is well founded.[7]

Irony as a means to show social submission while undoubtedly implying independent criticism is one among many features of a social system in which people know that things are not what they claim to be.[8] The principal rules concerning the relations between men and women, both in ancient and in rural modern Greece, may be summarized in a brief formula: women should not be seen, nor should they speak or be spoken of.[9] Yet even strict norms are not altogether unequivocal. Even if they are not actually challenged or are just circumvented, they may be handled in a number of ways. In brief, the rules may accommodate contradictory forms of behavior that might seem incongruent to an outsider, but that insiders explain as fully acceptable, and even as assumed and included within the terms of the norm itself. In classical Athens the social muteness that was required of women was not considered to be incompatible with the many women's voices that could be heard both in public and in private.

Whether someone will be heard and by whom, and what someone may say, depends entirely, of course, on where the speaking person is. In theory,

---

1987; Winkler 1990a; Hunter 1994; Walcot 1996 (defending cultural continuity); and most profoundly Cohen 1991: 35–69 (arguing for comparability instead of continuity). I fully agree with the latter's response to the criticism raised by M. Herzfeld, among others, of "Mediterranean" as a shorthand, encompassing concept: "I know of no other group of similarly well-documented societies which manifest the same patterns of social practices. . . . Despite many differences, there are typical patterns of social practices that characterize a wide range of Mediterranean communities" (Cohen 1991: 38, 40). Moreover, for the kind of history attempted here, which aims at understanding the mentality of ancient Greeks underlying the words and events documented in our sources, I strongly feel the need to *visualize* ancient society as a social system, essentially different from our own time and place. This envisioning depends on "thick description" and comparison, accounting for similarities as well as differences.

[6] Herzfeld 1991: 87–90.

[7] Ibid.: 87–88, 91.

[8] "A society where, people claim, one can never know what goes on in another person's mind" (ibid.: 90, with references); "*Meaning* is opposed to *verbality*, even in male contexts" (ibid.: 96); "One has no choice but to lie. If you don't, you can't manage" (quoted in Cohen 1991: 51); on lying as a structural ingredient of classical Athenian society, ibid.: 96; particularly in its lawcourts, Cohen 1995; on the "science" of physiognomy to read the truth behind people's appearance, Gleason 1990.

[9] For modern Greece, cf. Herzfeld 1991: 96: "Women . . . are constantly and curtly told by their husbands and fathers, *Mi milas* ['Do not speak!']."

an ideal survey of women's voices in classical Athens would need to situate all instances on the coordinates of two sets of intersecting axes. One set of axes would designate space. The axis indicating real space would run from the center of the home to the threshold, then to the streets of the neighborhood and its marketplace into the fields outside of town. Its parallel axis, indicating conceptual space, would signify at one end private space, next an ambiguous sphere both private and public, then an unequivocally public sphere, and finally domesticated nature bordering the wild. The other set of axes would designate time: a smaller one to signify the hours of the day, and a larger one to indicate the days of the year, even so as to include the four-year span of the large festival celebrations. This ideal survey would reveal that women could not be seen or heard on the street around 8:00 A.M. or 5:00 P.M., but could quite easily be found around 10:00 A.M.—that is, when the men were going to and coming back from their work, the street and market would be a male domain, but when they were gone women would cross to visit a friend or do some shopping, making a perfectly acceptable use of the same public areas.[10] Public and private space are relative concepts, whose meaning is determined by use, and hence by time. Anthropologist Rayna Reiter calls this time-regulated pattern in the gendered use of space in Mediterranean villages and provincial towns a coordinated choreography.[11] Since a full description of the Athenian choreography is impossible to attain, the present chapter entails a provisional sketch based on a few representative cases. I trace women's speech predominantly along the axis of space, specified as much as possible by indications of time.

As soon as the question of speech and mobility is raised, one should define precisely whose speech and mobility one is discussing. It is generally assumed that in ancient Greece different groups of women followed quite different unwritten rules as to when they could be in what place. For instance, even allowing for changes over time, older women and slaves were freer to move about than younger citizen women because of the different positions they occupied with respect to procreative sexuality, respectability, availability, and protection. In Greece as a whole, Spartan women were held

[10] To some extent, the city of Athens must have differed from the rural villages in that urban labor and sociability retained a number of men in the public areas, thus in practice limiting women's mobility. However, to possess a house in the city usually included possessing landed property plus house in the countryside (Osborne 1985: 184–87), hence requiring men's frequent absence from the home, like Euphiletos in Lysias 1.11, 13, 39; in Menander's comedies it is taken for granted that the men, wherever they live, are habitually away to work their fields.

[11] Reiter 1975b: 257; cf. Cowan (1991: 187), who speaks of "the moral geography of public leisure space" in Sohos, a town in central Macedonia, indicating the areas where men and women may or may not be without incurring censure for immoral conduct. A full description of this choreography would include the movements and speech of men in public and in private; e.g., male family members gathered indoors at home in the evening and stayed overnight until the following morning; in winter men were more indoors than in summer.

to have enjoyed the greatest freedom, Athenian citizen women to have faced the strictest limitations. However, although I do not doubt that in classical Athens a flute girl would be in places at times that no respectable citizen wife would ever consider, the recent work on comparative basis just mentioned encourages a thorough reconsideration of this matter. In contemporary Greece, the relations between men and women form variations on a distinct theme. The degrees of male authority over the women, of men's acknowledgment of women's contributions to the household and the community, of women's loyalty either to their menfolk or to other women of the community, and the range of movement and exchange are correlated with patterns of household formation (viri- or matrilocal), of providing for dowries, and of inheritance policies.[12] It will require a more extensive analysis to determine which variations on the same theme the city of Athens and the rural villages of Attica exactly represented.[13] For the time being it is useful to adopt an open approach to the question of how distinctions in age, class, and status were effectuated in daily life. I focus here mainly on the "average" Athenian woman.[14] The difference between citizen and metic status was only occasionally relevant, for instance in certain religious

---

[12] Strong pressure and limitations imposed on young wives in virilocal communities in Greek Macedonia, Danforth 1991: 102–5; almost total separation of men and women in social life combined with a relative freedom of speech and movement for women in matrifocal, neolocal villages on Lesbos, Papataxiarchis 1991: 157; frequent separation of men and women combined with nearly paranoid authority of men over women on Crete, Kennedy 1986: 122–26.

[13] Foxhall's (1989) analysis of households within the Athenian community, corroborated by Hunter (1994: 9–42), fits well with the structure of Vasilika, a village in Boeotia described by Friedl (1962, 1986) where, given the structural limitations of Mediterranean village life, women enjoy relative freedom of movement and speech. Conversely, the very strict rules in Hatzi, a mountainous village in Crete described by Kennedy (1986), do not openly condone women even to visit female friends; in this respect, the Cretan situation is clearly different from that in classical Athens. The structure of housing and neigborhoods, and the relation between village and farmlands described by Osborne (1985), fit well with the "Mediterranean" pattern examined by Cohen (1991: 47–54). Likewise, the varied patterns in locality of burial (Osborne 1985: 130–31; Cox 1998: 38–67) suggest types of marriage, residence, and linkage that would allow classical Athenian women a mobility more resembling that of women in Vasilika than in Hatzi.

[14] One should even ask to what extent the distinction "urban/nonurban" came to influence the other categories. Considering that, by the late fifth century B.C.E., of an estimated 22,000 households, about 5,000 owned no land at all, and another 5,000 owned less than a "subsistence-portion" (Foxhall 1992: 156), a large number of male and female citizens had to earn their living by other occupations, which probably were proportionally more often located in the city than in the rural communities. Other factors, too, gradually added to differences in "lifestyle"; Sommerstein (1995: 83) concludes that some marked distinctions in speech sounds between men and women had to do with dialectic innovations that were adopted by women in a natural way but that were counterbalanced in the case of men by the formal speech used in the Assembly and lawcourts by dominant, educated speakers.

activities. In day-to-day practice, people were probably more interested in the distinction between respectable and not respectable.

Finally, one more factor is of vital importance: the question of whether the discourse pertaining to a certain time and space is likely, or even allowed, to be recorded.[15] Women's voices in classical Athens may be recovered in some primary material, yet for the greatest part are to be inferred from circumstantial evidence. It is through acquaintance with Greek rural communities today that we may envisage just how much of ancient life, including women's speech, is obscured by the limitations of our sources. By assessing the scope of mobility, exchange, and recording, we may tentatively map the opportunities for (citizen) women to speak and be heard.

PRIVATE SPACE

The *oikos* ("household" and "family") was regarded as the proper space for free, respectable women. Considering that their domestic roles defined their lives and that they were expected to stay indoors, one would expect to find women's voices documented predominantly in situations inside the home.[16] However, this is not the case. Not only could women's voices be heard in public areas, but it is almost exclusively in public areas that *any* voices, including those of women, may be heard in our sources. This phenomenon cannot satisfactorily be explained by supposing that it is men's speech, and therefore public speech, that was documented.[17] Rather, it is

[15] There is yet another category: voices that were recorded but hardly ever intended to be heard by human beings, namely curse tablets (*defixiones*), spells, and prayers for justice, written down, probably read aloud, and then buried or deposited in a sanctuary or similar, appropriate place (Gager 1992 for the material; Versnel 1998, with full bibliography on recent interpretations, arguing for the term "prayer for justice"). In spite of the formulaic character of the actual texts, these spells allow a valuable insight in the private life and thoughts of ancient men and women. However, since this discourse was addressed to the deities in charge and was rarely meant to reach a wider mortal audience, it is not included in the discussion.

[16] Harding (1975) even argues that talking makes up a great part of women's domestic task in a Mediterranean village, in that childrearing, shopping, exchanging household utensils, and sharing experience with friends and neighbors all involve using words to get the job done; compare Dubisch 1991: 38–40 on "kin work."

[17] True, the voices raised at men's symposia in songs and conversations have been amply recorded and seem to be an exception to the rule that chiefly public speech is preserved in writing. However, it makes more sense to regard the *andrōn* ("men's dining hall"), where this sympotic discourse belonged, as an instance of public space inside the home; Humphreys [1983] 1993: 16–17. Cf. Bourdieu on a Kabylian house: "It can be divided into a male-female part and a female-female part" (quoted by Cohen 1991: 44). The architecture of Greek houses reveals flexibility in usage of space, the *andrōn* being the only room designated for specific use by (male) guests (Jameson 1990a and 1990b; Hunter 1994: 75–81). The modern equivalent of the *andrōn* as a center of male discursive sociability is the *kafenion;* cf. Papataxiarchis 1991.

speech in private space that was *not* documented; and women were inti-mately connected with the notion of privacy, which entailed precisely that part of family life that should not be talked about.[18]

Maintaining this privacy by silence was meant to look like the perfectly natural expression of a family's autonomy and self-restraint (*sōphrosynē*).[19] The *oikos*, being the foundation of a family's existence, concerned the fam-ily's men in particular in that the house, its (landed) property, and the lin-eage were inherited along male lines. Yet the women were the ones who guarded and maintained the *oikos* by their care, their economic manage-ment, and the continuity of the family. Women's performance both within the home and without was crucial to the family's social status. If the women were successful in their material responsibilities and in handling their rep-utation, the *oikos* thrived; for politically ambitious men, a prosperous *oikos* was vital.[20] If anything went wrong, be it mismanagement leading to debt or such female behavior that the neighbors would gossip about adultery, the family lost its honor for an indefinite time. The desire of both men and women to shield the life of the *oikos* against inquisitiveness increased their reluctance to report what went on inside.[21] Private family life thus became one of the best-kept secrets of Athenian history. No scene in classical drama is ever situated within the home; though the innards of the *oikos* whose for-tune is the subject of the play may be revealed onstage, the threshold of the house was respected as a boundary.[22] Attic drama presents many women talking, and even talking back, but never doing so indoors. Conversations between husband and wife, which in reality would never have been con-ducted in public, are presented as taking place on the street in front of the respective dwellings, be they palaces, houses, or huts.[23] Only incidentally

---

[18] The most famous ancient phrasing of this rule is probably Pericles' advice (in Thucy-dides' words) to Athenian women that they should not be spoken of, neither for praise nor for blame (Thuc. 2.46).

[19] On the delicate balance between the openness and privacy of a family, Cohen 1991: 60, 80–81; on privacy: 83–97.

[20] For men's dependence on and collaboration with women, see Foxhall 1989; for men's re-sponsibility, see, e.g., Creon's words to Haemon in Soph. *Ant.* 661–62: "The man who acts rightly in family matters will be seen to be righteous in the city as well," a poignant remark by a man whose disregard of his *oikos* leads to the ruin of his city. (I owe this reference to André Lardinois.)

[21] On the damaging effect of gossip, Hunter 1994.

[22] On innards (*splanchna*), the vital parts inside a human being where the emotions reside, as strongly associated with the feminine, Padel 1992: 106–13; Zeitlin [1985] 1996; and Mau-rizio's contribution to this volume.

[23] For example, Soph. *Trach.*: Heracles' house in Trachis; Eur. *Med.*: Jason's house in Corinth; Eur. *Alc.*: Admetus' palace in Pherae; Eur. *El.*: the hut of the peasant to whom Elec-tra is married; Ar. *Eccl.*: the house of Blepyros and Praxagora; Men. *Epit.*: in front of two houses of common citizens. Even two women are presented talking with each other on the street; Men. *Georgos* (ed. Sandbach 1990) 22–87.

are voices in private mentioned in a public context, like a reference in passing to the kinds of song traditionally sung to accompany routine jobs like
spinning and weaving.[24]

The few instances where events inside the home, including what was
being said by men and women, were recorded in writing often serve a purpose other than faithfully reproducing what had happened. Judicial orations
are a case in point.[25] Euphiletos, defending himself in a speech written by
Lysias for the killing of his wife's lover, described the orderly way his household was organized and his conversations with his wife in such detail as to
impress the jury with his integrity and sensible management. Conversely,
since a regular way to discredit someone's claims in court was to vilify his
character, a litigant would present as much inside information damaging to
his opponent as he could think of.[26] The fact that what was said was to a
large extent determined by when and why it was said is exemplified by the
conversation between the model gentleman-farmer Ischomachus and his
young wife in Xenophon's dialogue *Oeconomicus*. Although the dialogue
demonstrates why and how the *oikos* as a production unit of goods and children is as much the concern of the man as of the woman,[27] the conversation itself is not a credible representation of daily life, and probably does
not claim to be so. The picture drawn by Xenophon of an omniscient
Ischomachos instructing his initially ignorant wife how to run their *oikos* is
far from the truth, as is obvious to anyone who knows anything about traditional agricultural households.[28] Instead, Ischomachos and his wife figure as actors in the role-playing typical of the dialogue as a genre. Because
the dialogue form as a means of education involved question-and-answer
between equal individuals, the dialogue was basically considered the province

[24] Ar. *Nub.* 1358: an old woman singing while grinding grain is mentioned as a usual event;
cf. Ath. 14.618ff., listing spinning songs, laments, lullabies, and wedding songs as women's
songs, and compare Plato *Lysis* 205D: epic stories sung by old women.

[25] On judicial orations, see Gagarin's contribution to this volume.

[26] For many fine examples, see Hunter 1994: 96–119; for the political context of representation in oratory, Ober 1989; for the social context, Cohen 1995: 87–118 ("litigation as
feud"); and see Gagarin's contribution to this volume.

[27] Conversely, one could argue that the success of the *oikos* was of such importance to the
polis that *oeconomia* formalized women's status and power in a way that cut across the division
between public and private spheres; this is argued for modern rural Greece concerning the
nikokyrio ("household economy") by Salamone and Stanton (1986).

[28] Although in modern rural Greece girls, whose labor is important both in the home and
on the fields, often marry at a later age than is reported for the elite of classical Athens (as, for
instance, Ischomachos' wife), throughout it is clear that young women learn household management from their mothers from an early age, and not from their husbands; cf. Friedl 1962:
42–43; Salamone and Stanton 1986; Dubisch 1991: 36–38. There is no reason to assume that
the situation in ancient Athens was any different in this respect. Xenophon justifies his implausible picture by having Ischomachos explain that his wife's knowledge of household management was not absent, but deficient (7.5–6).

of upper-class men.[29] As a woman, especially a young one, Ischomachos' wife cannot fully count as an equal, and at first she is rendered only as a *tabula rasa* to be inscribed by the useful admonitions of her husband.[30] When finally she draws her own rational conclusions, Socrates expresses his satisfaction, saying that Ischomachos demonstrates that his wife has a masculine mind by her understanding (*dianoia*: 10, 1). *Oeconomicus*, then, does not want to offer a portrait drawn to nature of an Athenian couple privately talking about their household, but rather seeks to demonstrate the superior value of rationality in the production of knowledge and in the management of private affairs.

Against the men's privilege to exercise authority both over the members of the household and over public discourse,[31] women in contemporary rural Greece have created a powerful weapon: emotional pressure. Inside the home they vent an ongoing reminder to their menfolk that it is thanks to them, the women, that they, the men, prosper, keep their honor, are provided for, that without the women the men would be good for nothing—indeed, that the men are utterly dependent on the women for their well-being.[32] The men, for their part, may really feel threatened by women's vocal force.[33] This discourse of self-righteous rebuke seems to have been a familiar device of classical Athenian women, too, as it appears to be echoed in Aristophanes' *Thesmophoriazusae* (785–847). After initial mockery, a reversal of men's abuse of women, the women's chorus points out to Mnesilochos, Euripides' kinsman who has intruded into the women's festival, that the men have lost the weapons they received from their fathers; but the women safely keep the ancestral possessions and work the looms they inherited from their mothers. By claiming that they "saved the father's heritage" (*ta patrōia sōizein*) while the men lost their spear "from the *oikoi*" (*ek tōn oikōn*, 819–26), the women also reverse the gendered distribution of

[29] The participants usually were men, the most famous exceptions being Diotima, a priestess from Mantinea who instructs Socrates on the true nature of *erōs* in Plato's *Symposium*, and Aspasia, Pericles' Milesian wife, who is one of the main speakers in Plato's *Menexenus* and is also referred to in the *Oeconomicus* (3.14). It is a matter of dispute, however, whether these women should be regarded as reflecting historical reality or as fictitious figures who are mainly the exponent of alternative points of view in these dialogues; cf. Halperin 1990b.

[30] Though Ischomachos calls the conversation with his wife "conversing" (*dialegesthai*: 7.10, 8.23), Socrates defines it as instruction on Ischomachos' part (*didaskein*: 7.9, 9.1) and obedient listening on hers (*hypakouein*: 9.1), and initially so does Ischomachos himself (7.7). For an interesting view on women's alleged incapacity of rationality, Padel 1992: 111–12.

[31] Herzfeld 1991: 94: "Men are the idealized masters of language."

[32] Friedl 1986: 52. In Attic comedy, women use *philos* and *philtatos* (usually in the vocative case) in the sense of "dear" or "dearest" far more often than men (Sommerstein 1995: 72); this habitual expressing (invoking, confirming) of affectionate relationships can easily shade over into the kind of pressure discussed here.

[33] Hirschon 1978: 84–86.

properties. However, the women in the chorus find that the assets in their lives deserving the greatest praise are the sons they bear to fight and die for this same fatherland.

SEMI-PUBLIC SPACE

Beside tearing their hair, shrieking, and wailing, the nearest female relatives of the deceased ritually expressed their loss in poetic laments. From Homeric epic through the present day, Greek women have voiced their grief for the dead in these orally composed songs.[34] In ancient Greece, when a family member died, the first lamenting was raised inside the home, around the bier where the corpse was formally laid out. Probably the *prothesis* had traditionally taken place outdoors until the restrictive legislation of the sixth and fifth centuries forced the laying-out to be held in the courtyard of the home.[35] It seems as though the principal laws, traditionally attributed to Solon, were aimed at curbing aristocratic display at funerals, but were not really effective in repressing female mourning practices, as may be inferred from the continuity of these scenes in vase-paintings (see Fig. 3).[36] By the late fourth century, *gynaikonomoi* were appointed, officials who had to check if the limits imposed on funerals were observed.[37] After the *prothesis*, the funeral procession to the tomb brought the visual and audible signs of mourning into the public domain. At the tomb, where sacrifices and libations were made, women again lamented the dead. After the funeral proper, the dead were remembered on the third, the ninth, and the thirtieth days, and after a year. A combined public and private remembrance took place yearly at the Genesia, a festival that had been changed from a family-based ritual for deceased parents into a mourning day observed by the whole community.[38] Even if death came at unpredictable moments, gradually it was enclosed into a structured time.

[34] On the ancient and modern Greek lament from a comparative perspective, see Alexiou (1974), who moreover argues for continuity from antiquity to the present, and Holst-Warhaft 1992; on modern laments, Danforth 1982 and Caraveli 1986; for lament in tragedy, Foley 1993; on men's laments, Dobrov 1994; for an entirely different approach than that pursued here, Loraux [1990] 1998; for resonance in other kinds of poetry, see the contributions of Lardinois and Stehle to this volume.

[35] Alexiou 1974: 4–23; Holst-Warhaft 1992: 108–19; on the role of women in the death rituals, Stears 1998.

[36] Alexiou 1974: 17–19, 22.

[37] The institution of the office of *gynaikonomos*, which also supervised weddings and women's festivals, indicates both the lack of success in curbing ostentatious mourning at funerals and the growing tendency toward bureaucratic "solutions" for civic problems; cf. Garland 1981: 177–79.

[38] Deubner 1932: 229; Parker 1996a: 48–50.

Fig. 3. Funeral *prothesis* (laying-out of the corpse) on a black-figure plaque, c. 510 B.C.E. A male corpse is laid out on a bier, surrounded by female mourners who lament by striking their head and tearing their hair. To the left, two men extend their right arms with palms out, a gesture of farewell to the dead that may have been reserved for males: see Rehm 1994: 24 and 105. The lower level shows a chariot race.

The performance of laments, however, defied the boundaries between public and private space, accompanying the deceased from the domain of Hestia to that of Hermes.[39] The content of the songs was even more disturbing. Fiercely personal, they bewailed the deceased as a loss to the nearest (female) kin, not as a departed useful member of (male) society. The feelings of misfortune frequently turned into anger, pointing to others— officials, enemies, evils—as being guilty of this death and asking for retribution. Laments thus could create an atmosphere of revenge and often evoked social agitation. These effects have been documented at the performance of laments in the nineteenth and twentieth centuries,[40] but several

[39] Cf. Vernant [1965] 1983 for the classical analysis of Hestia and Hermes as the deities of the static feminine and the mobile masculine sphere respectively, here also representative of the movement from family/life to underworld/death.

[40] Caraveli 1986; Alexiou 1974.

critics have pointed to similar conditions in archaic and classical Greece. Then as well as now, the death of her husband robbed a woman of one who embodied her access to social respect and protection.[41] More generally, women were considered the true lamenters because they were thought both by men and by themselves to be the ones who suffered the greatest pain, indeed as the ones who knew the truth of fate and grief.[42] A striking example of social disturbance resulting from a woman's mourning is offered by Sophocles' *Antigone*. When King Creon has forbidden her to bury and lament her slain brother Polynices, Antigone acts on the spur of her personal loss instead of obeying the orders of the state, thus enforcing a conflict between the realm of the dead and that of the public city.

It is no coincidence that Sophocles chose women's responsibility for the death rituals to mold into a tragic theme. The overwhelming role played by death and retribution in tragic material incorporated the experience of grief and the performance of laments and dirges into the tragedies themselves.[43] The creation of tragedy, beside the institution of the Genesia, exemplifies the increasing involvement by the community in the mourning rituals in the sixth and fifth centuries. This tendency is revealed most conspicuously in the Athenian public funeral of the war dead and the oration in their honor given by a carefully selected speaker.[44] In this public ritual, the focus had moved entirely from the family toward the polis. The *epitaphios logos* ("funeral oration") claimed that it was for the community that the soldiers had died, and that the memory of the dead was to be publicly consecrated: they were to be praised, not lamented.[45] The women, having lamented before the public funeral, could no longer reenact the memory of their lost ones afterward, for the common war grave of the fallen soldiers buried tribe by tribe prohibited contact with individual dead. In tragedy and in the funeral of the war dead, the shift toward public fashioning of mourning meant allocating women's symbolic roles to the community of male citizens, while excluding women as active participants. Still, if the commemoration of the war dead effectively drove women to the margins of ritual mourning, this was not the case with the numerous deaths due to causes other than the bat-

---

[41] Holst-Warhaft 1992: 49–52.

[42] For modern Greece, see Caraveli 1986: 171–78; in classical tragedy, Alexiou 1974: 110–18; Foley 1993.

[43] Aeschylus: Cassandra in *Agamemnon;* the protagonists of the *Suppliant Women;* Electra and the chorus in *Choephoroi.* Sophocles: Ajax; Jocasta and Oedipus in *Oedipus Tyrannus;* Antigone; Deianira in *Trachiniae;* Philoctetes. Euripides: Alcestis; Hecuba and Polyxena in *Hecuba;* Medea; Phaedra in *Hippolytus;* Andromache in *Troades;* and Electra. All of these characters lament their own fate and death. Cassandra's description of burial and mourning ritual, *Tro.* 353–405; cf. Alexiou 1974: 112–13.

[44] On the change in classical mourning patterns, Holst-Warhaft 1992: 114–70; on the funeral oration, Loraux [1981] 1986.

[45] Holst-Warhaft 1992: 120–21.

tlefield. Burial and lamenting remained a family affair,[46] a ritual gaining momentum when women's voices filled the house and the graveyard.

Perceived from afar, a wedding procession could resemble a funeral.[47] A great number of people were involved, among whom women, notably the mothers of the bride and groom, played a prominent role. Loudly shouting, carrying presents, and holding torches, the participants in a wedding moved from a private home into the streets, thus apparently behaving like the affines of a recently deceased. Indeed, as a family ritual absorbing public space and attention, weddings became an object of supervision by *gynaikonomoi* just as funerals were by the late fourth century.[48] But at closer sight and hearing, mistaking the one for the other would be impossible. Central in the wedding train was the bride, veiled and decked with flowers, and flanked by at least two male kin or friends and one female friend.[49] Many others thronged around the central little group, dancing and singing as in a *kōmos* (see Fig. 4).[50] If the families involved were wealthy enough to afford it, a cart and horses, attendants on horseback, a girls' chorus, parade boys, jesters, and acrobats could be part of the festive procession. Onlookers would gape at the noisy celebrants, and could join in the festivities by throwing fruits, leaves, and flowers on the bride. Although some fine descriptions of a wedding procession and hymns sung at such an occasion have been preserved in writing,[51] the best representations of the wedding events are to be found in vase-paintings. They show how in this festive ritual the bridal couple were held to be close to the gods, who finally provided the soft persuasive words (*Peitho*) that would secure harmony in the home.[52]

A marriage being a private arrangement between two households in the first place, it was only by the public celebration that the union was recognized as a formal bond. The crossing of the boundaries between private and

---

[46] They became increasingly so when, in the wake of the public funerals, even poor citizens came to aspire to a grave monument; Humphreys [1983] 1993: 121–22.

[47] Rehm (1994) has argued that in tragedy, wedding and funeral rituals were conflated, as a way to create in the audience an intense and ambivalent response to events of this kind onstage. I cannot be persuaded by this view; weddings and funerals have only a few general features in common, which are based on their structure *qua* ritual (cf. Zeitlin 1995b), and many more features that are so distinctive that any "conflation" would ultimately create bewilderment and displeasure rather than insight. Likwise, Jenkins (1983) had pointed to analogies between abductions and weddings in vase-paintings, even though the social meanings of these events were fundamentally different.

[48] On the *gynaikonomoi* supervising weddings of the elite, see Patterson 1998: 189.

[49] The description of the wedding is foremost based on Oakley and Sinos 1993.

[50] Cf. Oakley and Sinos 1993: 27.

[51] For instance, Eur. *Alc.* 918–19, *Hel.* 722–24; Hyp. *Lyc.* 3–5. Descriptions of wedding feasts are numerous in New Comedy; hymns such as Sappho's fr. 44, and new ones, were sung. See also Lardinos' contribution to this volume.

[52] On Peitho on wedding scenes, Oakley and Sinos 1993: passim.

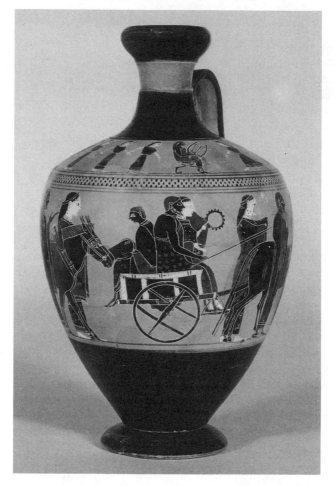

Fig. 4. Detail of a wedding procession (Attic black-figure *lekythos*, attributed to the Amasis painter, c. 560 B.C.E.). The groom and his bride, grasping her veil and a wedding wreath, sit on a mulecart that brings them from her family's home to his. They are escorted by various male and female figures. The dance scene on the shoulder shows wedding celebrants participating in various musical activities. See Oakley and Sinos 1993: 25, 29–30.

public space, the creation of festivities shared by women and men, and the marking of the event by the jubilant singing were prerequisites for recognition of the marriage as a legal union, and hence as the basis of legal offspring. Weddings could take place throughout the year, though the month Gamelion may have been a favorite period. At the Apatouria, the newborn citizen children—probably all boys and occasionally girls—were included in the phratries, and their mothers were ritually celebrated for having given birth to new citizens.[53] Like the Genesia with its commemoration of the dead, the Apatouria confirmed the relationship between private and public events, including nature's unpredictable moments within the larger timetable of the *polis*.

VOICES IN PUBLIC

Returning to the original premise that the possibility of being heard has everything to do with where someone is, we should now ask when (respectable) women were actually present in the streets of Athens and the Attic villages, and whether they made themselves heard so as to be somehow recorded.

The social rule in force with more or less strictness in Mediterranean societies that women ought to stay indoors does not necessarily mean that women actually stay indoors.[54] It means that women go out only if they have a distinct and socially accepted purpose, when it is the right time to do so, and if they can behave in such a way—for instance, by being in the company of other women, children, or male kin—as to prevent the neighbors' gossip. When in Aristophanes' comedy *Ecclesiazusae* Praxagora returns home from being out just before daybreak, she cuts short her husband's suspicious grumbling by telling him she has assisted a friend in childbirth—one of the few acceptable missions involving absence from home at an unusual, even unpredictable, hour.[55] A clear picture of the wariness roused by a woman walking alone is sketched in a few lines ascribed to Theognis:

[She:] I hate a base (*kakos*) man, and having veiled myself I pass, with a heart light as a little bird's.

---

[53] On the debated issue of female phratry membership, see Lambert [1993] 1998: 178–203; on the Apatouria as a festival celebrating young mothers, Schmitt-Pantel 1977.

[54] For description and analysis of the separation of the sexes in Mediterranean societies, see the references in notes 5 and 12 above. The differences in speech between men and women in classical Athens should also be understood as a constructive element of a social distance that is separation underlying hierarchy rather than hierarchy tout court (as Sommerstein 1995 suggests). Walcot (1994), though referring to anthropological material, misses the point by comparing the Mediterranean model (traditional, sociocultural separation of the sexes from each other, with hardly contested dominance of males over females) with the separation practiced by radical feminists and blacks in the 1970s (voluntary, politically motivated separation by one group from the other, aspiring to a reversal of social dominance). On the flexibility of the category "female," notably in relation to the politics of space, see Herzfeld 1986.

[55] Ar. *Eccl.* 528–34.

[HE:] But I hate a woman who always strays about, and a lascivious man who
wants to plough another's land.[56]

The poem not only indicates the woman's timidity and her attempt to be
invisible while the man interprets her presence immediately as a sign of pro-
miscuity, but foremost it exemplifies how reputation depends less on actions
than on glances, suspicion, and rumor. Adroit manipulation of appearances
might cover up misconduct, while conversely the name of an innocent person could be ruined by mere gossip. The following brief discussion of
women's movements outdoors in classical Athens thus fundamentally qual-
ifies the rule to "stay indoors," but does not deny its validity, nor does it implicitly argue that women could be in public areas as frequently or as easily
as men.[57] If women appear to have been far more outdoors than has often
be assumed, the basic pattern still entails that men could be outside whenever they pleased, while women had to negotiate their movements with distinct limitations on the penalty of ruinous gossip.[58]

Although there is no evidence indicating the hour of the day when
women would go out to visit friends, given the structural choreography of
Mediterranean life it seems plausible that women did so when the men had
more or less left the streets. The same rule no doubt applied to fetching
water at the well, a popular meeting point for women better known from
vase-paintings than from written evidence.[59] If a woman had to be outside
at a different moment, for instance because she needed to borrow household utensils, clothes, or foodstuffs,[60] and she could not send a child or a
slave, she either would make something of a display of the unavoidable
causes that made her leave the house, or she would try to be as unconspic-
uous and furtive as suspicion could tolerate. Contacts within the neigh-

---

[56] Thgn. 579–82. It is uncertain if the two lines following the four quoted here ("Yet, while
what has been done in the past cannot be undone, what belongs to the future should be guarded
with care") are to be connected to the previous lines or not. M. L. West's changing of ἔχουσα
to ἔχοντα (West 1989–92: ad 580) is not supported by the manuscripts and seems to me unnecessary. The relationship between the woman and the man speaking in these lines is unclear,
and need not be anything specific. Martin (1997: 156–57) perceives here elements of "a traditional insult duel: the exactly structured pair of couplets is formally equivalent to modern-
day Cretan *mandinadhes*, which are also used extensively in negotiating male-female relationships."

[57] For a more elaborate discussion of this theme with many references to women's activities, cf. Cohen 1989; Just 1989: 105–25; Hunter 1994: 9–42.

[58] On the effects of gossip about women on women themselves and their kin, see Hunter
1994: 111–16.

[59] These women were not only slaves or poor women, but included well-to-do women;
Mankidou 1992–93. For a list of these fountain scenes, see Webster 1972: 98, including scenes
showing men molesting women at the fountain, an outdoor spot where women were surely to
be found.

[60] On lending and borrowing, Ar. *Eccl.* 446–49; Theophr. *Char.* 10, 13.

borhood, seeing friends, or just asking the woman next door to lend her a few coins gave Athenian housewives ample opportunity to speak with each other, thus contributing to the ongoing murmur of gossip that shaped neighborhood relationships.[61] Thus women's voices were often feared, though obviously the men were equally involved in the "politics of reputation."[62]

Beside meeting with friends and relatives, most women of course had to leave their homes to work.[63] In the villages of the Attic countryside many poorer women worked in the fields,[64] and in cities like Athens they manufactured all kinds of goods, either at home or in workshops. Wares produced either by their own crafts or by others' were to be sold, as was the case with homegrown fruits and vegetables, cheese, and similar products. Again, women went to the market to set up their stalls or spread out the blankets on which to display their wares, probably before the men would fill the streets, and women merchants may have occupied a different part of the market area from the men, as in many Greek markets today.[65] This did not mean that market women waited silently for someone to notice them and their wares; female sellers of potherbs, omelettes, bread, and the like who yell, shout, or scold are stock characters of Attic comedy.[66] Housewives came to the market to buy goods and foodstuffs if they had no one else to do this for them, and probably many women had to do their own shopping. In this bustle, men and women mingled more than formal morality would allow.[67] Although the frequency of markets was no doubt influenced by the

[61] Lending some money: Ar. *Eccl.* 447; on gossiping, Harding 1975: 295–305; Cohen 1991: 83–90; Hunter 1994: 96–119.

[62] Cohen 1991: 54–69. In Eur. *Tro.* 651–52, Andromache, expounding the highest virtues of women, which she, too, accomplished in Hector's house, says she never let women's words into her home; conversely, see Theophr. *Char.* 28 for the male scandalmonger. Manipulating the reputation of the (male) litigants was a structural ingredient of Athenian lawsuits; cf. Hunter 1994: 96–111, 118–19; Cohen 1995: 61–87.

[63] For an overview of the many crafts and jobs performed by women, see Herfst [1922] 1979; Cohen 1989; Brock 1994, with references.

[64] Scheidel 1995 offers an impression of women's agricultural work.

[65] Theophr. *Char.* 2.9, 22.109. Cf. Herfst ([1922] 1979: 36–40), who also argues for a different meaning of the *agora gynaikeia*.

[66] Ar. *Plut.* 427–29, *Ran.* 857–58, *Lys.* 561–64, *Vesp.* 497–99.

[67] Respectable citizen women on the marketplace probably for shopping, Ar. *Lys.* 561–64; a girl getting out to sell a cock, Ar. *Ran.* 1350–51; cf. Brock 1994. Whether the difference between respectable and unrespectable would be observed by all parties concerned is not so easy to say, precisely because it was a socially contestable issue. Any woman who was outdoors or visible in such a way as to rouse criticism was typically accused of being adulterous, a whore, or both; cf. Dem. 57.30ff., where Euxitheos defends the honor of his mother, a market merchant; Ar. *Eccl.* 522, where Praxagora anticipates her husband's rebuke; Theophr. *Char.* 28.3, on the slanderer who accuses every woman of being a streetwalker. Cf. Cowan 1991 on the moral battles fought in a modern Greek provincial town over women who want to visit a *kafeteria*.

seasons, a market took place on the first day of every month, Noumenia, which was a religious feast day. Many Athenians gathered on the agora on this day, which was also a day for symposia and sporting, and people burned frankincense at the statues of the gods.[68]

Religious feast days, or more precisely women's festival days, are usually mentioned by scholars as one of the few opportunities for respectable women to get out of doors. It seems to be far less known, however, just how many feast days there were and that women were involved in the majority of them.[69] The Noumenia is a good example of the regular, minor religious feast day dedicated to a divinity and celebrated every month: beside Noumenia (on day 1), there was a day given to the *agathos daimōn* (day 2), to Athena (day 3), to Heracles, Hermes, and Aphrodite (day 4), to Artemis (day 6), to Apollo (day 7), and to Poseidon (day 8). Day 16 was the day for private offerings to Artemis, and day 30 for the same to Hecate. Certainly "festival days" of this kind did not mean "holiday" in the sense of a non-working day, which applied only to the largest and most important festivals.[70] These included the great festivals celebrated by the whole community all over Attica, many of them lasting for several days, like the City Dionysia, the Thesmophoria, the Panathenaia, the Anthesteria. A number of minor religious events may be added to these, such as small-scale rituals that were only celebrated in certain demes, by individual families, or by the numerous cult communities. In sum, the total number of feast days in Athens amounted to about 170; there were almost as many festival days as nonfestival days, and far more festival days than the 145 attested meeting days of the Assembly.[71]

Religious activities were thus ruled by time, since most festival days were regulated by day, month, and in some cases by year in the religious calendars.[72] The calendars explicitly prescribed when a sacrifice would be made, what kind it would be, and by whom it would be made. The average Athenian would probably choose the specific day of the divinity to whom this day

[68] Mikalson 1975: 14–15.

[69] All references to Athenian festivals are based on a combined use of Deubner 1932, Mikalson 1975, Simon 1983, and Parker 1996a. I am aware that the religious calendar of Athens, which even presupposes a unified polis such as only emerged by the end of the sixth century, depends entirely on attempted reconstructions, and that the extant calendars of Thorikos, Erchia, Marathon, and the Salaminioi (references in Parker 1987; van Straten 1995: 171–73; Scullion 1998) are often at odds with the surveys drawn up for Athens. My description of religious events only serves the focus of this chapter.

[70] As a rule, meetings of the Assembly did not take place on festival days, though there were some exceptions, and the council did meet on religious feast days if necessary; Mikalson 1975: 186–204.

[71] Ibid.: 182.

[72] Cf. Brumfield 1981 and Foxhall 1995 for the relationship between women's festivals and the agricultural year.

was sacred to donate some offerings or to address oral or written prayers. Countless small votive offerings, prayers, curses, and other dedications have been found in the sanctuaries all over the Attic countryside and in the city of Athens.[73] These donations were offered by men and women alike, and obviously women went to these shrines to deposit their gifts to the gods.[74] On the monthly Artemis' day, for instance, several smaller and larger festivities in honor of the goddess took place in which women in particular were involved.[75] On this day many women would visit a shrine or sanctuary dedicated to Artemis to make a modest votive offering. Hymns and other songs to honor the goddess, performed by informal groups or by a chorus, accompanied the festivities.

Concerning the actual participation of women and men in cult, men seem to have been more involved with male gods and women with female goddesses, but the pattern is blurred by many exceptions.[76] For instance, Demeter and Kore were the foremost women's goddesses. Only women swore "by the Two,"[77] and three of the five most important festivals celebrating Mother and Daughter were exclusively women's feasts.[78] Two festivals dedicated to the Two, then, were also open to men: the Great Eleusinia welcomed everyone of each sex and status who spoke Greek, and

[73] Women's religious activity as testified by votive offerings is an important (corrective) addition to the evidence of sacred laws, which *as laws* represent men's exclusive authority over written documents. For a different interpretation of these laws, see Cole 1992.

[74] Although it is often impossible to identify the gender of a dedicant, and taking the literacy among women to have been lower than among men, the number of identifiable female donors (identified by typically feminine votives like pins, fibulae, and necklaces) is still revealingly large; cf. Kron 1996: 155–71 (I owe the reference to this invaluable article to H. S. Versnel). Even in "mixed" cults, female dedicants range from approximately 45% (Parthenon, Erechtheion) to a majority (Asklepieion) (Kron 1996: 165, with references); to these extant gifts, the offerings of perishable material, like cakes, fruits, and wooden objects, should be added.

[75] Mikalson 1975: 18.

[76] Likewise, access to temples and participation in sacrifice were regulated by a variety of prescriptions, in which gender played an important role. Cole (1992) argues for asymmetry in favor of males concerning availability of priesthoods and access to cults and sanctuaries; I am more convinced by Kron (1996: 140–49), who argues for more equal roles based on abundant material, and Osborne (1993), doing the same with additional theoretical arguments, although it seems impossible to define unambiguous criteria on which to decide (cf. Richlin 1993 on the dilemma between a "pessimistic" or an "optimistic" view).

[77] This fact was frequently used by Aristophanes in his transvestite scenes: Mnesilochos, having wormed his way in female disguise into the Thesmophoria, fittingly swears by the Goddesses to escape detection (*Thesm.* 594); a woman who swears by the Two when the women have gathered on the Pnyx disguised as men is rebuked by Praxagora for giving them away (*Eccl.* 155–59).

[78] On the Thesmophoria as a feast of citizen wives, cf. Versnel [1992] 1993; on women's joking at these festivals, see O'Higgins' contribution to this volume.

the cultic personnel consisted of both male and female officials.[79] There were many Athenian festivals about which we simply do not know whether they were celebrated by men or women only. If sufficient evidence is lacking, it is certainly unfounded to assume that major groups, like all men or all women, were prohibited from participating.[80] A number of Athenian festivals were undoubtedly celebrated by men or women only; indeed, it appears that about twice as many festivals were celebrated exclusively by women than by men.[81] The same pattern of both exclusive and mixed participation applies to cult communities and small-scale cult practices on a local level.[82] In sum, a survey of all religious activities in classical Athens reveals that women were involved in most of them, by a very rough estimate around 85 percent of all religious events.[83] So on more than one out of every three days, a number of women, ranging from a few elite wives to all women, would leave their homes,[84] enter the public area on their way to

[79] Similarly, Poseidon seems a typically masculine god, yet the Posidonia festival included a plunge into the sea by both men and women (cf. Theophr. *Char.* 28.4). This was of course an opportunity to see and be seen, as illustrated by an anecdote about the *hetaira* Phryne's economy of visibility, quoted by Davidson (1997: 134) and by Rosenmeyer (in this volume).

[80] I agree with Foxhall (1995: 108–9): "Despite Detienne's [(1979) 1989] assertion that women were excluded from the act of sacrificing most of the time, it certainly does not follow that they were excluded from participating in civic festivals." For fundamental criticism of Detienne, see Osborne 1993; for material contradicting Detienne, Bremmer 1994: 78.

[81] The following overview is based on Mikalson 1975 and compared with Deubner 1932; the lists even of these scholars are not exhaustive, and the evidence on many festivals is inconclusive. The following results are therefore utterly tentative and provisional. Certainly or very probably attended by women only: Stenia, Thesmophoria in Halimous, Thesmophoria, Skira, Haloa, Theogamia, Adonia, Tauropolia, Brauronia. Certainly or very probably attended by men only: Theseia, Dipolieia, Olympieia, Demokratia. Certainly or very probably mixed (numbers of each sex could range from a few to a majority): Artemis Agrotera, Delphinion, Kronia, Synoikia, Panathenaia, Genesia, Eleusinian Mysteries, Anthesteria, Bendideia, Plynteria, Chalkeia, City Dionysia, rural Dionysia, Apatouria, Lenaia, Mysteries at Agrai, Proerosia, Oschophoria. On the role of women in the Apatouria, see Schmitt-Pantel 1977; in the Oschophoria, Deubner 1932: 144. No attention is paid here to the distinction between citizens and noncitizens.

[82] E.g., many sacrifices involving women in the deme of Erkhia, Mikalson 1975; women's festivals in Piraeus, *IG* II².1177, cf. Nixon 1995: 77; women as members of cult communities (local and private religious associations), Parker 1996a: 328–42.

[83] Analogous to the current revision of the views on Athenian women's economic activities and resources, recent work on women's religious significance calls for a similar change in perceptions on gender and religion. Men's prerogative in political decision-making was counterbalanced by women's prominence in religious matters, a juxtaposition of flexibility and action (Hermes) with permanence and reproduction (Hestia). This structure of complementary, asymmetrical responsibilities resembles modern rural Greece, where men dominate public worldly matters while women are considered to be the representatives and guardians of the spiritual in daily life, identified with the Mother of God; cf. Du Boulay 1986, 1991; I could not consult Hart 1993.

[84] For comic exaggeration of (old) women's religious activity, see Men. *Dys.* 260–63: "My

a sanctuary, and join in the celebration. They would raise their voices in saying prayers, singing hymns, and shouting as tradition required,[85] often accompanied by the singing of girls' choruses.[86]

CONCLUSION

The opportunities for women in classical Athens to speak, be heard, and find their words recorded were determined by a set of rules, or rather by a hierarchical system of values. Within this system, the separation of the sexes ranked highest. It was sustained by a spatial and conceptual distinction between public and private spheres, a distinction functioning as a complementary opposition.[87] Private was predominantly associated with femininity, public with masculinity, but by no means exclusively so. Usage of space and hence its gendered definition depended on time, occasion, and context. The interior of the classical Athenian house was considered unequivocally private; if necessary, private space could be divided into men's and women's areas. The public domain entailed in principle everything beyond the threshold of the house, though landed property in the countryside (fields) was again a more or less private space. Flexibility characterized the usage of public space due to the preferred separation of the sexes: if men were crowding the streets, women would stay indoors; women went to a sanctuary or the agora when men were occupied elsewhere. People knew this coordinated choreography and stuck to it as much as possible; violation of its precepts was a sure way to risk public censure. Two types of occasion exemplify the ambiguities within this system: men's sociability in the *andrōn*, and the burial procession accompanied by women's laments. The first case seems to be a "public" area within the house, the second a "private" event intruding into public space; in this latter respect, the wedding procession resembled the burial.

---

mother going all around the district sacrificing"; *Misogynes* (F 326 *CAF,* 277 Körte [1957–59]): "We [a man describing women] are sacrificing five times a day" (cf. F 601 *CAF,* 796 Körte [1957–59]). Compare the mockery of the overcrowded sacrificial calendars in general in Ar. *Av.* 864–903.

[85] Women were required to utter a scream on the *moment suprême* of the sacrifice (Zaidman and Schmitt-Pantel [1989] 1992: 35). Ritual screaming by women, e.g., to the gods (wailing for Adonis) and in other cultic contexts, could signify both joy and mourning (cf. LSJ s.v. *ololuzein;* Collins 1995).

[86] On girls' choruses, Calame [1977] 1997; although initiation rituals lay at the heart of girls' choruses, their performances were not limited to events of this kind, as exemplified by the girls' singing during the *pannychis* of the Panathenaia (Calame [1977] 1997: 130–31), and at feasts like weddings; cf. Lardinois 1998a.

[87] "Complementary opposition": a term coined by Herzfeld (1986), and reconsidered by Cohen (1991: 36–37 and passim).

The evidence strongly suggests that what happened and what was said in private was in principle not recorded; exceptions on the whole appear to have served a specific purpose. A great part of women's lives and hence of their speech belonged to this private sphere, and thus did not survive in written evidence. Yet numerous duties and interests on behalf of the *oikos* and the polis brought women into the public domain. Since it was events in the public area that in principle were liable to be recorded, indeed publicized, women's presence there can be traced in extant sources. *Provided it was the right time and the right occasion*, women were perfectly entitled to be in public space;[88] they would not by definition lose their respectability by being there, nor was the public area suddenly changed into a feminized sphere. Of course, these occasions were fewer and more complicated than was the case for men, and women's voices were for the greater part represented in male discourses with all its consequences; but this does not invalidate the general pattern. This pattern is well illustrated by the numerous dedicatory inscriptions on votive offerings, honorary statues, and similar objects adorning the streets, temples, agora, and Akropolis of Athens and sanctuaries in the countryside. If the women who dedicated these objects were not present any more in the flesh, they proudly mentioned their names and the reasons for their gifts. Passersby were expected to read the inscribed words aloud. So the self-conscious words of the washerwoman Smikythe, who dedicated a water basin to Athena, and of Xenokrateia, who dedicated a sanctuary to the river god Kephissos to commend her little son,[89] could be reimbued with life—and they still can.

[88] Obviously I disagree with the view that women had by definition no right to any voice in public; instead I argue that at accepted occasions like chorus performances, women's voices in public did not require an apology; cf. Lardinois 1998c.

[89] Kron 1996: 162–63, 166–68, with references.

CHAPTER SEVEN

Antigone and Her Sister(s)

EMBODYING WOMEN IN GREEK TRAGEDY

MARK GRIFFITH

1. FEMALE IMPERSONATION ON THE TRAGIC STAGE

The playwrights of the fifth century B.C.E. who competed each year in the Theater of Dionysus in Athens, with a series of three tragedies and one satyr-play, were each assigned the same level of human resources: two or three actors, a chorus of twelve or fifteen, and a variable number of non-speaking extras. All these cast members, like the playwright himself, were adult males. Thus there were no women's voices to be heard in the Theater of Dionysus.[1] Yet over one-third of all speaking roles (including choruses) are female, and in several plays more than half the lines are delivered by women (e.g., Aeschylus *Suppliant Women, Choephoroi, Eumenides;* Sophocles *Electra;* Euripides *Medea, Andromache, Trojan Women*).[2] The "voicing" and impersonation of women thus comprise a major part of the dramatic enterprise of Greek tragedy.[3]

Playing female roles was not in itself a specialized activity, for it seems to have been expected of all actors and chorus members. Actors often switched back and forth between male and female roles within the same play; and likewise the chorus members would be required during the course of each trilogy to take on three quite different choral identities, at least one of which

---

[1] Actors and chorus members were generally citizens, and often of high standing (in contrast, for example, to Roman professional/foreign actors, singers, and pantomime performers). It is not known whether or not the theater audience was likewise exclusively male: the evidence is conflicting and inconclusive; see Podlecki 1990; Henderson 1991; Goldhill 1994b, 1997: 62–66. In general, on the original conditions of performance, see Pickard-Cambridge 1988; Csapo and Slater 1995.

[2] None of Shakespeare's or Webster's tragedies (in which female parts were played by boys) approaches this ratio, still less Marlowe's; by contrast, Racine's and Ibsen's (where the parts were played by professional actresses) show similar ratios.

[3] For general discussions of the representation of women in Greek tragedy, see esp. Gould 1980; Foley 1981b; Easterling 1988; Des Bouvrie 1990; Zeitlin 1996; and McClure 1995, 1999, with further references.

would usually be female. (In the fourth play, of course, the chorus members were always satyrs.)

As far as we can tell, no particular physical or vocal characteristics were preferred for actors and choreuts, nor was the vocal training very specialized (in contrast to the theatrical traditions of, for example, India or Japan), though it became more so as the fifth century progressed and acting turned into more of a virtuoso performance in its own right, especially in the lyric modes. For the most part, male and female characters are found in tragic dialogue to employ the same metrical and linguistic forms, and the small differences of expression that can be observed are mostly quite subtle and sporadic: no sharp or consistent differentiation was made in the mode of delivery.[4] References in tragedy to "sharp, high" tones often denote intensity and distress, but not necessarily femininity; and male actors and choruses seem not to have made any thoroughgoing attempt to speak or sing "like" women (i.e., by adopting a falsetto delivery, or modifying their voices in any systematic way). In Aristophanes' *Thesmophoriazusae* 86–278, for example, the poet and actor involved in constructing and playing female tragic roles (Agathon and Mnesilochus) are clearly expected to adopt distinctive attitudes and movements, along with their costumes, and to sing certain kinds of songs; but the advice "Be sure you do a good job of being a woman with your voice!" (ὅπως τῷ φθέγματι / γυναικιεῖς εὖ, 267–68) does not indicate how specifically this is to be achieved. In lyrics, distinctions between male and female expressions and modes of delivery could be more sharply drawn, but even here we cannot be sure how realistically the intonation and mannerisms of Greek or foreign mourners, princesses, slave attendants, goddesses, and other female characters were represented onstage.[5]

In general, "female impersonation" relied more heavily on gesture, gait, dance step, and bearing, and on changes of costume, than on distinctively feminine voice or language. An expert actor could change "character" in just a few seconds: masks and wigs concealed the actors' beards, and the long-sleeved, ankle-length garments conventionally worn for the leading roles, in addition to conveying the appropriate opulence and dignity of the Bronze Age heroes and heroines of myth, would also cover hairy, muscular arms and legs. Thus, overall, the most distinct features of any role, female or male, were conveyed in the first place through means other than the voice:

[4] On details of "female speech," esp. in Euripides, see McClure 1995; also, for Aeschylus, Hall 1989: 204–10; McClure 1997; for Sophocles, Kitzinger 1976; Foley 1996; and below, pp. 121–23, 126–36. For discussion of the language and representation of (predominantly female) lamentation on the tragic stage, see note 11 below.

[5] We may recall that, in the case of Elizabethan theater, the dialogue and songs of an Ophelia or Desdemona were normally delivered by boys whose voices were still unbroken, an option not regularly available to Athenian playwrights (though children did serve as extras, and may occasionally have sung short lyrics: e.g., in Eur. *Alc.* 394–403, 406–15; see Kassel 1991: 32–55, esp. 43, 49–50).

a Nurse, or Queen, or Slave Chorus was recognizable even before a word was spoken, from mask, costume, posture, and movement.

Training in use of the body (with or without the voice) in performance of this or that social role, whether in play or in ritual (or even in athletics and war), was second nature to most Greeks. Different age and gender groups were distinguished by their own formations, songs, and dances, and in some cases their rituals also involved impersonation of one kind or another as part of the group's process of self-definition and self-presentation.[6] Athenians were thus quite accustomed to recognizing, and selectively adopting, various conventional patterns of behavior, or performativities, appropriate to this or that context and role, each with its distinct and distinctive semiotic code.

Indeed, rites of passage and initiation, athletic and military training, distinctions of sex/gender, class, and ethnicity, would be empty and ineffectual without such systems of linguistic, aesthetic, and bodily citation and (re)inforcement. Girls' and women's, boys' and men's choruses must not present themselves in the same ways, or they could not succeed in instituting their members into their proper social roles, and investing them with all the entitlements and restrictions to which they are due.[7]

[6] We hear of "Little Bears," "Tortoises," "Fillies," and other kinds of "herds" (*agelai*) being represented by children's groups and choruses (Lawler 1964: 58–73; Calame [1977] 1997: 98–101, 214–17; Lonsdale 1993: 98–99, 200–202); also, of course, satyrs (half horse or goat). At Delos during the archaic period, female choruses knew "how to imitate the voices of all kinds of human beings" (*Hymn. Hom. Ap.* 162–63); at Sparta, "maiden songs" (*partheneia*) were composed by men (such as Alcman) for girls to sing and dance, while at Athens, "boys' dithyrambs" were part of the annual series of competitions at the Great Dionysia, and these choruses may have involved an element of "impersonation" of the characters from the mythological stories they recounted: see Calame [1977] 1997; Herington 1985; Winkler 1990c; Lonsdale 1993; Stehle 1997. For comic references to the verbal, gestural, and musical imitation of men by women, see Ar. *Eccl.*, esp. 149–50, 268–78; and for aspects of the stage impersonation of "old men," see esp. Ar. *Vesp.* and *Eccl.* 277–79.

[7] This process of institution may involve posture, gesture, musical modes, dance steps, clothing, adornment, and other paraphernalia, as well as more or less formulaic verbal expressions, all of which need to be specifically marked for this or that occasion, gender, age, audience/addressee, and social function. For archaic/classical Greek examples of group self-presentation and ritual institution, see esp. Alcm. frs. 1–62; Pl. *Leg.* 2.652–674, 7.788–8.835; Arist. *Pol.* 7.1333–8.1342; and Calame [1977] 1997: passim. For fuller discussion of the processes of "self-presentation," see Goffman 1959; Gleason 1995: xvii–xxix; Carlson 1996: 34–50; Stehle 1997. For the notion of "performativity," as a mutually reinforcing combination of speech acts and behavior that both constructs and confines an individual within a previously authorized system of social categories, see Butler 1993: 2–16; Parker and Sedgwick 1995: 1–18. ("Performativity . . . is always a reiteration of a norm or set of norms, and . . . conceals or dissimulates the conventions of which it is a repetition," Butler 1993: 12.) For an alternative formulation, we may compare Bourdieu's *hexis* and *habitus* (Bourdieu [1980] 1990: 52–79), along with his accounts of "authorized language" and "rites of institution" (Bourdieu [1977–84] 1991: 107–26): "Bodily hexis is political mythology realized, *em-bodied*, turned into a permanent disposition, a durable way of standing, speaking, walking, and thereby of feeling

Athenian tragedy draws upon many of these choral and ritual performativities, even as it assimilates them to its own consistent and authoritative conventions and style. Thus, while iambic trimeters and lyric strophes impose their unique and inviolable stamp on every utterance (Persian Messenger or Theban King, slave Nurse or Bacchante Chorus, they all speak good Attic Greek), nonetheless the tragic plots present a strikingly diverse array of contexts and "characters." For this reason, tragedy may often preserve, or even reinvent, particular performative modes that were otherwise becoming socially obsolete or suspect;[8] and this may be one of the reasons why women, whose public roles in democratic Athens were very limited, except in the sphere of religious practice,[9] are given such prominence in the stage drama of the fifth century.

Just as tragedy employs an array of conventional masks to represent different (recurring) "types" of character (King, Old Tutor, Nurse, Young Princess, Blind Prophet, etc.), so we might look for a repertoire of associated performativities, incorporating specific details of idiolect, gesture, costume, musical modes, and choreography, by means of which a playwright could construct for each of his characters and choruses their proper person and "voice," a voice distinguished (if at all), not by pitch, regional/class accent, dialect, or even timbre,[10] but by rhetoric and patterns of speech.

---

and thinking. The opposition between male and female is realized in posture, in the gestures and movement of the body, in ways of eating. . . . When the properties of the body are socially qualified, the most fundamental social choices are naturalized and the body, with its properties and its movements, is constituted as an analogical operator establishing all kinds of practical equivalences among the different divisions of the social world—divisions between the sexes, between the age-groups, and between the social classes" (Bourdieu [1980] 1990: 69–71). Also: "The act of institution is thus an act of communication, but of a particular kind: it *signifies* to someone what his identity is, but in a way that both expresses it to him and imposes it on him by expressing it in front of everyone (*katēgorein*, meaning originally, to accuse publicly) and thus informing him in an authoritative manner of what he is and what he must be" (Bourdieu [1977–84] 1991: 121).

[8] Choral lyric is itself perhaps one example; others are lamentation and personal supplication, both of which were prominent in the mythical tradition inherited from the archaic period, but no longer commonly practiced in mainstream civic contexts (Alexiou 1974; Foley 1993; Gould 1973). Likewise, direct encounters with Olympian divinities, which were common in Homeric epic and easily reproducible onstage, were (presumably) not a part of normal everyday life.

[9] But see now Josine Blok's contribution to this volume for a reminder of the several ways and places in which women might in fact be seen and heard in public.

[10] By contrast with Aristophanic comedy, where Persian, Scythian, or Spartan attempts to utter grammatical and intelligible Greek may be mercilessly garbled and ridiculed, tragedy makes no attempt to reproduce regional variation: thus, even when Orestes and Pylades explicitly agree to disguise themselves as Phocians and speak in Phocian dialect (Aesch. *Cho.* 563–64), they continue to sound (so far as we can judge from the extant manuscript) perfectly Attic-Athenian. Only rarely do barbarians (panic-stricken Egyptians, Asian mourners, etc.) emit non-Greek sounds: Euripides' Phrygian slave (*Or.*) is an exception that proves the rule. See further Kranz 1933; Seidensticker 1982; Hall 1989.

So, what distinctions do we observe in our surviving tragic texts? What specific performative conventions, verbal mannerisms, and rhetorical strategies (in addition to the use of grammatically feminine word-endings) could be employed by the playwrights to assist their actors in representing women onstage? Can we identify particular types of utterance, linguistic usages or styles of delivery, modes of argument or self-presentation, that are marked as exclusively, or primarily, "feminine"? Did/do "women" have (a) distinctive voice(s) in Athenian tragedy?

The answer (predictably) is: Yes and no—but perhaps more "no" than "yes." It is true that certain kinds of emotive expression are usually reserved for female (or "barbarian") characters: in particular, ritual lamentation (*goos, thrēnos, kommos*) and actor's "monody" (solo aria). Such highly colored expressions of emotion, though they might once have been acceptable Attic practice, and were still to be found in several non-Attic Greek communities, were felt to be extravagant and unmanly by classical Athenian standards.[11] Likewise, certain kinds of agonized exclamation are largely confined to women—or to men who are explicitly said to be suffering from debilitating, or Orientalizing and "feminine," loss of self-control.[12] Yet these distinctions are not hard and fast: a Prometheus, or Philoctetes, or Heracles may "sing" (or "wail"?) briefly, when he is to be imagined as being in the most extreme throes of victimization and agony; and when the young Argive prince Orestes joins the Asian slave-chorus and his own sister, Electra, in a wild, extended lament and invocation of their dead father (Aesch. *Cho.* 306–478), it is impossible at times to distinguish his male voice from the two female voices with which he is alternating, so univocally are their words, meters, self-representations, and rhetorics merged and integrated.[13] Thus the (collective, nongendered) voice of "aristocratic family lament" and "children's cry for vengeance," in this case at least, proves stronger than the distinctive strains of "female utterance"; or, to put this another way, a man may—under circumstances of exceptional stress—have access to a language, or a "voice," normally, or selectively, restricted to women and/or foreigners. If a man gives in too completely to this mode of utterance, he

---

[11] On ritual lamentation, see esp. Alexiou 1974; Holst-Wahrhaft 1992; Foley 1992; Hall 1989; Griffith 1998: 49–52; see also the essays of Worman, Lardinois, Blok, and Stehle in this volume. It is uncertain how closely *goos* ("lamentation") and *goēteia* ("conjuring, incantation") were generally associated in fifth-century Athens, and whether the latter should be regarded as an importation from the North (Thracian shamanism?), or as an indigenous Greek practice; see further Burkert 1965; Kingsley 1994; Griffith 1998: 49–52; and Johnston 1999: ch. 3. On actor's monody, see Barner in Jens 1971; Hall 1999. On the disturbing capacities of the *aulos* (the instrument that accompanied almost all lyrics in the theater), see Anderson 1966: 64–66, 132–38; West 1992; and P. Wilson 1999.

[12] McClure 1995; Loraux 1990 [1998]; Hall 1989, 1993.

[13] The attribution and reading of several stanzas, or parts of stanzas, in this *kommos* scene of the *Choephoroi* remain uncertain; see Garvie 1986: ad loc.

may indeed run the risk of being seen as effeminized (as Heracles does at Soph. *Trach.* 1070–75, or Xerxes in Aesch. *Pers.*). Yet, in the artificial world of the Theater, forbidden practices from past eras, or repressed fantasies normally excluded from public male discourse, might surface and find exciting and (temporarily) legitimate expression.[14]

Conversely, in Aeschylus' *Seven against Thebes*, we find a chorus of Theban women passing quickly from panic-stricken shrieks and rhythmic tattoos of terror in the face of enemy attack, to sensible advice and relatively calm attempts to deter Eteocles, their general and king, from plunging into a course of crazed self-destruction; then, after his death, they relapse into exclamations of antiphonal grief typically associated with "mourning women." Thus, while their status as "women of the city" remains stable, their voice shifts register, back and forth, in response to, and definition of, Eteocles': they may be "female" to his "male," or "sensible" to his "crazed," "normal" to his "Oedipally cursed," within the same drama. And such alternations are common. For, just as a "man" is also—and is perceived to be, and interpellated and treated as—a soldier, a father, a brother, a citizen, etc., so is each "woman" potentially the site of several overlapping, alternating, or even competing performativities. Neither in drama nor in real life should we expect an individual always to speak with the "same" voice.[15] And of the multiple voices that may be available to a single person, some may be conventionally gendered, others not: indeed, the gendering may itself be a subject of contention—as Athenian tragedy is ever quick to demonstrate.

The Greeks themselves often asserted that women should be judged by different behavioral, moral, musical, and verbal standards from men.[16] In general, a woman's "virtue" (*aretē*) was often declared to be different from a man's, just as a slave's is different from a master's; and words—especially

---

[14] For the strong pressure in fifth-century Athens to curtail public expressions of female grief, see Loraux [1981] 1986; Holst-Warhaft 1992; Foley 1993; and for the effeminate characteristics of many wailing barbarians on the Athenian stage, see Hall 1989, 1993, 1999. (Hall goes too far in claiming that the shrill "wails" of grief connoted by the *kōku-* root invariably imply effeminization, for Creon and Haemon in Soph. *Ant.* 1079, 1206, 1227, etc., present decisive counterexamples.) Attitudes and conventions surrounding male expressions of grief seem to have been subject to change from place to place and period to period: see Loraux [1981] 1986; Monsacré 1984. For discussion of the Theater's function as a site for exploring forbidden or dangerous fantasies and experiences, see Montrose 1980; Zeitlin [1985] 1996; Goldhill 1990; Griffith 1998.

[15] Goffman 1959. I realize that "voice" is an ambiguous term here, involving both "speech patterns" and "positionality" (or what Goffman terms "front" and "routine"). But I think the ambiguity is appropriate to the contexts of Athenian tragedy.

[16] For typical statements of the fundamental differences between male and female morality, behavior, and upbringing, see, e.g., Plato *Ion* 540b; Arist. *Eth. Nic.* 8.1162a25, *Pol.* 1.1252a–1253, 7.1331bff. Certain musical modes and dances were felt to be distinctively "feminine": Anderson 1966; West 1992; Lonsdale 1993.

certain kinds of assertive, defiant, courageous, independent-minded words—that would be fine and admirable for a man to utter might be improper, foolish, even outrageous for a woman.[17]

Some of the most distinctively female patterns of speech in tragedy are obvious enough: lyric expressions of fear and grief; prayers to the gods for help; other ritual formulations, such as supplication, prophecies, curses, and various perlocutionary chants of damage or benefit;[18] references to domestic activities such as making and washing clothes, fetching water, making offerings, taking care of young children; descriptions of the miseries of slavery and loss of homeland and family; references to the intimate relations between child and mother or between sexual partners—all these are usually found coming from female characters rather than male. Thus, whereas in Homer's *Iliad* it is a male family retainer, Phoenix, who describes the homely details of Achilles' childhood, in the *Choephoroi* it is the Nurse who recalls Orestes as a baby (*Cho.* 750–62); and female speech is more likely than male to describe a child's appearance or upbringing (Eur. *Med.* 1071–77), to provide a delicate periphrasis for sexual intercourse (Cassandra and Apollo, at Aesch. *Ag.* 1202–12, or Io at *Prom.* 645–72), or to talk positively about the effects of erotic desire (Soph. *Trach.* 436–49, 497–530; Aesch. *Ag.* 1434–37, *Danaids* fr. 44 Radt). Accordingly, in Sophocles *Antigone*, it is the conventionally "feminine" Ismene, not Creon or Haemon himself—nor the "unfeminine" Antigone—who refers to the bond of affection between Haemon and Antigone (*Ant.* 570): male references to the power of Eros usually characterize it as an affliction or disease.

Another characteristic associated by the Greeks more with women than with men is silence; and a silence that would be shameful or cowardly in a man might conventionally be thought to confer an ideal air of "modesty" and "good sense" upon a woman. Indeed, one of the most distinctive signs of "femininity" on the tragic stage is failure to speak at all (Sophocles' Iole, Aeschylus' Iphigenia or Helen, Euripides' veiled Alcestis),[19] or inability to keep on speaking—whether this silencing is brought about by intimidation, by rhetorical convention, or by physical removal (Sophocles' Chrysothemis

---

[17] Aristotle, in his discussion of *ēthos* in tragedy (*Poet.* 15.1454a20–32), is especially concerned with this issue.

[18] In many of these operations, the speaker (speech-actor) is someone disadvantaged, someone whose own physical strength and/or political power is inferior: the paradigmatic figures are Hesiod's (female) songbird (*Op.* 202–12) and Archilochus' mother fox (frs. 174–81). Both suffer violence from lordly males (hawk, eagle), and both have recourse to vocal complaint, including explicit or implicit cursing in the name of Zeus. Similarly, cursing in tragedy is especially associated with victims, and hence with female characters, from Clytemnestra's embodied *arai* ("curses") in Aesch. *Eum.* to Antigone's and Eurydice's final words at Soph. *Ant.* 927–28, 1304–5 (see below).

[19] On these four, see esp. Wohl 1998.

or Tecmessa, Euripides' Phaedra or Alcestis, Aeschylus' Cassandra, Io, or—ultimately—Clytemnestra).[20]

By contrast, tragedy presents a select number of female characters whose "masculine" speech arouses the horror and/or admiration of other characters and critics alike. Among these we must count Aeschylus' Clytemnestra, Sophocles' Electra and Antigone, and Euripides' Medea.[21] In all four of these cases, it is striking that we find the character described both as typically or exaggeratedly "womanly," and as shamefully bold and "manly." Aeschylus' Clytemnestra, for example, even as she confirms her reputation for having a "male-counselling, expectant heart" (*Ag.* 11) by hacking her husband to death, and subsequently by calling for "a man-slaying axe" to deal with her avenging son (*Cho.* 889), is also criticized by the male chorus for her female flights of fancy, and later reveals her "feminine" susceptibility to sexual temptation: "No expectation of fear steps in my house, as long as Aegisthus warms the fire on my hearth" (*Ag.* 1434–35; cf. *Cho.* 893). She also mentions (effusively, but with some irony) her dependency on her husband (*Ag.* 855–913), and her maternal concern for her daughter (genuine) and son (perhaps feigned: *Cho.* 691–99; cf. 737–43). Likewise, her eerily knowledgeable vision of distant events at Troy gives her a "prophetic" air (not unlike, e.g., Theonoe's in Eur. *Helen*), and her obvious relish for deception conforms to the feminine stereotype established with/by Hesiod's Pandora.[22]

Medea similarly combines a "masculine" determination to exact revenge on her enemies at any cost with a passionate jealousy directed against her husband's new bride, and an explicit commitment to the traditional "womanly" resources of deception and trickery (*Med.* 393–409):

> I myself, taking a sword, even if I end up being killed,
> will kill them; I will proceed to resolute and bold action.
> For nobody—by the Mistress whom I revere above all
> and have chosen as my ally, Hecate,
> who resides in the inner chamber of my house—
> none of them will hurt my heart and escape unharmed. . . .
> Come Medea . . . , now the test is of your courage;
> . . .You must not let yourself be laughed at

[20] For Sophocles' Ismene, Antigone, and Eurydice, see below. For female modesty and reticence in general, see esp. Eur. *Heracl.* 475–83; also Soph. *El.* 518; Eur. *IA* 830–54, *El.* 343–44, *Or.* 108, *Phoen.* 1276, *Andr.* 877–79, fr. 521 Nauck. I am grateful to Laura McClure for several of these references.

[21] Athena, in Aesch. *Eum.* and elsewhere, perhaps deserves a separate category of her own, since, despite her title of Maiden (*Parthenos*), she is barely "female" at all; indeed, goddesses in general may belong to a separate, mixed category.

[22] On Clytemnestra's peculiar mixture of masculine and feminine language, see esp. Goldhill 1984; McClure 1997: 115–21.

as a result of this Corinthian marriage of Jason's,
when you yourself are born from a noble father, and from the Sun.
You know what is required; and furthermore, we are women—
most helpless for good, but the cleverest architects of all evils.

And as the play proceeds, we see her steel herself to murder her own children, in a nightmarish combination of cold-blooded rage (at their father) and tender concern (for the children's future without her—and for their very survival).[23]

Some of the most agonizing and introspective scenes of indecision in tragedy are focused on women: in addition to Medea herself, we may point especially to Phaedra (Eur. *Hipp.*), Iphigenia (Eur. *IA*), and Deianira (Soph. *Trach.*). That is not to say that men never experience such moments,[24] but the most searching explorations of impossibly conflicted inner feelings (as opposed to conflicting societal expectations) tend to be attributed to women.

Perhaps the most illuminating example of such indecisiveness comes in the scene where Deianira shares with the chorus (trusted women of the town) her anxieties about the magic robe she is sending to her husband (Soph. *Trach.* 582–87):

> May I never know or learn about evil acts of daring;
> and I loathe women who dare to perform them.
> But in the hope that somehow I may outdo this girl [= Iole]
> with magic charms and spells for Heracles,
> the deed has been planned and set in motion (*memēchanētai*)—
> unless I seem to you to be doing something irresponsible:
> if so, I shall stop at once.

Desperate to win back Heracles' love, yet acutely conscious of the impropriety (especially in an erotic context) of a woman's taking the initiative to force an issue and assert her wishes (*tolma*, "daring"), and aware, too, of the dubious admissibility of resorting to magic, she hovers between describing the "deed" as already done and out of her control ("it has [already] been contrived," *memēchanētai*), and asking her friends for advice and (in effect) permission to carry it out ("unless I seem to you . . . if so, I shall stop").

In response, the women of the chorus offer just enough reassurance and

---

[23] On Medea's combination of "heroic-male" and "passionate-female" language, see esp. Knox 1979; Bongie 1977; Foley 1989; Boedeker 1991. Thus, on the one hand, she dwells like a man on (dis)honor, revenge, and the prospect of gloating over her enemies, and she practices effective guest-friendship with the king of Athens; on the other hand, she sings a monody of grief, discusses her sexual feelings, and addresses the bodies of her children, all characteristically "feminine" modes of utterance.

[24] E.g., Pelasgus and Agamemnon in Aeschylus, Ajax and Neoptolemus in Sophocles, Creon and Agamemnon (*IA*) in Euripides.

encouragement to allow her not to undo what she has tentatively begun to do, though they are as evasive as she is about assuming responsibility, and they employ the same rhetoric of perfect passive and impersonal verb forms (*Trach.* 588–93):

> [Cho.:] If there is any trust [or "reliability," *pistis*] in what is being done (*tois drōmenois*),
> you seem to us not to have been badly counseled (*bebouleusthai*).
> [Dei.:] There is this much trust, at least: it seems good (*dokein*)—
> but I have never yet put it to the test.
> [Cho.:] Well, one must (*chrē*) know for sure [only] by doing it.
> For even if you seem (*dokeis*) to have [something good],
> you could never have a sure proof without testing it out.
> [Dei.:] Well, we shall soon know; I see Lichas coming.

With their tentative references to "seeming" and "knowing," "testing" and "doing," and their eloquent omission of the terms that might assign the personal responsibility and origin (or even specify the precise nature) of the "deed," the women collaborate to confirm their mutual support for one another, even as they implicitly deny their right to take positive action. All is conditional, and tautological: If what is being done succeeds, it will prove itself successful (and therefore good?). If it doesn't succeed, . . . what then? Will not "the things being done" by Deianira stand condemned as "boldness"? Neither Deianira nor the chorus can bring themselves to voice the possibility of failure: yet both, through their language and reticence alike, hint strongly at its likelihood, and at the culpability that will be Deianira's as a result of her misguided, half-spoken agency.[25]

2. THE THREE WOMEN OF *ANTIGONE*

Sophocles' *Antigone* provides a rich and instructive sampling of the range of possibilities for women's voices in tragedy, exemplifying, on the one hand, the multiplicity of "female" attitudes and modes of expression available, and on the other, the impossibility of isolating any particular quality as belonging exclusively or quintessentially to the category "woman," or "female." Woman as daughter, as sister, as bride, as wife, as mother: each has a distinct performativity and rhetoric, some of them overlapping, others diverging and even contradicting one another. We can learn much from tracing the interweaving strands of these discourses.[26]

---

[25] For a fine analysis of the ways in which Deianira's subjective desires are represented and foreclosed (and at times projected onto the silent Iole), see Wohl 1998: 17–56.

[26] The list could obviously be extended: woman as citizen or outsider, Greek or foreigner, young or old, parent or childless, free or slave, elite or commoner, etc.—none of which is specifically a gendered identity.

Three women appear in the play: the two sisters, Antigone and Ismene, and Creon's wife, Eurydice (mother of Haemon).Each of these three speaks with a distinctly, even radically, different voice; furthermore, in addition to their own words, each also has her speech and behavior imagined and described in her absence, or even in her presence, by other speakers in the play. Thus, in each case, "woman" is constructed as a speaking subject in conjunction with, or in opposition to, other characters, male and female.

The opening lines present the two sisters in close contact and collusion; but this closeness is almost immediately ruptured. Symptomatic of this troubled closeness—and of the uncomfortable and intricate family history and relations that produced it—is the frequent use of the dual ("we two," "our two brothers," etc.: 2–3, 13–14, 21, 50, 55–57, 58, 61–62), and of the *auto-* root, whose associations of "selfsame, very own, mutual" can be positive ("very own sister") or negative ("self-inflicted," "incestuous": 1, 49–52, 55–57; later 306–7, 511–13, 863–65, 900, 915, 1172–75, 1315).[27] As the scene progresses (1–99), Antigone in particular begins to employ the first- and second-person pronouns and verb-endings increasingly in opposition to one another (31–32, 37–38, 45–46, 71–72, 76–77, 80–81, 83, etc.), and even to threaten Ismene with "hatred" (86, 92–93). The siblings' hoped-for identity of interests and persons thus disintegrates into bitter opposition, and this is reflected in the contrast between the speech patterns of the unassertive, reasonable, and conventional-minded Ismene, and those of the uncompromising and single-minded Antigone. Antigone's speech favors blunt direct questions (2–3, 9–10) and future indicative statements (esp. 37, 46, 71–77, 80–81, 93), shorter and less complicated sentences, often enjambed (especially in the staccato phrases of her indignant rejection of Ismene at 69–77); and she prefers simple vocabulary and insistent repetition (2–3, 32, 73, 93–94; negatives at 4–6). Ismene speaks in more elaborate periods (esp. 49–68), with more ornate diction,[28] preferring potential and conditional utterance and a greater degree of generalization (61–62, 67–68, 92): she is seeking to establish a measured and balanced basis for decision-making, a set of principles that will make it possible for the remains of their family to recover themselves after this latest calamity, while Antigone sees only what lies directly before them—a body, her brother's body, to be buried: "Do you know . . . ? Have you heard . . . ? Or are you unaware . . . ?" (*Ant.* 2, 9–10); "Be what it seems best to you! I shall bury him" (*Ant.* 71–72).

This directness of expression continues to characterize Antigone's speech throughout the play; and it is further emphasized at times by a heavy use of

[27] See further Knox 1964: 79–80; Loraux 1986; Griffith 1999: nn. on lines 1, 2–3, 170–72, 488–89, 561–62, 769–70, 1226–27.

[28] A numerical measure of the difference: in 69–77, Antigone's nine lines employ sixty-two words, whereas Ismene's nine lines at 49–57 employ only forty-five.

negative particles and sarcastic dismissals of the suggestions of others.[29] Her language is contrasted not only with Ismene's, but also to an even greater degree with Creon's frequent *gnōmai* and generalizations, preference for the abstract over the concrete, and extensive use of analogies, metaphors, and similes, all of which characterize him as one who thinks in terms of rules, of hierarchies, and of predictable and controllable orders.[30] Several critics have remarked on this contrast of speech patterns, and some have seen it as conforming to a more general gender-based distinction: men are more logical and abstract, women more intuitive and concrete (or, as a refinement of this, the male-dominated sociopolitical world requires more absolute, generalizable rules, while women are usually called upon to make their moral decisions in contexts that require more particular and provisional judgments, often made *ad hominem*).[31] From another (less overtly gender-charged) perspective, Creon is viewed as representing men's (or humans'?) futile attempts at ruling the world by their own laws, extrapolations, and institutions, whereas Antigone speaks and acts in the name of higher (divine) truths incapable of rational exposition and capable only of direct or intuitive apprehension.[32]

Some such distinction is confirmed by the differing usages of words of "knowing," "learning," and "being aware": Creon, along with the other male characters (especially Haemon and the chorus), constantly harps on the need for "intelligence, good sense, planning" (*phronein, gnōmē, bouleuma, euboulia, nous*, etc.) and "learning, understanding" (*manthanein*), whereas for Antigone to "know" (*eidenai, epistasthai*) seems to involve a more immediate, less intellectual state of awareness, or "certainty" (18, 89, 447–48, 460, 521; 471–72, 480):[33]

> [CREON:] Did you know (*eidēstha*) it had been decreed not to do this?
> [ANT.:] I knew (*eidē*) . . . ; how could I not? It was clear to all. (447–48)

> [ANT.:] I knew I was going to die; of course I knew (*exeidē*) (460)

> [CHO.:] She does not know (*ouk epistatai*) [how] to yield to troubles. (472)

Yet before we assign Antigone's mentality and language too confidently to the category of "female," against Creon's "male," we should recall the

[29] See esp. 69–70, 450–60, 469–70, 515, 538–39, 905–7, 927–28, with Griffith 1999: ad loc.; also Kitzinger 1976: 75–85, 175–80.

[30] For these patterns in Creon's speech, see esp. Goheen 1951; Kitzinger 1976: 143–57.

[31] Foley 1996, with reference to Kitzinger 1976; Gilligan 1982.

[32] Reinhardt [1947] 1979; Whitman 1951, etc. See further Oudemans and Lardinois 1987: 160–69. The implicit or explicit attribution to females of a more direct contact than males with divine truths and revelations (through prophecy, possession, ritual activity of various kinds) is common in classical Greek culture, as in many others; see Padel 1983; Foley 1993, 1995.

[33] Kitzinger 1976; Nussbaum 1986: 51–82; Foley 1996: 57–59, 64–68; Coray 1993: 58–80; see further Griffith 1999: 41–43, 51–54.

ways in which her speeches earlier clashed with Ismene's milder and less aggressive style and diction. Each sister thus speaks in a manner that is characterized as distinctively "female"—yet, as we have seen, their respective
manners of speech are sharply differentiated from one another.[34] Indeed,
as Antigone asserts her intention of going off to bury the body, in defiance
of Creon's edict, Ismene reminds her (*Ant.* 58–62):

> So look and consider, now the two of us are left on our own,
> how miserably we will perish, if we violate the law
> and transgress the vote and authority of the rulers.
> We must bear in mind that we were born women,
> so we must not try to fight against men.

This is sensible advice; nobody could blame a young woman for submitting
thus to an official edict, however harsh—nobody, that is, except Antigone
(*Ant.* 69–70): "I won't tell you what to do. In fact, even if you should want /
to do it now, I wouldn't want to let you join me in carrying it out!" In her
anger at Ismene's caution and reserve, she rejects her completely, a reaction
that is repeated later in the play. Thus her subsequent claim, "I was born to
share in love, not in hate" (523), is seen to have a very limited application—
her "love" is for her father and her brother, but it extends no further; indeed, it is converted into hate as soon as it encounters resistance (86, 93,
etc.). Despite Ismene's subsequent offer to join her in opposition to Creon,
and risk death along with her, Antigone continues to reject her (536–60),
and later describes herself as "the last" of Oedipus' family (895), as if Ismene no longer existed. And indeed, Ismene soon fades completely from
the scene, and from our consciousness (she is never mentioned again after
line 771, the point at which Creon relents and agrees to punish only
Antigone). Her role has been to articulate "normal," conventional female
attitudes and expectations, in order to throw into even sharper relief
Antigone's extreme and unconventional behavior and views. And once
Antigone's portrait is complete, and her fate sealed, Ismene has no further
function to perform.

Antigone herself is one of the most discussed and most admired figures
of Greek literature, at least since the nineteenth century.[35] A young woman
who chooses to die for her brother, in lone resistance to an oppressive state
government; a woman sentenced to a dark and solitary "marriage to death,"
who takes her fate in her own hands and commits suicide, to be joined in

---

[34] To confuse things still further, there are some resemblances between Ismene's diplomatic
generalizations and Creon's, though the latter's language is distinguished from the former's
particularly by its harsh imagery and tone (Goheen 1951; Kitzinger 1976: 143–57; Griffith
1999: 34–43).

[35] Steiner 1984; McClure 1993, with further references.

death by her youthful fiancé; a woman who rejects human (institutional) authority in the name of divine law; yet at the same time one whose incestuous origin reasserts itself in her privileging of father and brother over sister or potential husband and children—she is a complex and contradictory figure. To some, she has appeared a passionate, loving sister and daughter, inspired by commitment to a higher and more perfect set of ideals than anyone else around her; to others, she is an inflexible but confused rebel, or fatal victim of a family's curse. Her voice is unusually individual and insistent, and it carries with it associations that are both manly and feminine, dutiful and transgressive, enlightened and narrow, typical and unique.

This is at least in part because Antigone's—and her family's—identity is itself so peculiar: "Oh common, self-sistered head of Ismene" (῏Ω κοινὸν αὐτάδελφον Ἰσμήνης κάρα, 1). All four of the brothers and sisters, and their father, too, are indeed "common and self/same-siblinged," an identity to which Antigone will sacrifice anything else in the world, including her own life. For her devotion to her *philoi* ("loved ones, nearest and dearest") knows no limits: "In love, I shall lie with him, with my loved one, having committed a holy crime." (φίλη μετ' αὐτοῦ κείσομαι, φίλου μέτα, / ὅσια πανουργήσασ᾽, 73–74). The "crime" to which she refers here, with consciously scornful paradox, is violation of Creon's edict forbidding burial of her brother's body. In this devotion to kin, and her resolute observance of proper funeral rites (washing a family member's body, wailing and lamenting over it), Antigone is performing a characteristic and proper female role; and she insists that by this action she is recognizing and honoring a universal obligation to the gods below (450–60). The fact that this brings her into collision with the legitimate political authorities and jeopardizes her own prospects of marriage, and even of life itself, does not deter her (*Ant.* 461–67):

> If I am to die before my time, I count that as a profit;
> Anyone who lives as I do, amidst many evils,
> doesn't this man (*hode*) derive profit by dying?
> So it is no pain for me to meet this end;
> but if I had left my own brother's corpse unburied,
> at that I would have felt pain.

Late in the play, when she is about to be led off to her living tomb, Antigone stipulates that she would not have acted so for a husband or child, but only for a brother, since, with their parents dead, he is irreplaceable (900–912). Some critics (especially those who take Antigone's earlier claims as representing "family" against "state") have seen this argument as a sign of youthful or "feminine" inconsistency, or loss of nerve, or special pleading, evidence that Antigone is not in fact acting on rational principles, but out of a semi-articulate spirit of sisterly devotion or divine enlightenment.[36] But her words here are not inconsistent with her former claims—merely more narrowly specific about her absolute commitment to natal family. In that respect, she is voicing (and enacting) a preference, or a contradiction, that lies at the heart of Greek gender relations, yet rarely finds overt expression: to which of her two families does a woman (bride, mother) owe stronger allegiance, that of her parents (including her siblings), or that of her husband (including her children and in-laws)? If exogamy (the exchange of women between households through marriage) is designed ideally to enable families to develop and extend their kinship ties, this institution brings with it an inherent conflict of interest—a conflict that men do not face, since they are never required to leave one household (their father's) to take up residence in another (their spouse's).[37]

Thus the deep-seated male fear that a wife will betray her "new" family out of loyalty to her "old" one finds its confirmation in Antigone's defiant statements, which amount to a resounding rejection of the institution of marriage itself. This rejection finds repeated expression in her observation (echoed by others) that her living entombment constitutes a "marriage to Death": her rocky "tomb" is her "bridal chamber underground," and she will be (re)united there with her dead parents, and above all with her beloved brother. These phrases, and the haunting spectacle of her being led off to her new "bridal chamber" (891, *numpheion*, etc.), underline the paradoxical character of a woman who is at the same time the most loyal daughter and the most impossible bride imaginable. Antigone never mentions Haemon; and she remains silent when his name and their planned marriage are discussed by Ismene and Creon (561–76). It is not Antigone but her more conventionally feminine sister who alludes to their "attachment" (570, *hērmosmena*) and cries out on behalf of "dearest Haemon" (572); and Creon recognizes this in his retort ("You and your [talk of] marriage are causing me pain," 573).[38] It is no coincidence that the only character who addresses or refers to Antigone as "woman" (*gynē*) in the play is Creon:[39]

---

[36] E.g., Knox 1964; Reinhardt 1979. Some have even argued for excision of the lines; but see Murnaghan 1986; Neuburg 1990; and Cropp 1997, for a convincing defense of them.

[37] See Seaford 1987, 1990; Rehm 1994; Wohl 1998.

[38] Some editors have given 572 to Antigone: but this would (as we have seen) be out of character (and would violate the normal stage conventions; see Griffith 1999: ad loc., with further references).

[39] E.g., "Don't ever lose your wits for the pleasure of a woman!" (648–49), "You woman's slave, don't try to cajole me!" (756); cf. his earlier outbursts, "A woman won't rule while I am alive!" (525), "Take them inside, attendants! From now on, they must be women, and not roaming loose" (578–79), etc.

to the others, she is always "child" (*pais*), "girl" (*neanis* or *korē*), "bride" (*numphē*), or "maiden" (*parthenos*), or else plain "Antigone."[40] *Gynē* implies "adult woman" or "wife," but it is also the regular term used in binary opposition to *anēr* ("man"), and therefore the most suitable for misogynistic insults; hence Creon's repeated use of the term in his confrontation with Haemon (649, 651, 678, 680, 740, 746, 756; cf. 694).

Just as Ismene earlier characterizes Antigone's speech and behavior as unfeminine, Creon, too, accuses her of usurping "the man's" role (*Ant.* 480–85):

> She knew how to commit outrage (*hubris*) then,
> when she overstepped the established laws;
> and this is a second outrage (*hubris*), on top of her action,
> that she boasts about what she did, and exults in it.
> Certainly I am no longer the man—she is the man,
> if authority (*kratē*) is to be overturned like this with impunity.

By conventional male—and political—standards, it is a serious "outrage" (*hubris*) to flout the law and perform a forbidden act, especially out in public, on the open plain;[41] but for Creon it seems almost more "outrageous" that she "voices so vehemently and gleefully" (*epauchein kai gelān*, 482) her responsibility. By this point in their confrontation, he has been riled by her dismissive tone and her scornful remarks (e.g., "If I seem to you to be acting foolishly, I can hardly be found guilty of foolishness by a fool!" 469–70). But even in her first words to him, neutral as they are, she has transgressed (*Ant.* 442–43):

> [CR.:] Do you say, or do you deny, that you did this deed?
> [ANT.:] I say that I did it; I don't deny it.

To see a woman stand her ground, look up at the city's chief officer, and thus break silence; to hear her lay claim publicly to an act of direct opposition to political authority; this can only happen in the Theater. Yet, unlike Clytemnestra's or Medea's stridently defiant claims, or Deianira's or Phae-

---

[40] *Anti-gonē* seems to mean "In return for birth"; the name is perhaps coined for this quintessentially Oedipal character, and does not recur at all frequently in other mythical or historical contexts (although the masculine, Antigonos, becomes very popular after the third century B.C.E.). By contrast, *Ismēnē* (or perhaps more properly *Hismēnē*, see Mastronarde 1994, on Eur. *Phoen.* 101) seems to connote "native of Thebes" (like the river [H]ismenus). Thus their names, like their patterns of speech, serve to distinguish the two sisters, one as unique and biologically/psychologically inseparable from (her peculiar) family, the other as more normal and typically Theban, and thus fully integrable into her community.

[41] The act itself could be said to be both supremely feminine (lamentation over a corpse, pouring of water) and also shockingly masculine (physical manipulation of the earth, usually the men's role in the burial rites).

dra's self-accusatory disclaimers, Antigone's simple assertion of responsibility carries a disconcerting air of absolute authority.[42]

The third female voice in this play is that of Creon's wife, Eurydice. She says very little. In fact, her speaking role is the shortest (except for Aeschylus' Pylades) of any named character in Greek tragedy (1183–91), though a few more words and cries of hers are later reported by a Messenger (1302–5). Her chief function is to receive the news of Haemon's death, and then by her suicide to become another component in Creon's downfall and final misery. Yet, short though her part is, it is in several respects typical of many female roles in tragedy, and illuminating both for what it (she) says, and for the way(s) in which she falls silent. Here is Eurydice's entire speech (*Ant.* 1183–91):

> All you citizens, I heard the news
> as I was coming up to the doorway,
> to go and present prayers to the goddess, Pallas Athena;
> I happened to be loosening the bolt of the gate,
> when the voice of disaster to our house struck right through my ears.
> I fainted in terror, and lay there in front of my servants, struck dumb.
> But tell me again what the news was;
> I am not inexperienced in disasters; I will listen to this, too.

The opening apology (why is she here at all, in public, out of the house? cf. 18–19), the allusive reference to previous miseries, and the steeling of herself to take in the grimmest news possible (the death of her only surviving son) are all common motifs from female characters in tragedy. What is unusual here, and highly effective, is Sophocles' decision to have Eurydice rush from the stage without a word, once she has heard the full news of Haemon's death (*Ant.* 1244–45):

> [Cho.:] What would you guess? The woman has gone back inside again, before saying anything, good or bad.

The Messenger and chorus debate for a few lines what to make of Eurydice's sudden departure (*Ant.* 1253–56):

> We shall soon know whether she is concealing
> something hidden in her raging heart,

---

[42] The only other voice in this play to speak with equal or greater authority than Antigone's is that of Teiresias. The feeble old blind prophet (presumably played by the same actor that played Antigone) in some respects comes to eclipse Antigone's earlier claims to divine insight, as he enunciates the gods' anger and Creon's impending punishment—a quasi-perlocutionary speech act that both is, and is not, a vindication of Antigone's earlier words and actions. (Teiresias does not explicitly mention Antigone at all; nor, after the messenger speech, is there any reference to her in the closing scenes of the play.) On the roles of Teiresias and the chorus in reclaiming some measure of male authority for the continuing polis, and the concomitant silencing of Antigone and Ismene, see further Griffith 1999. 52–66.

if we go inside the house; you are right:
there is a weight of danger even in excessive silence.

Their suspicions are well founded: she has killed herself—but not before uttering a final curse on her husband (*Ant.* 1301–5):

> Pierced by the sharp sword, near the altar, . . .
> she closed her darkening eyes, bewailing (*kōkūsāsa*)
> the empty marriage bed of Megareus,[43]
> who had died in the past, and now Haemon, too;
> and finally she sang out evil-doings (*kakās praxeis ephumnēsāsa*)
> against you, the child-killer.

This woman is defined entirely by her role as wife and mother, and when both of her sons have been taken from her (both, it seems, as a result of something her husband did), she has nothing to live for. Her anger, despair, and bitterness are channeled into two violent, yet typically "female," acts (an act and a speech act): suicide and curses on her husband. Like Antigone, she succeeds in hurting Creon even in and after her death; and like her, in so acting/speaking, she commands the strongest sympathy and approval from the theater audience.

Nonetheless, for all of the powerful impact of Eurydice's brief appearance and death, and all of Ismene's value as a foil to Antigone (and as a representative of "normalcy," too, amidst so much extravagant and misguided behavior), it is Antigone's voice that resonates most strongly from the play (at least in modern times), her personality that makes the most memorable and disturbing impression on the theater audience and the reader. So it is with Antigone that we should conclude. Is hers a voice of resistance, of potential liberation? In opposing a misguided political regime, breaking with conventional stereotypes of female submission and obedience, and asserting her own ineradicable right—as a human being, regardless of gender or status—to carry out such a universal obligation as burial of kin, does she not succeed in challenging and overthrowing Creon's short-sighted and bigoted version of male supremacy and political expediency? And if so, isn't her voice thereby proven to be "truer," or "higher," than Ismene's, the voice that recommended caution, compromise, and accommodation? If so, is it more—or less—"feminine" than Ismene's?

Or are we to conclude that it was Antigone's own transgressive and uncompromising ("unfeminine"?) temper that brought about the fatal collision and catastrophe ("Your own self-willed temper destroyed you," 875), together with her obsessive devotion to father and brother, to the exclusion

---

[43] The correct reading and reference of 1301–2 are disputed; see Griffith 1999: ad loc. But there is no doubt about the reference to her first son's death.

of other "normal" objects of devotion, such as sister or future husband? Or (extending this possibility a little further) is her position and behavior to be explained entirely in terms of her incestuous origin, from that archetypally Oedipal family in which the "daughter" can only imagine herself as loving (and "lying with") her own father and brother—and therefore must be consigned (must consign herself) to death?[44]

During the course of the play, Antigone embodies all these possibilities, or performativities. Her voice speaks loudly, piercingly, and effectively— but not univocally. Indeed, Athenian tragedy provides an extraordinarily richly textured, and often contradictory, babble of rival voices, as the various characters are embodied, masked, and endowed with speech by their authors and actors. Dramatic impersonation is a form of contestation and pretension, of laying claim to and trying out voices and roles that are not normally our own. Antigone's voice, and Ismene's, and even Eurydice's, are allowed to formulate queries and complaints, propose and violate norms, cite and blur this performativity and that, and thereby bring about shocking and edifying results. This process appears to have been useful, even necessary, to Sophocles and his male fellow-citizens, for representing and critiquing their society, as it is, as it might be, as it is imagined to be, for Dionysiac tragedy was the most admired and highly valued cultural event of the Athenian year.

What did Athenian men believe, or fantasize, about their daughters, their mothers, their sisters, their wives, their slaves? What did they want to believe? What did they fear? The roles that the tragedians wrote to be played out in the Theater by themselves and their fellow actors and choreuts remind the audience constantly how fragile and tormented the family relations are out of which they all come, and within which they all continue to function, even as they pursue their careers within the city as soldiers, competitors, and politicians. By giving voice—outspoken voice—to any and all of those family members, including the ones who normally keep quiet, stay out of public view, and "mind their own business," they allow unconscious anxieties to surface, unspoken contradictions to be stated, and unmentionable issues to be aired. Tragic "women" are especially good for that: for while real-life Athenian women would not dream of talking about (let alone acting on) the kinds of conflicts and fantasies that these plays explore—and conversely there are certain things that men in real life are not expected to say, certain sounds they cannot be allowed to make, if they are to remain sufficiently different and distinct from women—in the Theater the power

[44] Lacan [1986] 1992: 270–87; Johnson 1997; see too Butler 2000. I should like to thank Judith Butler, Victoria Wohl, Princeton University Press's two anonymous readers, and above all André Lardinois and Laura McClure, for helpful comments on earlier drafts of this chapter. None of these should be held accountable for its final form or content.

of disguise, and the license of impersonation, allows extraordinary liberties to be taken.

As for us, nowadays, what we end up making of these impersonated "women," how we evaluate their words and performativities within the drama that each inhabits, is open to discussion: it is up to us. Certainly, no neatly defined portrait of "woman" emerges (from this play, or from any other—or from Greek tragedy overall): no comfortable confirmation of preexisting distinctions of gender, of predictable mannerisms of speech, or of the natural divisions between male and female. For the term "woman" is too clumsy an umbrella for too many separate categories (daughter, sister, virgin, bride, wife, mother, princess, captive, etc.), whose several duties and expectations cannot be expected to cohere tidily—nor to separate themselves out conveniently and invariably (essentially) from those of son, brother, youth, husband, and father. The urge (within some of the play's characters, and perhaps within many members of Sophocles' audience, as with some readers in our own day) to find and maintain distinctions, to listen for the authentic voice of "woman," and to seize on particular formulations and enunciations as proof of inherent difference (whether inferiority, or superiority, or mysterious complementarity) is found to lead in circles: women do all speak alike (any more than men do); and they do not always speak as "women"—though sometimes their words will be misheard, or heard in a particular way, or not heard at all, precisely because all that is heard, or noticed, is a "woman's" voice.

CHAPTER EIGHT

Women's Cultic Joking and Mockery

SOME PERSPECTIVES

D. M. O'HIGGINS

IN THE HOMERIC *Hymn to Demeter*, Demeter wandered the earth, disguised as an old woman "remote from childbearing and the gifts of wreath-loving Aphrodite" (101–2), after discovering that Hades had abducted her daughter, Persephone.[1] Following her arrival at Eleusis, near Athens, a serving woman, Iambe, assailed her with mocking jokes:

> She stood on the threshold, and her head
> grazed the ceiling, and she filled the doorway with divine light.
> Metaneira [queen of Eleusis] was seized by reverence and awe and pale fear.
> She yielded her chair and bade the other to sit.
> But Demeter, Seasongiver, She of Glorious Gifts,
> did not wish to sit on the shining couch
> but remained silent, with her lovely eyes cast down,
> until decorous Iambe placed a jointed seat,
> and above she threw a silvery fleece.
> Then sitting down [Demeter] held her veil before her, in her hands.
> Long she sat on the stool, sorrowing and silent,
> nor did she welcome anyone by word or sign,
> but unlaughing and without touching food or drink
> she sat, pining in longing for her deep-girt daughter
> until decorous Iambe, with jokes
> and many a mocking jest moved the holy lady
> to smile and laugh and have a cheerful heart.
> Even afterwards she [Iambe] used to cheer her moods.
> To her Metaneira offered a full cup of sweet wine,
> but she refused. It was not right for her, she said,
> to drink red wine. But she bade her mix barley and water

---

[1] The *Hymn to Demeter* probably emerged between the seventh and the early sixth centuries in Attica. Like the other *Hymns*, it perhaps was meant to be sung at a festival—on its own, or as a prelude to a longer piece. On the date, see Richardson 1974: 5–11; Padgug 1972; Janko 1982: 181–83; Osborne 1985, Foley 1994: 29–30, 169–78.

with tender mint, and to offer this to her, to drink.
Metaneira prepared the drink and gave it to the goddess, as bidden,
and mistress Dēō accepted it, for the sake of the ritual.[2]

Demeter responded to Iambe by laughing, drinking the *kukeōn* (the "mixed drink" described in the *Hymn*), and then treating with fire and ambrosia Demophoon, Metaneira's infant son, while remaining among the women of Eleusis. This miraculous sojourn ended when Metaneira, suspicious of her strange nurse, interrupted the fiery baptism whereby Demeter planned to render the boy immortal.Demeter angrily returned to a grief and rage more bitter and destructive than before—until Zeus was forced to intervene. Despite its relative brevity, however, we should take stock of that interval between jest and interruption, during which Demeter abandoned her grief and dwelled with mortal women.

Just as Demeter's bereavement had brought her to the mortal world, so her laughter was the human kind, not Olympian. It recalls the laughter of Sarah, Abraham's eighty-year-old wife, when she discovered that she was pregnant.[3] When Demeter laughed, together with mortal women she celebrated life's renewal in the face of age and death. Demeter saw women— like herself—whose sexual and reproductive powers belied appearance. Like Queen Metaneira, who had borne a son—"late born, beyond all hope" (219)—like decorous Iambe, surprising in her mocking humor, so this decrepit old woman revealed incongruous energy.[4]

The Iambe episode, which occurred within a group of women, served as aetiology for bawdy jesting and ritual mockery, obscenity and insult (*iambos*) by women in secret Demeter cults, celebrated all over the Greek world. The ritual joking purportedly instituted by Iambe's mockery inspired—or at least influenced—the male-centered, and often misogynistic, genre of literary *iambos* or satire.[5] This and similar ritual obscenity and insult also con-

---

[2] *Hom. Hymn Dem.* 188–211. The translation is mine.

[3] See Di Nola 1974: 52, citing Proclus, for the laughter of the gods as a sign of their plenitude. Sarah's story is in Genesis 18. In the excellent analysis of Gilhus 1997: 24–26, Sarah's laughter, and Jaweh's reaction to it, reflect changing views of the role of women's laughter in religious worship.

[4] Iambe receives no description in the *Hymn* except *kedna eiduia* ("knowing worthy things"). Parallels from the *Odyssey* and the other *Hymns* (there are none in the *Iliad*) suggest that the formula affirms Iambe's sexual restraint. It appears at *Od.* 1.428, where Laertes is accompanied by the "reliable" Eurykleia; at *Od.* 19.346, Odysseus requests some aged and "reliable" woman to wash his feet; at *Od.* 20.57, 23.182, and 23.232, it describes Penelope. In *Hymn. Hom. Ap.* 313 Hera reproaches Zeus for dishonoring her, even though he has made her his *kedna eiduia* wife; at *Hymn. Hom. Aphr.* 44 the expression is used (by the poet) of Hera, as Zeus' loyal wife. Iambe is described as an old woman in Apollodorus 1.30; Philicus (in Page 1941: no. 90); Choeroboscus on Hephaistion—a source that is probably derived from Hipponax (Hipponax test. 21a Degani [1983]).

[5] I deal with the question of whether any women created literary iambic in my forthcoming book on women's joking and laughter in archaic Greece. Sappho is the woman most likely

tributed a crucial element to Old Comedy. In this chapter I concentrate mainly on women's ritual joking. I have selected the Thesmophoria as a representative cult, because we know something about it and because the jesting and the drinking of the *kukeōn* in the *Hymn* probably referred to the Thesmophoria.[6]

BAUBO

Parallel stories regarding Demeter's trip to Eleusis, from the Orphic tradition, depicted a woman called Baubo making an obscene gesture to Demeter, with similar results.[7] Thus, the speech of Iambe, and of the women who imitated her, was the verbal equivalent of Baubo's gesture.

There are two sources of evidence for Baubo: "Orphic" literary fragments, and inscriptions and figurines.[8] The archaeological evidence dates to the fourth century B.C.E. or later and derives from several places in the Greek world, but not from Attica itself. Orphic poems cannot be dated precisely, but they probably existed by the time of the *Hymn*'s composition, that is, by the late seventh or early sixth century B.C.E.[9] The Orphic material has survived mostly in descriptions by the church fathers of Demeter's cult;

---

to have participated in iambic (cf. West 1989–92; 2: 97). Horace (*Epist.* 1.19.28) may suggest that she did: *temperat Archilochi Musam pede mascula Sappho.* I follow Bentley (1869) and most modern commentators in translating "Masculine Sappho tempers her Muse with the meter of Archilochus." It is not clear why Horace calls her masculine. His focus here is metrical/literary tradition, and the room it leaves for originality. Porphyrio (ad loc.) speculates that *mascula* appears "*because she was famous in the craft of poetry, in which men are more often famous*—or because she is defamed as having been a tribad" (Sappho test. 17 Campbell [1982–93]). Sappho, a lone woman on Horace's list, participates in a tradition built by Archilochus and inherited by Alcaeus—and eventually by Horace himself. Horace's words better sustain the meaning that *iambic* (rather than poetry in general) was a medium without a place for "normal" women. Maximus of Tyre (*Or.* 18.9; Sappho test. 20) situates Sappho (like Socrates) in the center of a web of literary, intellectual, and social relationships—both affectionate and adversarial. Some of the extant fragments of Sappho (e.g., frs. 37, 55, 57) are unequivocally hostile.

6 Clinton (1992: 28–37) argues that the jesting, drinking of the *kukeōn* and nursing of an infant fit more closely with the Thesmophoria than with the Eleusinian Mysteries. He argues (35) that the *kukeōn* probably was not part of the Mysteries.

7 *Hom. Hymn Dem.* 197–205. For the Orphic tales, see note 8.

8 For the various Orphic tales, see Richardson 1974: 79–86; Burkert [1972] 1983: 285–86; Kern [1922] 1963: 115–30; Graf 1974: 174–75. For Baubo (and Iambe), see Di Nola 1974: 19–53; Devereux 1983; Olender 1990: 85–115; Gilhus 1997: 33–37.

9 Clay 1989: 224: "I would like to go further [than Richardson, who merely acknowledges the possibility of preexisting Orphic poetry] and suggest that the *Hymn*-poet assumes a knowledge of this common version on the part of his audience and has deliberately modified it. Moreover he draws attention to his modifications by short-circuiting the expected narrative connections and reshaping the story to his own purposes." Foley (1994: 99–100) concurs in the opinion that the Orphic tales probably predate the *Hymn*.

though they clearly wish to discredit the pagan rites, the events conform to fertility myths elsewhere.[10]

In the longest fragment (Kern no. 49) Baubo seems to be the mother of the infant Demophoon, and queen of Eleusis. In others, she is merely a local rustic, one of a cast of characters that includes her husband, Dysaules, the cowherd Triptolemus, the shepherd Eumolpus, and the pig-keeper Eubouleus.[11] In Clement's version (Kern nos. 50 and 52) Eubouleus and Triptolemus saw their animals being swallowed in the earth with Hades' chariot, and so they were able to tell Demeter—who had wandered to Eleusis searching for Persephone—what had happened. Demeter's reward to the people of Eleusis was twofold: instruction in agriculture and the Mysteries.[12]

Details of Baubo's gesture are found in Clement and Arnobius.[13] After failing to cheer Demeter with words, Baubo lifted her skirts to reveal her genitals—and perhaps also the child Iakkhos, who had his hand under her breast.[14] Hesychius under "Baubo" suggests that, according to Empedo-

---

[10] Richardson (1974: 216–17) and Di Nola (1974: 19–90) cite parallels from Egypt and Japan.

[11] The *Hymn* mentions Triptolemus and Eumolpus in a list of local dignitaries given by Callidice, daughter of Celeus, to the disguised Demeter (153–55). At 477ff. Demeter instructs local leaders (including Triptolemus and Eumolpus) in her Mysteries. The *Hymn* does not mention Dysaules, Baubo, or Eubouleus. For the range of Baubo's roles, see Olender 1990: 84. Baubo is a nurse (τιθήνη) in Hesychius (s.v. Baubo); a maenad in a first-century C.E. inscription from Magnesia on the Meander (Kern 1900: 215a32–40); a slave in a scholion to Nicander (*Alex.* 130); a demon of the night in a fragment preserved in Psellos (Kern [1922] 1963: 52).

[12] The *Hymn* prescribes the Mysteries only; agriculture already exists.

[13] See Kern [1922] 1963: 126–29. This gesture may be either positive (related to fertility) or negative (turning away an enemy with the magical potency of what is normally hidden). Gilhus (1997: 1–5) discusses the two fields of meaning (creation and joy; destruction and repression) in which laughter may be interpreted. Di Nola 1974 is the earliest and fullest account of the ways in which the Baubo incident may be viewed. See Zeitlin 1982a: 145 on Medusa, whose "genitalized" face can turn men to stone. Vernant ([1985] 1991a: 112–15) discusses the Gorgon Medusa as a terrifying emblem of a genitalized female face, capable of killing those who confront her. Cixous' famous essay (1976) portrays the laughing Medusa as a symbol for the open, abundant bodies of women. Similar apotropaic revelations occur in Plutarch *De mul. vir.* 246 a–b; Rabelais *Pantagruel: Le quart livre* 47; and the Irish epic *Táin Bó Cúalnge*, lines 1186–93 (O'Rahilly 1970). King (1986) discusses the *anasyrmos* ("pulling up," "exposure") as a conservative gesture, used repressively by women toward men to establish social order and gender roles.

[14] Festugière (1952) understood the child's image to have been drawn on Baubo's belly. Graf (1974: 196) argues, from Diels, that the word *iakhos* in Athenaeus was equivalent to *khoiros* ("cunnus"), but, as Marcovich ([1986] 1988) shows, this argument is based on a misunderstanding of unreliable evidence. Marcovich argues that, of the two principal texts describing the gesture (Clement *Protr.* 2.20.2–21.2 and Arnobius *Adv. nat.* 5.25), Arnobius, with the details of manipulation of genitals to create the image of a child, has no basis, deriving from a misunderstood and badly emended text of Clement.

olog, the name means "abdomen" or the body's cavity (κοιλία). Devereux and others have argued for an identification with the vulva.[15]

In addition to the fact that she gestured—instead of speaking—Baubo differs from her counterpart in being of childbearing years, whereas when Iambe's age is specified in the post-*Hymn* literary tradition, she occupies one of two extremes: girl or crone.[16] As a girl Iambe suffered humiliating retribution for her iambic outburst, and was compelled to commit suicide.

Iambe, as crone or unwed girl embracing death, reflected the situation she confronted: an old woman and a prematurely dying girl. In both manifestations she was the antitype of the mature female, and yet she restored wholeness to the mother goddess. In its very incongruity the miracle was the more uncanny. She conjured life—human and agrarian—through speech, while she herself seemed destined only for the grave. As we shall see, in Demeter's cult of the Thesmophoria, dead piglets—an extraordinary catalyst comprising unripe and overripe—formed an analogous part of the women's ritual.

On the other hand, Baubo embodied female sexuality and fertility, the power of the mature female displayed in a bold—even aggressive— epiphany. She revealed to the world what was normally hidden. Two types of terracotta figurine dating from the fourth to the first century B.C.E. are linked with Baubo.[17] The Priene type features a nude woman, whose face— which is also her belly and vulva—is supported directly by two stumpy legs.[18] The other type—"of Egyptian origin"—also shows a nude woman, this time with an anatomically correct body. Her belly is swollen, her legs splayed. She appears to be about to give birth, although in one example she is riding a pig, the animal sacred to Demeter.[19]

Inscriptions on Naxos and Paros and in Dion (Macedonia) testify to Baubo's cult status in these places. The fourth-century inscription from

[15] Devereux 1983: passim; Clay 1989: 234. Herodas (*Mim.* 6.19) uses the term *baubōn* to mean "phallus." For "dildo" as a possible explanation, see Olender 1990: 84; and Devereux 1983: 70. Zeitlin (1982a: 145–46), following Rohde and others, suggests the "bark of a dog, the latter animal being another term applied to the female pudenda," but Devereux (1984: 72– 74) dismisses this onomatopoeia as fanciful. See Olender 1990: 98, for references to the theory that *baubō* is a babble word, spoken by nurses to fretful infants.

[16] Most evidence on Iambe is Hellenistic or later, but the number and variety of the stories suggest a long history. Sophocles wrote a satyr-play called *Iambe*, but unfortunately we know nothing else about it. For Iambe as crone, see Hipponax test. 21a–x Degani 1983. Philicus in Page 1941: no. 90; Apollodorus 1.30. For Iambe as *korē* ("girl"), see schol. ad Hephaistion 281.8 Consbruch [1906] 1971. Eustathius (ad Od. 11.227) linked the suicidal Lycambides to a similar story about Iambe, a *korē* who ended her life after she had been insulted.

[17] See Karaghiorga-Stathacopoulou 1986 for details (and pictures) of both kinds of figurine.

[18] Reinach (1912: 117) suggests that in some cases the framing device may be Baubo's clothing, rolled back to reveal her face/vulva.

[19] Karaghiorga-Stathacopoulou 1986: 1.88. The pig-riding Baubo is Berlin Staatl. Mus. TC 4875.

Naxos associates Baubo with the principal deities of Eleusis: Demeter, Kore, and Zeus Eubouleus.[20] A similar inscription appears on Paros.[21] At Dion, the (Hellenistic) inscription, on top of a marble table, reads: "Menekrite, daughter of Theodorus, having served as priestess to Babo [sic]."[22] Nonnus preserves the story that Demeter herself performed just such an obscene gesture.[23] Like Iambe, Baubo revealed to Demeter something belonging to Demeter's own sphere and function, something present in Demeter herself. Baubo may be said to be a version or aspect of the goddess she confronts.[24]

Baubo clearly existed as both a cultic and a literary figure. Iambe, by contrast, has not shown up in inscriptions or in any archaeological context.[25] Iambe was "cultic" only in the sense that she epitomized a cultic activity: the exchange of insults or *aischrologia*. In fact, the evidence suggests that Iambe was the invention of the composer(s) of the *Hymn:* the necessary catalyst in the Eleusinian drama, but one who avoided the crude pantomime of the traditional cultic tale. Within the *Hymn* she was the solitary servant in a royal cast, of whom one member at least was worshiped in local cult.[26]

THE JOKING: CONTEXT, AND MALE PERCEPTIONS

In Athens, men and women engaged in bawdy exchanges during the Eleusinian Mysteries and Dionysian cults. Most evidence for exchanges involving both men and women derives from places other than Athens, however.[27] At the Hybristica at Argos men and women exchanged clothes and

[20] *Praktika tēs en Athenais archaiologikēs hetairias* 1950: 280; 1954: 336; *SEG* 16.478.

[21] *IG* XII.5.227. All three are described as χθόνιοι ("chthonic"). See Di Nola 1974: 30, where he discusses the infernal aspects of Baubo. He refers to Kenyon (1893: 77) for a fourth-century B.C.E. papyrus in which a funerary Hermes is called Ortho Baubo. Di Nola suggests that the resemblance to a dog's barking heard in the name may have a funerary aspect: cf. Johnston 1989: 134–42.

[22] *SEG* 27.280, 34.610.

[23] Nonnus *Dion.* 36.1028. The euphemistically worded passage refers only to her "thighs," but the meaning seems obvious. See Di Nola 1974: 44.

[24] Olender 1990: 99.

[25] Peredolskaya (1964) argues for an identification of one of the Taman peninsula grave figurines with Iambe. I think it is reasonable to see the naked woman portrayed as carrying a phallos and sitting on an altar as fulfilling a role analogous to Iambe's, but there is no certain basis for naming her Iambe rather than, say, Baubo.

[26] Celeus is mentioned in an Attic inscription as a recipient of honors: Sokolowski 1962: suppl. 10.72. It is likely that his wife Metaneira also existed as an Eleusinian cult figure.

[27] On male-female hostilities, see Gernet and Boulanger 1932: 52–54; for dances with opposed choruses of men and women, Nilsson 1906: 184ff. Burkert ([1977] 1985: 244) suggests that there must have been intergender insult exchanges associated with the cults of Demeter, as well as all-female ones.

fought; according to myth, the fight commemorated a victory by the women of Argos, led by the poet Telesilla, against the Spartans.[28] Leadership by a poetess suggests that there were verbal exchanges in addition to ritual fighting, and perhaps a woman's tradition of abusive poetry, now unfortunately lost. At Pellene in the Peloponnese, choruses of men and women hurled insults at each other at a festival of Demeter Musia.[29] At a sacrifice for Apollo Aigletes on Anaphe, an intergender exchange of insults occurred, supposedly because maidens given by the Phaeacian queen Areta to Medea had once "mocked the nobles" (presumably those accompanying Jason).[30]

Coarse humor occurred in an all-female context during Demetrian festivals: the Stenia and Thesmophoria, Haloa and the Eleusinian Mysteries.[31] At the Stenia, which preceded the Thesmophoria, Photius tells us that the women abused each other (he uses the verb *loidorein*).[32] Hesychius mentions that the women at the Stenia "blaspheme and mock" (*blasphemein, diaskoptein*).[33] In Epidauros and Aegina women similarly honored local versions of Demeter and Kore.[34] Belief in the generative power of women, produced among themselves through mingled solemnity *and* raucous joking, was powerful, both in Greece and elsewhere.[35] Ancient Egypt, Scandinavia, and Japan all produced traditional stories in which a woman or goddess cheers a mourner by making obscene jokes or by exposing herself.[36]

At the Haloa in Eleusis, a midwinter festival of the ploughed fields, the women gathered by themselves and whispered "shameful and irreverent" things to each other, standing at tables laden with earth's bounty, and held

[28] Plut. *De mul. vir.* 4. See also Paus. 2.20.7–8 on Telesilla's victory. Adrados ([1972] 1975: 295) suggests that there were two *komoi* or representative groups, each with its own leader.

[29] Paus. 7.29.9. See Farnell 1907, 3: 99.

[30] Nilsson 1906: 175–76 discusses the Apollo Aigletes ritual; cf. Ap. Rhod. *Argon.* 4.1710–30; Apollod. *Bibl.* 1.9.26.

[31] For the Athenian Demeter festivals, I have used Brumfield 1981. For rituals elsewhere in Greece, Fluck 1931 is still valuable.

[32] Brumfield 1981: 80 for details; cf. Photius s.v. Σήνια (sic) (Kock 1880–88, 2: 164).

[33] Hesychius s.v. Στήνια, στηνιῶσαι.

[34] Herodotus 5.83.

[35] Versnel ([1992] 1993) is incorrect in thinking of the women's joking at the Thesmophoria as rightfully male—something usurped by women during the carnival atmosphere of the festival. The Thesmophoria may have had "lawless" elements, but the joking and laughter of the women was not a misappropriation of male prerogative.

[36] See Richardson 1974: 216–17 for the non-Greek sources. Plutarch tells of a Boeotian Hera cult (the Daedala) in which a priestess of the goddess tears the veil from a statue on an ox-cart, and then bursts out laughing. The mythical commentary on this, that the goddess herself was originally duped into jealous rage by Zeus' mischievous construction of a veiled statue, resembling a bride, and that her laughter was in relief at her discovery of the wooden dummy and not a real girl, does not necessarily have anything to do with the ritual or its "original" meaning(s). One may note here also the "exposure" motif (in modified form), followed by laughter. Reinach (1912) discusses the Plutarch passage, which is found in Eusebius *Praep. evang.* 3.1.6. Cf. Paus. 9.3.

up representations of male and female organs —while outside the building or sacred area the (male) archons, who had prepared the tables within for the women, spoke of the gifts of Demeter to mortals.[37] The symmetry suggests that men and women felt themselves to be cooperating on the same project, and engaging in analogous activities. At the same time, women could joke with greater freedom in the absence of men. Winkler's essay on the Adonia has begun a fruitful line of speculation about such joking. Among other things, women in such cultic contexts might have joked about the relatively insignificant role of the male in the reproductive process. Winkler acknowledged, however, that he might still be "overly preoccupied with phallic issues of interest to men."[38]

Legitimate Greek established semantic and behavioral boundaries, whereas this cultic speech broached boundaries—of decorum and respect for others. In a competitive society the dangers of ricocheting mockery were great—for men as well as for women—and ancient theorists stressed norms of responsible behavior.[39] Mockery, insults, and obscenity were tolerated even for men only in certain contexts—cults, festivals, and banquets. Suspension of adult responsibilities and restraints was temporary; as Anacharsis, Solon's friend, said: "Be merry, that you may be serious."[40]

What applied to "respectable" men applied even more strictly and narrowly to "respectable" women, although in the case of women the philosophers usually did not engage in direct admonitions, which were seen as the responsibility of a woman's male relatives. It was the literary iambic tradition that explicitly enacted control of women's behavior. This seems paradoxical at first glance, given iambic's origin in outrageous speech, especially among women. But cults' excesses, in their very extravagance, emphasized the different norms in the world outside cult. Indeed, the iambic literary tradition was constructed around a series of imagined exchanges in which the iambic poet proved himself by quelling someone who had insulted him. Thus iambic literature not only exemplified excess, it defined the field of reference, set the limits, and spelled the consequences of excessive speech

[37] Schol. to Lucian *Dial. meret.* 6.1 (Rabe 1906: 279–81).

[38] Winkler 1990b: 206. But see Abu-Lughod 1986: 129, where she describes an old Bedouin woman mocking the male lack of a womb (and, therefore, lack of compassion) and the inadequacy of the penis as a womb substitute.

[39] See Grant 1924. E.g., Periander 10 ζ 15 DK: "revile with the expectation of becoming a friend"; Pythagoras 58 D 6 DK (on avoided excesses of mirth or gloom); Plato *Leg.* 7.816–17 (serious men should understand the comic in order to appreciate the serious, but they themselves should not participate actively in the comic); Plato *Resp.* 2.388E (the Guardians should not indulge in laughter, and worthy people and gods should not be represented as overcome with mirth). See also Arist. *Eth. Nic.* 1128a1–b9 on the need for restraint in mockery (this passage is discussed in Edwards 1991). Aristotle contrasts *aischrologia* as Old Comedy's source of humor with *hyponoia* ("innuendo") in New Comedy.

[40] Arist. *Eth. Nic.* 1176b33 cites the quote from Anacharsis.

and behavior. Stories succeeding the *Hymn to Demeter* portrayed the suicide of the *korē* ("young girl") Iambe, *aischrōs hubristheisa*—"shamefully abused" —by some unnamed practitioner of iambic *hubris*—undoubtedly the literary kind.[41] Similarly, the poet Archilochus punished Neobule ("Miss Change of Heart") daughter of Lycambes for her rupture, or her father's rupture, of her betrothal to Archilochus. According to the Archilochean tradition, the "Daughters of Lycambes" committed suicide following the poet's insults.[42] We also hear of male victims of iambic (Hipponax prompted the suicides of the sculptors Bupalus and Athenis when he responded to their caricatures of him). These tales vaunt the superior firepower of the iambic poet over the visual artist, whereas the Iambe and Lycambid stories seem different in implication. *Hubris* or "stepping over the line" for women tended to fall within the field of sexual morality; sexual speech or sexual initiatives resulted in being branded a slut by the iambic poet.[43]

Women were believed to require control because they were not self-regulating, like men.[44] Beginning with Pandora, women were portrayed as unwholesomely verbal.[45] Yet their worrisome proclivities meant that their use of obscenity was believed to have a power denied to men. Sexual and transgressive natures gave them an affinity with sexual and transgressive speech. At the same time, since the rules governing speech were more stringent in the case of women, the power released by women breaking those rules was proportionately greater.

Women also held within them potentially explosive secrets, knowing— as no one else could—the paternity of the children they brought to birth. "Speaking the unspeakable" (*aporrhēta* or *arrhēta*), the repressed or concealed thing, mirrored their ability to unlock the womb and its secrets: the power to give birth, and to affirm or deny paternity.

Men's sense of tension between the nuisance and value of women and their speech is tellingly witnessed by Semonides' iambic diatribe against wives.[46] The poem opens with the word "Apart" (*khōris*): "It was apart (*khōris*) that

---

[41] Schol. Hephaistion 281.8 Consbruch [1906] 1971. See West 1974: 26; Eust. ad *Od.* 11.227. In these suicide stories, Iambe is described as a girl. Others, deriving from the Hipponactean tradition, portray her as an old woman whose insults to Hipponax inspired him to name the iambic meter, without any ill effects for Iambe (see Rosen 1988; Hipponax test. 21 a–d Degani 1983).

[42] West 1989–92, 1: 63–64; 1974: 25–28.

[43] Neobule is harshly characterized as a coarse slut in Archilochus fr. 196a (the Cologne epode), for example.

[44] Carson 1990.

[45] On modern Greek perceptions of women as gossipmongers, together with some ancient evidence, see Hunter 1994: 99. Hesiod (*Op.* 78) describes how Hermes invested Pandora with "lies and wheedling words."

[46] Semonides fr. 7, cited by Stobaeus 4.22. Hubbard (1994) argues for a late sixth-century date.

god made the mind of women."[47] Beneath an apparent link between men and women lay a gulf. *Women's actions and speech invariably sprang from an alien source.* The following lines divide this "foreign matter" into its constituents. The female mind derives from the pig, vixen, dog, mud, sea, donkey, weasel, mare, or monkey. These "types" are variously hateful and hatefully verbal; the dog woman is gossipy and loud (12–20); the vixen utters an unpredictable mixture of bad and good things (7–11); nearly all women like to gossip about sex (90–91); all wives pick fights at home (103–5).

The bee is the last creature specified, the (arguable) exception that proves the rule (Sem. fr. 7.83–93, my italics):

> And one kind of woman (he made) from a bee; in getting her
> a man is lucky; on her alone blame does not alight.
> At her hands life blooms and grows.
> In affection she grows old with her loving spouse,
> having borne a fair and glorious family.
> She is distinguished among all women,
> and a divine grace encircles her.
> She takes no joy in sitting among women,
> *where they speak of sexual things.*
> Wives such as this Zeus gives as a grace to men,
> the best and the most *resourceful.*

The bee's final epithet—*poluphradestatē*—means "most resourceful," "most eloquent," "most talked of," or "most intelligent." In general, of course, being talked about was not a desirable quality in a wife. If one considers the other interpretation, there are problems as well. In Hesiod's *Theogony* the epithet describes the deceitful words of Gaia, which enabled Zeus to defeat Cronus when the father mistook stones for his own offspring.[48] Bergren describes this trick as "the primary *mētis,* the first imitation, one that seems to symbolize a suppositious child." *Mētis* was a type of discriminatory intelligence—as well as a type of trickery—that was characteristically female, and that underlay women's power over language: "Only the female has the knowledge necessary to tell the true from the false heir, but it is this very knowledge that also makes her able to substitute for the truth, a false thing that resembles it."[49]

Semonides' own language thus was freighted with misogyny that per-

---

[47] Lloyd-Jones (1975: 63) explains that *khōris* may mean either "apart" from men or "in discrete categories," "apart from each other." He prefers the former because then the poem makes a weightier opening statement, and the singular genitive "of woman" makes more sense if the poet is beginning with a single category and not many.

[48] Hesiod *Theog.* 494. The only other occurrence of the word in early epic poetry is in Hesiod fr. 310 M-W, where the Muses are described as making a man πολυφραδέοντα . . . θέσπιον αὐδήεντα ("very eloquent (?), marvelous of voice").

[49] Bergren 1983: 74 and passim.

vaded the Greek literary tradition. Indeed, the poem concludes with a powerful warning: the wife who seems most impeccable is destined to betray her husband (109–11).

The bee woman causes life to flourish, nonetheless. The words *thallei* ("blooms") and *epaexetai* ("grows") evoke Demeter's patronage of human and agrarian fertility. A scholiast to Pindar noted that the name *melissai* ("bees") was given to priestesses of Demeter—and by extension priestesses of other divinities were called bees "because of the creature's purity."[50] Apollodorus of Athens observed that priestesses of Demeter were known as bees since Demeter had taken refuge with king Melissos and his sixty daughters on Paros following the rape of Persephone.She gave the girls the cloth that Persephone had been weaving (*ton tēs Persephonēs histon*), and told them first of Persephone's fate and about the mysteries. Whence comes the name "bees" for women who celebrate the Thesmophoria.[51]

Greek women ideally stayed home, prepared and preserved household stores, and avoided public notice and speech, literary or political. *Aidōs* ("shame")—a sense of one's "place"—was the moral equivalent of this thrift and reticence. In reality, however, women needed constantly to move in and out of the house—like bees, whose accumulation of nectar required them to cross the threshold of their home.[52] Most of all, religious cults obliged

[50] For bees in antiquity, Cook 1895 is thorough, although he does not include Apollodorus (see next note). Bees were associated with Artemis and Demeter. Pindar (*Pyth.* 4.60) calls the Pythia "the Delphic Bee," to which the scholiast (ad loc.; Drachmann 1910, 2: 112 13) remarks: "Elsewhere he [Pindar] calls those involved with divine and mystic affairs 'Bees' [Pindar fr. 158]; he rejoices in the sacred bees. Mnaseas from Patrae [?] is the first to mention that they called those who perform sacred duties 'Bees,' since they caused flesh-eating men to cease, persuading them to turn to the fruit of trees; at this time a certain Melissa, having been the first to discover the honey comb, ate it, and mixing it with water, drank it, and she taught the other women. She called the creatures *melissai* after her own name, and she built the greatest fortification [for them?]. They say that these things happened in the Peloponnese. For the shrine/cult of Demeter is not honored without *numphai* [young, marriageable girls/bee-pupae] because these were the first to inform [people] about fruit and to end cannibalism and to contrive clothing from raw materials, because of their modesty; nor is any marriage celebrated without *numphai*, but we worship these first, because of the tradition." The scholion goes on to mention the fact that priestesses of Demeter are most properly called "Bees," even though priestesses of other divinities are named "Bees" by extension of the use.

[51] Apollodorus of Athens *FGrH* 244 F 89 (Jacoby 1923–58). Detienne ([1974] 1981: 100) discusses the story. Callimachus (*Hymn to Apollo* 110–12) describes certain Melissai—only those who are pure—who perform a *hydrophoria* ("water-carrying") in honor of Dēō or Demeter. At Theocritus *Id.* 15. 94, Persephone is addressed by the euphemistic title *Melitōdēs* ("Honey-sweet Lady"). A scholion to this passage notes that Melitodes was a euphemism for Persephone because her priestesses were known as bees. Persephone is called *Meliboia* by Lasus of Hermione, who is cited by Athenaeus (624e).

[52] Vergil in the *Georgics* (4.33–36) describes the ideal hive; it should be made of bark or willow patched with clay, and its entrances should be as narrow as possible to preserve an even temperature within; a nice balance between containment and accessibility.

women to engage in public activities vital for the community, but necessarily compromising the "ideal" self-containment of the *oikos* and the women in it.[53]

A story told by Servius exemplifies this tension between containment and useful interaction with the world.[54] An old woman living at the Isthmus, Melissa, refused to divulge the secrets of Demeter's rites, entrusted to her by the goddess. The local women, enraged when she refused to tell them, tore her apart. Demeter sent a plague to the neighborhood, and caused bees to be born from Melissa's body. Her body, emblem of courageous reticence *and* extreme disclosure, became a hive (the first?) in this account.

Semonides railed against women from the standpoint of the single household, where *one* woman was both necessary (for children, above all) and an embarrassment or nuisance. Yet bees are the only truly *communal* animal on his list. Their usefulness depends on cooperation with each other outside their individual homes.

The bee's characteristics, expressed and unexpressed by Semonides, evoke contradictions in women's roles. Semonides commends "bee women" as superior because they do *not* enjoy talking about sex (*aphrodisioi logoi*), yet sexual speech was central to the Thesmophoria and other cults of Demeter.[55] The poem's recognition of women as agents and speakers within the cult that inspired iambic is perceptible as a faint outline beneath the harsh iambic cartoons.

THE JOKING: CONTENT

We lack evidence regarding the *content* of women's sexual and abusive speech, only characterizations of it, often by men distant in time and unsympathetic to Demeter's cult.[56] Women's oaths and their use of formal speech differed slightly from those of men, inasmuch as we can judge from our (male) sources.[57] It is impossible to determine whether the actual obscene terms used by the women would have differed from those employed by men in cults of Dionysos and elsewhere.[58] When one looks at obscen-

---

[53] See Sissa [1987] 1990; Reeder 1995 (esp. Lissarrague 1995) on women as containers, women and containers. I am not suggesting that Greek women did not leave their homes, but that there was an ideology of "containment" pertaining to respectable women. See Cohen 1991 on this distinction, and Josine Blok's contribution to this volume.

[54] Servius ad Verg. *Aen.* 1.430.

[55] Bees were reputed to reproduce asexually; see Arist. *Gen. An.* 10.759–60; Verg. *G.* 4.198–99.

[56] But see note 5 on Sappho (above).

[57] On distinctive aspects of women's speech in Euripides, see McClure 1995.

[58] On distinctive aspects of women's speech in general, see Sommerstein 1995.

ity in the comic poets and orators, one uses mostly double entendres, drawn from everyday life.[59] The category of what we call "four-letter words" is relatively small. It is possible that women developed an exclusive vocabulary of such words, now inevitably lost, but I suspect that such a vocabulary, if it existed, was not large. We know from a fragment of Eupolis that women's word for the chamberpot was *skaphion;* no doubt there were a few such terms circulating among women.[60] The vessel used by men, the *amis,* may have had a narrow opening at the top and thus been unsuitable for women. In fact Mnesilochus, disguised as a woman in Aristophanes' *Thesmophoriazusae,* speaks as if an *amis* were preferable, thus betraying himself as an imposter, through his use of the man's term.[61]

Generally speaking, women's obscenity probably drew on their everyday vocabulary, words connected with spinning, weaving, food production.[62] Thus the section in the *Lysistrata* in which one woman wants to return home to "spread wool on the bed" and another wants to "shuck her flax" employs words describing routine domestic work—but of course, each expression bore a sexual double entendre.[63]

Plutarch cites a story about Thales of Miletus.[64] When Thales was in Eresos he heard his hostess singing to her handmill:

> Grind mill, grind;
> for Pittacus used to grind (or grinds)
> as he ruled mighty Mytilene.

The poem made a political joke—probably an obscene one, if *halei* (grind) means more than "oppress." It accompanied grinding grain in a pestle—a job usually done by a woman before baking. This "work song" relieved the effort and monotony of pounding grain: a humble task, and an appropriately satirical song for Demeter. Old comic fragments indicate that there were many such songs, sung by women as they ground barley or kneaded dough.[65] They were not performed in expressly cultic contexts, yet they surely echoed cultic *aischrologia.*

---

[59] Davidson (1997: 220) cites Aeschines on Timarchus (Aeschines 1.80). His (unintended) double entendre revealed him for the prostitute he was.

[60] Eupolis 53 KA—from the *Autolycus,* as cited by Pollux 10.45.

[61] Ar. *Thesm.* 633; see Henderson 1975: 191 for discussion.

[62] Henderson 1975: 2 and passim.

[63] Ar. *Lys.* 731–39. Holst-Warhaft (1995) cites modern Greek parallels from Tsouderou 1976 and Kassis 1980.

[64] Plutarch *Septem sapientium convivium* 14. See Campbell 1967 (*Carm. pop.* 869). The meter is lyric (choriambic).

[65] At Ar. *Nub.* 1357ff., Strepsiades recounts how his pretentious son refused to sing a Simonidean song during dinner, saying that to sing during meals was crude and old-fashioned "like an old woman grinding corn." In a fragment from the Aristophanic *Centaur* (287 KA), there is a reference to a kneading dance or *maktrismos,* performed by several women. The second *Thesmophoriazusae* of Aristophanes contained a reference to a song by women winnowing

THE THESMOPHORIA

Of Demeter festivals, the Thesmophoria—a fall sowing festival—is the best known and the most widespread, attested in at least thirty cities in Greece, Asia Minor, and Sicily.[66] It followed closely upon the Stēnia, and the series of rituals was believed to correspond with the events surrounding Demeter's loss of her daughter. Only women took part, although the festival enjoyed the financial and moral support of the men in the community. At the end of summer's drought, women called Balers (*antlētriai*) descended or lowered ropes into underground chasms (*chasmata*) or "chambers" (*megara*) and retrieved ritual remains thrown down earlier: piglets (tossed in live), pastries in the shape of male and female genitals, and pine branches.[67] These now-decayed objects they mingled with the seeds of next year's crop and spread on the ploughed fields in anticipation of the crucial fall rain and winter harvest.

Khoirion/khoiros ("piglet") was also a term for the vulva, and so the magical core of next year's crop was a symbolic and potent mixture of extremes: fertility, and death; the unripe youth of the piglet, and its decomposition: sexual immaturity, and overripeness or decay. The snakes thought to inhabit the underground pits and feed on the offerings similarly expressed paradoxical meaning. They were associated with death—but also with the

---

or hulling barley (352 KA). In a lost play by Nicophron (8 KA), someone calls on a flute girl (probably) to "play a pounding song." Some of these songs were probably obscene in nature: see Henderson 1975 on *spodein* ("crush") and *derein* ("flay"). Pherecrates' *Savages* (10 KA) describes the "good old days" before women had slaves and servants to do their housework, and before dawn you could "hear the whole village re-echo the sound of their grinding." Barley (*krithē*) could refer to the penis (*Peace* 962–67), and the term *heustra*, used of roasted barley, also applies in comedy to the *pudenda muliebra* or the loins (Cratinus 409 KA).

[66] See Lowe 1998 passim. Brumfield (1981: 70ff.) also discusses the difficulties in the principal source, a scholion to Lucian's *Dialogues of the Courtesans*. Parke (1977: 82–88) also discusses the Thesmophoria. See also Deubner 1932: 50–60; Prytz-Johansen 1975; Versnel [1992] 1993. Prytz-Johansen also disputes the connection of the festival with agrarian fertility by observing that on Delos and at Thebes, the Thesmophoria occurred two months earlier than in the rest of Greece. He sees in it a women's initiation rite. Foxhall (1995) also argues persuasively that women's relations with each other were crucial to the festival. Brumfield (1981: 79) notes difficulties of interpretation: "Any religious rite bears many meanings, and it is pedantic to insist on a single exact equation. That the main thrust of the rite was to regenerate the powers of fertility at the time of sowing, is evident." Humphreys ([1983] 1993: xxiv–xxv) makes a more skeptical statement about the festival and our readings of it: "It should not be taken as self evident that if a ritual refers to political organization, social categories, and agricultural processes, its 'original' concern must have been agricultural." Humphreys' skepticism notwithstanding, I believe, with Brumfield, that the evidence supports an agricultural basis to the Thesmophoria.

[67] Theodoretus (*Therapeutica* 3.84) mentions that models of female genitals were worshiped by women at the Thesmophoria.

miraculous ability to shed age and regain youth; the word *gēras* meant both old age and the skin that a snake sloughs off every spring.[68] The old age of the snake was a husk, from which youth reemerged The underground chasms or chambers, emblems of the vagina, simultaneously evoked the formlessness of decay, absorption, and death on the one hand, and fertility on the other.[69]

During the Thesmophoria the women withdrew to a place of their own and imitated an "ancient" way of life.[70] In some cases they built huts of leaves and pine branches; in Athens a building on the Pnyx, the Thesmophorion, was designated.[71] The women slept on couches of the *vitex castus* or withy. The Thesmophoria took three days at Athens (sometimes longer elsewhere): the Ascent, the Fasting or Middle Day, and the Feast of Fair Offspring. On the Middle Day, prisoners were released, lawcourts and council meetings were suspended, and the women lamented, fasted, and cursed anyone revealing the "things that may not be spoken."[72] They also joked and abused each other. The jesting among the women—who probably came from all walks of life, including slavery—drew them together and focused their generative powers.[73] Cleomedes compares the speech of the Thesmophorian women to that used in a brothel.[74] Diodorus Siculus—

[68] Aristotle *Hist. an.* 549b25. Aristophanes wrote a play called *To gēras* ("Old Age"—or "The Snakeskin"), datable perhaps to 412, and featuring a chorus of old men miraculously rejuvenated. On snakes and death, see Burkert [1977] 1985: 195.

[69] Aristophanes made reference to the "deep destruction" (*olethron ton bathun*) and "pit" (*barathron*) as terms for the female genitals (Ar. 332 KA and *Plutus* 431); cf. Henderson 1975: 139, on *barathron* as a term for the female genitals. See also Brumfield 1996: note 27, on the affinity between the vagina and the chasms of the Thesmophoria. Edwards (1991) discusses the connections between filth and decay on the one hand and fertility and wealth on the other, in the poetics of Aristophanes.

[70] Diodorus Siculus 5.4.7. On Eretria the women refrained from using fire, according to Plutarch (*Quaest. Graec.* 298b–c).

[71] In Athens the Thesmophoria was celebrated both at the city level and in at least four demes. See Osborne 1985: 171; Brumfield 1981: 70. MacDowell (1995) disputes the Pnyx as the site of the city Thesmophoria. See Henderson 1996: (92–93) for discussion and arguments in favor of the Pnyx.

[72] For the fasting at the Thesmophoria, see Plutarch *Mor.* 378E, *Dem.* 30.5. Holst-Warhaft (1992: 101) notes that modern Greek laments (made by women) also contain a strange mixture of elements: "The paradoxical nature of modern Greek laments, where anything from ribaldry to political satire can be woven into a dirge, remind us that Eros and Thanatos, like tears and laughter, were intimately associated in antiquity." See also Lardinois in this volume on wedding laments.

[73] Brumfield 1981: 84–88, for the evidence. Her conclusion is: "The festival was open to all women, and in a sense was the responsibility of all; the community's life depended on it" (88). See also Prytz-Johansen 1975: 81 (in contrast to Detienne's influential [1979] 1989 piece).

[74] Cleomedes 2.1 (p. 166.7 Ziegler [1891]). Yet ritual chastity was required of the female participants. Schol. ad Soph. *OC* 681; Pliny *HN* 24.59. With regard to the Skira (for which there is no explicit evidence for *aischrologia*), Philochorus, a fourth-century Attidographer, mentions that the women ate garlic so as to remain chaste (Photius s.v. *Tropēlis*). In some ver-

describing the Sicilian Thesmophoria—and Apollodorus explain the festival's coarse abuse in terms of the joking that cheered Demeter when she was grieving for Kore (Persephone). The women also beat each other with pieces of bark (the *morotton*)—a ritual associated with fertility magic.[75]

It is likely that the women broke their fast by drinking the *kukeōn*, a mixture of partially ground barley and pennyroyal in water, drunk in cultic and sometimes in secular contexts.[76] The pennyroyal in the *kukeōn* was known for its various reproductive functions, including opening the uterus for cleansing, hysteria, stimulating the onset of menses, abortion, stimulation of childbirth, and the expulsion of the afterbirth. As many ancient writers observed, and as some modern studies suggest, the *vitex castus* also had gynecological functions, including regulation of menstruation, encouragement of conception, labor, and lactation, treatment of uterine and ovarian problems, abortion.[77] Pine, which featured both in the sacrificial pits and in the temporary structures, also had a regulatory role in gynecological processes. Pine was known in antiquity as a contraceptive and an aid in lactation. Pomegranate seeds, whose chief function seems to have been as contraceptive and abortifacient, apparently also were consumed by the women at the Thesmophoria. Clement of Alexandria noted that the women were forbidden to eat "those seeds that had fallen on the ground"—presumably therefore they were eating others.[78] I suggest that those that fell on the ground were understood as being sacred to Persephone, the famously infertile bride of Hades, who consumed pomegranate seeds in the *Hymn*. Nixon concludes: "The references to pennyroyal and pomegranate in the *HHD* [the *Hymn*] (and to pine and vitex in allusions to the Thesmophoria) imply that any woman with knowledge of these plants could regulate her own reproductive life as she chose."[79] Nixon argues that, in the eyes of the women participants, the object of the festival need not have been "fertility" pure and simple, but rather a fertility that women controlled and managed. The "fair offspring" that were the festival's most publicly acknowledged objective might have been so precisely because of management and choice by women. Thus the Thesmophoria's objective for women need not simply have been the production of male heirs within a strongly patriarchal system, but also the handing down of critical and empowering gynecological

---

sions of the Thesmophoria, the women slept on the antaphrodisiac *lugos*—the *vitex castus* (agnus) or withy.

[75] Hesychius s.v. *morotton*.

[76] See Clinton 1992: 35; Delatte 1955: passim. Aristophanes refers to the *kukeōn* at *Peace* 712, where it is offered as a means of transition from abstinence (from sex and from nature's bounty generally) to indulgence.

[77] Nixon 1995.

[78] Clement *Protr.* 11.19.3.

[79] Nixon 1995: 92.

knowledge from older to younger women.[80] If one remembers Baubo's revelatory gesture, one may imagine how the analogous obscene joking fulfilled an educational function, among others.

We should expand our notions of what was possible at the Thesmophoria and similar festivals—beyond what seems broadly to serve the common weal: good harvests and new generations of citizens. First, as Nixon has demonstrated, we need to distinguish between "fertility"—broadly defined as "lots of children" or agricultural plenty—and *managed* fertility. Moreover, the Thesmophoria undoubtedly had the effect (and among women, the purpose) of re-forming and strengthening bonds among women, bonds that marriage might otherwise attenuate. Mothers, daughters, sisters, friends, and cousins would find each other at this and other festivals, even if geography and other constraints of married life had made it difficult for them to see each other daily. Joking rekindled and enhanced these bonds, as it does for us, at reunions of family or old friends.

Material evidence enhances our understanding of the Thesmophoria. A priestess's grave collection from the Taman peninsula includes terracotta figurines of grotesque old women and men; old women holding infants; a rooster, a sheaf of corn, and a pig; young women wearing crowns, or bearing vessels or baskets of loaves or fruit. Peredolskaya, who published these terracottas, judged them to be associated with the Eleusinian Mysteries. Clinton argued that the Taman figurines in fact were more likely to have been related to the Thesmophoria.[81] In addition to the Taman collection there are examples from Argos, Olynthus, Tarentum, the sanctuary of Demeter and Kore on the Acrocorinth, the necropolis at Meligunis Lipara in Sicily, Pantikapaion (Kerch), and other graves of the Bosphorus and Black Sea region.[82]

Peredolskaya described the grotesque face of one old woman as resembling a caricature mask of Old Comedy.[83] The bodies also, male and female, resemble the lumpish figures of comic actors. Thus the old women figurines display a protruding belly. Some scholars have argued that this is comic rotundity, but in a woman such a silhouette inevitably evokes a pregnancy—however incongruous.[84] Bakhtin saw their large bellies as a super-

[80] Ibid.: passim. Obscene joking can fulfill a similar instructive role on playgrounds today, as parents can attest.

[81] Peredolskaya 1964; Clinton 1992: 36: "The terracottas, however, insofar as they do suggest a Demeter cult, really show nothing that definitively pertains to the iconography of the Mysteries; they express fertility and parody, and point therefore to the Thesmophoria."

[82] Peredolskaya (1964: 5) cites finds at Argos, Olynthus, and Tarentum. On Acrocorinth, see Stroud 1968, and Bookides and Stroud 1997. The figurines on Acrocorinth have not been formally published.

[83] Peredolskaya 1964: 17.

[84] Webster ([1978] 1995) has studied a variety of grave figurines, among other artifacts, to cast light on Attic comedy. See also Bernabò-Brea and Cavalier 1965, and Orlandini 1967, for

natural pregnancy, the grotesque fecundity of a woman who seems destined only for the grave:

> In the famous Kerch terracotta collection we find figurines of senile pregnant hags. Moreover, the old hags are laughing. This is a typical and very strongly expressed grotesque. It is ambivalent. *It is pregnant death, a death that gives birth.* There is nothing completed, nothing calm and stable in the bodies of these old hags. They combine a senile, decaying and deformed flesh with the flesh of new life, conceived but as yet unformed. Life is shown in its twofold contradictory process; it is the epitome of incompleteness. And such is precisely the grotesque concept of the body.[85]

Given the Thesmophoria's paradoxical mixing of decay with premature life, and given the *Hymn to Demeter*'s tale of an ancient woman with unexpected powers of fertility, I believe with Bakhtin that these figurines expressed women's uncanny reproductive powers, agrarian and human. They are pregnant crones. These and other figurines represented characters in recurring cultic "dramas," now lost to us. One of the jokes that the pregnant crones represent is the discrepancy between women's own aging and often unlovely bodies and the ever-renewing life cycles over which they keep watch.

ANGER

In addition to mock hostility directed by the women at each other, Thesmophorian myths hint at serious hostility toward men.[86] Herodotus mentions that the Danaids brought the Thesmophoria from Egypt to Greece.[87] The Danaids were the fifty daughters of Danaus, who had quarreled with his brother Aegyptus over their joint rulership of Egypt. Danaus fled with his daughters to Argos, and foiled his brother's efforts at *rapprochement* by requiring his daughters to murder their husbands—Aegyptus' fifty sons—on their wedding night. All of the girls except Hypermnestra complied.

---

figurines of hags with swollen bellies in cultic contexts. Some scholars have interpreted this feature as "comic fat person" padding that actors wore, padding that remained the same whether or not they wore a female mask. But I believe that by insisting that (a) such figurines can *only* represent the comic actors of the Dionysian stage (as opposed to cultic "dramas," now lost to us), and that (b) the silhouette can *only* denote comic rotundity, we risk misinterpretation.

[85] Bakhtin 1968: 25–26, discussing the aesthetic of the grotesque—the antithesis of classical beauty.

[86] Burkert [1977] 1985: 244.

[87] Herodotus 2.171.

At Cyrene, King Battus is said to have been castrated by the Thesmophorian *sphaktriai* or "Sacrificers" because he attempted to spy on them.[88] The "Chalcidian Pursuit" was the name given to a mysterious element of the Thesmophoria that celebrated the pursuit of the enemy, following prayers of the women.[89] Yet at the same time, Aristophanes' parody of the Thesmophoria—with its tale of a male spy's *escape* from harm—was also true to the festival. Pausanias tells how Aristophanes of Messenia was overpowered and captured by the women celebrating the Thesmophoria— but that he was saved by the priestess of Demeter, who fell in love with him, a tale corresponding to the famous story of the rebellious Danaid, Hypermnestra.[90] Thus, Detienne's theory, that the stories of women's violence expressed male fear of gynocracy and of women wielding sacrificial knives, does not account for the complex meanings of the cult.[91] True, the Thesmophoria expressed the belief that an all-female group was essential to the functioning of the cult. At the same time, the mixed outcomes of the infiltration stories suggest that interaction between men and women might be bloody—but counterforces of trust, affection, and sexuality also operated. And interaction occured, albeit in defiance of prescribed rules. This paradox underlay the premise of "women alone."

Nonetheless, we would do well not to underestimate the Thesmophoria's darker side. There is a risk of attributing to Thesmophorian women *only* those thoughts and interpretations which somehow conformed to the official roles laid down for women by their society's public voice.[92] I wish to expand our notions of the Thesmophoria—*beyond* the perspective of what served the community: good harvests and "fair offspring," however defined. The abusive speech and flouting of other norms also may have been an end in itself, not only a means to the goals of the festival—which of course mattered to women as well as men. Perhaps such speech and action celebrated *grotesquerie* within a set of norms and values that was semi-

---

[88] Ael. fr. 44 = Suda A 4329, Θ 272, Σ 1590, 1714. Detienne [1979] 1989 talks of the bloody aspects of Demeter's rites.

[89] Semus, *FGrH* 396 F21 (Jacoby), and Hesychius s.v. χαλκίδιον δίωγμα.

[90] Pausanias 4.17.1.

[91] Detienne ([1979] 1989: 135) argues for a connection between the right to blood sacrifice and political power.

[92] In her work on the poetry of modern Bedouin women, Abu-Lughod distinguishes between a public discourse (belonging largely to men) and a private discourse, which includes *ghinnawa*—a poetry of sentiment, belonging especially to women and youths. The tender and vulnerable feelings expressed in such poetry are completely at odds with the more aggressive and honor-bound language of public discourse, including heroic poetry. She has criticized Bourdieu because sometimes he "takes a position granting official ideology a totalitarian role in structuring experience. The existence of two Bedouin discourses leads us to conclude that the dominant ideology of honor does not set the limits on the 'thinkable and the unthinkable,' or perhaps the 'feelable and unfeelable'" (Abu-Lughod 1986: 256).

independent of the male world. Alternatively, women's cultic speech may have included a more subversive agenda.

Scott has studied how "dominated" classes speak among themselves, and how this speech—the "private transcript"—differs from what they permit themselves to speak in public contexts.[93] Because such speech, often angry, contemptuous, and vengeful, is by definition dangerous if voiced in a public arena, historians—who typically belong to elites—ignore it, or may not even know about it. Rarely, under conditions such as revolt or carnival, such voices become publicly audible, so as to enter the permanent record. I suggest that the women of Athens—though not universally as downtrodden as some of the slave and serf societies studied by Scott—were, broadly speaking, a "dominated" group, and that their cults allowed a discreet but focused expression of such a "private transcript." The story of the murderous Danaids, the castration of Battus—and Aristophanes' angry Thesmophorian women using the festival to devise ways of punishing Euripides for revealing their naughty secrets—all reflect a genuine function of the women's festival that did not conform to "official" ideology. Moreover, such talk did *not* necessarily serve (the interests of those holding power) as a "safety valve," allowing women to "vent," before returning to their officially submissive roles.[94] As Scott has suggested of carnivals elsewhere, such occasions can be subversive, and always have the potential for getting out of hand.

In Aristophanes' *Lysistrata*, an outraged magistrate claims to recognize in the women's impromptu gathering on the Akropolis a "typical" women's cultic orgy, with drums and yelling for Sabazios and Adonis.[95] He apparently remembers how a group of women on the rooftop keened and yelled drunkenly for Adonis—the young consort of Aphrodite and a Semitic import god—*at the very time that* Demostratus—whose wife was one of the Adonis worshipers—was proposing troops for the Sicilian expedition in the Assembly.

Such expressive cults afforded women an opportunity to decry catastrophic political decisions. The Adonia was confined to women, yet ob-

---

[93] Scott 1990.

[94] I do not agree with Burkert ([1977] 1985: 258–59) and others who maintain that festive activities invariably reinstate societal order. For example, Aristotle (fr. 558) tells of how a *kōmos* arranged by some young men to the house of the widely envied Telestagoras on Naxos led to riots and the establishment of a new regime on the island.One of the Pisistratids, Hipparchus, insulted Harmodius, who had rejected his love, by refusing to allow Harmodius' sister to carry a basket in the Panathenaea (Thuc. 6.54–58). Harmodius and Aristogeiton then planned to overthrow Hipparchus on the day of the festival, "since they could bear arms without exciting suspicion" (Thuc. 6.56.2). Thus we see that even a great state-sponsored festival could furnish both an inspiration and an occasion for revolution.

[95] Ar. *Lys.* 387ff.

servable by men, since it took place on rooftops.[96] In fact, this "jinxing" of the Sicilian expedition by women's voices probably was contrived by Aristophanes, and was not historical.[97] Yet if Aristophanes invented the connection or was hinting that the magistrate had imagined it, it is nonetheless suggestive. Mock lamentation for a boy prematurely slain assumed new meaning in the dark days of the war.[98] The Adonia was celebrated informally by neighborhood women in summer; they could choose exactly when to hold it. The "memory" that eerie wailing and laughter had interrupted a crucial session of the Assembly suggests that the city's center of power was perceived to have shifted, or lost its integrity. Women's voices were being raised—and heard—in unnerving counterpoint to the men's debate in the Assembly.

WOMEN'S "SHAMEFUL" SPEECH—AS PERCEIVED BY WOMEN

Women's obscene and abusive cultic speech was variously described in ancient sources: *aischrologia, arrhēta, aporrhēta,* and verbs connoting abuse, mockery, and blasphemy: *loidorein, blasphēmein, diaskōptein.* The terms *arrhēta* and *aporrhēta* refer to what should not or cannot be spoken. This taboo was interpreted in different ways. The subject was not supposed to be divulged, and/or the words were so shameful as to make it virtually impossible to utter them under normal conditions.[99] Both readings of *arrhēta* challenge the modern scholar.

Obviously, taboos on speech or reference impede the transmission of information and render suspect the accounts that do survive. If we consider the implications of *shameful* speech—*aischro-logia*—we also face difficulties.[100] Whose notion of shamefulness are we seeing? The famous debate between Creon and Antigone illustrates how a woman, focused on her obligations to family, contested the king's rebuke for breaking the law: "Are you not ashamed (*ouk epaidei*)?" "No," she answers, "it is no shame (*ouk ais-*

---

[96] Winkler 1990b. In the Adonia, the women's joking formed part of Aphrodite's worship.

[97] Servais 1981.

[98] On the changing meaning of carnival, see Gilmore 1987: ch. 6. See also Simms 1998 on the Adonia.

[99] Brumfield 1996: 67.

[100] Henderson (1975) has argued that the Roman notion of the obscene (*obscaenum*) differed from that of the Greeks. The Romans, like ourselves, viewed the obscene as something filthy, contaminating, whereas the Greek focus was on shame. Yet the Greeks did worry about corruption. Aristotle at *Politics* 1336b4, in talking of the education of small children, recommends banning *aischrologia*, since talk can develop into action. Plutarch (*De liberis educandis* 9F) cites Democritus as saying that "the word is the shadow of the deed" in the course of Plutarch's own recommendation to keep one's sons from using foul language.

chron) to revere one's blood kin."[101] Their lethal conflict is reflected in their opposing applications of virtually the same term.

Another episode reflecting different notions of shame appears in Athenaeus' *Deipnosophistae* ("Cultured Diners"), in which the diners exchange stories about witty courtesans. Lais, an Athenian Mae West, was renowned in such (pseudo?) biographical stories and celebrated by the comic poets:

> They say that Lais, the Corinthian woman, once saw Euripides in a garden, having his writing tablet and stilus hanging by his side. "Tell me, Mr. Poet," she said, "what did you have in mind when you wrote in a tragedy: 'Get out, you evildoer'?" Euripides was stunned by her gall and said: "As for you, what are you, madam? Are you not an evildoer yourself?" She laughed and replied: "But what is evil, if it does not seem so to those who engage in it?"[102]

Lais asks Euripides to explain to her what he intended when he had Jason call Medea an *aischropoios* ("evildoer"). Thus the famous Corinthian *hetaira* considers a dramatic insult delivered to another famous—and infamously assertive—foreign woman. Lais' reply to the poet's rebuke also quotes Euripides, a line from the lost play *Aeolus*.[103]

The insult directed by Jason at Medea occurs at the end of the play, after she has revealed the children's bodies to him. His use of the term is unambiguous, but Lais is leading the poet into a trap, because *aischropoios* can also mean "fellator/fellatrix," a meaning that Euripides is quick to acknowledge as he retorts, "And that's what you are yourself!"[104] Lais does not deny the charge—but she disputes the meaning attributed by Jason to *aischros*. One's evaluation of behavior will depend on one's perspective. She repudiates Euripides' definition of shameful behavior and reveals—at least as ancient audiences might see it—inconsistencies in his thinking. How could he, the (in)famous moral relativist, insist on a transcendent value to *aischros*?

Lais was a foreigner and a *hetaira*. In her verbal cleverness (for which the great *hetairai* were famous) and in her relativistic argument she resembles the sophists.[105] Euripides himself was regarded as something of a sophist, making her trap for him ironically apt. Yet she was also a woman living in Athens, someone with whom Athenian women could have felt an affinity—just as the women in Euripides' play first expressed sympathy with Medea when they discovered how Jason had treated her. She would have participated in some religious festivals, together with Athenian citizen women of

---

[101] Soph. *Ant.* 510–11.

[102] Athenaeus 582c–d.

[103] This line was also mocked by Aristophanes at *Frogs* 1475.

[104] Eust. *Il.* 2.677, line 16; Hesychius D entry 687, line 1; Sch. in Ar. *Nub.* 296b1; sch. in Ar. *Plut.* 314–15; Suda Θ entry 204, line 1.

[105] See Davidson 1997 on *hetairai*.

all ranks, and slaves.[106] Her questioning of a male poet's use of *aischros* in a dramatic address by a male character to a female raises the possibility that a term like *aischrologia* reflected a male perspective. Women need not have felt shame in their Thesmophorian speech, characterized as being like that used in a brothel. They would have recognized its shock value within the larger (male-run) culture, but this does not mean that they themselves fully subscribed to the values of that culture.

CONCLUSION: WHAT THIS SPEECH COULD DO

If we look again at the story thought to inspire women's cultic *aischrologia*, we see how it subverts "real world" logic. Demeter abruptly ceased from lamenting her dead daughter; Iambe spoke with disrespect to a (divine) guest. The somber *Mater Dolorosa* turned into genial Aphrodite, indifferent to sexual embarrassment.[107]

With her jokes Iambe also could be said to have restored to completeness Demeter, the mother goddess shorn of her child. She caused Demeter to acknowledge her continuing role in the world and her undiminished powers of life. Demeter had disguised herself—almost as her own opposite. Yet in describing the old woman, the poem signals not a crone, antithesis of the earth goddess, but a double presence. She is old and young, feeble and strong, beautiful and a stranger to Aphrodite; she is a giver of life and an omen of death. Most importantly—as Iambe reveals—Demeter is a childless mother, simultaneously fertile and infertile, an elderly woman who can breastfeed an infant.[108] In causing her to laugh, Iambe evokes Demeter's persistent strength—within her feeble age.

This fantastic "doubleness" confronted a widespread pattern of distinction and antithesis, which shaped Greek logic, and structured most speech

[106] See note 73 above. I believe, following Brumfield (1981: 84–88), that the evidence does not support the conclusion that the Adonia festival was confined to wellborn women. See, e.g., Menander *Samia* 35–48, where a Samian *hetaira* became friends with, and celebrated the Adonia together with, Athenian women.

[107] I am thinking of the tale of Ares and Aphrodite, narrated at *Od.* 8.266–366. Only the male gods chose to witness the trap in which Hephaestus had snared his faithless wife Aphrodite with her lover, Ares. The goddesses all stayed home "out of *aidōs* [modesty]." The male gods laugh their "unquenchable laughter"—and Aphrodite herself, when released and hastening away to Paphos, is called *philommeidēs* or "laughter-loving" by the poet.

[108] The daughters of Celeus use the term *ektrephein* (166) when they speak of Demeter's role in the life of the child Demophoon; Metaneira asks Demeter to nurture (*trephein*) Demophoon, so that he might reach the *hēbēs metron*, or "marker of maturity." *Trephein* and *ektrephein* refer to the early nurturance of children: a term that includes, but is not confined to, breastfeeding. On the other hand, Demeter's reply, in which she claims to be taking on the responsibility "as you instruct" (226), includes a promise to place the child beneath her breast, and employs the term "nurse" (*tithēnē*, 227), which tends to be restricted to the sense of "wet nurse."

except that of cult. Praxiteles made two statues: a weeping matron and a laughing whore.[109] In the literary world, tragedy abstracted certain themes from cult's *mélange*, comedy and satire accruing motifs from the other end of the spectrum.[110] Yet the women of the Thesmophoria, in remembering Demeter and reenacting Iambe's words, *mingled* grief and raucous laughter; their reaction constituted a shifting chiaroscuro of outrage and hilarity, despair and hope, rage and tenderness. Within a world organized and articulated by antithesis (expressed by Greeks' ubiquitous particles *men* and *de*), the Thesmophorian women derived energy from this doubleness.[111]

This subversiveness extended to time itself. In the "real world" the future rolls continuously into the present and the past, and nothing obstructs or deters it. In the real world all things end, and every accomplished task evokes that final ending, which is death. Yet cults could interrupt or even reverse the running of the clock.[112] Demeter gave to the women of Paros the cloth that Persephone had been weaving at the time of her abduction— surely an *incomplete* web, symbolizing both the nuptial veil and the shroud for which she was not ready and never would be ready.[113] Persephone thereafter lived between the living and the dead. The women celebrating the Thesmophoria commemorated her suspended state, and that of her mother, whose laughter at Iambe's jests established the magical timelessness of the cult. Their recurring mockery and jokes took place in this timeless state, and indeed recreated a parallel universe, in which the crude, the unfinished, the unhierarchical prevailed, and the "shameful" workings of reproductive processes emerged ebulliently into the light.

---

[109] Pliny *HN* 34, 70.

[110] Adrados [1972] 1975.

[111] Bergren (1983) argues that in archaic Greece, the female was perceived as the source of both truth and lies. This power was then appropriated by the male, who typically wished to demonstrate the truth of his own speech.

[112] Csapo and Miller (1998) analyze ancient concepts of time, as handled by classicists in the last century. They distinguish between "aristocratic" time, that of an unchanging ideal past, reproducing itself in the deeds of noble families (as per Pindar), and "democratic" time, reflecting change and distance from the past. "Cultic" time, as I am analyzing it here, is closer to aristocratic time, reenacting a moment—like that of Demeter's laughter—that steps outside of time's river, and stands still.

[113] Penelope's nightly unraveling of Laertes' shroud also surely is ritual magic, not just a trick; she turns back the clock. In art, one of Persephone's attributes was the *kalathos*—a wicker basket with a narrow base and broad mouth, used for storing raw wool. See Lissarrague 1995: 95–96. The *kalathos* is portable—suitable for Persephone's peripatetic existence. Also, the *kalathos* represents the earliest stage of wool's processing. Persephone has moved back from weaving to the process that turns raw wool into thread. Winkler (1990b: 208) mentions rituals of North African women weaving cloth and their connection with birth, child-rearing, and death. Zeitlin (1982a) cites Artemidorus 3.36 in this context: "Weaving on a loom is like life; he who dreams he is just beginning to weave is predicting a long life; he who is at the moment of cutting off will have a short one; and the cut-off cloth signifies death."

CHAPTER NINE

Women's Voices in Attic Oratory

MICHAEL GAGARIN

IN SEEKING information about the lives of women[1] in classical Athens, scholars have long looked to the speeches of the Attic orators (c. 420–320 B.C.E.), which commonly portray women as restricted, physically to their homes and socially to the company of other women, children, and a few close male relatives. One speaker, for example, protests his opponent's intrusion into the women's quarters of his house, where the intruder encountered "my sister and nieces, who have lived such proper lives that they are ashamed to be seen even by close [male] relatives" (Lysias 3.6).[2] This picture of seclusion was first challenged by Gomme, who cited (among other things) the strong independent women of Athenian drama.[3] In subsequent studies, the differences among scholars' views of women's lives in classical Athens have in part depended on the different weight given these two sources—those who draw on tragedy are in general more "optimistic" about the power of women, while those who rely on oratory tend to grant women a more limited, largely powerless, role.[4]

Whichever one's view, it is generally assumed that in comparison with that of drama, the evidence of oratory can be taken more at face value, at least with regard to general social rules and attitudes, since litigants presumably wish to appear (at least) to be upholding the rules and values of the community,[5] whereas sentiments expressed by dramatic characters may or may not be consistent with community standards. But how different, in fact, are the two genres in this regard? Scholars recognize that standards such as the extreme seclusion of women implied by the speaker in Lysias 3 (quoted

---

[1] Unless otherwise specified, "women" will hereafter designate female citizens (or, if "citizens" is thought to apply only to males, then daughters of citizens).

[2] I will not include the Greek text except where the specific words are important. For the orators I use the Oxford Classical Texts except for Antiphon, where I use Gagarin 1997.

[3] Gomme [1925] 1937: esp. 91–96.

[4] See Pomeroy 1973: 140–43; Just 1989: 4–5. As some scholars are beginning to recognize, the roles assigned to women are actually not so dissimilar in the two genres (Gould 1980; Seidensticker 1995). On the representation of women in tragedy, see also Griffith's contribution to this volume.

[5] See Dover 1974: 13–14, on the evidence of oratory being unreliable for what in fact happened, but reliable (within limits) for what an ordinary Athenian could believe had happened.

above) are ideals, and further that these ideals are sometimes more persuasive than descriptive and may not correspond to actual values held by the jurors.[6] Moreover, in some respects the characters portrayed in oratory are just as much their authors' creations as are the characters in drama.[7] Specifically with regard to women and the voices they are sometimes given, we must bear in mind that, just as in drama, these words were authored by a male (the logographer or poet), were performed by a male (the litigant or actor), and sought the approval of an entirely or predominantly male audience (the jurors or spectators).[8] Thus, the relation of these characters and their words to reality[9] is problematic.

In light of these considerations, some recent reassessments of the evidence of oratory may need to be questioned. The most forceful challenge to the traditional view that women in oratory are essentially powerless comes from Walters (1993), who argues that women had more power than is generally realized. His prime example is the daughter of Diogeiton in Lysias 32, who "was able to motivate events in her male-dominated world, indeed to take control of events, not the least of all by having her say" (199–200).[10] Like virtually all respectable women in oratory, this woman is unnamed,[11] and to avoid the repeated circumlocution "daughter of Diogeiton," I will call her "D's daughter," or "D. d." (Didi) for short. Walters draws especially on the long speech Didi gives on behalf of her children (32.12–17), which he considers an "outstanding example of female eloquence" (195) that must have had "both credibility and verisimilitude" (199).

Walters does not explicitly defend his assumption that the evidence of oratory represents "social reality," but he contrasts oratory with tragedy, in which, he argues, representations of women are fictional in part "because they are totally and solely the product of Athenian men" (194). As noted above, this distinction is questionable at best, and some recent critics of the

---

[6] See, e.g., Dover 1974: 14, on the standard of propriety that women did not use makeup for a month after a death in the family: "This passage [Lysias 1.14] tells us . . . that the speaker wished . . . to insinuate into the jurors the idea that they too took it [this standard] for granted." Dover also acknowledges (14 n. 10) that speakers may misread the jurors' actual values.

[7] It may be going too far, however, to conclude that "the daughter of Diogeiton [in Lysias 32—see below] is a character created by Lysias, just as the Samian woman is a character created by Menander" (Vial 1985: 59).

[8] In my view, citizen women did not attend the theater, though some metic women probably did; see Goldhill 1994b.

[9] For the reality of "reality," see Searle 1995.

[10] Cf. Just (1989: 131), who maintains (citing Lacey 1968: 172–74) that Diogeiton's daughter and other examples confirm that "the relationship between a man and his wife, sister, mother, or daughter could be extremely close and could also allow a good deal of *de facto* female authority."

[11] See Schaps 1977.

orators have developed a greater degree of skepticism about the verisimilitude of the events they portray; these may not be utterly fantastical or impossible, but a compelling narrative may succeed in disguising the essentially fictional nature of an event or character. Such skepticism underlies the very different approach to the portrayal of Didi taken by Foxhall (1996), who contrasts her with another widow with small children in the care of an unscrupulous guardian, namely Demosthenes' mother Cleobule.[12] This situation, as described in Demosthenes 27–30, is similar in many ways to that of Lysias 32, but in Foxhall's speculative but not implausible reconstruction, the two widows behaved very differently: Cleobule took control of the household after her husband's death, refusing to remarry and resisting her son's guardians at every turn, whereas Didi forfeited her authority by remarrying and raising a new family. Foxhall suggests that Didi's speech is "a fabrication" and that she was "given a script" by her children and son-in-law (should she not say by Lysias?), but she does not confront the paradox that the allegedly powerful Cleobule plays almost no role in Demosthenes' speech, whereas the apparently powerless Didi has a prominent role in Lysias' speech.

Clearly an assessment of Didi's real power will depend in part on the reality of her speech. Other opinions about the speech tend to range between the poles of realistic representation and complete fabrication,[13] but no one has established good grounds for holding any of these opinions. Perhaps we can never know for certain just what (if anything) Didi really said, but I think we can go beyond pure subjectivity. First, we can examine all instances of women "speaking" in the orators to determine whether any common features or patterns might provide clues to the reality of these voices. The number of such passages is relatively small. Although litigants frequently mention that a woman or women uttered some words,[14] in only nine cases are we given a significant number of actual words spoken by a woman, either in direct speech or in indirect speech that seems closely to represent direct speech.[15] I shall examine all nine. Second, we can seek to determine in each case what controls there might have been on the speaker's repre-

---

[12] We know Cleobule's name from a later Life of Demosthenes, not from his speeches.

[13] E.g., "Since all that she says is what we would expect under the circumstances, we may reasonably suppose that something along these lines was said, though the words will be those of Lysias" (Carey 1989: 211)—is there here an echo of Thucydides' famous assessment (1.22) of the speeches in his own work as representing "what was needed" (*ta deonta*) in words that are his own but keep as close as possible to the original? Cf. Usher 1976: 39: this speech "must rank as one of the finest pieces of female Athenian oratory outside Aristophanes, though it is scarcely credible for its realism."

[14] For example, "a woman claimed that he was her slave" (Lys. 23.10); "the seals were acknowledged by both his wife and mine" (Dem. 41.21); etc.

[15] These are (in the order discussed below) Lys. 32.12–17; Lys. 32.11; Lys. 1.15–16; Dem. 47.57; Antiph. 1.15–16; Dem. 55.24; Hyp. *Ath.* 1–4; Dem. 59.110–11; Lys. 1.12–13.

sentation—for example, how many other people witnessed the scene? As we shall see, in some cases there is no control at all; and even where the opposing litigant was at the scene, in no case would the speaker be constrained to cite a woman's words verbatim.

I begin with Didi's speech (Lysias 32.12–17), which is by far the longest. The case concerns the conduct of a certain Diogeiton. After the death of his brother Diodotus, Diogeiton became trustee of his estate and guardian of his young children, whose mother is Diogeiton's own daughter, Didi.[16] Thus Diogeiton is at the same time the orphans' paternal uncle and maternal grandfather—a not-surprising arrangement in fourth-century Athens. Although the speaker does not emphasize the fact, he provides enough information for us to learn that Didi has remarried and has children with her new husband, Hegemon. When the wards reach maturity, they accuse Diogeiton of fraudulently depleting their father's estate, and the case is presented to the jurors by their sister's husband (not by their stepfather Hegemon!). The speaker relates how, when the elder boy came of age, Diogeiton announced that the estate was almost entirely depleted, so that he could no longer care for the children, who would henceforth be on their own. This led to a family conference, in which their mother Didi criticized her father's treatment of his wards and urged him to take pity on them. The speaker devotes a sizable portion of his speech to this scene:

[12] When we had gathered, the woman [Didi] asked Diogeiton how he had the heart to treat the children in this way. "You are their father's brother and my father, making you their uncle and grandfather. [13] Even if you have no regard for any human being," she said, "you should have feared the gods. He gave you five talents on deposit when he set off—and I am willing to go anywhere this man may designate and swear an oath to this by the lives of these children and my later ones. I am not so wretched or so concerned about money that I would try to obtain my father's property illegally, and live out my life to the end having sworn a false oath by my children." [14] She then continued her indictment, showing that he had received nautical loans worth seven talents and 4,000 drachmas, and she displayed the accounts for these loans: for when the household was being divided and he was leaving Collytus for the

[16] A family tree may help sort out the complex relationships.

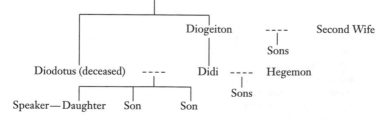

house of Phaedrus, the boys brought her a discarded ledger they had found. [15] She showed that he had also received 100 minas in mortgages on rental property and an additional 2,000 drachmas and furniture of considerable value; and further that they received grain from the Chersonese every year. "With all this money," she said, "you dared to claim that their father left just 2,000 drachmas and thirty staters, which had been left to me and which I gave to you when he died? [16] And then you thought you could just throw them out of your house, these grandchildren of yours, their clothes in tatters, without shoes, with no attendant, with no bedding, with no cloak, with none of the furniture their father left them, and without all the property he deposited with you. [17] And now you are raising the children you had with my stepmother in great comfort, with lots of money. This is the right thing to do, of course, but you do my children an injustice when you throw them out of your house and seek to have them appear without honor, in rags instead of riches. For this sort of conduct you have no fear of the gods, no shame before me (who knows everything), and no regard for your brother. You value every one of us less than money."

Although Diogeiton is apparently unswayed, the rest of the company departs in stunned silence (32.18), and almost all critics today find the speech very moving. Indeed, it employs many of the techniques of other forensic speeches and a full range of rhetorical effects, such as parallelism, repetition, anaphora, asyndeton, and direct address of the accused.[17] In fact, this is a miniature forensic speech encapsulating the full case against Diogeiton: Didi begins with a preliminary appeal referring to the intricate dual relationships in the family (cf. 32.5) and evoking a sense of piety. The narrative begins in 32.13 with the first specific figure (five talents) but is interrupted by Didi's offer to swear an oath, a common strategy of (male) litigants.[18] The narrative continues in 14 with more figures and (apparently) the presentation of documentary evidence.[19] It is picked up again at the beginning of 15, perhaps with more documentary evidence.[20] The speech ends with an extended peroration, including a direct appeal to Diogeiton, and again invokes fear of the gods.

In short, Didi here delivers a forensic speech in appropriate forensic language and style. To be sure, the scene is an informal private arbitration, and is thus quasi-forensic, so we may feel that this sort of speech would be ap-

---

[17] Cf. Usher 1965: 118: "The asyndetic anaphora with which [Diogeiton's daughter] describes the complete destitution of her family at his hands is one of the most forceful and pathetic passages in Lysias: in this passage there also seems to be a deliberate effort to avoid trochaic and iambic rhythms in favour of the nobler dactylic, spondaic and cretic."

[18] See Gagarin 1998: 43–45.

[19] Note 32.14: "she displayed" (*apedeixen*).

[20] 32.15: "she showed" (*apephēne*) may indicate a combination of speech and evidence.

propriate and is likely to represent what Didi actually said. But how did a respectable Athenian woman learn to speak in the language and style of forensic oratory? We have no evidence that women were educated in rhetoric; indeed, their ignorance of proper rhetoric is parodied in Aristophanes *Ecclesiazusae* (110–245), where the women in the Assembly instinctively use clearly marked women's talk[21] and have to be taught to speak like assemblymen. Only Praxagora already knows how to speak in the Assembly, and she gives the rather contrived explanation that she used to live near the Pnyx (where the Assembly met) and could overhear the speeches given there. Similarly, Lysistrata offers the explanation that she used to listen to her father's discussions with his male friends.[22] Both scenes strongly imply that women did not as a rule know how to speak on public issues.

Most men, of course, did not learn rhetoric through formal education but rather from direct experience in the Assembly or the courts, but women—at least citizen women—were not normally present in court any more than they attended meetings of the Assembly. It is not impossible that citizen women, particularly poor women, attended court in special situations, but social norms, reinforced by the rules of judicial procedure, prescribed a woman's absence.[23] Another possibility is that Didi may have learned rhetoric from the men in her family. Xenophon has Ischomachus say that his wife often listens to him practicing his pleadings and then gives her verdict on them (*Oeconomicus* 11.25), and the woman is such a model of virtue that he can never persuade her of something that is not true. But this little morality tale fits so neatly into Socrates' denunciation of rhetoric as making the weaker case the stronger (while at the same time reinforcing the picture of the woman's incorruptibility) that it seems unlikely to represent actual experience. The scene emphasizes the moral excellence of Ischomachus' wife and shows that good jurors cannot be persuaded by lies; it is not a paradigm for the training of Athenian women.

Finally, it seems very unlikely that women learned to speak this way among themselves in their not infrequent gatherings at festivals and other ritual occasions. In addition to the evidence of comedy noted above, modern research across many cultures shows that women speak differently among themselves than they do in the presence of men,[24] and nothing we know about Athenian women's participation in ritual events indicates that these would have provided them with any training in forensic speech.

[21] Marked primarily by their swearing oaths to female deities (155, 189). See further Sommerstein 1995; and McClure's introduction to this volume.

[22] Ar. *Lys.* 1126–27.

[23] See Gagarin 1998.

[24] Even in modern Western cultures where women's and men's lives are not so separate as they were in classical Athens, the two genders talk differently; see, e.g., Coates [1986] 1993; Tannen 1986.

Aristophanes' parody in *Ecclesiazusae* (see above) may not accurately represent features of women's speech, but his point that women do not know the male language of public discourse is probably correct.

It thus seems very unlikely that Didi, who (we are told) had never before spoken in front of men even in her own family, could really have delivered this typical forensic speech. And when we consider that Didi's speech encapsulates nearly all the main arguments of the larger speech of which it is part, even though at the time she could not have known even that a suit would be brought in the case, let alone the details of such a suit, the conclusion seems inevitable: Didi speaks as she does because Lysias wrote her speech in the language that was familiar to him, his client, and his audience—the language of forensic oratory—in order to provide the strongest possible support for his client's case when it was presented in court. He was not trying to report accurately what she actually said.

The other examples of women's voices suggest the same conclusion. For instance, earlier in this same case, the speaker reports that Didi came and asked him to hold a family gathering: "Even if I have not previously been in the habit of speaking in front of men, the extent of this disaster will compel me to reveal to you the full extent of our hardships."[25] There are at least three forensic commonplaces here: "I am not accustomed to speaking," "circumstances compel me to act," and "I will reveal everything." In this case, even if Didi knew how to speak in forensic language, she would have no reason to address her son-in-law in this fashion. Lysias has given her a forensic voice, because she is, in fact, speaking not to her son-in-law but to the jurors; here, too, the words are not hers, but Lysias'.

We may draw the same conclusion from Lysias 1.16. The speaker, Euphiletus, relates how one day, when he was still ignorant of his wife's affair with Eratosthenes, an old woman approached him: "'Euphiletus,' she said, 'don't think I'm being meddlesome by approaching you;[26] the man who is insolently disgracing (*hybrizein*) you and your wife happens to be an enemy of ours. If you take and interrogate your maid who does the shopping and serves you, you'll learn everything. The culprit,' she added, 'is Eratosthenes of Oe. He has corrupted (*diaphtheirein*) not only your wife but many other women. He makes a profession of it.'"

Usher comments that this is one of "three passages [in Lysias 1] written in a very artificial style,"[27] and notes the reminiscence of "a litigant's commonplace claim that he is not litigious." But there is more: to the disavowal

---

[25] Lysias 32.11; the words are reported in indirect speech, but I have converted them to direct speech.

[26] Literally: "It is not through any *polypragmosynē* ["meddlesomeness"] that I approach you."

[27] Edwards and Usher 1985: 224. The other two are 1.26 (see below) and 1.18.

of meddlesomeness the old woman adds the equally common justification that her adversary is a personal enemy, implying that her motive was revenge, which was proper, not something like financial gain, which was not. Moreover, she describes Eratosthenes' adultery from Euphiletus' perspective with the same terms he himself uses repeatedly in denouncing it to the jurors—*hybrizein* (1.3, 1.4, 1.25) and *diaphtheirein* (1.4, 1.8, 1.38, cf. 1.33). Her language is thus more appropriate for making Euphiletus' case to the jurors than for giving him information, even though at the time she could scarcely have envisioned that he would be making this speech in court.[28]

Similarly directed at the jurors are the words of the plaintiff's wife in Demosthenes 47.57. The speaker recounts how during a series of earlier disputes with the defendant, Euergus, he lost a judgment for more than 1,300 drachmas. Euergus then came to his house in his absence, seized sheep that were worth about the amount owed, and in addition took some furniture from the house. All this despite the fact that "my wife told them they were not to touch it [the furniture], and said it had been included in the value of her dowry and that 'you have fifty sheep, the slave boy and the shepherd, which are more than the value of the judgment you were granted (ἔχετε . . . πλείονος ἄξια ἢ κατεδικάσασθε)'; for one of the neighbors had knocked on the door and reported this to them. She also said that their money was on deposit in the bank, for she had heard this from me. 'If you wait for him,' she said, 'or one of you goes after him, you will leave with the money right now. But leave the furniture and don't take any of my property, especially since you have the value of the judgment you were granted (ἔχοντες ἄξια τῆς καταδίκης).'"

This is indeed a moving scene—a woman bravely confronts an intruder and explains the legal situation to him. To make the scene more plausible, we are even told how she learned the details she mentions. If her language sounds legalistic, perhaps we should only conclude that she knows the law and speaks accordingly. Note, however, that she not only presents the same facts and arguments her husband presents to the jurors, but uses some of his actual words. In particular, her expression, "you have the value [or, more than the value] of the judgment you were granted," is not found in any other surviving speech, but it does recur at the end of this speech in the speaker's own plea to the jurors (47.81): "They are so brutal and vicious that they entered my house in the presence of my wife and child, though they already had the sheep and servants, which were more than the value of the judgment they were granted (ἔχοντες . . . πλείονος ἄξια ἢ κατεδικάσαντο)." Here, too, then, it seems likely that the logographer has tailored a woman's words on an earlier occasion to fit the needs of the present case.

[28] It is possible (though surely unlikely) that she had figured out what arguments would most appeal to Euphiletus, and that these are the same arguments he thinks will most appeal to the jurors. But this would not account for her use of forensic commonplaces.

The same is true of one other passage, Antiphon 1.15–16, where a woman's reported speech can only have come from the plaintiff's (or the logographer's) imagination. The speaker accuses his stepmother of poisoning his father and his father's friend Philoneus in collusion with Philoneus' *pallakē* ("concubine"). According to the speaker, his stepmother realized that Philoneus "was treating the *pallakē* wrongly, and so she summoned her and, when she arrived, said she, too, was being treated wrongly by our father. If the woman followed her instructions, she said, she was capable of renewing Philoneus' love for her and my father's love for herself. She added that her job was to contrive the plan, the woman's was to carry it out. She asked the woman if she was willing to help, and she agreed—without hesitation, I think."

For the moment let us consider only the end of this conversation, in particular the stepmother's insistence that she would contrive the plan, while the *pallakē* would assist her. It is crucial for the speaker's case that the true agent of this crime be his stepmother, not the *pallakē*, who has already been executed for giving the men the poison (1.20). On this point, however, there is no evidence apart from this alleged conversation. Thus the woman must be heard to convict herself, so to speak, of being the true agent of the crime. In reality, the stepmother would have had no reason to tell the *pallakē* explicitly that she, the stepmother, would contrive the poisoning while the *pallakē* would only be the servant, since this would be evident in their relationship; but to strengthen his case, the speaker puts these words in her mouth.

These five passages show that the logographers regularly create words for women that are designed to support their client's present case, even though the women's words were spoken long before the case was brought. The women use specific words and phrases that are important to the litigant's case and often employ standard rhetorical techniques and commonplace forensic arguments. Since it is unlikely, however, that any of these women could or would use this forensic language, or that at the time they knew what the speaker's arguments in court would later be, the logographer must be creatively rewriting words the women actually spoke, or in some cases perhaps creating speeches from nothing.

The stepmother's speech in Antiphon 1 is certainly creative fiction. The speaker was not present during the conversation he reports between the two women, and neither the stepmother nor the *pallakē* could have described the scene to him.[29] In two other scenes, the old woman's information about the adultery (Lysias 1.16) and Didi's request for a conference (Lysias 32.11),

---

[29] Before her execution, the *pallakē* may have given a general account of the stepmother's role in the affair, but if she had included this kind of detail in her account, the speaker would surely have mentioned this.

the woman's words were heard only by the speaker. There was no other witness who might testify, and the speaker does not offer to torture the slave woman or have Didi swear an oath, which might confirm at least that these speeches were delivered.[30] Since Didi had remarried and was raising a new family, it seems unlikely that she took as much initiative in the matter as the speaker represents; and the motivation alleged in Lysias 1, that her mistress is seeking revenge for being jilted, fits too neatly into the sexual stereotype being promulgated by the speaker, namely that adultery has so corrupted its victim that she is angry and seeks revenge when the adulterer leaves. Thus we cannot help but suspect that much in these speeches is fictional. And even if these women did say something along these lines, there was no reason for either to use the forensic language Lysias gives them. As we have them, then, these two speeches are probably Lysias' creation.

In Demosthenes 47, since the speaker's wife is represented as speaking to the defendant in this case, Euergus, the scene is probably not completely imaginary, for Euergus would have a chance to protest if it were. But it would not be worth his while to dispute the precise wording of the woman's speech as reported, if she had said anything remotely similar. Thus, it is quite possible that she simply told Euergus to leave since he had already taken enough; it seems unlikely, however, that she would have echoed the speaker's case so closely or used the rather technical language he gives her. Similarly, Didi's long speech was made in the presence of both the speaker and the defendant (and others), and thus it seems likely (though not certain) that the meeting actually occurred and that the woman uttered at least a few Greek words.[31] Whether her actual plea was as extensive as her reported speech is more doubtful; and surely she did not deliver the polished forensic performance Lysias so effectively portrays.[32]

It might not be so surprising that in these cases the woman's voice conforms to the language of forensic speech and the needs of the particular case, if the same is true of men's voices in oratory, as Bers has recently argued. Bers claims that speakers are not misrepresenting men's voices even

[30] For the challenge to swear an oath, see below, note 37.

[31] It is not impossible that the scene of a family gathering is completely imaginary and that Lysias reasoned that since no one else present would now testify for Diogeiton, the jurors would be more likely to believe his vivid description than Diogeiton's protest that no such meeting was held. Even if most of the speech is fictitious, Diogeiton would hardly wish to draw attention to the family scene by protesting that Didi had not spoken precisely as reported.

[32] Bers (1997: 145–46) argues that Didi could have prepared her words to sound not much different from the speaker's case; but since there was no case at the time, how could she know what the case would be? Bers also argues that the woman who informs Euphiletus in Lysias 1 may have wanted to make a quick impact; but "your wife has a lover" would surely work better. Bers is trying to argue that there is not such a gap as usually thought between formal rhetoric and real speech; he may have a point, but he neglects several significant difficulties with this view (see below).

when the language seems extremely formal, since men may actually have spoken in such terms. For example, Euphiletus' words to the adulterer Eratosthenes just before he kills him are certainly formal: "It is not I who am going to kill you, but our city's law, which you have transgressed and regarded as of less account than your pleasures, choosing rather to commit this foul offence against my wife and my children than to obey the laws like a decent person" (Lysias 1.26).[33] Bers argues that, however artificial these words may strike us, the quasi-judicial setting might in fact have called for such words. This seems unlikely: Euphiletus may have spoken the opening words ("not I but the law"), for these were something of a cliché that could be used of many different acts.[34] But the remainder of the speech is specific to this unusual situation, and, even if Euphiletus was not the unsophisticated farmer he claims to be, it seems unlikely that he heard language like this often, let alone was able to use it himself.

Moreover, even if Euphiletus could have known and used the kind of language he reports himself speaking, the same is not true of the women we have been considering. Bers argues that both Didi and the old woman who approaches Euphiletus could have prepared their words ahead of time so as to create the greatest effect, but he does not seek to explain how either woman learned to speak in this formal way even if she had time to prepare,[35] or how either could have composed a speech that so closely supported a legal case that had not even been imagined (at least in the case of Euphiletus) at the time of her speech. Even if Bers is correct that there was not such a gap as is usually thought between formal rhetoric and actual speech (and the hypothesis may be impossible to prove or disprove), the special circumstances of these women's voices make it unlikely that the orator's version represents what they actually said.

Not all women's voices (or all men's voices, for that matter) speak the language of forensic oratory. In two other passages, women speak in what appears to be ordinary, everyday language. In the first, Demosthenes 55, the defendant is contesting a suit for damages brought by his neighbor Callicles. As evidence that Callicles has inflated the damages, he reports his mother's first-hand observation: "She said that she saw and was told by the mother of these men that less than three *medimni* of barley had gotten wet (and she herself saw them drying it), and about half a *medimnus* of wheat flour; and that a jar of olive oil had tipped over but had not been damaged"

---

[33] Bers 1997: 146–47. I have kept Lamb's Loeb translation, which Bers uses.

[34] Cf. Ar. *Eccl.* 1055–56: "It is not I who arrest you, but the law." Bers (1997: 146–47) cites his own experience, when he once uttered "Is there a doctor in the house?" rather than "Any physicians here?" but the words he uttered are also a well-known cliché, hardly a parallel for the bulk of Euphiletus' speech.

[35] Bers 1997: 145–46. Ironically, Bers claims that, in his own experience (above, note 34), he would have spoken less formally if he had taken more time (146 n. 44).

(55.24).[36] He later adds that to confirm this report he challenged Callicles to let both mothers swear oaths (55.27).[37] Since the mother's words in this case (as we can reconstruct them) are both appropriate, since only she has first-hand knowledge of important facts, and nontechnical, she may well have actually spoken as reported. We should bear in mind, however, that (as we should expect) her words clearly support the speaker's case, and that no one else was present during the conversation who could challenge his report.

Another woman's voice that is nontechnical and helps support the speaker's case comes in Hyperides 3, the speech *Against Athenogenes*. The speaker, whose name is probably Epicrates, describes himself as the victim of a type of swindle that still is widespread today.[38] As Epicrates tells it, he was unaware that the swindlers, Athenogenes and a prostitute named Antigone (almost certainly a metic), were working as a team, when Antigone came to him and offered to help resolve a dispute he was having with Athenogenes over a slave, Midas. He trusted her and accepted her help. "Later she sent for me again and told me that after considerable pleading with Athenogenes, she just managed to persuade him to release Midas and both his sons to me for forty *minas*, and she instructed me to get the money as quickly as possible, before Athenogenes changed his mind in any way" (3.4). Epicrates does as she says, and before long he has not only lost all this money but is saddled with enormous debts as well. How much of the story is true, we will never know, but like Athenogenes, Antigone is portrayed quite simply as a swindler. Here, too, her language is nontechnical, and her words seem appropriate to her character, but again, there is no one else present during the conversation, and her voice here lends support to the speaker's case. Thus we cannot know how closely (if at all) Hyperides represents what she actually said.

Antigone is different from the other women who speak in one important respect: in the first six examples discussed above, the women all speak about domestic or family matters, an area where a woman's voice would ordinarily carry weight. Antigone speaks in a case involving a disputed contract of sale, in which she plays an important role. She can do this because she is a metic, and although metic women were excluded from certain public affairs, they otherwise engaged in a broad range of activities not available to citizen women,[39] who speak only about family matters.

[36] The passage is in indirect discourse, but the mother's original words are easily recoverable.

[37] The challenge to swear an oath, which is virtually always refused, often serves to confirm the testimony of a woman, who would not appear as a witness; see Foxhall 1996: 143; Gagarin 1998: 43–45.

[38] The basic pitch is: "Have I got a deal for you. You'll make millions. Just give me a little cash up front."

[39] Todd 1997 shows that, from a legal perspective, the pattern of strong separation between males and females characteristic of Athenian citizens did not apply to metics.

The domestic role for citizen women is also evident in another, rather different evocation of the female voice in the speech *Against Neaera* (Demosthenes 59). Toward the end (59.110–11), the accuser Apollodorus raises the awful possibility of an acquittal:

> And what could each of you [jurors] actually say when he goes home to his own wife or daughter or mother after acquitting this woman, when she asks you: "Where were you?" and you say "we were trying a case." "Whom?" she will ask at once. "Neaira" you will say, of course (what else?) "because though she is an alien she is living in marriage with a citizen against the law, and because she gave in marriage to Theogenes who served as King-archon her daughter who had been caught in adultery, and this woman carried out the secret sacrifices on behalf of the city and was given as wife to Dionysos"; and you will narrate the rest of the charge against her, saying how memorably and carefully each detail was presented. And they on hearing this will ask: "So what did you do?" and you will say: "We have acquitted her." So then the most decent of the women will be furious with you, because you thought it right that this woman should have the same share as they in public life and religion; while to all the foolish ones you are giving a clear signal to do whatever they please, since you and the laws have given them complete freedom. For it will seem that you too by treating the matter in a casual and indolent way approve of this woman's way of life.[40]

This is the only passage in which women's voices are imagined in the future, not reported from the past. It is sometimes used to show that Athenian husbands regularly asked for and respected their wives' opinions on public matters, but it is no better evidence for the actual behavior of Athenian men than the scene in *Lysistrata* (512–15) where a woman asks her husband about his day in the Assembly and he replies, "What's it to you; won't you shut up"—which she does. Both passages confirm, however, that citizen women were expected to remain home while their husbands handled the legal and political affairs of the city. Women could have a voice in public matters only at their husband's discretion—or, in the case of Demosthenes 59, at the discretion of the male logographer who allows them to speak. Goff has noted that in the middle of this passage, Apollodorus switches from singular to plural. This is the only instance in oratory where a collective women's voice is present, and Goff suggests that by invoking the voice of these women as a collective, suggestive of the ritual activity of the Thesmophoria, Apollodorus is evoking not just the special moral authority sometimes accorded Greek women,[41] but also the power of women massed together in ritual activity.[42]

[40] The translation is from Carey 1992.
[41] So, too, in Lys. 32, Dem. 47, and Xen. *Oec.* 11.25 (all discussed above).
[42] Goff 1997.

We noted that in oratory, citizen women only speak on domestic issues, but here in Apollodorus' speech, Goff argues, the women "emerge from their domestic roles to occupy positions within a public discourse about the city's cultic identity." On matters involving civic ritual identity, she adds, "the speaker experiences a need for the women's voice so great that he actually imitates it" (should we not rather say he "creates it"?).[43] We must note, however, that this collective female voice is evoked on an issue that, although brought into public discourse by Apollodorus, specifically concerns female behavior and the role of women in creating Athenian citizens. When the issue is not specifically domestic or concerned with women's behavior, the same rhetorical trope is used to invoke a male response, as we see near the end of Aeschines 3, which is concerned with public policy: Aeschines imagines a juror who votes for Ctesiphon's acquittal going home not to his wife or daughter, but to his son; when he tries to educate him, the son refuses to obey a father who by his vote has shown such disregard for honor and justice (3.245–46).[44]

It is hardly surprising that all the women's voices we have examined thus far support the speaker's case and even echo his arguments, most often in formal forensic language. The speaker is evidently in control and his purpose—presenting the strongest possible case—is transparent. Our final example, however, may entail some ambiguity, perhaps unconscious. In Lysias 1.12–13 Euphiletus describes how one day, before learning of his wife's adultery, he returned home unexpectedly and was about to go to bed after dinner, when their baby started crying. "I told my wife to go down and feed the baby, to stop it crying. At first she refused, as if glad to see me home after so long. When I became angry and ordered her to go, she said, 'You just want to stay here and have a go at the slave-girl. You felt her up once before when you were drunk.' I laughed at this, and she got up and left. She closed the door behind her, pretending to make a joke out of it, and bolted it. I had no suspicions, and thought no more of it, but gladly went to bed, since I had returned from the country."

Euphiletus later (1.17) tells us that he realized in retrospect that his wife was going to meet her lover, but readers today understand the episode differently—as portraying a domestic situation that might well induce a woman to take a lover: her husband, after a long absence, rejects her overture for sex and laughs off her concern about his affair with the maid. We cannot be certain that any of the male Greek audience would hear it this way, but we may still wonder why Lysias allows this woman to speak in (ap-

[43] Ibid. The quotation is from the unpublished typescript of the talk.

[44] For the same trope, cf. Aeschines 1.187 and Dinarchus 1.66–73, which also envisage a male response to an unjust acquittal. Lycurgus takes the idea even further, evoking the country, its trees, dockyards, and city walls as all appealing for a conviction (1.150).

parently) her own voice? True, her complaint provides an excuse for lock-
ing the door; and Euphiletus' admission of weakness may make his persona
more believable.[45] But elsewhere he conceals his wife's role in the affair and
blames only Eratosthenes. Why should he (or Lysias) give any hint here
that his wife might have a legitimate grievance? Perhaps their male-centered view of domestic life makes them unaware of this underlying implication. Or perhaps they are aware but unconcerned, reasoning that few jurors would notice and those who did would think nothing of it. At the very
least we can say that sexual matters generally create ambivalence, and that
a sexual double standard is well established in the mythological tradition
and was generally accepted, at least by men. Women in oratory never
openly protest this or other standards governing their lives, and so this is
one of the very few passages where a woman may truly be speaking in her
own voice, even if obliquely. If Euphiletus had ambivalent feelings about
his wife—both as guilty of adultery and as innocent victim—perhaps he
could not fully conceal the fact, even with the help of a logographer.

A similar ambivalence may be present in Antiphon 1.15–16, which we
considered earlier. The speaker begins his description of the conversation
between the two women by noting that his stepmother "realized that
Philoneus was treating the *pallakē* wrongly, and so she summoned her and,
when she arrived, said she, too, was being treated wrongly by our father."
There is no further indication of the nature of the injustice the stepmother
is suffering (the *pallakē* is about to be forced into prostitution), but presumably she feels that she (like Euphiletus' wife) has lost her husband's
love.[46] Antiphon's task is difficult, since unlike Euphiletus' wife, the stepmother must be given some motivation for her alleged crime, and so it may
have been important to mention her grievance, even if this also allows her
to be seen as a victim. Similarly, the *pallakē* must appear to be both guilty—
she was, after all, executed immediately—and the innocent victim of the
stepmother's plot. Thus, as in Lysias 1, Antiphon allows a woman's voice to
give a hint of the dilemma confronting a woman who loses her husband's
love, even though the effect on his case may be problematic.

Lysias 32 suggests that a widow faces a different dilemma: whether to remain faithful to her late husband's family or take a new husband and start a
new family. Here, too, the logographer, by mentioning Didi's new family,
has provided just enough evidence to let us suspect that his picture of the

---

[45] So Carey 1989: 70. Euphiletus acknowledges other faults, such as gullibility and quick-
ness to anger, that help support his case, whereas his apparent dalliance with the maid does
not.

[46] The verb for "treat wrongly" in Antiphon 1.15–16 is in both instances *adikeō*, which is
used of unrequited love in archaic lyric poetry: Sappho 1.20; Theognis 1283 (and perhaps
1282); cf. Archilochus 779a (Diehl 1949) = Hipponax 115 (West 1989–92). See further
Gagarin 1974.

faithful widow may be masking a woman who in fact did not support her orphaned children as she might have.[47] Indeed, Lysias may give her such an extended voice precisely in order to compensate for her lack of more substantive action on behalf of her orphaned children. Demosthenes pursues the opposite strategy with regard to his mother Cleobule, who apparently acted forcefully in support of her orphaned son but has little presence in his speeches. Can we conclude that under such conditions a woman's true power is indicated not by the presence of her voice in the public discourse of oratory but by its absence?

Women's voices in the public discourse of oratory pose a dilemma for logographers. Athenian public culture is largely a male culture.[48] It is also an oral culture in which virtually all communication, debate, deliberation, and decision-making is conducted by means of spoken *logoi*. True, logographers compose written speeches, but their clients deliver these speeches orally in the public arena of the lawcourt. In such a culture, speech is the means of exercising authority. Women (at least citizen women) do not normally participate in this culture or in this male public discourse; and from all indications, Athenian men would largely agree with Pericles' view that the best women are those who are least evident in public discourse (Thuc. 2.46).

Forensic discourse, however, at least in private cases, often requires the presence of women. For the most part, the (male) logographers keep these women nameless (unless they disapprove of them) and speechless, but on occasion, when they wish to represent women as having authority, they give them voices. Women probably had their own language of oral communication, as the scene in *Ecclesiazusae* (discussed above) indicates, but the logographers do not mark their voices as female, for women's language would have little or no authority in the male context of the courts. So, the logographers generally give women voices that are male, that is, that are marked by the features of male forensic rhetoric, for this is the voice of authority. Sometimes a woman's voice is neutral or unmarked, and on rare occasions a woman will speak in (apparently) her own voice and will express concerns that are not shared by the male culture. But women like Didi, whose speech makes them appear powerful, almost certainly did not really speak like this, and indeed, may not have spoken much at all. The women with real power, like Cleobule, may be those who, as Pericles recommends, have the least presence in this public discourse. Thus, although women's voices in Athenian oratory may occasionally hint at the reality of a woman's situation, they are generally an unreliable guide to her real status or authority.

---

[47] So Foxhall 1996.

[48] The main exception is religious matters. Cf. Blok's and O'Higgins' contributions to this volume.

Part Three

THE LATE CLASSICAL PERIOD AND BEYOND

CHAPTER TEN.

The Good Daughter

MOTHERS' TUTELAGE IN ERINNA'S DISTAFF *AND FOURTH-CENTURY EPITAPHS*

EVA STEHLE

THE FEW women's "voices" that we have from ancient Greece often speak about relationships among women. Sappho, Nossis, and Anyte celebrate friendship or love among women and respond to women's beauty. Erinna fits this description as well, for her major poem, the *Distaff,* takes the form of a lament for her childhood friend Baukis, who died shortly after marriage. These poets have left us, along with beautiful, influential poetry, a different perspective on women's lives from that of the dominant culture and insight into the richness of women's mutual attachments. But Erinna, in addition, opens a window for us on another aspect of women's experience for which there is scant evidence, the relationship of mother and daughter. It must have been an important artistic as well as emotional tie; mothers passed on craft traditions, storytelling traditions, poetic traditions of lament and song to their daughters. Marilyn Skinner sees a reflection of this process in Nossis' epigram (*Palatine Anthology* 6.265) naming three generations of women, two of whom dedicate a woven garment together.[1] But seldom do Greek cultural artifacts depict mother and daughter, and the few that do give us a male rendering and the mother's perspective.[2] Erinna gives us a woman's and a daughter's view of girls' education in adult sexual and social roles under the tutelage of mothers. Hard to decipher as it is, her poem therefore offers a unique account of this aspect of women's lives.

---

[1] Skinner, this volume. Sappho frs. 132 and 98b mention her daughter Kleis but do not reveal much about their relationship.

[2] Loraux ([1990] 1998) treats mother and daughter in myth. She finds that a mother's wrath expresses itself in different ways with daughters and sons (55): "In accordance with the tradition of the 'race of women'—which the *andres* ['men'] rouse when they want to feel both terror and fascination—the mother lives with her daughter in a closed circle, but feminine wrath threatens the son, because he stands in for the father." Cf. 64–65 for the reversal by which the daughter substitutes for the son, whose bodily connection with his mother is too easily eroticized. The "closed circle" of mother and daughter is, on this analysis, one of a series of displacements in fantasy for mothers' attachment to sons.

There is another untapped source of information on mothers and daughters: grave inscriptions. Though not very illuminating in themselves, they prove to be informative as background for Erinna's poem: they reveal the sort of exemplary relationship that won public approval among the relatively wealthy and educated.[3] I believe that Erinna sets her lament off against exactly this idealizing public image of mothers and daughters.

GRAVE INSCRIPTIONS

Because they provide context, I begin with grave inscriptions. My main interest is the fourth-century epitaphs, which are roughly contemporary with Erinna, but to appreciate the new sensibility they exhibit it is helpful to look first at earlier inscriptions.[4] In the sixth and fifth centuries, one common formula for epitaphs was, "X set me/this marker (*sēma* or *mnēma*) up for Y," in which X might be the name of the setter-up, the relationship of the setter-up to the deceased, or both.[5] The formula allows us to see who had the authority to set up markers for whom and therefore to deduce something about family relationships.[6]

Women, it appears, use this formula to set up markers almost exclusively for sons who die young.[7] But fathers more often commemorate sons, and only once, in an instance really belonging to the following period, does an

[3] See Sourvinou-Inwood 1995: 170ff., on the conformity of archaic epitaphs from all over the Greek world; these reflect the ideology of the (commissioning group within the) community.

[4] The metrical inscriptions of the sixth and fifth centuries B.C.E. are collected in the first volume of Hansen 1983–89 (abbreviated *CEG*). The second volume contains the fourth-century inscriptions. I confine my study to these (and exclude nonmetrical inscriptions) because they represent fuller sentiments. The dates and provenances I give are taken from Hansen.

[5] See Lausberg 1982: 106–11 on this form.

[6] Of course, a family member may have set up a gravestone without recording the fact in the epitaph. But epitaphs that do indicate who set up the marker or who mourns tell us something about the public view of family relationships. For family relationships as deducible from funerary art, see Bergemann 1997. The identity of figures in the images is difficult to determine, although the possibility that the mother was depicted even when not named would be relevant here. Much of Bergemann's interest is in family members who share a grave, a different line of inquiry from mine.

[7] See next note for examples. Women do not (using this formula) set up markers for fathers. There are three possible but no certain cases of a woman recording her setting up a marker for her husband: *CEG* 1: no. 74, but the name of the setter-up is lost, and Hansen thinks it was more likely a male friend of the man; no. 124, where a woman sets up a marker for a man but no relationship is given; no. 136, where the deceased is called an *anēr agathos* ("good man" or "good husband"), but his youth is stressed, so he might be the woman's son. Humphreys ([1983] 1993: 126 n. 18) counts *CEG* 1: no. 43 in this category, but I follow Hansen's view (ad loc.) that only the son was named. *CEG* 1: no. 37 is a sister's marker for her brother.

epitaph name both father and mother as memorializing their son (CEG 1: no. 102, c. 400?, from Attica).[8] We may guess that a mother provided her son's grave marker if his father was absent or dead; his overriding need for a memorial justified her initiative.

Women who died young almost never received poetic epitaphs. Fathers set up markers for daughters in two cases (one restored).[9] There is one instance in *CEG* 1 of a mother mentioned as grieving on a daughter's monument (no. 153, c. 450?, from Amorgos, without the setting-up formula or her name). A woman named Metriche mentions a daughter (and a brother) after the lines stating that she set up a marker for her sons (*CEG* 1: no. 94, c. 410–400, from Attica). In addition, mother and father together set up a marker for a daughter (*CEG* 1: no. 119, c. 450?, from Thessaly), and possibly two examples exist of mother and father jointly memorializing their son and daughter.[10] The numbers are much too small to take as statistically significant, but, for what it is worth, most of the few daughters commemorated seem to be connected in inscriptions with their mothers. In the two (?) epitaphs for daughter and son, the mother may have been included to acknowledge her interest in the daughter.

On the other hand, there are also two or three isolated examples of women memorializing nonkin women in *CEG* 1, one from the sixth century (no. 38, c. 530?, from Attica) and one or two from the end of the fifth (no. 97, end of fifth century?, from Attica, and perhaps no. 92, c. 420–400?, from Attica).[11] The latter two belong to the period when Attic grave monuments reappeared after virtual nonexistence for seventy years, and so could

---

[8] I count nine examples in *CEG* 1 of mothers memorializing sons, fourteen of fathers. Humphreys ([1983] 1993: 126 n. 18) lists *CEG* 1: nos. 35 and 43 as Attic examples of mothers setting up markers for sons; I add no. 94 (not certainly Attic) and, from outside Attica, nos. 108, 114, 117, 138, 157, 169. Humphreys lists nine Attic instances of fathers memorializing sons: *CEG* 1: nos. 41, 42, 46, 50, 53, 55 (restored), plus three that are not in *CEG* (*IG* i³ 1263, 1266; *SEG* 15. 69). I add *CEG* 1: nos. 14, 32, and 71, and from outside Attica, nos. 113, 121, 122, 137, 152. There are also dubious cases, cases where the name and gender-marker of parent or child is missing, and cases without the setting-up formula. Men who died young were the most common recipients of epitaphs; see Lausberg 1982: 118.

[9] *CEG* 1: no. 18 (?; male name restored) and 161. Men relatively seldom record their setting up markers for other than children, but they do commemorate fathers (*CEG* 1: nos. 61, at the behest of the mother, 96, 111; in the last two the the setters-up are *paides*, which usually refers to male children) and friends (40?, 58), occasionally also brother (70), wife (54, where the mother's name may have been added, 167), sister (156), or unspecified woman (66).

[10] *CEG* 1: no. 84 (for a brother and sister, without the setting-up formula), and possibly 25 (also for a brother and sister, judging from the relief). The latter is damaged; it *may* have said that the father set the marker for the son and the mother for the daughter (see ad loc.). However, it is also possible that the mother was deceased as well.

[11] In the case of *CEG* 1: no. 92, "companions" (*hetairoi*) "crown" the grave of Anthemis; note the language of male athletic glory. The word is masculine, but the "companions" may be female anyway. Two women were pictured in the accompanying relief, now lost.

be counted as representing the beginning of the next stage. I cite *CEG* 1: no. 97:

> πιστῆς ἡδείας τε χάριν φιλότητος ἑταίρα
> Εὔθυλλα στήλην τήνδ᾽ ἐπέθηκε τάφωι
> σῶι, Βιότη· μνήμηγ γὰρ ἀεὶ δακρυτὸν ἔχοσα
> ἡλικίας τῆς σῆς κλαίει ἀποφθιμένης.

For the sake of faithful and sweet friendship your companion Euthylla set up this stele on your grave, Biote. For having always tearful memory of your perished youth she cries.

Philotēs does not exclude kin relationship, but since female kin (other than mother and daughter) do not seem to represent themselves as memorializing one another, it shows that friendship was the important stimulus. This inscription is the closest the epitaphs come to the relationship of "Erinna" and Baukis in the *Distaff*.

With the end of the fifth century, a change of style emerges. More people receive inscribed grave markers, which now more generously describe emotions.[12] Women now receive poetic epitaphs far more often than before, often with praise, especially of their *aretē* ("virtue") and *sōphrosynē* ("chastity, inconspicuous behavior"). But I am investigating the living who memorialize the dead. The setting-up formula is no longer used in Attica, though it is still found in a few other places. Instead of naming the source of authority for the monument, epitaphs now often list the inner circle of mourners. And prominent in the newly expanded group is the mother. In the majority of epitaphs that mention the father's grief for a son, the mother joins him, a real change from the earlier style.[13] And the mother lithically mourns her daughter far more often. Mother and father, together with the girl's siblings, appear in *CEG* 2: no. 591 (c. 350–325?, from Attica) for a twelve-year-old girl (lines 9–12):

> ὦ μελέα μῆτερ καὶ ὁμαίμονες ὅς τέ σ᾽ ἔφυσεν
> Μειδοτέλης αὐτῶι πῆμα, Κλεοπτολέμη,
> οἳ γόον, οὐ θάλαμον τὸν σὸν προσορῶσι θανούσης
> θρῆνόν τε ἀντ᾽ ἀνδρὸς καὶ τάφον ἀντὶ γάμου.

O wretched mother and siblings and Meidoteles, who begot you as a grief for himself, Kleoptoleme, who behold wailing, not your bridal chamber, since you have perished, and a dirge instead of a husband and a grave instead of marriage.

---

[12] See Humphreys [1983] 1993: 104–8, on the shift toward family feeling revealed in funerary relief sculpture beginning in the late fifth century; also Lausberg 1982: 136–39 on the more personal tone in epitaphs; and Sourvinou-Inwood 1995: 201–4.

[13] See, e.g., *CEG* 2: nos. 527, 629, 704, for good examples. I use the words "mourning" and "grief" fairly broadly to include cases in which the mourning is implicit, e.g., statements about the deceased "leaving behind" another.

The girl's death before marriage evokes a particular pathos. The mother is
melea ("wretched"), a poetic word that occurs mainly in the lyrics of tragedy.
The father's *pēma* ("grief") is poetic, too, and the whole quatrain is at the
register of high drama, but the mother is listed first. The grave monument
actually contains three inscriptions, of which this is the third; the second
singles the mother out, again as *melea* and also left with *penthos* ("sorrow").
Notice, on the other hand, that she is not named. The mother's name is
often not given in this style of memorial.[14]

A mother might also appear as a mourner, more surprisingly, in an epitaph for a married daughter along with the daughter's husband.[15] Even after
the daughter has left home, her mother's tie to her now wins public recognition. *CEG* 2: no. 543 is an example (c. 350?, from Attica, lines 7–10):

> πένθος μητρὶ λιποῦσα κασιγνήτωι τε πόσει τε
> παιδί τ᾽ ἐμῶι θνήισκω καί με χθὼν ἥδε καλύπτει
> ἡ πᾶσιν κοινὴ τοῖς ἀπογιγνομένοις·
> εἰμὶ δὲ Λυσάνδρου Πιθέως Ἀρχεστράτη ἥδε.

Leaving grief for my mother and brother and husband and child I die and this
earth covers me, earth that is common to all those who have passed away. I am
this Archestrate, daughter of Lysandros of Pithos.

Natal and marital families come together, the mother again holding first
place. Here, too, there are three inscriptions. This time the first one singles
out the husband, to whom, along with their *philoi* ("friends"), Archestrate
has left *pothos* ("longing"). The second mentions Archestrate's dutiful and
chaste life (*eusebēs* and *sōphrōn*).[16] It seems that the elements of a woman's
conventional ideal life are assembled: son, loving husband, and virtue. In-
clusion of the grieving mother increases the pathos of her early death but
also suggests that her mother continued to be an important figure in a
woman's life, along with husband and child. The father is far less often mentioned than the mother in epitaphs for married daughters; possibly he is already deceased, but the epitaphs may also reflect the mother's closer tie with
her daughter and prominence as a mourner.[17]

[14] Mothers are also grievers in epitaphs for (explicitly or presumably) unmarried daughters
in *CEG* 2: nos. 518 (with the father), 575, 599, 655 (with the father), 693 (with the father), 714
(damaged). I find no case of a father alone grieving for his daughter, although the father's name
may be given in the genitive for identification of the woman.

[15] It is possible that this occurs already in *CEG* 1: no. 54 (c. 510–500?, from Attica). Humphreys ([1983] 1993: 126 n. 18) cites also *IG* i³ 1229 (= *SEG* 25.59), a nonmetrical inscription.

[16] Cf. Pircher 1979: 30–31 on this epitaph.

[17] Father and mother both appear in *CEG* 2: nos. 529 and 604 ("parents") for married
daughters. The mother without the father appears in nos. 486, 513, 536 (no grief expressed
but the woman is identified through her mother), 689, in addition to the inscriptions cited. I
count fifteen definite or probable epitaphs in which a husband grieves for his wife but her
mother is not mentioned (nos. 530, 539, 555 [?], 566, 573, 576, 590, 603, 669 [?], 680, 690,

Another example evokes the performance of lament at the tomb (*CEG* 2: no. 686, fourth century?, from Chios):

> αἰαῖ, σεῖο, Κομαλλὶς, ἀποφθιμένης ἀκάχηνται
> μάτηρ θ' ἁ μελέα κουρίδιός τε πόσις,
> πᾶσά τε συγγενέων πληθύς σ' ἀδινὸν στεναχίζει
> δρυπτόμενοι χαίτας τοῦδε πάροιθε τάφου·
> ἦ γὰρ δαίδαλά τε ἔργα χεροῖν καὶ σώφρονα κόσμον
> ἤσκησας, μῶμος δ' οὔτις ἐπῆν ἐπὶ σοί.

Alas, Komallis, your wretched mother and your legitimate husband are grieved at your death, and the whole crowd of relatives loudly groans for you, tearing their hair in front of this tomb. For indeed you practiced clever work with your hands and chaste decorousness, and there was nothing blameworthy in you.

Here mother and husband are individually mentioned, leaving the other relatives to a collective rubric. The mother is again *melea* ("wretched").[18] In a kind of counterpoint, the unrestrained lament is set against the skillful labor and chaste decorousness of Komallis. I shall return to this.

Occasionally a mother alone grieves for her lost daughter, as in *CEG* 2: no. 587 (post c. 350?, from Attica, lines 2–5):

> οὔ σε γάμων πρόπολος, Πλαγγών, Ὑμέναιος ἐν οἴκοις
> ὤλβισεν, ἀλλ' ἐδάκρυσε ἐκτὸς ἀποφθιμένην·
> σῶι δὲ πάθει μήτηρ καταλείβεται, οὐδέ ποτ' αὐτὴν
> λείπουσι θρήνων πενθίδιοι στεναχαί.

Hymenaios, attendant of marriages, did not bless you in the house, Plangon, but wept for your perishing outside. Your mother dissolves at your misfortune, nor do the sad groans of lament ever leave her.

Note the contrast between "in the house" and "outside." Whether or not Plangon perished outside the house, the emotional valence of the contrast is clear: inside is safety and happiness, while outside is grief. This is one of only three epitaphs in *CEG* 2, however, in which mothers independently mourn for daughters; unaccompanied mothers still set up markers or grieve for sons more often.[19] The point is that the mother-daughter bond gains vis-

---

726, 728, 731 [?], 738 [?])—less than twice as many. In no. 522 three generations of women are named.

[18] In *CEG* 2 the adjective occurs only in no. 729 (possibly again of a mother) in addition to the two instances I have cited. This epitaph is notably Homeric in its language.

[19] See above, notes 14 and 17, for cases of mother mourning daughter. Mother without father mourning son: *CEG* 2: nos. 557, 593, 636, 650, 687, 706, 709. A woman alone is still not portrayed as grieving for father or husband. There are a few cases of wife and children mourning the husband, e.g., *CEG* 2: nos. 512, 586, 640.

ibility, but within the patriarchal family context.[20] Even in this inscription, the focus of the mother's grief is the daughter's missing out on marriage.[21]

One might expect in the new atmosphere that women's nonfamilial relations with other women would be more frequently foregrounded. They are not. A woman's *philoi* are occasionally included among the mourners (as in *CEG* 2: no. 543 above), but no named nonkin woman recognizably commemorates another in verse in the fourth century. Family relationships are pervasive; men sometimes set up markers or grieve for friends and comrades, but women are represented as grieving exclusively (so far as I can tell) for family members. What we see in the epitaphs is that in the fourth century women's domestic virtue becomes a matter for public praise, that the emotional impact of loss is far more freely portrayed than before via evocations of lament or poetic language of suffering (as well as in an ordinary vocabulary of grief and longing), and that the attachment of a mother to her daughter is highlighted for the public to share in the context of a daughter's death. The mothers' names are frequently not recorded; it is rather the generic figure of the lamenting mother that elicits public pity.

ERINNA'S *DISTAFF*

We are now ready to look at Erinna's *Distaff*. Erinna was an important figure in the transition to the Alexandrian literary flowering.[22] Eusebius gives a mid-fourth century B.C.E. date for her, and most of the various places named as her homeland were in the southeast Mediterranean cultural orbit.[23] She was widely praised for the *Distaff*, a hexameter poem said to be 300 lines long, of which a fragment containing parts of fifty-four lines has come to light.[24] It turns out to be a lament for Baukis, the childhood friend

[20] Mothers had always had a recognized role in deciding on the daughter's marriage. Cf. the *Homeric Hymn to Demeter* and Euripides' *Iphigeneia in Aulis* 456–59, where Agamemnon comments on Clytemnestra's coming "unsummoned" to Aulis with Iphigeneia. In Euripides' fragmentary *Erechtheus*, the mother, Praxithea, consents to the sacrifice of a daughter to save the city.

[21] On this theme in tragedy, cf. Rehm 1994.

[22] For her fame, see especially *Anth. Pal.* 7.12, 713; 9.190.

[23] See Gow and Page 1965, 2: 281–82; Scholz 1973; West 1977: 95–96 on the "biographical" information. Her homeland is identified as Teos, Tenos, Telos, or Rhodes (as well as Lesbos, to put her into Sappho's milieu), of which Tenos, near Rhodes, seems the most likely choice. I have not seen Neri 1996.

[24] For a technical description of the papyrus, see Neri 1997: 57–68. The fragment is actually four pieces: line-ends 1–14 are separate; the beginnings and ends of lines 15–34 are on separate fragments with no join; and line 35 begins a new fragment. I take the text from Lloyd-Jones and Parsons 1983 (*Suppl. Hell.* no. 401) and have added supplements that they deem plausible. Neri favors a few divergences from this text, but nothing that affects the meaning. See Levin 1962: 201 n. 3, for earlier bibliography.

of "Erinna" (the first-person speaker in the poem). Erinna's literary lineage and influence have been effectively studied, especially by Marilyn Skinner and Kathryn Gutzwiller. Skinner compares her lament with those for Patroclus and Hector in *Iliad* 22 and 24, and Gutzwiller points out her innovative combination of Sapphic first-person perspective with the subordinate genre of lament in epic.[25]

The most influential interpreter of the situation in the fragment has been Sir Maurice Bowra, whose reading has guided all subsequent scholarship.[26] According to it, Erinna nostalgically recalls two scenes of playing with Baukis in childhood, but then she accuses Baukis of forgetting her after Baukis marries. Now that Baukis has died, Erinna regrets that she cannot attend the funeral, perhaps because she is a priestess. Bowra's analysis emphasizes the pathos of the poem but presents it as listing a series of causes for lament one after another in a paratactic litany: Baukis has died, I remember our childhood games, Baukis forgot me, I cannot go to her funeral. Any reading of the badly damaged fragment, itself only a sixth of the poem, must be speculative, and Bowra's study is very important in bringing illumination to an obscure text. But because I give close attention not only to Baukis and Erinna but also to the various mother figures in the poem, I believe that I can detect a tighter logical connection among the various scenes and a theme of daughters reacting to mothers, real and folkloric, who shape them for their adult role. The fourth-century epitaphs also provide a new context for the poem, although Erinna's poem bears a message about the relationship of mothers and daughters that is far more ambivalent than the ones found in the epitaphs.

The extant fragment comes from the end of the poem, so about 250 lines preceded it.[27] Epigrams in the *Palatine Anthology* alluding to the poem supply some information and allow some inferences about what was in the missing part.[28] According to *Anth. Pal.* 7.11 and 9.190, Erinna was a nineteen-year-old *parthenos* ("young unmarried woman"). This must be the persona presented by the speaker in the poem; it is appropriate for a composition whose dramatic moment is directly after the death of Baukis.[29] Two

---

[25] Skinner 1982; see also Skinner, this volume. Gutzwiller 1997: 203–4, 210–11 (while Murnaghan [1999] sees women's lament as a different voice within epic). Rauk (1989) compares the *Distaff* to Sappho fr. 94 and proposes to read it as Erinna's *propemptikon* ("farewell song") for Baukis, recalled with grief in the context of her death.

[26] Bowra [1936] 1953.

[27] Neri 1997: 62–63; West 1977: 112.

[28] See Snyder 1989: 87–91, for discussion of the epigrams.

[29] See Arthur [Katz] 1980: 55–58, for refutation of West's idea (1977: 116–19) that we should take it as a literary forgery by a male poet because the poem was not likely composed under the circumstances described in it (and in the epigrams). Also Pomeroy 1978: 19–20. I suscribe to the view of Snyder 1989: 96: "Whether or not 'The Distaff' was in any sense autobiographical, we can safely assume that it is a genuine record of female experience transmuted and transmitted through the medium of poetry."

epigrams attributed to Erinna (*Anth. Pal.* 7.710 and 712) mourn the death of Baukis shortly after her marriage; Erinna must have made the timing of Baukis' death a focus of grief. Two lines quoted by Stobaeus 4.51.4 (*Suppl. Hell.* no. 402) speak of the "empty echo" reaching Hades and the silence and darkness there, so Erinna included thoughts about the futility of her own communication with Baukis. An introduction to the girls' childhood relationship and their families must also have stood in the missing lines, along with much more, probably, about Baukis — her character and qualities, her marriage. But most informative and most important for me are lines 5–6 of the anonymous *Anth. Pal.* 9.190, whose picture of Erinna I will make use of later; they show that Erinna also mentioned her relationship to her mother and the circumstances under which she composed the *Distaff*.

The fragment we have is plausibly addressed entirely to Baukis, just as three of the epitaphs quoted above address the deceased in a fiction of continued communication. It is divided into three sections, punctuated by a break-off apostrophe with *tu* (you [accusative]), Baukis' name, and a word for bewailing (lines 18–20, 31 [with name in 30], and 47–48), and followed by a final farewell passage (49–54). In the first section (5?–17) the subject is the game of *chelichelōnē*, in the second (21–30) household scenes and Baukis' marriage, and in the third (32–46) "Erinna" herself. The first two sections are narrative, recollections of childhood, and the third seems to be "Erinna's" explanation for her mode of mourning Baukis. In each section a mother figure and the theme of mobility versus immobility serve to focus Erinna's depiction of a daughter's training in her adult social role. I shall go through the fragment, quoting each section as I come to it.

Only of the last three lines of the first section is much preserved; I quote those along with the end of the previous line (14–17):

> ἐς β]α[θ]ὺ κῦμα[
> λε]υκᾶν μαινομέγ[οισιν ἐσάλαο π]ρσσιν ἀφ᾽ ἵ[π]πω[ν·
> αἰ]αῖ ἐγώ, μέγ᾽ ἄϋσα· φ[   ] χελύννα
> ἀλ]λομένα μεγάλας[κατὰ] χορτίον αὐλᾶς·

[Into the deep] wave / from white horses [you leapt] with maddened feet. / "Aiai," I cried loudly; . . . tortoise / [leap]ing . . . [down] the enclosure of the great yard.

Sir Maurice Bowra brilliantly identifies these, the first more fully extant lines, as a description of the children's game *chelichelōnē* or "torty-tortoise."[30] As Pollux describes it, one girl crouches down, while the others run in a circle around her and chant, "Torty-Tortoise, what are you doing in the middle?" The crouching girl answers, "I weave wool and Milesian thread." Those who are circling then ask, "What was your son doing when he per-

---

[30] Bowra [1936] 1953: 154, from the description in Pollux 9.125.

ished?" She answers, "From white horses into the sea he leaped." On the word "leaped" the crouching girl leaps up and tries to tag another, who will then be the tortoise.[31] The supplements given in the text above depend on Bowra's identification. This game appears to be the subject from at least line 5 of the fragment on (since "tortoise" appears at the end of lines 5 and 7).

The game contrasts immobile mother and mobile son. But before I incorporate it into my analysis, I want to note what we can deduce with minimal supplementation so that my analysis does not appear to be entirely derived from Pollux's account. In line 16 "Erinna" cries out in a phrase equivalent to "woe is me!" *Aiai* is a wail used in lament; it is found both in epitaph *CEG* 2: no. 686, quoted above, and in the last line of the *Distaff* ("*aiai*, wretched Baukis . . ."). "Erinna" must be reacting to the "maddened" action involving feet mentioned in the line before. It seems reasonable to assign this action to Baukis. If so, we see a difference in their emotional tendencies: Baukis madly moves (since feet are involved), while "Erinna" quickly yields to grief or fear.

We can now investigate how the game helps us interpret their emotional reactions. As Pollux describes it, the game encodes two social roles as physical positions: the "mother" crouches, a posture that could be linked to giving birth and is certainly immobilizing, while the "son" leaps into motion, up and out in rejection of the crouch.[32] The children's chant amplifies the contrasting kinetics: the mother is a tortoise, and the son rides horses. The tortoise is also suited to represent a mother because it carries its "house" with it, as Marylin Arthur [Katz] has pointed out, and therefore is always confined inside the house.[33] Furthermore, this "tortoise" weaves a shroud; wool-working and lament are identified with women. The "son" leaps from horses to his death—yet his leap also implies sexual desire, if leaping from white horses into the sea is a variant of a theme that Gregory Nagy has isolated, of leaping from a white rock into the sea to cure desire.[34] The leap from the white rock may kill, for it precipitates the leaper into unconsciousness, whether of relief from passion, drunkenness, sleep, or death.

[31] The crouching girl's leap is deduced, in part from the game of *chytra* (described in 9.113–14) to which Pollux compares this game.

[32] For mythic association of the female with immobility, the male with mobility, see Vernant [1965] 1983.

[33] Arthur [Katz] (1980: 58–61) gives Greek references to this idea, including a story in which *Chelōnē* (Tortoise) was a young woman who stayed home rather than go to Zeus's wedding; Zeus condemned her to be always "at home." She interprets the tortoise as a boundary figure. Pomeroy (1978: 18) notes also the connection with silence.

[34] Nagy [1977] 1990: 226–34. Horses are found in association with some references to the theme, and riding a "horse" is an image of intercourse in, e.g., Anacreon fr. 417. Griffith and Griffith (1991) cite Nagy but interpret the game as a metaphor for the young man catching a wife, who then becomes confined to the home and produces a son, who will catch a wife.

The chant therefore maps the complex of gender roles onto mobility and immobility. For girls who play the game, the cultural messages are clear: mobility—circling, leaping, running—makes the game fun to play but is attached to a role that will not be theirs, while the loser's position of immobilized mother represents their future. The game elicits pleasures that the chant implies are alien to women. At the same time, by equating movement and freedom of action and sexuality with death, the chant reinforces the strictures that will soon inhibit their movements. Not that the girls would necessarily recognize the leap as sexual, but they would experience it as free use of their limbs and release from tension.

Returning to Erinna's poem, as supplemented in light of the game, we can expand our analysis. "Erinna's" account, we must remember, is retrospective; it reflects the significance that the speaker now sees, following Baukis' death, in that episode. As "Erinna" describes it, Baukis leaps with maddened feet from white horses into the sea; she is fully identified with the son of the chant. The following lines, "tortoise / [leap]ing . . . [down] the enclosure of the great yard," should continue the description of Baukis, now in terms of her actual motion.[35] By interweaving the action of the game (leaping down the enclosure) with the words of the chant, Erinna invites us to transfer the action of the son in the chant to Baukis: Baukis leaps away from the mother's confined position and into sexuality and death. Her "maddened feet" convey intensity, as though she were desperate or possessed. And by putting the term "tortoise" in the sentence describing Baukis' actual motion, "Erinna" implies that Baukis really is (or should be) a tortoise. "Erinna's" oxymoronic image (for tortoises cannot leap) highlights the leap against the behavior expected of Baukis.

"Erinna" also contrasts her former self with Baukis. Her wail of "*aiai*" could be dismay at Baukis' impetuosity, or perhaps she was tagged. Either way, whether she laments Baukis' violence or her own fate, she identifies herself with the tortoise-mother. The two girls' different emotional tendencies can be detected in the minimally supplemented text; the game situates their reactions in the context of education in gender roles. Erinna surely did not include the tortoise game as a random childhood memory, but as a vivid prefiguring of their adult attitudes.

After the three-line refrainlike lament (18–20), "Erinna" begins anew (21–30):

δαγύ[δ]ων τεχ[   ]ίδες ἐν θαλάμοισι
νυμ[φ]αι. [   ]έες· ἅ τε ποτ᾽ ὄρθρον

---

[35] So Bowra [1936] 1953: 154. This is not certain; West (1977: 104) suggests that in these lines "Erinna" chases Baukis in turn, which would require great compression in the narrative. It is also possible that there was a high point after *chelunna* (*Suppl. Hell.* app. crit. ad loc.), but enjambement seems to me more likely after a previous stop at the feminine caesura.

μάτηρ αε[   ].οισιν ἐρείθρις
τηνασηλθ[   ]να ἀμφ' ἁλίπαστον·
.. μικραισ.[   ]γ φόβον ἄγαγε Μορ[μ]ώ
τᾶ]ς ἐν μὲν κο[ρυφᾶι μεγάλ'] ὦατα ποσσὶ δὲ φοιτῆι
τέ]τρ[α]σιν· ἐκ δ' [ἑτέρας ἑτέραν] μετεβάλλετ' ὀπωπάν·
ἀνίκα δ' ἐς [λ]έχος [ἀνδρὸς ἔβας τ]όκα πάντ' ἐλέλασο
ἄσσ' ἔτ[ι].. ηπιασ.. τε[ᾶς παρὰ] ματρὸς ἄκουσας,
Βαῦκι φίλα· λάθας.. ε.[ἐπέβα]σ' Ἀφροδίτα·

Of dolls . . . in bridal chambers / brides . . . ; and toward dawn / the mother . . .
to wool-workers / . . . *halipaston.*[36] . . . to (?) little girls . . . Mormo brought fear,
/ on [whose head are large] ears, and she comes and goes on feet / four and from
[one (form) to another] she changes her appearance. / But when [you went] to
the marriage-bed [of a husband], then you forgot all / that . . . you heard from
[your] mother, / dear Baukis; forgetfulness . . . Aphrodite [brought on].

We have no outside help in supplementing the first lines, so our analysis
must rely on significant words. In lines 26–29 the supplements fit well and
are not critical. In line 30 the verb supplied ("brought on") is speculative,
but Aphrodite as subject of a sentence containing the word "forgetfulness"
seems to call for a causative verb.

In this section we are still treated to scenes from childhood.[37] But this is
a later stage in the girls' education for adulthood, for the play is now realistic, not escapist: the words "dolls," "in bridal chambers," and "brides" appear in lines 21–22.[38] The girls are indoors, perhaps playing at marriage
and motherhood. A mother (whether "Erinna's" or Baukis') has something
to do at dawn with wool-workers, in which she may involve the girls also.[39]
The mother linked with house and wool-working recalls the tortoise-
mother of the game, but now there is no leap or escape, and play grades into
work. In this new stage in their training, the girls must conform to the roles
prescribed for women.

[36] The meaning of this word is unknown. Bowra ([1936] 1953: 157) suggests "salt-sprin-
kled meat." West (1977: 106–7) thinks of cloth interwoven with threads dyed purple (from
marine animals).

[37] Based on a restoration of lines 19–20 that creates a contrast between "these games" that
"lie still warm in my heart" and others that are "now ashes," West (1977: 105) takes these activities as earlier than the tortoise game. But whether line 20 contained a contrast with 19 is
uncertain.

[38] The word translated "brides" may refer to the dolls (cf. schol. Theoc. 2.110, quoted in
Suppl. Hell. ad loc., on *nymphē* as a word for this kind of doll) but certainly carries a reference
to the girls' future role.

[39] It is possible that the girls are close kin (e.g., cousins on their mothers' side) and are
jointly living for a time with the mother of one of them. *Erithoi* does not mean specifically
wool-workers (as Page [1981: 344] points out), but the word was often used of wool-workers
and they suit the female context; cf. Latte 1953: 84.

The culmination of these indoor memories is Mormo the bogey in lines 25–27, a female fright-figure with whom mothers threatened children. As in the tortoise game, Erinna uses an item from shared folklore to represent the gender formation that the culture impresses on girls. Mormo was herself a mother; according to the surviving story, she ate her own children and thereafter attacked children and parturient mothers.[40] Sometimes she is imagined in animal form, as here and in Theocritus 15.40. In the latter passage, from the mime poem "Women Going to the Adonia," one mother si lences the child that wants to go out with her by saying, "Mormo the horse bites!"[41] The mother of line 23 must similarly have silenced Baukis and "Erinna" by threatening them with Mormo.

What "Erinna" emphasizes is Mormo's mobility: she comes and goes and shifts shape as well. The relationship between the mother figure and mobility has altered since the previous scene. The "mother" herself is now mobile, but only because she is an evil mother who eats rather than grieves for children. Action as well as fiction is reversed: in the game the child could leap into motion, but escape from Mormo is won by immobilizing oneself in fear and obedience.[42]

Each of the first two sections sets out a detailed scene of the girls' activities as they engage through play and folklore figures with their adult social roles. And just as the first scene culminates in Baukis' leap, so the second scene, I believe, ends with her metaphorical "leap" from mother and constraint into sexuality (and death). After the lines on Mormo, "Erinna" continues, "but when [you went] to the marriage-bed [of a husband], then you forgot all / that . . . you heard from [your] mother, / dear Baukis; forgetfulness . . . Aphrodite [brought on]." Bowra paraphrases these lines to say that Baukis moved on to new interests with marriage, leaving "Erinna" behind.[43] He slights the words, "you forgot all that . . . you heard from [your] mother," and makes "forgetfulness . . . Aphrodite [brought on]" the main thought. Aphrodite he equates with marriage, forgetfulness with Baukis' at-

---

[40] See Johnston 1999: 173–83. Mormo is related to Lamia ("Devourer"), who lost her own children and now kills those of other women. I thank S. I. Johnston for showing me her work in advance of publication. Cf. also Bowra [1936] 1953: 158–59; Pomeroy 1978: 21, and Arthur [Katz] 1980: 64–65 on Mormo.

[41] So Johnston 1999: 179 (and cf. 182 for confirmation in the scholia). Others take "Mormo" as an exclamation, with "the horse bites" as an independent threat.

[42] Cf. CEG 2: no. 587 (quoted above), with its contrast of marriage inside the house and perishing outside. The child in Theocritus is scolded for wanting to go outside.

[43] Bowra ([1936] 1953: 159) says of these lines, "[Erinna] turns to Baukis's wedding, and says that with it Baukis forgot all that as a child she had heard from her mother. Then she goes on to mention Aphrodite by name and indicates that she played a part in causing this forgetfulness; in other words, wedlock brought a new life with new interests." Bowra then mentions Sappho and the "sharp pangs of parting when her followers were married and left her for a new existence." The slide from mother's words to friend is clear.

titude toward her earlier life and her old friend "Erinna." But this distorts the text, for *what* Baukis forgot was specifically what she heard from her mother, not her childhood games or companion. And Aphrodite leading a young bride to forget her mother's words might give a Greek reader more pause than Bowra allows.[44]

What does it mean that Baukis forgot all she heard from her mother? What did the culture imagine a mother communicating to a daughter that the latter should remember but that Aphrodite might erase from her mind? In the fourth-century epitaphs, the married woman's preeminent attribute is *sōphrosynē* ("chastity, self-control").[45] This quality, which popular culture most associated with a good wife, would by definition be threatened by Aphrodite.[46] Hippolytus makes a point of contrasting Aphrodite and *sōphrosynē* in Euripides' *Hippolytus*.[47]

Moreover, daughters learned *sōphrosynē* from their mothers. One epitaph indicates as much: *CEG* 2: no. 542 (c. 350?, from Attica) asserts that Peisikrateia "left her virtue and *sōphrosynē* to her children to exercise." Xenophon is more explicit. Ischomachus' young wife in Xenophon's *Oeco-nomicus* says, in her first speech about her wifely role, "My mother told me that my duty is to practice self-control (*sōphrosynē*)."[48] Ischomachus has already told Socrates (7.6) that his wife came to him knowing how to weave a cloak and apportion weaving to the slaves and "educated concerning the stomach" (i.e., to control her appetite, one part of *sōphrosynē*). In New Comedy also, another fourth-century expression of social mores, a mother may be intimately concerned with her daughter's virtue (trying, often, to protect her reputation and bring about a marriage after the girl has been raped).[49]

---

[44] I do not mean that Aphrodite had no place in marriage, but that Aphrodite in connection with "forgetting" would have a different resonance for a Greek audience from what it may convey to us. Scheidweiler (1956: 48) suggests that Baukis's mother died early and Baukis forgot her. Cf. note 54 below.

[45] According to statistics in Brulé 1987: 341–45, *sōphrosynē* is the most common attribute of married women in epitaphs, with *aretē* next. Women are often identified as *ergatis*, "worker," while few men are so identified; this probably refers to wool-working. Reliefs refer to women's beauty and labor. See also North 1966: 252–53 on inscriptions: *sōphrosynē* is the virtue most elaborately amplified for women in the later period.

[46] Cf. North 1966: 1 n. 2 on *sōphrosynē* for women throughout Greek history: "chastity, obedience, inconspicuous behavior." On 71, however, she discusses Euripides' use of the term more broadly to include the behavior of a good wife in general.

[47] Lines 640–68 and 993–1006 with 113.

[48] *Oec.* 7.14. Translation from Pomeroy 1994: 141. See her comment on the wife's training, 270 ad 7.6.

[49] In Menander's *Georgos* and *Heros* (for neither of which is the evidence extensive), the mother of a raped girl appeared as a character distressed by violation of her daughter. On the plot and characters of these, see Gomme and Sandbach 1973: 106–7 and 385–87. In *Samia* the mother did not appear onstage, but we learn that the young rapist has promised her that he will marry her daughter. Cf. also Sostrata in Terence's *Adelphoe*, adapted from Menander,

Therefore, coming as it does in Erinna's poem after the depiction of the girls playing house, a mother interacting with wool-workers, and fear of Mormo, the phrase "all she heard from her mother" must refer to instruction in domestic work and *sōphrosynē* similar to the teaching that Ischomachus' wife received from her mother. Erinna strengthens the contrast between her mother's instruction and Baukis' action by placing both Mormo and Aphrodite at line-end (25 and 30), preceded by a verb. Aphrodite's effect is the opposite of Mormo's; rather than frightening her victims into immobility, she lures them into motion.[50] Mormo, the image that the mother impresses on her child, is replaced in Baukis' case by Aphrodite, who erases the mother's warnings. "Erinna's" accusation therefore amounts to saying that Baukis treated marriage as a leap to freedom from the strictures of *sōphrosynē*.

Bowra's interpretation, that Baukis substituted new interests for old with marriage, also relies on the idea that marriage represented a strong break with a woman's natal family, that her new life would not include the natal family as a matter of course. But in the genres that offer context for Erinna's poem, this is not so. In Erinna's two major literary referents, Sappho and Homer, Aphrodite causes Helen to forget natal and marital families alike. Sappho says of Helen (16.8–12 V): Helen, "leaving the best of husbands went off, sailing to Troy, and remembered neither her child nor her parents in the least, but [Aphrodite] led her astray." Likewise in *Iliad* 3.139–40, when she comes to summon Helen to the wall of Troy to watch the duel between Menelaus and Paris, Iris undoes the effect of Aphrodite: "Having spoken, the goddess shot sweet longing for her earlier husband and city and parents into [Helen's] heart." Conversely, the fourth-century epitaphs reveal the mother's presence as a mourner at the married daughter's death, which argues for mother and daughter forming a continuing tie between the families. To look to New Comedy again, Terence's *Mother-in-Law*, taken from Apollodorus, depicts mother and recently married daughter maneuvering against the men of both houses to hide the results of a premarital rape.[51] A woman's Aphrodisiac forgetting undid the constraints of *sōphrosynē* and therefore threatened the reputations of both *oikoi* ("households, families").

What are we to imagine Baukis doing, what metaphorical equivalent of

---

especially lines 344–52. Rosivach (1998: ch. 3, "Mothers and Daughters") discusses a different plot-type in which a mother (or female guardian) arranges a liaison for her daughter, whether for profit or to provide the young woman with a home. This is the negative inverse of the mother's responsibility for her daughter's training and virtue.

[50] Cf. Andromache in Euripides' *Trojan Women* 647–50, who says, speaking to her mother, that she did not go out of the house, a thing that might compromise her reputation, but suppressed her longing (*pothos*) and stayed indoors.

[51] On the development of the mothers' roles in this play, see Goldberg 1986: 152–56.

her "mad" leap in the first section?[52] She surely was no Helen, but somehow she has refused the constrictions of the woman's role with its woolworking and housebound immobility. Perhaps she was physically too expressive or playful or assertive. Erinna may have provided the necessary clues earlier in the poem, but perhaps all she ever indicated is that once Baukis was away from her mother she deviated from conformity to the standards expected by her culture.

Baukis' behavior has cut her off from "Erinna," as the following section shows. The break-off marking transition to the third section does not employ even a full stop; rather, reduced to the apostrophe in line 30 and "bewailing you" in 31, it is woven into a continuing train of thought. I cite the relatively complete lines 31–35:

ϛῶ τυ κατακλα[ἰ]οισα τα[
ρὐ [γ]άρ μοι πόδες . . . . [ ] [
οὐδ᾽ ἐσιδῆν φαέε[σσι
γυμναῖσιν χαίταισιν[
δρύπτει μ᾽ ἀμφὶ πα[ρῆδας

τᾶ]λλα δὲ λείπω[·
] . . ο δῶμα βέβαλοι·
]κυν οὐδὲ γοᾶσαι
φο]ινίκεος αἰδὼς

Wherefore bewailing you (I) . . . and/but I neglect [the rest]; / for my feet are not . . . [from?] the house *bebaloi;* / and neither to see with my eyes . . . nor to lament aloud / with naked hair . . . crimson shame / tears me about the [cheeks].

"Erinna" connects the two sections with "wherefore." This "wherefore" has been too little noticed, but the logical connectives in this section are critical.[53] Let us consider the sequence of clauses as preserved: "Aphrodite . . . forgetfulness, *wherefore,* bewailing you, (I) . . . and/but I neglect [the rest], for my feet are not *bebaloi.*"[54] The "wherefore" shows that "Erinna's" attitude toward Baukis on her death is the result of Baukis' forgetting, and that

---

[52] In Euripides' *Cyclops* 164–72 (cited by Nagy [1977] 1990: 228 and 234), the Cyclops describes drinking wine as a leap from the white rock into the sea, leading to sexual satisfaction and forgetting of evils. The connection between Baukis' leap in the game and her forgetting under the influence of Aphrodite may have been evident to Erinna's original readers, based on this folk image.

[53] Skinner (1982) notes its Homeric tone. Latte (1953: 86) rejects the idea that "Erinna" blames Mormo for Baukis' death but does not give another explanation. Scheidweiler (1956: 48) conjectures "took revenge" in the lacuna and suggests that Aphrodite killed Baukis for forgetting; that seems too mythic for this poem.

[54] The missing first verb of this statement would determine how to take the participle. If its meaning contrasted with the participle, it would make the participle adversative and give us, e.g., "Aphrodite brought on forgetfulness, wherefore, although I bewail you, I stay home and neglect (your obsequies)." If the meaning of the verb complemented the participle, it would make the second verb adversative instead, e.g., "Aphrodite brought on forgetfulness, wherefore, bewailing you I sorrow, but I neglect (your obsequies)."

attitude seems to have two contrary strains, bewailing and neglecting.[55] The following clause, introduced by *gar* ("for"), explains what "Erinna" means by "neglect": she cannot do something with her feet (because they do not have the right quality), look on something, or lament aloud with unbound hair. Bowra deduced that she could not go to Baukis' funeral (including the formal lament during her laying-out), which seems right.[56] If we accept the restoration "the rest" as the object of "neglect," we can paraphrase the train of thought as follows: Aphrodite made you forget, wherefore, although I bewail you, I neglect the rest (i.e., the other expressions of grief that would be expected), for I cannot go to your funeral.

The poem must have provided a reason for "Erinna's" absence.[57] At this point I think we can see the possible relevance of *Anth. Pal.* 9.190.5–6, which describes Erinna as follows: "She stood at her distaff, out of fear of her mother, or at her loom, a menial laborer occupied with the Muses."[58] The portrait of Erinna must come from the *Distaff*, but no one has indicated how it might form part of her lament for Baukis.[59] Now, however, it is easy to connect the conclusion that Baukis violated *sōphrosynē* with the phrase "out of fear of her mother" in the epigram and deduce that "Erinna's" mother forbids "Erinna" to associate with Baukis by lamenting her in the company of others. The epigram implies that "Erinna" would rather be doing something else that would earn her mother's wrath, but that (unlike Baukis) she has accepted her mother's strictures. Just as she describes herself as under the influence of immobilizing mother figures, the tortoise and Mormo, in the first two sections, so she must show herself submitting to her mother in section three. Just as immobility is linked with wool-working in the first two sections, so it is here. This picture of "Erinna" also offers a completion of the theme of women's education that I have been

[55] Other translations of λείπω are possible, but it seems to have a direct object (restored as τἆλλα), a construction that calls for the general meaning "turn one's back on."

[56] Bowra [1936] 1953: 159–61, relying on *bebaloi* (on which see below), further suggests that "Erinna" was a priestess who was barred from looking on the dead. He adduces no parallel for such an exclusion, and Erinna would be using an impossibly awkward way of indicating the problem. For other explanations, see below.

[57] West (1977: 108–9) suggests that as a woman of childbearing age, she was legally prohibited, Skinner (1982: 268–69) that as nonkin she was barred. But the only known funerary legislation that specified the degree of kinship required for women to attend a funeral was Solon's; the other evidence relates to the kind and duration of mourning women could make and the degree of relationship required for women to return to the house after the funeral: see Garland 1989. Solon's legislation permitted women who were within the degree of second cousins to attend, and we do not know that Baukis and "Erinna" were not related. Latte (1953: 88), Scheidweiler (1956: 49), and Rauk (1989: 102–7) accept Wilamowitz's idea that Baukis had married someone from abroad and that "Erinna" must have been so ill as to prevent her even leaving the house.

[58] On this epigram, see Page 1981: 343–46.

[59] Latte (1953: 88) rejects its relevance out of hand.

tracing: "Erinna" has now taken on the woman's task, immobilized wool-working, that lies in her future in the first two sections.[60] Baukis, mean-while, has "leapt" away to death.

That the three sections visible in the fragment are parallel (which strengthens my claim to take the epigram as a reflection of the third section) is indicated by an overt sign: the word "feet" appears in all three, carrying the theme of mobility and immobility. In line 32, "Erinna" refers to her feet as not *bebaloi;* whatever the adjective means, the negative implies that her feet are not in use.[61] Baukis' feet are "maddened" in her leap in the first section (15), and Mormo ranges up and down on four feet in the second (26–27). By contrast, "Erinna" seems to have the feet appropriate for a woman of *sōphrosynē.*

The funeral, on the other hand, is described in surprisingly sexual terms. Not only does it require mobile feet, but, if she went, "Erinna" would "look on" [something] and lament "with naked hair."[62] The physicality condemned in Baukis seems to be freely expressed in the ritual. "Erinna" points out in effect that in lament women were permitted to shed bodily and verbal restraint: they could leave their indoor work, accuse and speak of longing, throw off their coverings.[63] Thus women, perversely, should only fully experience the pleasure of physicality in pain. Women also lamented together; if modern Greek lament provides a parallel, friends as well as relatives must have come together in an intense emotional experience.[64] But because Baukis has made physical expressiveness an issue, "Erinna" cannot freely engage in even this sublimated form.

Yet, as I pointed out earlier, "Erinna's" attitude toward Baukis has two contrary strains, which she names in the opening of the section: she *does* bewail Baukis even though she neglects the ritual lament. Likewise, *Anth. Pal.* 9.190 implies that "Erinna" would rather be doing something other than wool-working. In this final section, therefore, "Erinna" is not merely contrasting her own response to training in a woman's role with Baukis' but also

[60] It is possible that the scene of "Erinna" weaving was presented earlier in the poem and then alluded to in lines 36–46, or the mother's stricture may have been introduced in these lines. See below for remains of these lines.

[61] *Bebaloi* is difficult and may not be the right reading; see the apparatus for the doubts of Lloyd-Jones and Parsons. Applied to persons, *bebalos* means "uninitiated" or "impure"; applied to ground it means "unhallowed." If it is the right word, its meaning may be transferred from the religious to the sexual realm as "not abstemious" or "not respected" or the like. (Cf. Plato *Symp.* 218b and Theocritus *Id.* 3.51, both of which passages, in ironic reversal, call those who do *not* experience a state of sexual desire *bebaloi.*)

[62] The last image recalls Andromache in *Iliad* 22.468–72 throwing off her veil, symbol of modesty, when she hears of Hector's death. As to "looking on," cf. Ischomachus' comment in 7.5 that his wife came to him as a young girl who had been guarded so as to see and hear as little as possible.

[63] Cf. Holst-Warhaft 1992: 101, on ribaldry and satire as part of modern Greek lament.

[64] Cf. Alexiou 1974; Holst-Warhaft 1992: 28–29; Seremetakis 1991.

expressing the conflict she feels between her sense of propriety and her love for Baukis. This must be the cause of the surprisingly violent image of lines 34–35: "Crimson *aidōs* tears me about the [cheeks?]." *Aidōs* means both "modesty" and "respect for others"; it could refer both to "Erinna's" reverence for her mother and to her sense of bodily constraint.[65] *Aidōs* demands that she disavow Baukis—and yet it tears at her. *Druptō* is the verb used of women tearing their hair or cheeks in lament (as in *CEG* 2: no. 686, quoted above). It is as though her *aidōs* as well as Baukis' death were causing her to lament.[66] If this clause was connected to the previous clauses by an adversative (but, yet), then "Erinna" qualified her apparently firm renunciation of the funeral with an outburst describing her conflicted feelings.[67]

From the line-beginnings that survive from line 35 on, we can tell that "Erinna" continues to speak about her own state. Visible words in lines 36–45 include "before," "nineteen," "Erinna," "distaff," "know that" (imperative), "*aidōs*," "virgin" (dative-plural adjective), "looking," and "hair."[68] The lines must have expanded her description of emotional conflict. *Aidōs* in line 42 shows that she continues on that subject.[69] And the word "distaff" in line 39 suggests that she described (or reverted to) her mother's insistence that she remain home at her weaving. The three extant sections of the poem thus reveal not just progressive stages in women's training but also a progressive separation of Baukis and "Erinna" and an intensifying demand that she choose either Baukis or conformity to her woman's role.

In the first two sections, Baukis' leap (real or metaphorical) comes at the end. At the end of the third section (47–54), "Erinna" leaps: she breaks into a sustained eight-line apostrophe of final farewell (dear Baukis in 47–48, vocative ὦ in 51 and 53, Baukis in 54). Only line-beginnings survive, but the vocatives make this heightened finale closer to the style of performed lament than the more narrative and expository sections that preceded; emotionally "Erinna" has broken loose from her conflict and shifted into a full-throated cry to her friend.[70] Somehow she has resolved the conflict between

---

[65] For the connection of *aidōs* with women's sexual behavior, cf. Eur. *IA* 568–70 with Cairns' discussion of the passage (1993: 340–41); Gutzwiller 1997: 209–10.

[66] Bowra ([1936] 1953: 160) takes it to mean this (for a different reason). Lloyd-Jones and Parsons (1983: ad loc.) call it a remarkable image.

[67] The connective I am assuming before "*aidōs* tears me" is something like "nevertheless." Page (1962b: ad loc.) prints the conjecture *atar* in the lacuna, which suits exactly.

[68] The age nineteen, the spindle, and virginity are all associated with Erinna in epigrams referring to this poem, *Anth. Pal.* 7.11–12, 9.190.

[69] West (1977: 109–10) suggests that Erinna pictured *aidōs* personified as speaking to her. Arthur ([Katz] 1980: 62–65) sees Erinna's vision of a lonely old age as the burden of this section. Erinna's urgent desire to communicate with Baukis seems to me to make it more likely that she continues to address Baukis, and nothing indicates that "Erinna" is alone. On the contrary, she seems to be with her mother.

[70] "Erinna" may have mentioned Baukis' marriage in these lines, if *hymenaios* or the like is to be restored in lines 51 and 53. As Marilyn Skinner points out to me, "Erinna" must have

bewailing and neglecting, love of Baukis and *aidōs*, in favor of love and lament.[71] She introduces her apostrophe, significantly, with "wherefore" (47), echoing "wherefore" in line 31. The clause in 31 introduces her conflict, and this one signals its resolution.

The fragmentary text gives us no clue as to how "Erinna" resolved her emotional dilemma, but again *Anth. Pal.* 9.190 may help. I quote lines 5–6 again: "She stood at her distaff, out of fear of her mother, or at her loom, a menial laborer occupied with the Muses." The final words, a "menial laborer occupied with the Muses," combine wool-working and poetry. The phrase draws, of course, on the old association of poetry-making with weaving.[72] But in this context it does more: the oxymoronic phrase suggests a humble-looking figure with unexpected expressive power.[73] It implies that "Erinna" resolved the conflict by quietly weaving/composing a text that could go out into the world in her place and speak publicly of her love for Baukis.[74] And with this idea we realize the full significance of the title, *Distaff*. The distaff, which appears in line 39 and in the epigram, represents both "Erinna's" acceptance of her woman's role and her "leap" via weaving/poetry to mobility and expressiveness.[75] More, therefore, than lament, her poem is affirmation of Baukis.[76]

CONCLUSION

In retrospect we realize that the poem we have been reading is Erinna's answer to the constraint that women live under, reproduced generation after

---

evoked the motif of the bride of death, for it appears in *Anth. Pal.* 7.712. It could fit with Erinna's exploration of the social cost of female expressiveness. Michelazzo Magrini (1975) argues that the whole fragment is a description of Baukis' wedding (and not childhood scenes) and an expansion of the motif.

[71] Line 46, the final line of the section, refers to "gently speaking gray-haired women, who are the flower of old age" or (with Lloyd-Jones and Parsons [1983]) "gently-speaking grayhair, which is the flower of old age." But who the line refers to is obscure (alternative mother figures cast as Muses?).

[72] See, e.g., Bergren 1983. See Skinner, this volume, for other uses of the metaphor of weaving as poetry.

[73] There was a statue of Erinna in the Baths of Zeuxippos in Constantinople, described by the sixth-century c.e. Christodoros (*Anth. Pal.* 2.108–10) as sitting, "not handling the twisted thread but in silence letting fall drops of Pierian honey." Perhaps the statue captured the same passage in the *Distaff* as *Anth. Pal.* 9.190.

[74] Cf. the statement in *Anth. Pal.* 7.710.8 that Erinna engraved the poem on [Baukis'] tomb.

[75] Cameron and Cameron (1969) suggest that it refers to the spindle of the Fates. That is not incompatible with my suggestion.

[76] The unusual epitaph inscribed by Euthylla for Biote (quoted above) had a similar effect locally, whatever the background. Lament was the one medium in which women might express heterodox views. Foley 1993 discusses the implicit politics of women's lament in tragedy.

generation by the patriarchal demand that the mother inculcate *sophrosyne* in her daughter. The reader who invests emotional sympathy in "Erinna's" longing for Baukis comes to experience the progressive confinement of the girls in narrow social roles and the grief it brings both to the one who conforms and to the one who "forgets." Such a responsive reader must feel relief and pleasure when "Erinna" breaks into her apostrophe at the end. Seducing the reader out of making a conventional judgment, Erinna shapes her poem as a revelation of the hidden perceptions and feelings of women who are forced into outward conformity.[77]

Let us finally return briefly to the epitaphs. The epitaphs show us a young woman's bond with her mother even after marriage and help to make the case that what Baukis "forgot" was *sophrosyne*. In turn, Erinna's poem shows us that in an implicit exchange for ensuring the daughter's self-control, the patriarchal cultural system (to some extent) permitted mothers and other female relatives to become uninhibited in lament. We can therefore deduce the subtext of the epitaphs: the mother's foregrounded grief is confirmation of her daughter's virtue and also compensation for producing such a daughter. In *CEG* 2: no. 543 (quoted above), the deceased woman "speaks" to claim that she has exercised a "dutiful and chaste life"; her mother heads the list of grievers. The speaker of no. 686 (also quoted) says that Komallis exercised chaste decorousness, along with clever work of her hands. The latter must mean wool-working, the craft that women typically practiced; like "Erinna" and Ischomachus' wife, she listened to her mother and stayed at her loom. At her loss and because of her virtue (note *gar* in line 5), the relatives groan loudly and tear their hair before the tomb.[78] Their dramatic expressiveness contrasts with the impression we get of Komallis' restraint. Here, as in the *Distaff*, physical expressiveness is transferred from love to lament in women's actions. These memorials show that it was acceptable to present the idea of women acting out their grief bodily in public ("before this tomb"), while the wife's body is manifested only in virtue, child, and continuing ties with her mother.

Epitaphs provide the ideal against which we can understand the experience (whether fictional or not) of Baukis and "Erinna" in relation to their mothers, while Erinna sketches the pressure the social system put on women to achieve the ideal. Her poem brings us closer to the lives behind the facade of the epitaphs. Within the poem, Baukis and "Erinna" exemplify opposite reactions to the pressure, but "Erinna," the good daughter,

[77] Gutzwiller (1997: 210) reaches a similar conclusion from different arguments: she suggests that Erinna protests against being kept from the funeral and against men's dismissal of female friendships in general. For women's public enactments renouncing claim to their own sexuality, see Stehle 1997: ch. 2; and McClure 1999.

[78] These were predominantly female relatives, presumably, despite the masculine-plural participle, since women were the principal mourners.

makes her own indirect revolt the resolution to the poem's tensions and thus comes down on the side of Baukis. In this Erinna is in tune with her times: New Comedy sometimes explores harsh and unjust judgments leveled by men against women, and women were beginning to win more freedom of movement.[79] But in even insinuating defiance of the underlying value system that demanded women's conformity to narrow ideals, Erinna was a bold, if subtle, commentator on her society.

[79] For New Comedy, see Konstan 1995; Zagagi 1995; Rosivach 1998. For women's increased freedom, see Pomeroy 1977. I thank the editors and also Marilyn Skinner and Joseph Day for their helpful comments on an earlier draft of this chapter.

CHAPTER ELEVEN

Ladies' Day at the Art Institute

THEOCRITUS, HERODAS, AND THE GENDERED GAZE

MARILYN B. SKINNER

THANKS TO research undertaken during the past decade, a more detailed picture of ancient Greek women's literary activity has begun to emerge: although surviving texts are largely fragmentary and widely separated in provenance, they appear to display some common features.[1] As Lardinois observes elsewhere in this volume, female poetic production, both oral and written, is grounded upon female public speech genres such as hymns and laments. Consequently, the Greek woman poet chooses material associated with those forms of expression; Jane Snyder lists her preferred themes as "emotions, lovers, friendship, folk motifs, spiritual and ritualistic matters, various aspects of daily living, children, and pets."[2] One additional, and possibly unexpected, focus of her attention is the female viewer's aesthetic reception of *objets d'art*.

Within a wide selection of genres, ancient writers experimented with the device of *ekphrasis*, in which the reader is asked to visualize a scene or object through the eyes of a textually constructed focalizer.[3] This convention occurs in Homer (the obvious instance is the Shield of Achilles at *Iliad* 18.478–608); it is likewise found in archaic lyric (Sappho fr. 2; Ibycus fr. 286) and, as I discuss below, in fifth-century drama. From the Hellenistic period onward, it becomes a major preoccupation of epigram. The ninth book of the *Greek Anthology* contains hundreds of descriptive verses on all manner of subjects—including the notorious series of thirty-six poems (*Anth. Pal.* 713–42, 793–98) attesting to the realism of Myron's *Cow*. Chronologically, the contents of that book range from compositions by the earliest Hellenistic practitioners of the genre through representative pieces

---

[1] See especially Snyder 1989; essays in Martino 1991b; Williamson 1995: 16–21; Gutzwiller 1997 and 1998: 54–88; Lardinois in this volume. Citations of Theocritus follow Gow 1952; for Herodas, I use Cunningham 1971. Epigrams of Anyte, Erinna, and Nossis are cited from Page 1975.

[2] Snyder 1989: 153–54.

[3] On the ekphrastic focalizer, see Fowler 1991.

from each of the following centuries, right on down to predictable Byzantine variations on well-worked topics.

Women were among the first to write ekphrastic epigrams. Elegiac quatrains describing rustic shrines, landscapes, paintings, statues, and other artifacts encountered in a religious setting are attributed to the fourth- and third-century B.C.E. poets Erinna, Anyte, and Nossis. Feminist scholars have shown that these women adapted the traditional "voice of alterity" found in lament, and particularly in Sappho's lyrics, to the epigrammatic mode.[4] By doing so, they were able to articulate gender-specific responses to the changing political and social climate of the mid-fourth to early third centuries B.C.E. The present investigation proposes that they may also have appropriated conventional "viewing" situations and dialogue from mime and drama for the purpose of creating a female visual perspective. After canvassing that possibility, I explore two later manifestations in Alexandrian court poetry of a gaze marked as "other" than that of the typical elite male spectator, differentiated along the lines of gender and also, to a certain extent, of class. This textual gaze, I argue, is borrowed from, and alludes to, ekphrastic verse by women writers. To the extent that Hellenistic men addressing learned colleagues incorporated that gender-specific perspective into their own compositions, the Greek female poetic tradition may have had a pronounced impact on mainstream literary developments, more than has heretofore been supposed.

VIEWING WOMEN VIEWING

Let me begin by revisiting a new study of the ekphrastic moment in Alexandrian literature. In a key theoretical discussion, Simon Goldhill propounds that Hellenistic *ekphrasis* is a self-conscious exploration of the act of "seeing meaning" whose literary development constitutes "the history of the formations of a viewing subject." As the final step in his argument, he contrasts two well-known texts that place technical aesthetic criticism in the mouths of female characters looking at artworks. According to Goldhill, Herodas' fourth *Mimiamb*, in which a pair of farm wives comment upon a collection of statues and paintings housed in a temple of Asclepius, employs

---

[4] On Erinna's use of the female lament tradition in her major hexameter poem, the *Distaff*, see Stehle in this volume; cf. Rauk (1989) and Gutzwiller (1997: 207), who argues that, by invoking Sappho as an additional model, she "wrought a fundamental change in epic form." Nossis and Sappho: Skinner 1989, 1991a, 1991b; followed by Williamson 1995: 18–20. See now Bowman 1998; I regret that this essay appeared too late to be taken into account in my argument. The feminine sensibility of the persona projected in Anyte's epigrammatic laments is well characterized by Barnard (1991) and Gutzwiller (1998: 54–74); see further Greene 2000.

a sophisticated discourse of art appreciation essentially to amuse an edu
cated audience.[5] Conversely, Theocritus' fifteenth *Idyll*, the *Adoniazousai* or
"Women at the Adonis Festival," ironically evaluates the language of viewing itself. Here two women, the Alexandrian matrons Gorgo and Praxinoa,
again behold art in a religious setting as they admire the ceremonial tapestries for the Adonia displayed at the palace of Ptolemy Philadelphus and Ar-
sinoë. For Goldhill, Theocritus' poem constructs a multilayered system of
frames of reference through which to explore the process of visual appreciation. By juxtaposing the reactions of these women, "figures framed as
other," with contrasting perspectives—those of an irritated male bystander
and a hymn singer, as well as the royal patrons of the exhibition—it ultimately turns back on the reader "the requirement of evaluative response."[6]

Goldhill's otherwise illuminating analysis has, I think, a great hole at its
center where an intertextual citation ought to go. In what follows, I hope
to show that similarities between the poems of Herodas and Theocritus are
due to their mutual appropriation, although for different purposes, of a previously existing gendered focalizer. In the *Adoniazousai*, Gorgo and Praxinoa's knowledgeable appreciation of textiles can be construed as a programmatic exemplar for correct audience reception of the authorial text.
This self-referential application of the feminine gaze pays homage to the
symbolically charged parallelism between weaving and poetic composition
informing Erinna's most famous poem, the *Distaff*, and is then reinforced
by passing echoes of Erinna's epigrammatic imitator Nossis. In Herodas'
mime, on the other hand, the thrust of a whole sequence of veiled references to female poets is parodic. Close reading will reveal that these allusions ridicule the popularity of literary innovations developed by women
writers, especially that of the gendered gaze.

Because *Mimiamb* 4 and *Idyll* 15 are more or less contemporaneous,
Herodas' intertextual relationship to Theocritus, if any, is extremely hard
to pin down. Empirical data do not permit us to establish which poem was
written first. Relying upon internal clues, Gow conjectures that the *Adoniazousai* was composed between 278 and 270 B.C.E. and places the dramatic
action in August or September of approximately 272 B.C.E., while Cunningham dates Herodas' fourth mime, also on the basis of internal evidence,
to some point during the fifteen-year period between c. 280 and c. 265
B.C.E.[7] To complicate the picture, we cannot even claim that one of the two
poems *must* have given rise to the other, for the situational parallels can also

[5] Like Goldhill, I follow Cunningham (1971: 2) in referring to the mime writer as "Herodas" (= Ἡρώδιας, later Ἡρώδας). Masson (1974: 89–91) defends the form Ἡρώνδας.

[6] Goldhill 1994a: 222–23.

[7] Gow 1952, 2: 265, adding that Herodas' poem "seems connected, if not very closely, with
this Idyll" (266). On the date of *Mimiamb* 4, see Cunningham 1971: 128.

be explained by postulating independent borrowing from one or more common sources. Here the names of the Syracusan comic poet Epicharmus and his countryman, the mime-writer Sophron, both active during the fifth century B.C.E., are frequently invoked.

Epicharmus, the older of the two,[8] was primarily known for mythological burlesques.[9] However, stage action similar to that found in Theocritus' and Herodas' texts turns up in two citations of his *Theoroi* or *Spectators* (apud Ath. 8.362b, unfortunately quite corrupt, and 9.408d). In these short extracts, visitors to Delphi inspect, enumerate, and possibly express their admiration for assorted votive objects at Apollo's shrine. Epicharmus' observers are male, but, according to the *Suda*, the mimes of his follower Sophron were grouped into "those about men" (*andreioi*) and "those about women" (*gynaikeioi*). A scholiast informs us that Theocritus "adapted" (*pareplase*) his fifteenth *Idyll* from a mime in which women were most likely portrayed as "watching the Isthmian festival" (*Isthmia theōmenai*).[10] A generic topos common to both Hellenistic texts confirms Sophron's influence. In one quotation from his mimes, a female slave is rebuked as "wretched" (*talaina*) Koikoa (fr. 16 Kaibel), and this abuse is paralleled by Praxinoa's scolding of her maid at Theocritus 15.27–32 and Kynno's tirade at Herodas 4.41–51. Two other citations suggest that viewing scenes were a feature of his *gynaikeioi*. In fr. 26 Kaibel, a woman is addressed with the endearment *phila* and urged to "look" (*ide*) at shellfish and "perceive" (*thasai*) their ruddiness and smooth hair.[11] Fr. 32 Kaibel is even more suggestive of direct influence:

θᾶσαι ὅσα φύλλα καὶ κάρφεα τοὶ παῖδες τοὺς ἄνδρας βαλλίζοντι·
οἱόνπερ φαντί, φίλα, τοὺς Τρῶας τὸν Αἴαντα τῷ παλῷ.

See how many leaves and twigs the boys shower upon the men! Just as they say, dear, that the Trojans pelted Ajax with mud.

While the speaker may be watching an actual *phyllobolia* ("pelting with leaves") congratulating victors at the games (cf., e.g., Pind. *Pyth*. 9.123–24),

---

[8] Aristotle (*Poet*. 1448a33) states that Epicharmus was "much earlier" (*pollōi proteros*) than Chionides, named by the *Suda* as first to win the comic contest at the City Dionysia (486 B.C.E.), and Magnes, whose victory in 472 is attested in the didaskalic record (*IG* 2².2318). Evidence for his date is discussed in Pickard-Cambridge 1962: 230–39.

[9] See Pickard-Cambridge 1962: 239, and papyrus fragments of play lists (Austin 1973: nos. 81–82).

[10] Σ 15.arg.7–8 Wendel (1914). The title is not quite certain; Θεωμένων is Valckenaer's correction for mss. ἐκ τῶν παρὰ Σώφρονι Ἴσθμια Θεμένων.

[11] Ath. 3.106d–e cites this line for the form *kourides* instead of the regular *karides*, "shrimps"; a pun on *kouros*, "youth," is not out of the question. Moreover, the dildo praised by two women in Herodas 6 is also red (19) and smooth (71). If the putative crustaceans may be deemed suspect, they could furnish a precedent for the sustained joke on dildoes as shoes in *Mimiamb* 7. Regarding the latter, see Cunningham's exegesis (1971: 174–93).

it is equally possible that she is pointing out a detail in a picture to her companion, for this custom is alluded to in Attic vase-paintings.[12] If so, the original source of the literary motif of women looking at visual representations may well be Sophron.

Unquestionably, Hellenistic mimes featuring women as protagonists draw heavily, and perhaps quite independently, upon Sicilan predecessors. But this concession does not rule out secondary intertextuality. A much-discussed papyrus text of a satyr-play has been assigned to Aeschylus' *Theoroi* or *Isthmiastai*; as its title reveals, the drama must emulate Epicharmus, and possibly Sophron as well.[13] In one section, members of the satyr-chorus admire their own portraits, which they bring as votives to Poseidon's temple.[14] Each image or *eidōlon*, they rhapsodize, is a "Daedalic imitation" that "lacks only a voice" (τὸ Δαιδάλου μ[ί]μημα· φωνῆς δεῖ μόνον, 7); the resemblance is exact enough to fool one's own mother (14–17). The satyrs' remarks imply an interest in artistic verisimilitude and its psychological effects on the part of contemporary theater audiences.[15] As literary parody plays a large part in satyr drama,[16] this episode may caricature tragic viewing scenes, with the chorus' ludicrous pronouncements mocking the kind of deft but fatally misguided reading of graphic signs staged, for example, in the central episode (359–652) of the *Seven against Thebes*.[17]

[12] On the *phyllobolia*, see Eratosthenes apud Eur. *Hec.* 573 (*FGrH* 241 F 14 [Jacoby 1923–58]). Representative vase-paintings: Beazley, *ABV* 260/27 (Nauplion Archaeological Museum, Glymenopoulos Collection 1); *ARV²* 331/15 (Louvre G 296); *ARV²* 446/263 (Leningrad inv. 5576). Thanks to my colleague David Christenson for providing slides of such vases. Perhaps, however, the viewers are looking at a mural like those housed in the Stoa Poikile in the Athenian agora (Paus. 1.15.2–3).

[13] Aeschylus' activities in Sicily as playwright and producer, beginning in 470 B.C.E., are well attested (*Vit. Aesch.* 8–9, 16, 18). On Epicharmus and Attic comedy, see Pickard-Cambridge 1962: 286–88; for fifth-century literary exchange between Athens and Sicily, cf. Taplin 1993: 2.

[14] *P Oxy.* 2162.i.1–22. Sutton (1980: 29–33) offers a summary of the dramatic action with attention to various problems of interpretation. On this passage as evidence for the development of Greek portraiture, see Stieber 1994, with extensive bibliography.

[15] Note Aeschylus' comparisons of situations in tragedy to graphic representations. At *Ag.* 242, the image of Iphigeneia carried to the sacrificial altar resembles a figure in a painting (*prepousa tōs en graphais*), and in *Eum.* 50–51 the priestess equates the sleeping Furies with a picture of Harpies. For the emotive effect of images, cf. *Ag.* 416–17, where the attractiveness of statues (*eumorphōn kolossōn charis*) is painful to the husband deserted by the woman they depict. Stieber (1994: 108–14) discusses the latter passage in the light of the iconography of *korai* statues from the Athenian Akropolis. Concern about visual pleasure and the truth of art is well documented for the later fifth century: see Gorg. *Hel.* 18, on figures and statues as affording, paradoxically, a "pleasant sickness" (*noson hēdeian*) to the eyes; Xen. *Mem.* 3.10.1–8, on representing the internal disposition of the subject and on "the illusion of life" (*to zōtikon phainesthai*, 6) as art's most seductive pleasure. Discussion of Plato's well-known suspicion of the visual arts is beyond the scope of this chapter.

[16] Sutton 1980: 159–79.

[17] I am not, of course, claiming any direct parodic link between the two Aeschylean plays. For Eteocles as semiotician, see Zeitlin 1982b: esp. 44–49.

Scenes in Athenian tragedy featuring observers' spoken reactions to the perceived object, then, conceivably might reflect at least the indirect influence of Sicilian mime and comedy. Euripides' surviving plays contain several episodes in which onlookers respond to visual experiences.[18] The *Ion* has three closely related *ekphrases*. Two are purely descriptive: a messenger pictures the tapestries of Ion's tent (1132–65), and Creusa specifies the pattern she wove into the cloth in which Ion was wrapped (1417–25). During the parodos, though, spectatorship is enacted, as a chorus of slave women surveys mythic figures to be seen on the sanctuary façade at Delphi[19] and recognizes them from stories told at the loom (*emaisi . . . para pēnais*, 196–97). While the presence of the chorus of observers outside a temple recalls Aeschylus' *Theoroi*, repeated exhortations to look at particular images (190, 193, 201, 206, 209) and the use of *phila* in direct address at 193 and 208 is reminiscent of Sophron. Zeitlin accordingly suggests that the *Ion* parodos is itself indebted to the mime tradition and posits the likelihood of "an identifiable genre scene in which naive sightseers come to a temple precinct or another public place and feast their eyes on works of art."[20] While the existence of such a *tragic* type-scene must remain hypothetical, evidence discussed above indicates that the external surroundings of a temple often served as background for staged viewing episodes in *nontragic* genres and also implies that the female observer was something of a stock character in mime and comedy. When the woman poet modifies that character to create her focalizer, the scene of viewing also changes, and the prospect shifts to either the interior of the temple or the world of nature beyond it.

WOMEN VIEWING

Literary interest in female experience during the Hellenistic period may be traced back to widespread admiration for the mid-fourth-century B.C.E. poet Erinna, renowned as the author of the *Distaff*, a hexameter lament over the death of her onetime playmate Baukis.[21] Concentration upon the now-

[18] Some, in fact, rework other famous *ekphrases*. At *El.* 452–78 the female chorus offers at second hand a description of the armor Achilles wore on his voyage to Troy—reminiscent of, though significantly different from, the replacements for it fashioned by Hephaestus; and, in *Phoen.* 103–92, Antigone and her pedagogue perform a conflation of the Teichoscopia of *Iliad* 3 with Aeschylus' shield scene.

[19] In a fragment of Euripides' *Hypsipyle* (Diggle [1998] 4–5), one of Hypsipyle's sons similarly calls his brother's attention to a relief: ἰδού, πρὸς αἰθέρ' ἐξαμίλλησαι κόραις / γραπτούς <τ' ἐν αἰετ>οῖσι πρόσβλεψον τύπους ("Look, press on the sky with your eyes and behold the painted figures on the pediments").

[20] Zeitlin 1994: 147–48.

[21] West's claim (1977: 117–19) that the *Distaff* is a forgery by a male writer has not won support: see Pomeroy 1978 for rebuttal, and cf. the skepticism of Hutchinson (1988: 16 n. 32) and Hunter (1996: 14 n. 56). See also Stehle in this volume.

fragmentary *Distaff* has overshadowed the fact that its composer is further identified in the *Suda* as an epigrammatist. In the introduction to his *Garland*, an anthology of Greek epigrams compiled around 100 B.C.E., Meleager of Gadara lists "the sweet maiden-complexioned crocus of Erinna" among his florilegium of poets (*Anth. Pal.* 4.1.12); the three preserved epigrams attributed to her may originally have been attached to manuscripts of the *Distaff*.[22] The last of these, Erinna 3 (*Anth. Pal.* 6.352), appears to link earlier dramatic viewing scenes with subsequent ekphrastic epigrams:

ἐξ ἀταλᾶν χειρῶν τάδε γράμματα· λῷστε Προμαθεῦ,
  ἔντι καὶ ἄνθρωποι τὶν ὁμαλοὶ σοφίαν.
ταύταν γοῦν ἐτύμως τὰν παρθένον ὅστις ἔγραψεν
  αἰ καὐδὰν ποτέθηκ᾽, ἦς κ᾽ Ἀγαθαρχὶς ὅλα.

This picture is the work of sensitive hands. My good Prometheus,
  there are even human beings equal to you in skill.
At least, if whoever painted this maiden so truly
  had just added a voice, you would have been Agatharkhis entirely.

If Erinna's traditional date of 353/2 B.C.E. is correct,[23] hers is the oldest surviving epideictic epigram on a work of art. One more piece of evidence for its temporal priority is Meleager's editorial practice of placing imitations of an epigram after its model.[24] In the *Greek Anthology*, as part of a Meleagrian sequence, this quatrain leads off a series of variations that include two expansions of the theme by Nossis and an inversion of it by Leonidas, both traditionally dated to the first quarter of the third century B.C.E. Hence Herodas' figurative description of Nossis as Erinna's "daughter" (discussed below, pp. 216–17 and note 61) is generally understood to refer to literary filiation.[25]

One conventional pronouncement upon art found in the fragment of Aeschylus' *Theoroi* resurfaces in this epigram, though with some modification. The satyrs had identified each portrait as an "imitation" (*mimēma*) belonging to the legendary artisan Daedalus. There, for the first time in extant literature, we encounter an account of the craftsman uniquely Attic. In fifth- and fourth-century Athenian texts, Daedalus is a human sculptor proverbial for his ability to cast statues endowed with speech and move-

---

[22] Suggested by K. Gutzwiller *per litteras*.

[23] Eusebius assigns her *floruit* to Olympiad 106.4 or 107.1; although this date seems early, it is generally accepted in the absence of firm evidence to the contrary. See Gow and Page 1965, 2: 281–82. For literary analysis of Erinna 3, see Luck 1954: 171; Scholz 1973: 21–24.

[24] Gutzwiller 1998: 302.

[25] On Erinna's importance as a model for Nossis, see now Gutzwiller 1998: 76–78 and 86–87, contending that the latter nevertheless distances herself from Erinna's "maidenly" image by defining herself as an erotic poet following in the footsteps of Sappho.

ment.[26] The satyrs' assertion that the *eidōlon* lacks only a voice points to precisely that facet of his mythic personality. Erinna advances the same claim for the portrait of Agatharkhis but compares its maker to Prometheus rather than Daedalus. Replacing the mortal workman with the demigod enhances her analogy for artistic creation, insofar as Prometheus' action in molding humanity from clay involves not just achieving an illusion of life but producing life itself.[27] However, the explicit reference to Daedalus' skill has been lost: in gaining wider ekphrastic currency, the assertion of "lacking voice alone" has become mere hyperbole. In context, this alteration reveals that the prior tradition of literary viewing to which Erinna is indebted for her focalizer was probably that of classical Athenian drama.

There is a marked difference, however, between things observed earlier in a theatrical setting and the present painting of Agatharkhis. Onstage descriptions normally involve representations—mythic personages and events, for example, or celestial and natural phenomena—corresponding to no particular object in reality.[28] To be sure, Aeschylus presumably did allow his audience to see the images the satyrs were carrying and judge the degree of verisimilitude for themselves. Because the satyr-chorus spoke as a collective group, however, we should not assume that each figure was strikingly differentiated.[29] Agatharkhis, on the other hand, is ostensibly a distinct individual known to the speaker.[30] The supreme criterion of quality in fourth-century and later art criticism was the "realistic, *trompe l'oeil* representation of objects as they appear in nature."[31] Erinna's first-hand testimony to the accuracy of the portrait, based on her own acquaintance with the sitter, becomes crucial to any third party's appraisal of its artistic value.

[26] E.g., at Eur. *Hec.* 836–40, where Hecuba wishes to be endowed with a voice in every part of her body "by the crafts of either Daedalus or one of the gods," *ē Daidalou technaisin ē theōn tinos* (838). Morris (1992: 217–26) discusses the *Theoroi* passage in the light of other, mainly comic and Platonic, testimony to the artist as a maker of magic statues.

[27] Prometheus' creation of mankind was a highly popular theme in fourth- and third-century literature and art. The tale circulated orally as one of Aesop's fables (240 Perry [1952]); it is mentioned as a well-known story by Philemon (fr. 93 KA) and Menander (fr. 718 Körte). For examples of third-century seals showing Prometheus fashioning a human torso, see Gisler 1994: 2.428 (nos. 83 to 85a–h).

[28] Mythic and astronomical figures appear on Achilles' shield at Eur. *El.* 458–78 and are embroidered on tapestries at *Ion* 1143–65. Stylized illustrations of daily life are seen on the Shield of Achilles (*Il.* 18.490–606) and on Heracles' shield (Hes. [*Sc.*] 144–313), together with allegorical, mythic, and divine figures.

[29] For a contrary argument, see Stieber 1994: 92–93.

[30] Her name may allude to the famous fifth-century painter Agatharkhos, who, according to Vitruvius (*De arch.* 7 praef. 11), invented scene-painting for a production of an Aeschylean tragedy and wrote a treatise on the subject. For discussion of Agatharkhos' contribution to Athenian stagecraft, see Pollitt 1974: 234–39 and Rouveret 1989: 106–15.

[31] Zanker 1987: 47. On the assumptions underlying Hellenistic realism, see further Pollitt 1986: 141–42; for art as a visual deception, Onians 1979: 40–46.

As a female viewer, accordingly, she stands in a privileged position with respect to the reader of the epigram, for she alone can assure him of the picture's fidelity to life. Meanwhile, her enthusiastic reaction inscribes into a brief vignette the theatricality of dramatized viewing scenes, inviting the reader to participate vicariously in the excitement produced by the visual stimulus.

While following Erinna's lead in positing a female viewing subject, the next generation of women epigrammatists goes beyond her in creating an unconventional focalizer and presenting new prospects to her gendered gaze.[32] Perhaps the earlier in chronological order is the Arcadian poet Anyte of Tegea, whose *floruit* may be placed at the beginning of the third century B.C.E. Her twenty or so genuine epigrams initially seem no different from many others preserved in the *Greek Anthology*. Like her male colleagues, Anyte applies a "quintessentially allusive" style[33] to funereal and dedicatory themes, addressing her verse to the normative elite male reader. However, the poet employs a variety of strategies to project a distinctively regional, female literary persona. First, she chooses what was, at the time, atypical epigrammatic material: verses expressing pity for the deaths of young women and animals and affectionate delight in children far outnumber those glorifying masculine achievements.[34] As the acknowledged inventor of the pastoral epigram, Anyte introduces evocations of peaceful idyllic landscapes into the ekphrastic repertoire. Parallels in later poetry, both Greek and Latin, suggest that her picturesque settings may have carried secondary, programmatic implications: in poems 16 and 18, two descriptions of rustic enclaves, the implied male reader urged to enjoy the refreshment afforded by flowing water and shade may simultaneously be invited to project himself into a new literary sensibility encapsulated in the rural charm and peace of the countryside.[35]

Anyte's most important contribution to the construction of the female viewer is her "introspective" approach to *ekphrases* of paintings and statues. Far from offering a detached, strictly empirical report of visual experience, her *ekphrases* infer, from observed phenomena, the internal disposition of the object portrayed. Thus, according to Gutzwiller, Anyte "presents for us, not an accurate description of an artwork, but an imaginative interpretation that arises from her own unique perspective on the represented figure."[36]

[32] The following discussion of Anyte and Nossis, though conceived independent of Gutzwiller (1998: 54–88), is greatly indebted to her illuminating analysis of the role each writer played in the development of epigram collections.

[33] Geoghegen 1979: 9.

[34] On Anyte's particular interest in children and animals, see Barnard 1991.

[35] Gutzwiller 1998: 71–73; the association between the *locus amoenus* and the pastoral genre itself is clearly established in Theoc. *Id.* 1.1–3 (whose anaphora *hadu . . . hadu* may echo Anyte 18.2, *hadu . . . throei*) and in Verg. *Ecl.* 4.1–3 and 6.1–2.

[36] Gutzwiller 1998. 68.

Examples of this approach are poems 13 and 14, each addressing the artistic image of a goat: the observer guesses at the fantasies of the children playing with the animal in the former, and, in the latter, conjures up the goat's own pride in his appearance. A still more complex instance of this ekphrastic strategy is poem 15, on a precinct of Aphrodite overlooking the sea:

Κύπριδος οὗτος ὁ χῶρος, ἐπεὶ φίλον ἔπλετο τήνᾳ
   αἰὲν ἀπ᾽ ἠπείρου λαμπρὸν ὁρῆν πέλαγος,
ὄφρα φίλον ναύτῃσι τελῇ πλόον, ἀμφὶ δὲ πόντος
   δειμαίνῃ λιπαρὸν δερκόμενος ξόανον.

This is the site of the Cyprian, since it is agreeable to her
   to look ever from the mainland upon the bright sea
that she may make the voyage good for sailors. Around her the sea
   trembles looking upon her polished image.

The predominant dactylic rhythm of the opening couplet and the soothing alliteration of λ and ν in the first three lines reflect Aphrodite's benevolent mood, mirrored in the translucent expanse of water viewed from her headland and transmuted into solicitude for the mariners she beholds from afar. Dieresis after the fourth foot of line 3 marks an abrupt switch in perspective to the reverent tremor of the water as it, in turn, observes the goddess' glistening statue. Descriptively, the epigram presents a contrast of emotive reactions to separate ocular experiences linked by the mutual apprehension of a brightly sunlit surface. Anyte's efforts to create audience empathy with the visualized object blur strict boundaries between textual perceiver and thing perceived, and consequently between that perceiver and the reader.

Eleven surviving epigrams by one of Anyte's contemporaries, the south Italian poet Nossis, seem, upon examination, no less innovative. Seven of these are dramatic monologues expressing the speaker's reaction to the sight of painted portraits and other temple offerings made by women. These dedications would have been visible only within the sanctuary, beside the cult statue to which they were offered (cf. Herodas 4.19–20). Here, then, *interior* sacred space is established as the *mise en scène* of *ekphrases* incorporating a female perspective. Elsewhere I have argued that the epithet "woman-tongued" (*thēlyglōssos*) conferred upon Nossis by Antipater of Thessalonica (*Anth. Pal.* 9.26.7) characterizes her as a female voice speaking, like Sappho, to an audience of female listeners. This inference is confirmed by Nossis' own use of the matronymic, a woman-specific form of self-identification, in her quasi-autobiographical third poem[37] and by the opening line of poem 4, where the participle referring to the notional in-

---

[37] For identification through the maternal line as a speech trait characteristic of women, see Skinner 1987.

ternal audience (*althoisai*) is in the feminine plural. When the woman writer presents herself as conversing with women exclusively, conventional ekphrastic language takes on new functions. The speaker's assessments coincide with and indeed enunciate the collective judgment of her female community, most notably in praising the allure of the courtesans whose dedications are celebrated in poems 4, 5, and 6.[38] At the same time, recognition of the elegance of the consecrated object, whether tablet, headdress, or statue, spontaneously evokes memories of the donor, impressions of her individual bearing and personality permeated with homoerotic energy.[39] Through exhortations to "look," *ide* (6.3, 8.1) and *thaeo* (9.3), Nossis' reader is invited to share in those erotically charged sensations. For a male reading audience, such rhetorical strategies generate a vicarious experience of immersion within the emotive currents of a woman's world.

In addition to the choral hymns, epithalamia, monodies, and laments associated with Sappho and other archaic female composers, then, ekphrastic epigrams afforded Hellenistic women writers a new way to express a gendered perspective. Erinna refashions the stereotype of the woman viewer into an authoritative focalizer by reassuring us of the veracity of the painted representation, based on her personal familiarity with the individual portrayed. Assuming the literary persona of the gendered viewer, Anyte and Nossis subsequently explore radically different aspects of her alterity, although each deepens the subjectivity of the speaker and infuses her empirical descriptions with emotional tone and color. Furthermore, the qualities for which particular votive objects are admired—chiefly the fineness of their workmanship—define a specifically feminine aesthetic that may be traced back, again, to Erinna.

THEOCRITUS: VIEWING WOMEN VIEWING WEAVING

After a laborious journey through the streets of Alexandria, Gorgo, Praxinoa, and their maids press within the thronged gates into the palace grounds. Over the heads of the crowd, Gorgo glimpses the billowing tapestries surrounding the Adonis display in Theocritus' *Idyll* 15.78–79:

Πραξινόα, πόταγ᾽ ὧδε. τὰ ποικίλα πρᾶτον ἄθρησον,
λεπτὰ καὶ ὡς χαρίεντα· θεῶν περονάματα φασεῖς.

Praxinoa, come over here. Look first at the rich hangings,
how light and graceful they are! You'll think they're robes of the gods.

[38] Skinner 1991b: 23–27.
[39] Gutzwiller 1998: 80.

Praxinoa in turn is astonished by the detailed craftsmanship of the embroidery (80–83):

> πότνι᾽ Ἀθαναία, ποῖαί σφ᾽ ἐπόνασαν ἔριθοι,
> ποῖοι ζωοφράφοι τἀκριβέα γράμματ᾽ ἔγραψαν.
> ὡς ἔτυμ᾽ ἑστάκαντι καὶ ὡς ἔτυμ᾽ ἐνδινεῦντι,
> ἔμψυχ᾽, οὐκ ἐνυφαντά. σοφόν τι χρῆμ᾽ ἄνθρωπος.

> Lady Athena,what kind of weavers toiled on them,
> what kind of artists drew the patterns precisely!
> How truly they stand, how truly they move,
> breathing, not woven in. Man is a skilled creature.

In expressing her admiration for this workmanship, Praxinoa commends the achievement of a lifelike realism, and in particular of a *trompe l'oeil* effect. Her language recalls that of Erinna in its praise of truth to nature in drawing (*grammat' egrapsan . . . etyma*; cf. *etymos . . . egrapsen* at Erinna 3.3) and its celebration of human *sophia* ("skill"). These verbal correlations, together with the passionate enthusiasm of both women's aesthetic responses and the fact of their looking at dedications on display within a sacred precinct, suggest that Theocritus has appropriated the female focalizer developed by women epigrammatists.

But is an implied reader supposed to take their observations all that seriously? When Praxinoa proceeds to exclaim over an effigy of the young Adonis, it becomes too much for a male bystander, who tells the two women to "stop chattering endlessly" (*pausasth'. . . ananyta kōtilloisai*) and makes fun of their broad Doric accents (87–88).[40] For many critics, the bystander's rebuke leaves no doubt that the perceptions of Gorgo and Praxinoa are being discredited. According to Dover, their "thoughts and tastes" exist only "as strings of clichés"; similarly, Griffiths finds a "housewife's failure of imagination" in their enjoyment of a "mawkish spectacle, gotten up for the consumption of the masses."[41] Other scholars emphasize the disparity between the romantic stimulation afforded by the beauties of the festival and the dismal quality of the housewives' daily lives; a condescending attitude toward so fervent an appreciation of spectacle underlies their sympathy.[42] As Burton notes, then, readings of *Idyll* 15 "have traditionally endorsed the fictive eavesdropper's remarks."[43]

---

[40] Speaking in broad Doric himself, as the above quotation indicates. The inconsistency has baffled commentators: see Gow (1952, 2: 290 ad loc.) and Dover ([1971] 1985: 207), who broaches the possibility of satire.

[41] Dover [1971] 1985: 207; Griffiths 1981: 249.

[42] Hutchinson 1988: 151–53; Davies 1995: 153.

[43] Burton 1995: 107. Cf. her further observations on reader-response dynamics in the *Adoniazusai*: "Although the poem may start for some readers with an apparent collusion between the poet and the reader against the women, the tone of the *ekphrasis* encourages the abandon-

Yet no one subject position in the text should be deemed innocent or open to uncritical self-identification on the part of readers: at this point, irony is so all-pervasive that the patronizing bystander himself cannot escape it. Praxinoa rounds on him with a proud avowal of her native origins and a sarcastic corroboration of dialectal difference: "You're ordering Syracusans around. . . . We're Corinthians by extraction, just like Bellerophon. *We* prattle (*laleumes*) in Peloponnesian.[44] I daresay Dorians are allowed to speak Doric!" (90–93). The irony arises from two perhaps not unrelated circumstances: first, Theocritus, like Gorgo and Praxinoa, was himself Syracusan by birth; second, the epigrams on which he modeled their appreciative comments are all in Doric dialect. Thus the author's affiliation with his characters and literary models is both implicit and complicated. As literary mime, Hunter suggests, the *Adoniazusai* is an "imitation of life" that "inscribes possible models of its own reception in the text"; observing that the genre, too, has now emigrated from Sicily to Alexandria, he postulates that Gorgo and Praxinoa "act the rôle of the informing poet" and that their reactions to the tapestries set a standard for positive reception by the actual reading audience.[45] Burton, arguing along similar lines, cites considerable textual evidence for Gorgo and Praxinoa's appreciation of "fineness and delicacy" (*leptotēs*) along with variegation, craftsmanship, realism, and learnedness, and emphasizes that the qualities they value in the tapestries, and later in a hymn sung in honor of Adonis, are the very same ones "prized by aestheticised Hellenistic poets."[46]

In support of those claims, I would add that the women scrutinize the textiles with the eyes of practiced fabric workers. Although the palace hangings are of course much more sumptuous than cloth made by Gorgo and Praxinoa, references to the "full range of manufacturing processes involved" in preparing the weavings for the Adonis exhibit are carefully par-

---

ment of an implied reader who holds conventional elitist views about women's incapacity for elevated aesthetic response and expects Theocritus's representations of fictive women responding to art to reflect such attitudes" (219 n. 56).

[44] McClure (1999: 76–77, 81–82) demonstrates that both *laleō* and *kōtillō*, used earlier by the bystander, are verbs specifically associated with female volubility; the latter word also connotes guile and deception, as in Hesiod's warning to beware the seductress "babbling wheedling words" (*haimula kōtillousa, Op.* 374). Like Praxinoa's employment of *laleō*, however, *kōtillō* may be appropriated by a woman to characterize her own utterances positively: in her programmatic poem fr. 655.5 *PMG*, the Boeotian poet Corinna boasts that her native city of Tanagra rejoices in her "clearly chattering voice" (*ligourokōtilus enopēs*).

[45] Hunter 1996: 116–19.

[46] Burton 1995: 102–4, in a discussion of Gorgo's descriptive phrase *lepta kai hōs charienta*, which echoes a well-known Homeric formula (*Il.* 22.511; *Od.* 5.231, 10.223 and 544). This, she contends, is a conscious allusion on Gorgo's part and, for Theocritus, a vehicle for characterizing Gorgo's subjectivity. See Burton's further comments at 173–75, arguing that it is a specific reminiscence of the encounter between Odysseus' men and Circe.

alleled by "allusions to their own prowess at their women's work in all its different stages, from scouring the raw fleece to wearing the finished garment."[47] The dresses they don for the festival flaunt their household wealth and advertise their own industry. When Praxinoa cries out as her light summer wrap is stepped upon and torn (69–70), she is dismayed by the ruin of what represents, for her, an investment of considerable time and artistic energy. Conversely, when she and Gorgo rave over the products of the queen's workshops, the tribute awarded both craftspersons and royal sponsor comes from connoisseurs of the weaver's art.

In Theocritus 15, then, the female viewer is, among other things, a surrogate for the *trained* reader. The rare textiles she admires are symbols of the elegant court literature produced under Ptolemaic patronage. Since Homeric times, of course, poetic composition had been commonly associated with, if not necessarily described as, weaving.[48] Through Gorgo's and Praxinoa's declarations, the trope is embellished by association with the aestheticism of the Alexandrian academy. Expansion of the image of poetry as weaving to encapsulate an ideal of artistic refinement resonates with the contemporary popularity of Erinna's *Distaff*, which had revolutionized objective epic narration by developing the ancillary motif of female lament for fallen heroes into a "dominant and structuring form."[49] Graphic allusions to children's games, childhood bogeys, and wool-working perform complex semiotic functions in Erinna's narrative as they reflect upon basic aspects of Greek women's lives, including domestic duties, homosocial bonding, marriage, separation, aging, death, and creativity.[50] The cluster of meanings surrounding the titular organizing image is unusually dense: the figure of "Fate, mistress of the flax-spinning distaff" (*Moira, linoklōstou despotis ēlakatēs, Anth. Pal.* 7.12.4), casts a long shadow of mortality over the poem's realistic scenes of everyday life in the courtyard and women's quarters and its thematic preoccupation with textile/textual art.[51]

Later testimony confirms that the *Distaff* forged a tight metonymic bond between the fashioning of intricate polychromatic designs in wool or linen

[47] Whitehorne 1995: 70–71. Using comparative data from papyri in the Zenon archive, he establishes that the *fucus* and *natron* Praxinoa's husband was sent to buy (15–17) were not intended for cosmetic or household use but rather for dyeing and fulling.

[48] On Homeric applications of weaving imagery to song-making, consult Snyder 1981 and Bergren 1980: 22–23; but see now Scheid and Svenbro ([1994] 1996: 111–30), who attribute the invention of the metaphor of song as fabric to the choral poets.

[49] Gutzwiller 1997: 207; for the "foundational importance" of Erinna's *Distaff* in the development of a Hellenistic poetics of affect, see, in addition, 210–11. On Erinna's close adaptation of the woman's *goos* or lament in the *Iliad*, consult Skinner 1982; for a pointed contrast with the "constricted" language of actual tomb inscriptions commemorating women as mourners, cf. Stehle in this volume.

[50] Arthur [Katz] 1980.

[51] Levin 1962; Cameron and Cameron 1969; Pomeroy 1978.

and the arduous effort of composing a slender, but exquisite and touching, literary masterpiece. This correlation surfaces for the first time in an honorific epigram by Asclepiades, who characterizes Erinna's poem as "a sweet labor, not lengthy, but more influential than many others" (*glykys . . . ponos, ouchi polus men . . . all' heterōn pollōn dynatōteros, Anth. Pal.* 7.11). The inclusive term *ponos* ("labor") is chosen to permit an equivocation between loomwork and literary creation.[52] An anonymous imitator of Asclepiades also terms the *Distaff* a "beautiful labor of verses" (*epeōn . . . kalos ponos, Anth. Pal.* 7.12.5), and Antipater of Sidon favorably compares Erinna's "slight sound" (*mikros throos*) to the raucous noise of countless epigones (*Anth. Pal.* 7.713.7). Quite soon after its publication, then, Erinna's poem was already regarded as "a model of Hellenistic miniaturism"[53] and, by natural affinity with the women's work it celebrated, as a product of painstaking toil.

In Nossis 3 the poet programmatically represents herself as a girl who has learned clothmaking from her mother and now, in the older woman's company, offers a costly robe to Hera, presumably on the occasion of her own marriage.[54] This constellation of elements—a bride, her mother, the rite marking a transition from childhood to adulthood, and weaving as a reflexive emblem of the written text—looks back to the *Distaff,* where each motif had been prominently featured.[55] Nossis broadens the semantic range of the weaving trope, however, by inventing a beholder whose sensibilities are engaged by every kind of ornate and embellished handiwork. The phrase *chrysōi daidaloen,* "curiously wrought with gold," is applied to a wooden statue inlaid with gilding in poem 4.2; in poem 5.3, *daidaleos* is the descriptive term for an embroidered headdress fragrant with the owner's hair-perfume.[56] "Delicacy of fabric, intricacy of design, sweetness of scent serve to define a feminine aesthetic, standards of beauty held by the women known to Nossis and reflected in both their possessions and persons."[57] As we have already observed, interest in fine optical effects as a means of insuring the accuracy that guaranteed verisimilitude was a crucial preoccupation of fourth-century B.C.E. art criticism.[58] Nossis borrows intellectual ter-

---

[52] Hunter 1996: 15.

[53] Cameron 1995: 275.

[54] On the epigram as a self-conscious artistic pronouncement, see Skinner 1991b: 22–23.

[55] A. Lardinois reminds me that some of these elements are already present in Sappho fr. 102, in which a girl confesses to her mother that she is unable to weave on account of her desire (*pothos*) for a youth.

[56] Both adjectives are, of course, etymologically associated with the name "Daidalos," though their frequency, from Homer onward, precludes direct reference to the myth. For discussion of *daidaleos* and its cognates in epic, see Morris 1992: 3–35.

[57] Gutzwiller 1998: 82–83.

[58] On craft and elegance as dominant concerns of Hellenistic art and literature, see Fowler 1989: 5–22.

minology to sanction aesthetic pronouncements that reflect a female viewing eye trained for keen observation through textile manufacture.

Indebted to both Erinna and Nossis for the metaphor of the well-crafted text as a piece of elaborate weaving, Theocritus adapts from Nossis another component of his self-oriented analogy, namely the casting of the female focalizer as expert critic. Praxinoa's exclamation, "How truly they stand" (*hōs etym' hestakanti*, 82), referring to the figures embroidered on the tapestries, recalls Nossis' phrase, "How gently she stands" (*hōs aganōs hestaken*), said of the young woman Callo, subject of a portrait described in poem 6. Later in *Idyll* 15, Gorgo's identification of the "erudite performer" (*polyidris aoidos*) of the Adonis hymn through a reference to her mother (*ha tas Argeias thygatēr*, 97) again brings the Locrian poet to mind—for Nossis, in the same manifesto in which she depicts herself as an adolescent weaver-writer, also traces her noble ancestry back two generations through the female line, calling herself the child of "Theophilis daughter of Cleocha" (*Theuphilis ha Kleochas*, 3.3–4).[59] Theocritus' homage to Nossis indicates that the concentration on minute detail fundamental to Alexandrian, and more specifically Callimachean, poetics accords with the perceptions of her female observer.[60] By importing that gendered spectator into his own text and adopting her, however playfully, as the spokesperson for his own aesthetic presuppositions, Theocritus affirms the feminine ekphrastic tradition she embodies. Not only isolated motifs, then, but an entire complex of literary values, first configured as such in Erinna's *Distaff* and enhanced by an intermediary generation of female epigrammatists, was transmitted to the court poets of Alexandria and became the dominant poetics of the Hellenistic age. That the learned public was aware of the contribution to Alexandrian literary protocols made by women writers we now discover by turning to Herodas—a hostile witness if ever there was one.

HERODAS: VIEWING WOMEN WRITING

In the unblushingly obscene *Mimiamb* 6.20, a housewife refers disparagingly to *Nossis* . . . *Ērinnēs*, "Nossis, daughter of Erinna," as being in illegitimate possession of a leather dildo. To Herodas' readers, Nossis' unusual *sphragis*, her woman-oriented style of poetic identification, was apparently well known enough to be parodied outright.[61] This sign of familiarity with

[59] The scholiast identifies the singer as a poet, and Dover ([1971] 1985: 208) takes *polyidris* as a reference to her skill at composing her own songs.

[60] Burton 1995: 104.

[61] In Skinner 1991b: 35–36, I analyze the derogatory implications of Herodas' reference to both women writers. Without knowing my study, Neri (1994) arrives at similar conclusions,

Nossis' poetry on the part of both author and audience gives us a *prima facie* reason for exploring the possibility that the scenario of *Mimiamb* 4 may be based upon her ekphrastic epigrams. Nossis' poetic speaker has been described as a unique personality "who guides us, as it were, on a tour of an art gallery."[62] The objects that meet her imagined companion's eyes are identified as actual votive gifts, at least three of which are housed in a local temple of Aphrodite.[63] *Mimiamb* 4 presents one woman guiding another through a collection of statuary, paintings, and other votive objects found in a sanctuary of Asclepius—possibly on the island of Cos, though the locale has been questioned.[64] Parallels between the dramatic setting of the epigrams and the mime are too close, in my opinion, to be explained by coincidence. The reactions of Herodas' female speakers to the temple offerings also appear to parrot the ekphrastic language of both Nossis and her predecessor Erinna. Finally, the fact that the mime action takes place in a temple of Asclepius points to a further connection with Anyte and suggests that the victim of Herodas' satire is not only Nossis—though she is his principal *bête noire*—but women writers in general.

We can start with the ostensible allusion to Anyte. Pausanius (10.38.13) reports a foundation legend associated with a ruined sanctuary of Asclepius near Naupactus, supposedly built by a private citizen, Phalysius, in gratitude for a miraculous cure performed through the good offices of "the poet Anyte" (*Anytēn tēn poiēsasan*), who received two thousand gold staters as a reward. This anecdote appears to contain garbled testimony about a real hymn of thanksgiving to Asclepius, probably written to commemorate the dedication of Phalysius' shrine. The existence of the legend shows that the hymn itself was once better known, if not familiar to Pausanias. Since Kynno's opening prayer to Asclepius and related divinities (1–18) renders thanks for a cure performed by the god, it may be intended to remind the reader of Anyte's composition. As Cunningham notes ad loc., these lines closely resemble surviving cultic invocations to Asclepius; their only exceptional feature is Kynno's parenthetic apology for her meager donation (14–16). Her justification, "for we do not draw water abundantly or readily at all" (οὐ γάρ τι πολλὴν οὐδ᾽ ἕτοιμον ἀντλεῦμεν), should be taken as

---

plausibly adding that the designation of Nossis as Erinna's "daughter" implies she is an "inept imitator" (*imitatrice fallita*) of the more renowned poet (231).

[62] Gutzwiller 1998: 83.

[63] Contrary to Gow and Page's assertion (1965, 2: 438 and 4.1) that "nothing is known of a temple of Aphrodite at Locri," excavations have uncovered evidence of two such sanctuaries in the immediate vicinity, an archaic temple at Marasà and another shrine near Centocamere; it is unclear which one might be Nossis' shrine. For discussion, see Gigante 1974: 30–32 and Bagnasco 1990: passim.

[64] By Cunningham (1966: 115–17), who demonstrates the weakness of that claim. A telling counterargument is that none of the pieces discussed by the women can be securely identified with a known artwork, much less one associated with Cos.

a figure of speech, referring to an overall lack of household resources. If the entire passage is a burlesque of Anyte, the remark can also be understood, metatextually, as a snide allusion to a dried-up wellspring of poetic inspiration.

At line 19 the mimiambist turns to his primary target. Kynno instructs her companion, Kokkale,[65] to place a *pinax* to the right of a statue of Hygieia, a piece of stage business that brings Nossis' portraits to mind. Once that action has positioned us to observe the linkage, Kynno's further exchanges with Kokkale can be seen to travesty the relationship in Nossis' epigrams between the first-person speaker and the implied addressee. Kynno is the bossy figure who knows her way about the shrine and briskly supplies factual information about the objects on display, while her friend exclaims in naive astonishment at their verisimilitude. Their opening exchange gestures toward the basic framework of the dedicatory epigram. Kynno is asked for the names of the sculptor and donor of a statue group: "What workman made this piece and who set it up?" She replies, "The sons of Praxiteles— don't you see those letters on the base?—and Euthies the son of Praxon dedicated it" (21–25). Here the text calls attention to itself as a parody of another genre by poking fun at the convention that makes the epigrammatic speaker, standing in front of a consecrated object, proffer information her internal addressee could obtain merely by reading the accompanying inscription.

According to fourth-century B.C.E. academic criteria, excellence in painting and the plastic arts was conceived as the accurate realization of interior dispositions, whose truth to nature would then produce a corresponding pleasure in the viewer.[66] This is presumably the critical tenet informing Kynno's and Kokkale's educated appreciation of what they see.[67] When citing *Mimiamb* 4 to illustrate that aesthetic principle, however, scholars overlook the women's appetite for sensationalism and the irony that consequently pervades their laudatory remarks. To Kynno, for example, a figure of a girl gazing with longing at an apple conveys a greed so intense that its victim is on the point of fainting away (27–29). She proceeds to marvel, in

[65] Cunningham (1966: 118–19) believes the names "Kokkale" in line 19 and "Kottale" in line 88 (variant papyrus readings that must refer to the same character) are those of a slave, insofar as orders are being given. Here and in his commentary, he assigns Kynno's friend the name "Phile," which occurs as a vocative in 27, 39, and 72. We have seen above, however, that female speakers in Sophron's mimes and in the *Ion* parodos use the adjective as a term of endearment, as women addressing each other do elsewhere in Herodas (1.73, 6.31). Consequently I think "Kokkale/Kottale" is the second speaker's real name and *philē* another generic marker.

[66] Articulated at Xen. *Mem.* 3.10.8: imitation of the feelings (*ta pathē*) affecting physical agents gives rise to a kind of enjoyment (*tina terpsin*) in spectators. Cf. Onians 1979: ch. 2; Pollitt 1986: ch. 3; Zanker 1987: 42–44.

[67] Gelzer 1985: 115.

the same manner as Erinna and Theocritus' *Praxinoa*, at a marble likeness all but gifted with speech and speculates that human genius will someday put life into stone (32–34); but she produces those topoi in reaction to a realistic depiction of a boy strangling (*pnigei*, 31) a goose. The works of art she and her companion admire are either melodramatic in subject matter or capable of triggering overwrought responses that call their capacity for proper evaluation into question.

Mockery becomes overt in Kokkale's remarks about a statue of Batale, daughter of Myttes (*ton Batalēs . . . andrianta tēs Mytteō*, 35–36). In Erinna's paradigmatic epigram, human achievement in portraiture was compared to Prometheus' act of creation, and the image so truly (*etymōs*) depicted said to want only a voice. Batale's stance is so accurately rendered, Kokkale asserts, that one who has seen only the statue ought not to "be in need of the true woman" (*mē etymēs deisthō*, 38). Batale and her mother Myttes bear *redendere Namen* that may be translated as "Stammerer, daughter of Speechless." This use of the matronymic is another oblique allusion to Nossis' *sphragis*, while the combination of derogatory names hints at her artistic ineptitude. Both names have obscene connotations: Harpocration 44.9 defines *batalos* as "anus," while in Hesychius *mytis* is applied to someone given over to sex, *myttos* to a woman's private parts. As Cunningham (ad loc.) assures us, these are appellations "no respectable woman would bear."[68] Though Batale's actual pose is not described, one is therefore tempted to suspect the worst and to sense a sinister implication in the verb *deisthō* ("be in need of"). It seems reasonable to conclude that Nossis' epigrams celebrating offerings by courtesans are burlesqued in this passage.

Presently Kynno leads Kokkale into the sacristy to view the *chef d'oeuvre* of the temple collection, a depiction of a sacrifice by the great fourth-century master of illusion, Apelles. Kokkale's item-by-item comments on details of this painting (56–71) are an instance of *enargeia*, the descriptive effect that aims at bringing an event vividly before the senses so as to make the audience into a virtual eyewitness of what is narrated.[69] Yet her response to the piece as a harmonious composition betrays her inability to appreciate what she is privileged to behold. She instantly fixes upon the sensuality of one particular figure (59–62):

---

[68] The names of the two leading figures are no less pejorative. "Kynno" is obviously from *kynō*, "bitch," the epitome of female shamelessness (Hsch.), and "Kynne" is an actual *hetaira* name (Henderson 1975: 133). If the second speaker's name is "Kokkale," it may be derived from *kokkos*, "seed," which Hesychius identifies as a metaphor for "cunt"; if it is "Kottale," it would presumably be related to the sympotic game of *kottabos*, played by *hetairai* on the shoulder of *ARV*[2] 23–24/7 (Munich 2421), a vase reproduced on the cover of this book. For related puns in Aristophanes, see Henderson 1975: 134.

[69] So defined by Dion. Hal. *Lys.* 7. Walker (1993) offers a sophisticated analysis of the operations of *enargeia* in prose narrative; for its application to poetry, see Zanker 1981.

τὸν παῖδα δὴ <τὸν> γυμνὸν ἦν κνίσω τοῦτον
οὐκ ἕλκος ἕξει, Κύννα; πρὸς γάρ οἱ κεῖνται
αἱ σάρκες οἷα θερμὰ θερηὰ πεδῶσαι
ἐν τῇ σανίσκῃ.

This boy—the naked one—if I scratch him,
won't it wound him, Kynno? For in the panel
the flesh lies on him pulsing like warm, warm springs.

If we accept Kenyon's attractive supplement *ton*, which adds a second, emphatic "the," what engages Kokkale's rapt attention is the boy's nudity. Apelles' renowned capacity to transmit the impression of corporeal presence through his brushwork gives her pleasure, but not of an aesthetic kind—rather, it arouses her sadistic lust. Next, her admiration for one minor article, a pair of silver fire-tongs, is expressed in terms of the desire a thief would experience if he thought them real. What seems to be the central grouping is then recounted in three breathless lines: "The ox and the man leading him and the female attendant and this hook-nosed man and the fellow with the cowlick—don't they look like daily life?" (66–68). Lastly, her coy affectation of terror at the oblique glance of the sacrificial ox constitutes a *reductio ad absurdum* of the woman viewer's emotional immersion in the lifelikeness of an image. As presented through Kokkale's eyes, then, this muddled account of an ostensibly great painting frustrates the reader's attempt to visualize it as a totality and thereby underscores the focalizer's own incompetence.[70]

But Kokkale's mentor Kynno comes off no better. After decreeing, in language again reminiscent of Erinna 3.1–2, that Apelles' hands were "true" (*alēthinai*) in all his paintings (*grammata*), she commends him for his eagerness to attempt any subject that entered his mind.[71] To the reader, such backhanded praise conveys impulsiveness and lack of proper judgment. Through the vulgarity of Kynno's capping pronouncement, Herodas' deflationary aim is fully achieved: anyone who has not looked upon the painter's work rightly, she says, should be "hung by the foot and carded at the fuller's" (76–78). The form of punishment that springs to her mind denigrates the privileged association of textiles, textuality, and aesthetics with the female writer. At the same time, the eclecticism she imputes to Apelles may be thought to reflect no less poorly upon efforts by fourth-century women writers to introduce previously neglected elements of domestic and affective life into poetry. If the language of artistic verisimilitude in *Mimi-*

---

[70] My reading of this passage owes much to Burton 1995: 99–101.
[71] ὧι ἐπὶ νοῦν γένοιτο καὶ θέων ψαύειν / ἠπείγετ' ("Whatever came into his mind, he was eager to pursue quickly," 75–76).

amb 4 replicates the discourse of fourth-century academic art criticism, it does so only to benchmark the perceptual shortcomings of its female users.

CONCLUDING VIEWS

Herodas was no stranger to artistic polemic: *Mimiamb* 8 shows him to be a fully engaged participant in the literary controversies of the academy.[72] Yet, for reasons discussed above, it would be going too far to posit that the attack on women poets in *Mimiamb* 4 is directed at his colleague Theocritus as a rebuttal to the affirmation of the female viewer and the female voice in *Idyll* 15. My claim is more limited. I propose that the *Adoniazousai* is but one example of a current fashion in Alexandrian literature that the mimiambist sees as pernicious: the assumption by male writers of a feminized perspective, the sympathetic, romantic, or at the very least tolerant exploration of women's subjectivity. Given initial impetus by the affective and rhetorical power of Erinna's *Distaff*, this trend was accelerated when the epigrammatic collections of Anyte and Nossis presented other equally interesting subject positions with which a male reader could identify. The influence of Erinna, and of those woman writers who followed her, had apparently become pervasive enough to provoke a counterattack from Herodas.

My reading of *Mimiamb* 4 has focused upon a number of features not derived, as far as we can tell, from mime tradition: the choice of a temple of Asclepius as the setting; the characterization of the two protagonists as guide and protégée; the parody of dedicatory epigrams; the incongruous attribution of academic opinions on art to poor rural women; the equally incongruous mention of a famous artist and failed *ekphrasis* of his painting. In the same text, however, we also find typical elements of mime, most notably the presence of double entendre and even gross obscenity. That last element dominates Herodas' sixth and seventh mimes, which also refer in passing to Erinna and Nossis. Sardonic echoes of Kokkale's delight in "high art" are found in the admiration other female speakers express for leather sexual tools fashioned by the cobbler Kerdon (6.65–67, 7.115–17).[73] Burton demonstrates that similarities in language and thematic motifs, with particular emphasis on female interest in finely stitched artifacts, connect these three mimes closely, protracting the polemic trajectory of *Mimiamb* 4.[74]

Three out of eight of Herodas' more or less intact compositions lampoon a poetics of elegant, visually absorbing craftsmanship; in the process, they affiliate women writers with that poetics. What conclusions are we permit-

---

[72] Rosen (1992) explains *Mimiamb* 8 as Herodas' *apologia* for the mixed nature of his genre.
[73] Gelzer 1985: 102.
[74] Burton 1995: 110–12.

ted to draw about the prominence of such writers and their impact upon the contemporary literary scene? Suggesting that Erinna and Nossis could have exerted some influence upon literature at the Ptolemaic court is not entirely unheard of; twenty years ago Stern proposed that the two authors were castigated in *Mimiamb* 6 for "taking the art of poetry in wrong directions."[75] To invert Foucault's dictum, where there is resistance—and prolonged, acrimonious resistance at that—there *must* be power. Herodas would not have devoted so much energy to discrediting the poetic efforts of women if those efforts had not created what he and readers sympathetic to his opinions seem to have regarded as a controlling paradigm. Assessed two millennia later, his attack may be considered partly successful. The paradigm remains stereotypical of the era. But it has lost its overt ties to the female poetic tradition and became, simply, one key component of "the Hellenistic."

Because the loss of so many texts makes it difficult to grasp the extent of women's contribution to Greek literature, both traditionalist and feminist scholars tend to marginalize it: women poets, they believe, were few to begin with, and, except for Sappho, not widely read. Yet evidence contained in the work of male literary figures—Asclepiades' praise of the *Distaff*, Theocritus' use of the female ekphrastic focalizer, Herodas' successive burlesques—tells another story. When that evidence is closely studied, it becomes increasingly likely that the works of Erinna, Nossis, and Anyte were not peripheral curiosities but major counters in Hellenistic scholarly and aesthetic exchanges. Their surviving verses, then, must receive more meticulous consideration—if only to gain a fuller understanding of literary disputes as they play themselves out in canonical authors of the period. Accordingly, I hope that I have made a plausible case for entertaining, if not immediately accepting, a revisionist hypothesis concerning Hellenistic literary history—that, in that collective racket emanating from the notorious "birdcage of the Muses" at Alexandria, some of the Doric chattering was noticeably higher in pitch.[76]

---

[75] Stern 1979: 254; while the claim once seemed unreasonable to me (Skinner 1991b: 46 n. 46), I am now prepared to accept it and to concur in his view of *Mimiamb* 6 as a complex literary proclamation operating on several highly sophisticated levels.

[76] I wish to thank Kathryn Gutzwiller, André Lardinois, and Laura McClure for offering excellent suggestions on previous drafts of this chapter.

CHAPTER TWELVE

Windows on a Woman's World

SOME LETTERS FROM ROMAN EGYPT

RAFFAELLA CRIBIORE

TEEUS TO Apollonios her lord many greetings. First of all I salute you, master, and I pray always for your health. I was in no little distress, my lord, hearing that you had been ill, but thanks be to all the gods for they keep you free from harm. I beg you, my lord, if you so wish, to hurry back to us, else we die because we do not see you every day. Would that we were able to fly and come and pay respect to you, for we are anxious to follow you. So change your mind for us and hasten back to us. Goodbye, my lord. . . .

The powerful feelings that this woman, a servant, expressed are still vibrant on the page: her letter catches us unaware with its modern introspection and unabashed outpouring of affection. But apparently Teeus was not the only woman preoccupied with the welfare of Apollonios. At the beginning of the second century C.E., in the Egyptian cities of Hermopolis and Heptakomia, the lives of a circle of women revolved around a single man, who was respectively their son, husband, father, master, or social acquaintance. This chapter is concerned with these women. It not only considers what these women wrote to each other and to the man who was the center of their attention, but also inquires about the degree of authenticity and spontaneity of their personal voices and the education and literacy that their letters disclose. Moreover, it explores the habits and etiquette of correspondence that these letters reveal, which are fascinating since the evidence on women and writing in antiquity is extremely thin.

At the end of Trajan's reign and the beginning of Hadrian's, the Apollonios in question was *stratēgos*, head of the civil administration, of the district of Apollonopolites Heptakomia in Upper Egypt. When he laid down his office in 120 C.E. and went back to his property in Hermopolis in Middle Egypt, he followed the habit of other officials and took with him all his private and official papers that had accumulated in the period from 113 to 120. All the papers of this archive were found at the beginning of the twentieth century around Hermopolis, probably where one of the family's estates was located. Among these there are twenty-five letters of women who were related in some way to the *stratēgos*.[1] The papers contained in the archive were scattered among various collections of papyri. The whole archive thus was never thoroughly studied, and the women's letters in particular have so far earned very little attention.

The family of Apollonios belonged to the upper class of the Greek population of Hermopolis. Even though the names of some of its members betray an Egyptian influence, the family's culture and education were Greek. The archive shows that most of Apollonios' acquaintances and the people who worked directly for him were Greek, but that the *stratēgos* also maintained a friendly relationship with some influential Romans.[2] Apollonios' appointment as *stratēgos* is per se evidence that his family was of good standing. The papers of the archive, moreover, show that he owned a linen-weaving enterprise in Hermopolis that must have employed between twenty and fifty workers and that he possessed property in and around this city. One of the letters from his wife, Aline, and four other letters from the architect Herodes speak of the construction by Apollonios of a mansion in the countryside of Hermopolis at the conclusion of the Jewish War.[3] This house, which was constructed with choice woods and had a tower, receptions halls, many rooms of various kinds, and sanctuaries for cult,[4] gives an adequate idea of the wealth and power of Apollonios' family. In a letter to his architect, Apollonios himself gave him specific directions to build a mansion "worthy of his dignity and fitting his way of life."[5]

The office of *stratēgos* required service outside of the district of one's residence. The capital of the new district under the jurisdiction of Apollonios, Heptakomia, was a smaller city with less than a third of the population of Hermopolis.[6] When Apollonios took office, he transferred there with part of his family. His wife Aline followed him with the smaller children, who are mentioned and greeted at the end of many letters. Nothing is known about their age and gender. Thus the wish for a baby boy expressed in two letters, *P.Brem.* 63 and *P.Giss.* 77, may have been dictated by the fact that the couple's children were all of female gender. Certainly the oldest, Heraidous, who was the center of much attention and affection, was a girl. She did not follow the rest of the family to the new residence but remained in Hermopolis with Apollonios' mother, Eudaimonis. She was probably a

---

[1] Many of these letters are brief or fragmentary. In what follows I shall mention and/or translate the most interesting and continuous passages. Papyrus editions in this chapter are abbreviated in accordance with the "Checklist of Editions of Greek and Latin Papyri, Ostraca, and Tablets," 4th ed., in the *Bulletin of the American Society of Papyrologists* 7 (1992).

[2] See, e.g., *P.Brem.* 5, 6, and 10.

[3] See *P.Giss.* 20 (by Aline) and *P.Giss.* 67, *P.Brem.* 15, 48, and *P.Ryl.* II. 233 (by Herodes).

[4] See Husson 1983: 313–19.

[5] *P.Giss.* 67.4–5.

[6] See *P.Brem.* 23. Hermopolis must have had a population of about 25–30,000 people.

teenager who pursued studies beyond the elementary level.[7] It is likely that her parents' decision to leave her behind was dictated by the difficulty of finding a suitable teacher for her in the new district.

The distance between Hermopolis and Heptakomia—approximately 100 kilometers—could be covered in a two- to three-day journey by horse or boat on the river Nile. Mail between the two cities traveled fast: perhaps Apollonios' family was able to benefit from the government's postal service. The relative closeness of the two cities partly accounts for the conversational quality of some of the letters, which implies that regular contacts were maintained between relatives in Hermopolis and Heptakomia. When Soeris, writing to Aline, whom she calls "daughter," remarks rather peevishly after a few fixed stereotypes, "Why are you writing to me that you do not feel well? I was told that you are not ill. You make me so awfully worried. But see, I have been sick in my eyes for four months!" she seems to be engaged in a modern telephone conversation.[8] In spite of the word "daughter," Soeris was probably an older relative, perhaps an aunt of Apollonios, since this name seems to occur in his family. As usual, in fact, appellatives such as daughter, son, brother, sister, or mother in letters of Greco-Roman Egypt are not to be taken literally as indications of degrees of family relationship.[9] Even though Soeris should not be identified with Apollonios' mother Eudaimonis, as was suggested,[10] her brusque and outspoken attitude is reminiscent of the latter's personality. She certainly was on intimate terms with Aline, since she could afford to accuse the wife of the *stratēgos* of looking for sympathy and exaggerating the condition of her own health.

In spite of its title, the office of *stratēgos* implied only civil duties: Apollonios was the head of the administration of his nome and had to supervise the functioning of the taxation system. The great Jewish revolt of the eastern provinces of the empire, however, greatly changed the state of affairs[11] and deeply affected the lives of the *stratēgos* and his family. When the Jewish population's struggle first with their Greek neighbors and then with the Roman government escalated to a civil war, the *stratēgos* called out a levy of peasants and took the field with them against the Jews. According to Eusebius, the revolt of the Jews of Egypt, Alexandria, and Cyrene broke out in 115 and was finally crushed in 117 when the emperor sent a great contin-

---

[7] See *P.Giss.* 80 and 85 and *P.Brem.* 63.

[8] *P.Brem.* 64.

[9] Aline, for instance, always addresses Apollonios as "brother," and for some time it was maintained that theirs was one of those brother-sister marriages that were rather common in Egypt, about which see Scheidel 1996: 9–51. Aline, however, was not Apollonios' sister, as was proved conclusively by Schwartz (1962: 348–49).

[10] U. Wilcken suggested in the edition of the papyrus that Soeris could be the second name of Eudaimonis, but this proposition is untenable.

[11] See Modrzejewski 1995.

gent of forces, after much devastation and loss of life (*Hist. eccl.* 4.2). Apollonios often left Heptakomia during the war and once went as far as Memphis, taking part in a victorious battle, together with the Roman troops.[12] During the revolt his family went back to Hermopolis for at least some of the time, but in its final phases the Jewish revolt also raged in the district of Hermopolis, where many of the villagers were slaughtered by the "impious Jews."[13]

Apollonios' relatives were distraught that he had to perform military service in such a dangerous situation: after all, the event had no parallel in the history of the office. Writing to her husband at the beginning of the hostilities in 115, Aline appears torn by anxiety and exhorts Apollonios to shift dangerous duty to his subordinates, as the *stratēgos* of the Hermopolite district was apparently doing:

> Aline to the dear Apollonios, many greetings. I am very worried for you on account of the things that people reported about what is happening and because you left so suddenly. I take no pleasure in food and drink, but always stay awake day and night with only one thought, your safety. Only my father's care revives me and, by your safety, I lay without eating on New Year's Day, until my father came and forced me to eat. I beg you, therefore, to look after your safety, and not to face danger alone without a guard. But do the same as the *stratēgos* here who puts the burden on the magistrates. . . .[14]

In the rest of the letter, which is now very fragmentary, Aline still expresses her concern for her husband's well-being and for the danger that her own brother faces. Aline was staying in Hermopolis in the house of her parents. Apparently Apollonios, who had taken her there to celebrate the Egyptian New Year, had left suddenly for his district where some fighting had broken out.

Aline's well-written letter, which strongly conveys the impression of her devotion to her husband, also reveals something about this woman's upbringing and background. From the very beginning the war was conducted ruthlessly, and atrocities were committed on both sides. Aline was concerned about the gravity of the news that she had heard, "things that people reported (*phemizomena*)". The verb used was not part of colloquial language but was a more sophisticated choice. It is significant that it occurs in the papyri only one other time, in a well-constructed letter that a young man who was studying rhetoric in Alexandria in the same period sent to his father.[15] Aline's letter contains other refined words that have a literary fla-

---

[12] *P.Giss.* 27.
[13] *P.Brem.* 1.
[14] *P.Giss.* 19; *Corpus papyrorum Judaicarum*, 2: 436.
[15] *P.Oxy.* XVIII.2190.

vor, such as that used when she says that in her worry for her husband's safety she wished to go to bed "without eating" (*ageustos*). This term never appears in the language of the papyri, but occurs with the same meaning in the work of a contemporary writer, Lucian (*Tim.* 18). Again, when this woman says that only the attention of her father "revived" her in that dire circumstance, the choice of the verb *anegeirein* tells something about her education. This verb, which is found only one other time in the papyri—in the carefully phrased letter of a learned person—is a poetical term used by Homer also in the metaphorical sense, "to encourage."[16]

Two more letters written by Aline are preserved: one sent to her servant Tetes and one to Apollonios. It is unclear when *P.Giss.* 78, the short note to the servant, should be dated. Since at the time Aline was apparently in Heptakomia, and since her letter does not contain any hints of anxiety, it was probably written before or after the war. This letter is concerned only with domestic matters, specifically with the purchase of some cloaks. Tetes apparently had complained about the absence of her mistress, and Aline was responding affectionately, saying that she "had been torn away from her by reason of necessity." Since Aline calls Tetes "mother," the latter was probably an old servant whose judgment she trusted.[17] That is why at the very end of this epistle the mistress confides to her servant: "My little Heraidous, in writing a letter to her father, does not say hello to me, and I do not know why." Had Heraidous simply forgotten to remember her mother at the end of her letter, or was this a symptom of mother-daughter tension and of a teenager's mood? The latter supposition is more likely. Aline's comment indicates that the salutations in letters were not simply a polite and unnecessary addition but had the important function of maintaining family contacts. Numerous letters of Greco-Roman Egypt basically consist of salutations: after a quick introduction, the writer simply lists a sometimes disproportionate number of people who greet the recipient, usually a rather uninteresting addition even for the papyrologist. Perhaps letters were read aloud in a family circle, with people awaiting avidly for the mention of loved ones, for this was a guarantee of their well-being. Aline's concern was thus well grounded.

The second letter of Aline to Apollonios, *P.Giss.* 20, was sent when Aline was in the district of Hermopolis to supervise some work of reconstruction after the conclusion of the war. Back in Heptakomia, her husband was celebrating the crushing of a revolt, in which he had an important part.[18] Apol-

---

[16] *P.Congr.* XV 22.1.3.16. See, e.g., *Od.* 10.172.

[17] On the term "mother" indicating sometimes a bond of affection, see Dickey 1996: 78–79.

[18] *P.Giss.* 46 shows that Apollonios had purchased a costly breastplate and other items to parade in the celebrations; see Whitehorne 1994: 24.

lonios' conduct in that circumstance had been remarkable: he had responded to the call of duty with unusual promptness and unsuspected military talent. The revolt had caused extensive damage to property and land. A letter of the architect Herodes to Apollonios shows that it was practically impossible to travel by land at that time due to the devastations in the country: one could but rely on the river Nile.[19] A papyrus indicates that at a certain point Apollonios resolved to ask for a two-month leave of absence to set his own affairs in order, since his wife could not provide for everything.[20] In Hermopolis Aline was working hard. Family correspondence reveals that she became pregnant at the end of the war, and thus by now she had a new baby. This letter to Apollonios, which was written in response to a letter sent by him, is still concerned with his well-being, but naturally shows less apprehension. At the beginning, in fact, Aline expresses her gratitude to the gods who kept her husband safe. The tone of this letter is very different from that of the previous one, since Aline's mind was now occupied with practical affairs: workers were building their new house, and Apollonios had to be kept informed about various details. Apparently the couple had also corresponded in regard to a certain garment that she was preparing for him, about which she had a few doubts:

> I am working the wool, as you wrote . . . tell me by letter which color pleases you or send me a small sample of it. If you want your garment to fall in light folds, you should think of the purple. I was given a response by the Dioscuri of your estate, and a holy shrine has been built for them. Areios, the maker of votive limbs, provides the service to them. He says, "If Apollonios writes to me about it, I will serve free of charge." You really ought to write him a couple of lines, since he is a person worthy of you and the gods and came forward promptly. Your children are in good health and salute you. Write to me often about your health. . . .

As in classical antiquity, wool-working was still a typical woman's occupation.[21] Presumably Aline was unconcerned with the task of spinning, which was left to her slaves, but, like the young wife of Ischomachos in Xenophon's *Oeconomicus*, she was supposed to supervise their work, choose the colors, and perhaps cut and tailor the garments (7.36). The sanctuary dedicated to the Dioscuri was built on one of the family's estates. The Areios mentioned in the letter, who was a *koloplastēs*, a manufacturer of votive limbs used as offerings, probably volunteered to tend the sanctuary for free because he hoped to sell his votives to the eventual visitors. In building a heal-

[19] *P.Brem.* 15.

[20] *P.Giss.* 41.

[21] About wool-working as a prevalent occupation of women of all social classes, see Pomeroy 1978.

ing shrine at the conclusion of the war, presumably for the local war wounded, Aline showed her pride in her husband's accomplishments and her desire to keep alive the memory of his performance even in the district of Hermopolis.

Aline dictated the first letter to Apollonios to a scribe. Since the end is very fragmentary, her own signature, which must have been there, is not preserved. Her own handwriting, however, is visible in the salutations added to the letter to Tetes, which was dictated to a different scribe. Clearly a long and faithful relationship entitled Tetes to this epistolary courtesy. From what remains of the subscription, Aline's handwriting appears neat, small, and rather proficient and supports the assumption that she received a good education. The scribe she used to pen the letter for her husband is the same one who wrote another letter that her mother-in-law sent to Apollonios. Conceivably Aline went to Eudaimonis' house to dictate her letter and thus took advantage of the circumstance that someone was going to carry mail to the *stratēgos*. It is more problematic, however, to determine who penned her second letter to Apollonios. It is not inconceivable that this epistle was penned by Aline herself, since the handwriting appears rather uneven.

As a rule, the fact that a letter was dictated to a scribe does not tell anything about the literacy and writing ability of the sender. People who could pen letters were available in wealthy households. In a period of about eight years—from 113 to 120—Aline and Eudaimonis apparently employed nine different scribes to pen their letters, a very high number, indicative of the prosperity of the household. A literate man or woman of the upper class who had a certain volume of correspondence to discharge usually had recourse to scribes, but would add personal greetings at the end of a letter.[22] In some circumstances the same person might choose to write the whole text of an epistle directly. Dictation was fast, convenient, and offered advantages such as allowing one to attend to other things while dictating.[23] Another crucial reason why people of high social status may have found it distasteful to write in their own hands is that letter-writing required the employment of large, comprehensible characters without a high number of ligatures, which necessitated a certain amount of effort and time. Countless letters on papyrus show that, for the sake of legibility, epistolary hands were always slower, more careful, and of larger size than the hands that penned documents.[24] People who were able to write but valued their own time may

---

[22] McDonnell (1996), who argues that the Romans of the upper class often penned their own letters, only brings evidence concerning men of the highest social orders, such as Cicero, Atticus, or emperors, and no evidence concerning women.

[23] See, e.g., Pliny the Younger describing his uncle dictating while having a bath, *Ep.* 3.5.14.

[24] About differences in types of hands see Cribiore 1996: 4–7.

have disliked having to trace their characters slowly and painstakingly. Undoubtedly the practice of dictating one's epistles was an acquired habit of wealth: it is likely that a person did not have to think twice to opt for dictation when it was available, but at the same time this habit slowly impoverished his or her ability to write a letter fluently.

The evidence that the letters of this archive offer with regard to women's writing habits is without parallel in antiquity. The letters of the mother of the *stratēgos*, Eudaimonis, are particularly valuable because they form a considerable body of correspondence written by a single woman. Eleven letters of the archive were sent by Eudaimonis to members of her family: nine to Apollonios and two to Aline.[25] In eight of these letters, the main body was penned by a scribe, each one by a different scribal hand (see Fig. 5). The quality and characteristics of the different handwritings vary, but, by and large, they show that Eudaimonis relied on able, professional writers. Apollonios' mother added personal greetings and a date to three of these letters, which are preserved in their entirety. Since all the letters were addressed to close relatives, she must have subscribed even those that are now mutilated at the end. The preserved subscriptions show that Eudaimonis wrote greetings with relative ease. Her own correspondence, and the allusions contained in it to other epistles sent to various people, show that, as the matriarch of the family, she tried to keep in close contact not only with her relatives in Heptakomia but also with her daughters and with servants who needed her advice.

It is likely that Eudaimonis herself penned three other letters, *P.Giss.* 22 and 24 to Apollonios, and 23 to his wife. When penning a whole text, her handwriting shows a curious mixture of proficient and amateurish characters. The overall appearance is rather clumsy and uneven, with corrections and letters traced twice, and betrays Eudaimonis' relative inexperience in penning long texts. *P.Giss.* 24 was probably written at the beginning of the revolt: Eudaimonis is terrified that her son will be overcome and addresses all her prayers to Hermes, called *anikētos* ("undefeated"). The other letter to Apollonios is, however, a cry of triumph, written at the very end of the war. Eudaimonis claims that her religious piety was a determinant in bringing back Apollonios "free from harm and very happy." The letter to Aline, with its expressions of gratitude to the gods and the mention of a sanctuary dedicated to a local cult of Aphrodite Tazbes, could also relate to the same period. Why did Eudaimonis pen these letters in her own hand? It is not inconceivable that in those years of turmoil even this wealthy lady had a little more trouble finding suitable scribes and had to rely on her literacy. But perhaps it was the urgency of the moment and the need to feel closer to her

[25] *P.Flor.* 332; *P.Brem.* 60; *P.Giss.* 21, 22, 24; and *P.Alex.Giss.* 57, 58, 59, and 60 to Apollonios; *P.Brem.* 63 and *P.Giss.* 23 to Aline.

Fig. 5. This papyrus (*P.Giss.* 21) contains a letter of Eudaimonis to her son Apollonios. A scribe wrote the bulk of the letter, but Eudaimonis added salutations and
comments over the line notes, demonstrating that she was literate herself. The letter was written in the Hermopolite between 115 and 117 c.e. and is currently in the
Universitätsbibliothek of Giessen (Inv. P 26).

distant relatives and to express her solidarity with them that inspired her
personal effort.

Even the lives of wealthy people were deeply affected by the war. In Hermopolis, in the last phases of the revolt, Eudaimonis had her share of trouble. Aline had gone back to Heptakomia, probably because she wanted to
be close to Apollonios when giving birth. Her mother-in-law was left with
the responsibility of managing the family's weaving enterprise, the difficulty

of finding help, and the labor unrest of the family's workers, who requested higher wages. She actually forecasted a difficult winter and complained that her wardrobe was in a poor state. Life, however, went on. One of her daughters, Souerous, had given birth to a baby. The servant Teeus, who had accompanied Aline to help her deliver the baby and had left her own family behind, had done so on the advice of Eudaimonis. "Little" Heraidous kept studying diligently:

> Eudaimonis to her daughter Aline, greetings. Above all I pray that you may give birth in good time, and that I shall receive news of a baby boy. You sailed away on the 29th and on the next day I began to weave. I at last got the material from the dyer on the 10th of the month Epeiph. I am working with your slave-girls to the best of my ability. I cannot find girls who can work with me, for they are all working for their own mistresses. Our workers have been marching all over the city, eager for more money. Your sister Souerous gave birth.[26] Teeus wrote me a letter thanking you so that I know, my lady, that my instructions will be carried out, for she has left all her family to come with you. The little one sends you her greetings and is persevering with her studies. Rest assured that I shall not pay studious attention to god (*skholazein*) until I recover my son back safe. Why did you send me 20 drachmai in my difficult situation? I already have the vision of being naked when winter starts. Farewell, Epeiph 22.
> [postscript] The wife of Eudemos does not leave my side and I am grateful to her for that.[27]

Such was Eudaimonis: a grand lady, irascible, petulant, all-controlling, hard-working, and with an unbounded affection for that son whom in another letter she calls *philostorgotatos* ("tenderly loved").[28] Even her religious piety was subject to recovering Apollonios from the dangers he was facing. Eudaimonis was in charge and god (Hermes?) had to wait. Her mention of her studious granddaughter evoked in Eudaimonis' mind thoughts of school, diligence, performing one's duty, and reaping the fruit of one's perseverance. She had to be diligent, too, and continue praying and "paying studious attention" to god (*skholazein*). But just the thought of it made her rebel. She would not be good to god until god was good to her. The expression Eudaimonis uses to say that she wanted to recover her son back safe, *apartizein*, is quite interesting.[29] In papyri it only occurs once, in a contract of apprenticeship of a boy in shorthand writing, in which the teacher

---

[26] "Sister" is used for "sister-in-law."

[27] *P.Brem.* 63.

[28] See *P.Alex.Giss.* 59. The expression is quite unusual in papyri and must reflect Eudaimonis' personal use of language.

[29] Wilcken, the editor of this papyrus, was quite puzzled by the expression, whose real meaning also escaped A. Fuks, who reedited this letter in *Corpus papyrorum Judaicarum*, 2: 442.

was supposed to give a good preparation to his student and "make him per
fect" in his skill.[30] With the same meaning, the term occurs in the *Philogelos*, where the subjects of the joke are again a student and a teacher.[31] It is
not by chance that Apollonios' mother uses this curious expression. Eudaimonis was going to pray and be good to god only after she had recovered
her son and "made him perfect." It does not matter that recovering Apollonios was actually beyond her ability. This mother was now transformed
from student into teacher and wanted to believe that she was going to have
a say in the outcome of the situation.

All the letters of this lady strongly reflect the traits of her personality. The
letters written by scribes were dictated by her word for word and were entirely her own compositions. Original expressions and turns of phrase derive from Eudaimonis' own use of the Greek language. It is quite intriguing to follow the train of Eudaimonis' thoughts: her attention is channeled
in various directions but usually returns to the preoccupation of the moment. Another feature of her epistles, and in general of the letters of the
women of this archive, is the presence of postscripts added at the end or
in the margins.[32] The fact that in the archive only the letters of women
contain postscripts may underline a characteristic more pronounced in
women's epistles. It appears that, at least in this archive, men's letters were
more straightforward and proceeded directly to the conclusion, without af-
terthoughts, while women often felt the urge of adding something else. One
should keep into account, on the other hand, that the vast majority of these
letters written by men are formal and official. Not enough is known about
men's letters in general to make precise claims.[33]

A letter that shows to the full how Eudaimonis' mind worked, the emotions that gripped her, and the practical thoughts that prevailed in the end
and brought her to reason is *P.Flor.* III. 332. This time the danger that
threatened Apollonios was very close to home. Eudaimonis' brother Diskas
was menacing his sister and her son with a lawsuit about which we are not
otherwise informed.

> Eudaimonis to her son Apollonios greeting. You are aware that two months
> ago today I went to see the undisciplined Diskas, for he would not await your
> arrival. But now, together with some friends from the gymnasium, he is plan-
> ning how to attack me, since you are away, thinking that he can gain his end
> unjustly. I did what was up to me, and I have neither bathed nor worshiped the

---

[30] *P.Oxy.* IV.724.

[31] See Thierfelder 1968: no. 220.

[32] Five women's letters contain postscripts: *P.Flor.* 332, *P.Brem.* 60, 61, 63, and *P.Giss.* 23.
More epistles, however, may have included postscripts that are not preserved, since often a
surviving letter is mutilated after the beginning.

[33] Men's letters on papyrus were never collected together and studied.

gods in my fear for what hangs over you, if indeed it is impending. Let it therefore not remain impending, lest I too encounter trouble in the lawcourts. Before all I pray for your health and for that of my children and of their mother. Write to me constantly about your health so that I can have consolation for my trouble. Goodbye, my lord. Phaophi 3.

[postscript] At your wedding the wife of my brother Diskas brought me 100 drachmai. Since now her son Nilos is going to get married, it is right that we make a return gift, even if little questions are between us.

Eudaimonis dictated this letter with much anxiety. The letter starts abruptly, without the initial customary expressions, and moves immediately to its principal subject. Diskas is amusingly presented as a misbehaving student. The term that Eudaimonis employs to capture her brother's personality is *ataktos* ("undisciplined"). This adjective will appear only once more in the papyri, in the petition of a woman centuries later who complained of being abused by some "undisciplined, lawless" men.[34] The verb *ataktein* was used in school in reference to students who misbehaved, as the *Philogelos* and the grammatical examples employed by the second-century grammarian Apollonius Dyscolus reveal.[35] Like a naughty student, Diskas was planning his attack with the help of some friends from the gymnasium. The peculiar expression used by Eudaimonis, *gymnastikoi philoi* ("friends fond of athletics"), which seems to contain a hint of scorn, appears only here in the papyri. Again the grand lady shows that in time of deep trouble her reaction was to rebel against the unjust gods and not to perform any religious rites. To this she now adds a refusal to bathe that underlines her utter anguish.[36] This case was "impending" (*meteoros*). To underline how this threat hung over their heads and refused to go away, Eudaimonis uses this adjective three times, and close together.[37] But after this outburst of anger and anxiety, the thought must have occurred to her that she had never properly greeted Apollonios and his family: she thus reverts to proper formulaic expressions that usually occur at the start of a letter. The epistle ends, and Eudaimonis adds her own final greeting and a date. But the thought of Diskas resurfaces. This time it is a family celebration, the wedding of Diskas' son, that brings her back to her main preoccupation. In reminding Apollonios of the need to send him a suitable gift, Eudaimonis intends to show that she will not be as "undisciplined" as her brother but will stick to the behavior proper of a real lady. In her words now, the trouble is reduced to proper

[34] *P.Oxy.* L.3181, from the fifth–sixth century.

[35] Thierfelder 1968: no. 61; Apollonius Dyscolus *Syntax* 1.111.

[36] See Diod. Sic. 1.91.1: in times of grief the Egyptians plastered their heads with mud and refused to bathe. In a troubled letter to his beloved, *P.Oxy.* III.528, a man reveals that he did not bathe for a whole month out of anguish.

[37] Compare the anxiety of another letter where this expression appears often, *BGU* II.417.

perspective, *zētēmatia* ("little questions"), a term that does not occur any-where else in Greek.[38] Surely, in receiving her letters, Eudaimonis' relatives must have heard her actual voice in all its nuances.

Apparently Eudaimonis had brought up her own daughters at her school. Extroverted and eager to correspond, they seem to have absorbed much of their mother's personality. Apollonios must have resided in a large house in Heptakomia, since various family members and servants from Hermopolis spent time there. In a letter to her son, *P.Giss.* 21, Eudaimonis informs him that his sister Soeris had written to her from Heptakomia, where she was visiting him. Another sister, whose name is not preserved, seems to have been very close to her brother. Coming back from a visit to him, she dis-covered to her dismay that some thieves, profiting from her absence, had stolen a certain box. After being caught, the thieves wanted her to make a sworn statement about its contents. The incident so upset her that, exactly like her mother, she blurts out the whole matter, without using the com-mon introductory formulaic expressions. In the middle of her message, however, she realizes her lack of tact:

> How are you? Every day I am in anguish, hoping you are not sick again. Send me news about your health. I certainly value your well-being much more than the things that I am trying to recover. I know that you regard me highly and I can bear witness to the many favors you did to me. Greet Aline who is a sister to me and mother Eudaimonis and your children free from harm. I hope you are well; Pharmouthi 16.
>
> [postscript] You certainly are aware that that foolish man [*mōros*] is bothering me again and is so stupid [*mōrainein*] because of his mother and because you are not here to shake out his stupidity [*mōria*]. Please make sure, when I send you the children, Pausas and Kotteros, to advise them regarding that matter and bring it to an end.[39]

The postscript to the letter is reminiscent of certain outbursts of Eudai-monis. But who was that man, the *mōros* who kept on *mōrainein* in his *mōria*? An estranged husband, perhaps? The alliteration and repetition brings out all the indignation of Apollonios' sister. While the verb *mōrainein* only oc-curs here, the other two terms are also very colloquial and quite rare. Usu-ally ancient letters tried to keep an appearance of politeness and anonymity because of the difficulty of securing the private reception of a certain mes-sage. But this woman was a free spirit: the sound of the words that she spits out is still there for us to catch on the papyrus.

---

[38] See the correction by W. Clarysse in *Berichtingungsliste der Griechischen Papyrusurkunden aus Ägypten*, vol. 7, edited by E. Boswinkel, W. Clarysse, P. W. Pestman, and H.-A. Rupprecht (Leiden, 1986).

[39] *P.Brem.* 61.

The greeting and date that she adds in her hand are larger than the handwriting of the scribe. She uses letters that are completely separated, but that are nevertheless graceful and well formed and have some pretension of elegance. She was not exposed to the regular practice of writing long texts, but she had received a good education and was familiar with the type of writing used in copying books. The same papyrus that contains her letter also includes two more letters to Apollonios by male relatives, one of whom was the infamous Diskas. Both letters, which follow the woman's, are much shorter and are only concerned with Apollonios' health. It was probably Apollonios' sister who took the initiative to write; both men followed her example, profiting from the occasion that someone was leaving for Heptakomia.

The writer of another intriguing letter in this archive, *P.Giss.* 79, may have been a sister of Apollonios or a woman relative. The identification of the sender is difficult because of the epistle's fragmentary state. It cannot be excluded that this woman was Aline herself: the advice she provides with a sweet disposition would suit Apollonios' wife's personality.[40] The letter was written around 120. The years immediately following the conclusion of the war were difficult for landowners. After so much devastation, prices of agricultural produce were unstable, and landowners were disappointed. With time things improved, and when this letter was written wine sold so well that the prices for vineland were astronomical. The woman writer downplays her role of financial adviser to a man who was probably her husband:

> If I could take hold of the management of our property, I would not hesitate, but in any case, for I am a woman, I exercise every care. So far Epaphroditos does not neglect anything, but puts forth every effort for our sake and the sake of your affairs. . . .
>
> Just now the wine is very expensive, about three staters. Thus nobody is discouraged to sell property. But if god allows a large yield next season, soon, because of the low price of the produce, the landowners will be discouraged, so that we will be able to buy at a low price, as you wish.

Like the wife of Ischomachus in Xenophon's *Oeconomicus*, this woman, who displays an authentic desire to manage the family's finances, had learned her lessons well. After showing off shyly her financial ability in describing the cyclicality of commodities, she moves to a more controversial subject in the second part of the letter in which she offers advice in human behavior. Perhaps her husband was still supposed to take into account her modest words,

---

[40] In this case the Apollonios alluded to in col. 4 would not be the *stratēgos* but a namesake: after all, Apollonios was a common name. The letter is written entirely in one hand, reminiscent of the handwriting of *P.Giss.* 20 but more regular and even. This woman may have penned the whole epistle.

ὅτι γίαυί gyνῶ ("for I am a woman").[41] She writes: "I think you should be nice to everybody as you were to the people from the district, so that we depart from them on good terms with friendship and without giving offense." What is the reality behind these remarks? Has her husband behaved improperly? We will never know.

Literate women with interesting backgrounds can also be found outside of Apollonios' family. One of them was Philia. Very little remains of her letter to "the eminent stratēgos," *P.Brem.* 62, which was written by a scribe in an official chancery hand. It is likely that Philia's husband or father was a high official. It is the social background of this letter that is intriguing. It is striking that this woman took the initiative to write to Apollonios, presumably a man of comparable age, without the mediation of a male relative.

Another notable woman is "the mother of the poet" who wrote the *stratēgos* a letter mutilated at the beginning, *P.Brem.* 59. Apparently Apollonios had asked her to find some purple to make him a cover for his head. The woman responds:

> You wrote to me about the purple for your head and I looked thoroughly, but I could not find purple as shiny as you have. I found some of cheap quality and . . . of price. Then I was glad I did not find it, since the equipment is also of bad quality. Salute Camilla, my lady, your wife, and all your relatives. My son, "the poet with his own lyre," says hello. I pray that you are well.

Letter and greetings are all in one hand, a fact that makes one suspect that this woman wrote the entire message herself. The handwriting, moreover, would seem to support this hypothesis: the characters are stiff and a little shaky; the writer dipped her pen into the ink a little too often and made a few clumsy corrections. The background of this woman, and the fact that she could show a poet in her family, strengthen the supposition that she was able to write with relative ease. The editor of the papyrus commented about this woman's pride in her son's literary accomplishments, but motherly vanity does not fully explain the woman's remarks. She defines her son with the expression *poietēs autolyros* ("a poet with his own lyre"); the adjective does not appear anywhere else. In Lucian, however, the expression *onos autolyrizon* ("a donkey playing his own lyre") occurs as a derogative remark in reference to an old lover who attempted to sing, in spite of his few teeth.[42] From Lucian's text it appears that the "donkey who played his own lyre" was part of a proverbial saying. Thus the woman of this letter seems to make one of the few jokes that can be found in papyri, targeting the artistic pretensions of her son.

---

[41] This expression sometimes appears in the papyri as a cliché; cf. a petition from a wealthy widow, *P.Oxy.* I.71, who often invokes the "natural weakness" of women. Of course, it often corresponded to reality.

[42] *Dial. meret.* 14.4; cf. also *Ind.* 4, about a donkey listening to the lyre and wagging his tail.

It was not only women of high social status who kept up with their correspondence. Arsis, who wrote two letters in this archive,[43] was a businesswoman who worked in the linen-weaving enterprise of Apollonios' family. Even though both Apollonios' mother and his wife were somewhat involved in the work, Arsis participated in a professional capacity. Her son Khairemon was the director of the enterprise, while she herself was in charge of purchasing the material and handled considerable amounts of money. One of the reasons Arsis wrote to Apollonios in *P.Giss.* 68 was that her son had died suddenly: Apollonios was her only hope. "Besides god," she tells him, "I only have you, and I know the affection you had for Khairemon." Arsis must have been a relatively old woman, whose family was in the service of Apollonios' for a long time. It is significant that in a letter, *P.Giss.* 12, Khairemon addresses Apollonios as *teknon* ("child"), while Arsis calls him *huios* ("son").[44] It is likely that Arsis watched Apollonios grow up, get married, embark on a distinguished carrier: a long, close acquaintance entitled her to a warm relationship with the *stratēgos*. While her other business letter, *P.Brem.* 57, was dictated to a scribe who wrote in a professional literary hand, the epistle to Apollonios is written—greetings and all—in the large, backwards-inclined, and unprofessional characters of a left-handed person. Perhaps Arsis herself was responsible for penning it.

Some questions are inevitable: How representative of the condition of their sex are the women considered above with respect to education? What was the level of literacy normally attained by other women of their time? It is extremely difficult to answer. The literary sources provide isolated examples of women of exceptional social and economic status whose achievements are hardly indicative of the level of culture of other women.[45] While some examples of women who achieved signature literacy are known, a thorough study of women's letters, which may provide some answers, is still a desideratum.[46] In any case, women's—and men's—letters are usually isolated, and very little is known about the writers. In this respect, the women's epistles contained in the archive of Apollonios are invaluable because they provide precious details about the literacy of the women in the domestic circle of the *stratēgos*.

Some of the letters, moreover, differ in tone, content, and degree of formality. I believe that no different epistolary conventions applied to letters written by women to men and to other women, and that the gender of the

[43] *P.Giss.* 68 addressed to Apollonios and *P.Brem.* 57, a business letter addressed to a certain Kornas.

[44] Both terms, which are used for younger addressees, sometimes only indicate a long acquaintance; see Dickey 1996: 64–72.

[45] See Pomeroy 1977 and 1981: 309–16.

[46] I am currently engaged in the project of collecting women's letters on papyrus together with R. S. Bagwall.

person addressed did not reflect to a great extent on how a letter was formulated. The variations are mostly due to the identity and cultural background of the writer, the difference in social and economic standing of writer and addressee, and the circumstances in which an epistle was sent. The letters of the close relatives of Apollonios are more extensive and show a great variety of topics: family problems, disagreement between family members, the course of the war, Apollonios' safety, advice to him on a number of matters, and practical details of domestic life, such as the color of a certain garment or a gift to send. As one should expect, the tone is more formal and reverential when the women who address the *stratēgos* are his acquaintances or people who work for him. Likewise, letters addressed to one another by the women of Apollonios' family touch on many subjects, not only domestic life and family relationships but also the problems caused by the war, the operation of the family business, and the strike of some workers. In the correspondence between these women and female slaves or servants, however, social difference plays a role: the epistles are shorter and eminently practical.

But it is now time, as this survey of the women of the domestic circle of Apollonios comes to an end, to return to Teeus and the warm feelings she expressed for the *stratēgos*. What kind of special relationship did this woman have with her master? Besides this letter, Teeus writes another epistle to Apollonios, *P.Alex.Giss.* 50, and one to Aline, *P.Giss.* 77. The letter to Apollonios concerns his well-being and that of his wife, whom Teeus was going to assist in delivering the baby. The fragmentary letter to Aline is full of gratitude toward her because of the gift of a tunic. Heraidous and her greetings to her mother are also mentioned right at the start because Teeus is trying to impress Aline and make a nice gesture toward her. It was suggested that Teeus might have been a young slave with whom Apollonios had a sexual relationship. The reality seems to be different. Everything supports the idea that she was an old trusty servant. She may have raised Apollonios and may have been manumitted after caring for him during his childhood. While her two other letters were dictated to scribes, the first letter to Apollonios, *P.Giss.* 17, was probably penned by her. The shaky, clumsy handwriting, with the letters all separated, is the least proficient among those appearing in the archive. Maybe Teeus had learned to write together with Apollonios and the other children of the household, but had never practiced sufficiently. But now Apollonios was in danger: Teeus wanted to reach him and fly to him not only with her voice but also with the traces of her hand on papyrus.

CHAPTER THIRTEEN

(In-)Versions of Pygmalion

THE STATUE TALKS BACK

PATRICIA A. ROSENMEYER

μὴ δείσῃς· ἐξείργασαι γὰρ πάγκαλόν τι χρῆμα, οἷον δή τι οὐδεὶς εἶδε πώποτε πάντων τῶν διὰ χειρῶν πονηθέντων, τὴν σεαυτοῦ ἑταίραν ἱδρύσας ἐν τεμένει. μέσῃ γὰρ ἔστηκα ἐπὶ τῆς Ἀφροδίτης καὶ τοῦ Ἔρωτος ἅμα τοῦ σοῦ. μὴ φθονήσῃς δέ μοι τῆς τιμῆς· οἱ γὰρ ἡμᾶς θεασάμενοι ἐπαινοῦσι Πραξιτέλη, καὶ ὅτι τῆς σῆς τέχνης γέγονα οὐκ ἀδοξοῦσί με Θεσπιεῖς μέσην κεῖσθαι θεῶν. ἐν ἔτι τῇ δωρεᾷ λείπει, ἐλθεῖν σε πρὸς ἡμᾶς, ἵνα ἐν τῷ τεμένει μετ᾽ ἀλλήλων κατακλινῶμεν. οὐ μιανοῦμεν γὰρ τοὺς θεοὺς οὓς αὐτοὶ πεποιήκαμεν. ἔρρωσο. (Alciphron *Letters* 4.1: "Phryne to Praxiteles"[1])

Have no fear; for you have wrought a very beautiful work of art, such as no-body, in fact, has ever seen before among all things fashioned by men's hands: you have set up a statue of your own mistress in the sacred precinct. Yes, I stand in the middle of the precinct near your Aphrodite and your Eros too. And do not begrudge me this honour. For it is Praxiteles that people praise when they have gazed at me; and it is because I am a product of your skill that the Thes-pians do not count me unfit to be placed between gods. One thing only is still lacking to your gift: that you come to me, so that we may lie together in the precinct. Surely we shall bring no defilement on the gods that we ourselves have created. Farewell.

Alciphron invented this fictional correspondence in the late second or early third century C.E., reflecting his generation's view of the social and cultural context of fourth-century B.C.E. Athens. His corpus contains four books of prose letters imitating the voices and concerns of four distinct social groups: fishermen, farmers, parasites, and courtesans. The passage quoted above is the first letter of his fourth book. Each book contains between nineteen and forty-two letters, which vary in length from a few lines to several pages and resemble brief essays on the lives of the poor and humble: stereotypically hard-working country folk and the demimonde of the big city. For fisher-men, farmers, and parasites, Alciphron chooses eloquent "speaking" names:

---

[1] Text and translation are from Benner and Fobes [1949] 1979.

"Bon Voyage to Sea Lover" (1.21) or "Garlic Sniffer to Crumb" (3.25), for example. Unlike the vividly imagined but mostly anonymous lower-class men (and some women) who populate the first three books, courtesans, through their connections to great men, can achieve a measure of fame, and Alciphron's fourth book offers readers a glimpse of (in)famous women mentioned elsewhere in historical and literary documents: Menander's Glykera (4.2, 18, 19), Praxiteles' Phryne (4.1, 3, 4), and others.[2]

Curiously, we have more information (factual or fictitious) about the courtesans inhabiting these pages than we have about Alciphron himself, who is not mentioned by any ancient author; even his dates are guesswork based on his similarity to Lucian.[3] In a recent book on the Second Sophistic, Graham Anderson summarizes Alciphron as a "miniaturist" offering a sample of "the idiosyncratic repertoire of sophistic learning indulged in for its own sake or for purposes of learned entertainment"; he places both Alciphron's *Letters* and Lucian's shorter dialogues in the context of school exercises (*progymnasmata*).[4]

The similarity to such an exercise is obvious in *Letters* 4.1, in which Alciphron adopts the voice of a famous Athenian courtesan from the fourth century, writing to her lover, the sculptor Praxiteles. Alciphron imagines what she might say upon seeing the statue modeled on her body and displayed in a sanctuary of Eros at Thespiae. Along the way, Alciphron retells (with a slight twist) a familiar tale, namely that of the male creation of a female "ideal" form, as best represented by Ovid's version of the Pygmalion story.[5]

Yet the opening words of Alciphron's letter make it clear that his Pygmalion version is actually an *in*-version. The boastful *egō* is not the artist but the model, who does not depend on her creator for animation, since she already stands there in the flesh and "talks back." She, Phryne, is just as famous in antiquity as her renowned sculptor-lover, Praxiteles (although the body of the text gives only *his* name, either to abide by epistolary conventions of verisimilitude, or perhaps to enact Phryne's own words of reassurance: "For it is Praxiteles that people praise when they have gazed at me"). The female voice here may be unnamed, but it is far from powerless. Phryne comforts her audience ("have no fear"), gives commands ("do not be-

---

[2] Cf. R. Cribiore's discussion of real letters from ordinary women in Roman Egypt, included in this volume.

[3] Benner and Fobes [1949] 1979: 6–18.

[4] Anderson 1993: 10, 190–92.

[5] On Ovid's Pygmalion, see Sharrock 1991: 36–49; Elsner and Sharrock 1991: 149–82; Solodow 1988: 203–31. On representation in antiquity in general, see Goldhill forthcoming; the selections in Elsner 1996a, esp. the chapters by A. Laird, A. Sharrock, and Y. L. Too; Gleason 1995: 13–16; Kris and Kurz 1979: 61–90. On the implications of viewing representations, see Stewart 1997: 19–44, 100–106; Osborne 1994: 81–96; and Hurwit 1990: 180–97.

grudge"), and praises the statue. Phryne controls what we hear and "see" in these lines, not Praxiteles.[6]

I want to explore how the female voice in this passage challenges our expectations of hierarchy and power relations: of male and female, sculptor and model, viewer and viewed, even flesh and stone. The Phryne who was an object of the sculptor's gaze (as well as of his love) turns herself into an art lover, gazing at the marble reproduction with a critic's eye.[7] Unlike other economies of artistic reproduction, in which "original" and "copy" can be kept distinct, this statue does not just reproduce but actually replicates the self; the artist, invited to come to the sanctuary and embrace his beloved, is asked to imagine a choice between a living, breathing Phryne, and a marble statue begging to be brought to life at his touch. Pygmalion sculpted a statue and brought it to life; Praxiteles takes his live beloved and petrifies her in representation. But Phryne manages to retain control over both her own self and her statue: the artist may expect a mute and compliant Galatea, but instead, in writing her letter, Phryne slips back and forth between the voices of woman and statue, lending her voice to her representation in order to "talk back," to be the speaking subject. In Ovid's version, Galatea is marked by her silence, even after the marble turns to flesh. In Alciphron's inversion, the statue not only talks back, but has the last word, and Praxiteles is condemned to the marble silence of Galatea.

Yet this "last word," viewed from a slightly different angle, is a male fantasy: Alciphron's ventriloquization. Alciphron is as much in the business of representation as Praxiteles was, and Phryne may be interpreted as deprived of a specifically female "subjectivity" when he feeds her her lines. In the process of this chapter, however, I hope to recuperate some of the power of Phryne's own (fictional) voice.

The issue of the use of female characters as mouthpieces for invisible male authors and male concerns is, of course, not limited to texts of this period.[8] But Alciphron's contemporary Lucian presents us with a useful parallel: in his *Imagines*, admiring men invent an encomium as they gaze upon the body of another famous courtesan, Panthea; the woman objects to their praise, but is silenced by even more extravagant flattery, as the men compare her to the divine Aphrodite. Lucian buries Panthea's voice in the speech of the men, and her opinions are overriden by her "admirers," eager to prove their own rhetorical skills in this contest of the power of words ver-

---

[6] Cf., however, Too (1996: 133–52), who argues that being made into stone means allowing someone else to control your representation; it is a threat, a calcification. While Phryne praises her own image by Praxiteles, we can recover a sense of threat in her anxiety about her inscriptions (see below on Thebes) and her wish to discover what Praxiteles viewed as his best work.

[7] See M. Skinner's article in this volume on Hellenistic female viewing subjects.

[8] See the contributions of Worman, Martin, Griffith, and Gagarin to this volume.

sus art in the representation of beauty. By contrast, Alciphron foregrounds Phryne's persona to such a degree that Praxiteles seems forced to take on a role of submission and obedience; she is the one authorized to discuss his work of art, the one who invites the artist to admire his own product. Here the admired, rather than the admirer, is in the position of power. In Lucian's text, the men speak and the woman is said to respond; here the situation is reversed, and Praxiteles is invited to respond on two levels: first, by writing a letter in return, and second, by his very action of coming to meet Phryne in the sanctuary.

BACKGROUND: PHRYNE IN THE FLESH

Before rereading Alciphron's text, let us place Phryne in her historical context.[9] Athenaeus (13.590f–91a) reports that Phryne was the model for a number of artists' renditions of the goddess of love: she inspired Apelles to paint his Aphrodite "rising from the sea" (Ἀναδυομένη) and Praxiteles' famous Knidian Aphrodite (see Fig. 6). Praxiteles sculpted a marble statue of Phryne for a sanctuary of Eros in Thespiae, where it stood flanked by two other Praxitelean masterpieces, an Eros and an Aphrodite (Paus. 9.27.5; Alc. 4.1; Plut. *Mor.* 753f). This, presumably, is the group of statues referred to in Alciphron's text: Phryne declares that she stands in the middle of the precinct between Eros and Aphrodite, and that the Thespians gaze upon them all with great admiration. Finally, Praxiteles dedicated a gold statue of Phryne at Delphi, positioned prominently between statues of two kings, and inscribed "Phryne, daughter of Epikles, of Thespiae" (Ath. 13.591c; Paus. 9.27). The Cynic Crates is said to have seen the statute at Delphi and labeled it a memorial to Hellenic "decadence"—ἀκρασία (Ath. 13.591b; Plut. *Mor.* 401a).[10]

The honorific patronymic in the Delphic inscription fits with Phryne's image in antiquity as someone quite out of the ordinary. The comic poet Poseidippos (third century B.C.E.) calls Phryne "the most illustrious courtesan of her time (ἐπιφανεστάτη πολὺ τῶν ἑταίρων)."[11] Anecdotes about her abound. Let me emphasize, however, the seductive quality of such anecdotes: the levels of mythologizing of Phryne and her relationship with Prax-

[9] The anecdotes about Phryne and Praxiteles are collected in Overbeck 1868: nos. 1246, 1251, 1269–78; and Pollitt 1990: 84–89.

[10] The Greek is τῆς τῶν Ἑλλήνων ἀκρασίας ἀνάθημα. Cf. Diogenes Laertius (6.60), who ascribes the saying to Diogenes the Cynic.

[11] Kassel and Austin 1983–96: fr. 13: Poseidippos, *The Woman from Ephesos*, quoted in Plutarch (*Mor.* 849e), Athenaeus (13.591e), and Quintilian (*Inst.* 1.5.61, 10.5.2). See also Alciphron *Letters* 4.4.1, where Bacchis calls Phryne famous not only in Athens but throughout all Hellas.

Fig. 6. Statue of Aphrodite from Knidos by Praxiteles. Roman copy after a c. 350 B.C.E. Greek original, presently in the Vatican Museum. According to ancient anecdotes about her life, the courtesan Phryne modeled for this statue.

iteles are so convoluted that it is impossible to separate fact from fiction.[12] There probably was some historical person by that name; evidence about her, however, comes from sources centuries later. Our sources include literary anecdotes by male authors, sculpted images including later copies of

[12] See Havelock (1995: 39–54), who argues that their relationship was invented at a later time.

the Knidian Aphrodite, and literary descriptions of sculpted images. The heyday of literary epigrams on the subject, and a renewed interest in the Knidian Aphrodite itself, appear only in the later Hellenistic period; Pliny, Lucian, and Athenaeus write almost four hundred years after the original statue was carved.[13] But even if we question the historicity of Praxiteles' and Phryne's liaison, the literary anecdotes still tell us much about how one's reputation is made in antiquity. The stories allow us to explore what might have been at stake in the pairing of these two: Phryne, the most beautiful woman, and Praxiteles, the most skilled sculptor of his day. In turn, a reading of the literary sources may help us better interpret Alciphron's own construction of Phryne and his use of her voice in *Letters* 4.1.

The literary anecdotes are of two main types: those about Phryne's physical beauty, and those about her wit. Phryne is represented as having consciously "invented" herself in both areas. Stories of her beauty reveal a consistent modesty contrasted with occasional instances of public exposure. For the most part, Phryne was said to reject cosmetics, to conceal her body, and to shun public baths. Compare with this decorous behavior the reports of her baring her breasts at trial to elicit pity from the jurors, and her spectacular nude dips into the sea in full view of all the Greeks at the great assembly of the Eleusinia and at the festival of Poseidon (Ath. 13.590f–91e; Quint. *Inst.* 2.15.9). Both stories reveal the power of the narrative to highlight one aspect of the event and shape the reader's opinion accordingly. The anecdote of Phryne walking into the sea does not stress any religious purpose to her action, but rather emphasizes her shocking exhibitionism; the whole account has a sensationalist flavor. The court scene has been transmitted to us in at least three versions, each more lurid than the next. First Athenaeus reports Poseidippos' "chaste" version, in which Phryne elicits pity from the jurors by clasping their hands and weeping (13.591); then Plutarch (*Mor.* 859e) adds that her lawyer-lover, Hyperides, opened her dress and displayed her breasts to the jurors (Ath. 13.590); finally, Quintilian (*Inst.* 2.15.9) claims that she herself bared her breasts and overwhelmed the jurors with her sexuality. Over time, the single anecdote turns Phryne from a pitiful victim into an assertive woman, acting "in character" with her profession as courtesan by undressing in public, letting her body rather than her voice speak for her to gain acquittal.[14]

The combined stories of exposure show Phryne in control of her own

---

[13] See ibid.: 2–10; Havelock suggests (63–67) that the statue awakened new public interest when it was bid for by a wealthy art patron (King Nikomedes IV of Bithynia) and repositioned in a new setting.

[14] This evidence is discussed extensively by Havelock (ibid.: 43–46). The idea of the "speaking body" was suggested to me by A. Lardinois. Note the comparable power of Helen's bared breasts over Menelaus in Eur. *Andr.* 629–30 (cf. Ar. *Lys.* 155), which supports the idea of a stock scene.

body; she does not allow the general public to "see" her when she is disinclined, but is perfectly willing to reveal her nude body when she can make a show, have an effect. Nudity itself is a form of dress, a kind of display, a statement.[15] A passage in Xenophon presents a comparable situation of the power politics of bodily display (*Mem.* 3.11.1–3).[16] Socrates and his friends go "to view" (θεᾶσθαι) a woman named Theodote, a courtesan so beautiful that artists flock to paint her portrait. It is unclear whether we are meant to imagine her posing nude: she is said to show the painters "as much of herself as was right" (ὅσα καλῶς ἔχοι), but Socrates notes that she is πολυτελῶς κεκοσμημένην (3.11.4): either "sumptuously dressed," or "adorned [only] with jewelry." At the very least, we may imagine her dressed to attract, to seduce. Socrates poses the question of profit: who gains more from the interaction, the viewers or the viewed? He concludes that Theodote herself comes out ahead in this exchange. She profits by exposing her body to public display and becomes adored by all: the viewers' desire to touch her stays with them even after they depart, and they become her adorers, praising her to all they meet. Modern readers might view such a scene as exploitation, the powerless woman defined by her body, a victim of men's prying eyes.[17] But Theodote is not a common prostitute, not for sale to just anyone, nor under the control of a male "owner." As a courtesan, she participates in a complex system of sexual economics that, while demanding that she persuade or seduce her clients to begin with, still allows her to bestow and withdraw favors, to be in ultimate control of her self and body.[18] Xenophon presents her in this scene controlling the men around her: painters try to immortalize a beauty that cannot be described in words, and Socrates and his companions flock to feast their eyes on her body.

Lucian's *Imagines* gives us another example. In this dialogue, two men offer composite portraits of Panthea, a woman from Smyrna who was the favorite of the emperor Verus (c. 165 C.E.). One speaker describes a statue of Panthea looking back at her viewer, drawing him to her as if she were a magnet attracting iron, taking him away wherever she wishes (*Imag.* 2). The viewer will be turned to stone, as if the object of his gaze were a Medusa rather than the statue of a beautiful woman. Lucian's Panthea plays the same game as Xenophon's Theodote, using the power of eros to challenge the self-determination of the men who view her. The male gazer, thinking himself the subjective viewer of an artistic tableau, is overpowered by the beauty of the object, and finds himself at its service. Panthea attracts her viewer to

---

[15] See Stewart 1997: 24–42, also quoting Berger 1972 and Clark 1956.

[16] On this passage, see Goldhill 1998. See also Henry 1995: 48–50, on whether Theodote is a figure for Aspasia.

[17] This is also Plutarch's view (*Mor.* 142c–d) in the case of a respectable woman.

[18] Cf. a grimmer view of a courtesan's life in Dem. 59.18–20, 26–34 (*Against Neaera*).

herself as she stares back at him, and leads him wherever she will: Theodote enslaves her admirers, inspiring them to go away still desiring her, singing her praises abroad. So, too, the anecdotes about Phryne show her shifting perspective from the object of male eyes, to the subject of her own "staging," controlling the men who gaze upon her.

When Lucian's characters in the *Imagines* create their composite portrait of the ideal woman, they divide their praise into two segments: one on her physical beauty, and the other on her spiritual or intellectual qualities, her soul (*Imag.* 23). Anecdotes about Phryne fall into this same pattern of external and internal virtues. Stories of Phryne's wit and intelligence reflect an independence of spirit parallel to her self-determination on the physical level. Athenaeus (13.583c–85f) is our main source for dozens of witty exchanges between *hetairai* and their companions at symposia, and Phryne is prominent among them. In one example (Ath. 13.591b; Paus. 9.20.2), Phryne reinvents herself as an art collector. She is said to have asked Praxiteles for the most beautiful of his statues; he agreed but refused to tell her which one he considered his masterpiece. So she staged a report of a fire in his studio, and he exclaimed that all was indeed lost if his Satyr and Eros were burned. After admitting her ruse, Phryne took the Eros and set it up as a votive offering in Thespiae, one of the three statues we meet in Alciphron's letter.[19]

Another anecdote tells us perhaps even more about Phryne's self-image. Having amassed a large sum of money, she offered to rebuild the walls around Thebes if the city would write an inscription on the stones in her honor, reading "Alexander destroyed Thebes but Phryne the *hetaira* built it back up" (Ath. 13.591d).[20] Phryne, in charge of her own money, wants to outdo the great Alexander. She reminds us explicitly that she is a *hetaira*, leaving no doubt about the origins of her wealth. She defines herself through sex, and emphasizes again the connections between eros, money, and power. Her own publicity agent and biographer, she carefully designs the image she wishes the world to see: that of a wealthy *hetaira*, a public benefactor, a woman of intelligence and power.

As if in response to this extravagance, Plutarch (*Mor.* 336d, 401a, 753f) writes on perversions of power represented by women acting as men. He points to the infamous Semiramis, and follows that story with Crates' criticism of Phryne's gold statue at Delphi, discussed above. To his mind, female rulers and gold statues are two sides of the same coin: an unnatural waste of resources. The issues of gender, money, and power return when he

[19] See also *Anth. Pal.* 6.260, 16.204–6.

[20] Ἀλέξανδρος μὲν κατέσκαψεν, ἀνέστησεν δὲ Φρύνη ἡ ἑταίρα. Athenaeus (13.591d) records Callistratus *On Courtesans* as his source, as well as references to Phryne's wealth in Timocles (*Neaira*) and Amphis (*The Dresser*); see also Propertius 2.6.5–6.

reports, in the context of a dialogue on love, a disapproving male voice commenting on the statue of Phryne at Thespiae, saying, "Goodness, that woman down there who shares a temple and worship with Eros, whose gilded statue stands in Delphi with those of kings and queens, what dowry had she to subjugate her lovers?" (Plut. *Mor.* 753f). Phryne, according to Plutarch, memorialized in gold as if she were royal or divine instead of "merely" a courtesan, challenges the myth of male self-sufficiency, threatens her male lovers with "subjugation," and flaunts in our faces the power of eros. Plutarch (*Mor.* 753) compares her to Bilistiche, the Macedonian mistress of Ptolemy II, whom the king elevated to cult status as Aphrodite Bilistiche, and in whose honor the Alexandrians dedicated shrines and temples.[21] He obviously sees this as a dangerous breakdown in social hierarchy, if slave women become the new gods.[22]

In reading the literary anecdotes about Phryne, I see a common interest in a strong female personality using all her skills to control her own image, manipulating the men who in turn wish to manipulate her as a courtesan. By controlling her own self-representations as far as she is able, or by choosing for whom she will model, these versions of a historical (and transhistorical) Phryne invent a self to be remembered and admired. Her obsession with power, whether controlling others through eros or herself through representation, encourages me to read her story in Alciphron as an extension of this game, yet another carefully planned and executed "staging" of her life. But the question remains whether this is ultimately (the fictional) Phryne's staging or Alciphron's.

ALCIPHRON *LETTERS* 4.1

Turning to the representation of Phryne in Alciphron *Letters* 4.1, we are faced first with a gap. Some words appear to have been lost at the beginning of the letter, which begins in mid-sentence. At one level, this uncertain beginning mirrors the state of all epistolary exchange: there is always an assumption that something has come before, something that we are not privileged to see, as we imagine the contents of a previous letter, or a preexisting correspondence. I have attempted to fill in the gap in the previous section, alluding to other versions of the story of Phryne and Praxiteles in antiquity. The best we can do now is forge ahead with the surviving text. Alciphron's Phryne begins with a direct address to Praxiteles.

[21] On Bilistiche, see Cameron 1995: 243–46.

[22] Consider the permeability of mortal and divine status in later periods: see Carradine and Price 1987. The issue of mortals identifying with deities in literature and the arts is discussed in Havelock 1995: 128–30. Aphrodite herself had long been the patron divinity of both queens and courtesans, so Bilistiche unifies two aspects of the goddess more usually kept apart.

Have no fear; for you have wrought a very beautiful work of art, such as nobody, in fact, has ever seen before among all things fashioned by men's hands:
you have set up a statue of your own mistress in the sacred precinct.

The speaker, Phryne, commends Praxiteles, the "you" of the passage, on
a statue he has made, which is really an image of herself. Her instruction
not to be afraid leads us to ask why she assumes in the first place that he
should be. The next sentence makes it clearer. The work of art is called
πάγκαλόν τι χρῆμα,[23] a most beautiful thing, more lovely than anything
else anyone has ever seen; the exact phrasing, to translate literally, is "of all
things crafted laboriously (πονηθέντων) by [human] hands." This artisanal
term suggests a contrast between "natural" beauty, namely, that with which
one is born or the "ideal" beauty of the divine, and "constructed" beauty,
the artist's attempt to approximate perfect human or divine shape. Praxiteles' statue of his mortal beloved is so perfectly crafted that it is considered
worthy to stand beside his images of the divine, Eros and Aphrodite. Praxiteles puts a human, profane image where an immortal, holy one should be;
perhaps this is why Phryne tells him not to fear. She is not afraid to be placed
amongst the gods; in fact, she positively glories in it.

Lucian's second essay on portraiture, a response to his *Imagines* entitled
Pro imaginibus, shows how differently Panthea views her situation. She responds to the men who compare her to the Knidian Aphrodite with violent
shuddering, weeping, and fear: she considers it a sacrilege (ἀσέβημα) and a
sin (πλημμέλημα), claiming that it cheapens the goddess to be compared to
a mortal woman (*Pro imaginibus* 8–15). Lucian offers a sophistic defense of
his speaker's behavior that cuts to the heart of the matter of representation
(*Pro imaginibus* 23):

> It was not with the goddesses I compared you, my dear woman, but with mas-
> terpieces of good craftsmen, made of stone or bronze and ivory; and what man
> has made, it is not impious, I take it, to compare with man. But perhaps you
> have assumed that what . . . Praxiteles made in Knidos not many years ago is
> actually heavenly Aphrodite?

Lucian goes on to undo this argument by saying that, even if he had compared her to the very goddesses themselves, he would only be following in
a well-trodden path first used by Homer, with whom not even Aristarchus
found fault on that score (*Pro imaginibus* 24). He goes on to praise Panthea's
beauty even more excessively, effectively silencing her protests.

Alciphron does not overtly draw such a connection between excessive

---

[23] This is a common term of description in the Second Sophistic; see esp. Longus' *Daph-
nis and Chloe*, where it is applied to the painting in the grove, the garden paradises, even Daph-
nis himself.

praise and sacrilege, at least not beyond the hint in Phryne's injunction to Praxiteles not to be afraid. And it is telling that Phryne herself has no fear; the artist appears to need reassurance here, not the model. To model Phryne on Aphrodite (or vice versa) does not necessarily denigrate the divinity or put the mortal in a dangerously hubristic role, but the placement of the mortal statue does suggest competition among the beautiful marble bodies. It is the representation of Phryne that, we shall see below, stands in the middle of the precinct, as if it, rather than the statue of Eros or Aphrodite, should receive the spectator's full attention.

Distance is created between the woman speaking and her marble image, as well as between Phryne and her lover, as she says, "You have set up a statue τὴν σεαυτοῦ ἑταίραν"—not "of me," but "of your own mistress." She presents herself as an objective viewer, admiring Praxiteles' erotic art without revealing any connection to herself or her own erotic feelings. Praxiteles has made his beloved into a goddess, literalized an erotic metaphor so familiar from Roman elegiac poetry. But instead of being "like a goddess" to the lover alone, he metamorphoses her into a public Aphrodite: she becomes a statue for open viewing and worship, frozen in one pose, unable to change position or talk back to those who gaze upon her.[24] Phryne's careful distinction between herself and Praxiteles' mistress, in this instance, allows her to keep moving, talking, and shifting perspectives even as her statue "self" cannot.[25]

One of the epigrams in the *Greek Anthology* (*Anth. Pal.* 16.160 "Plato") presents Aphrodite in exactly this situation:

> Ἡ Παφίη Κυθέρεια δι' οἴδματος ἐς Κνίδον ἦλθε,
>   βουλομένη κατιδεῖν εἰκόνα τὴν ἰδίην·
> πάντη δ' ἀθρήσασα περισκέπτῳ ἐνὶ χώρῳ,
>   φθέγξατο· "Ποῦ γυμνὴν εἶδέ με Πραξιτέλης;"

> The Paphian Kytherea came through the waves to Knidos,
>   desiring to look upon her own image.
> Once she had viewed it from all angles in its open shrine,
>   she cried, "Wherever did Praxiteles see me naked?"

The goddess comes as any tourist might, eager to see a famous sight.[26] She is amazed at the accuracy of the representation, assuming that Praxiteles must have seen her naked without her knowledge. She acts precisely as

---

[24] See *Anth. Pal.* 16.166.1–4, where Praxiteles makes his Aphrodite "visible to all the Knidians, proof of his art."

[25] Note the tellingly different result in the Narcissus story discussed by (Elsner 1996b: 255): "His objectification of self turns the subject into an object and results in an absorbed paralysis of self, a self-absorption whose only end is death."

[26] The naïve, often female viewer appears as a stock motif in the Greek literary tradition; see M. Skinner in this volume.

Phryne does: marveling, uttering words in praise of the statue, moving around its base to admire it from all perspectives. There is a marked lack of prurience or fetishizing here, as also in the case of Phryne: no list of body parts, no suggestion that Aphrodite is embarrassed by her own nudity.[27] Aphrodite's specific concern here has more to do with the injunction against a mortal viewing a goddess naked (e.g., Actaeon, Tiresias) than with disapproval of nudity itself.

Phryne swiftly changes perspective again in the next line, as she trades the distancing third person for the immediate first.

> I stand in the middle of the precinct near your Aphrodite and your Eros too. And do not begrudge me the honour. For it is Praxiteles that people praise when they have gazed at me; and it is because I am a product of your skill that the Thespians do not count me unfit to be placed between gods.

After praise of the artist comes a sudden burst of first-person boasting at odds with the speaker's affirmation that people praise Praxiteles alone. It is as if Phryne's conventional (and therefore expected) deference as woman and model is struggling to retain control over her assertive stance as speaker/writer. *I* stand in the precinct, she says, people admire *me*—oh yes, and they praise Praxiteles as they gaze at me, for his representation of a beauty so great that it goes beyond the mimesis of a mortal woman, and is considered fit to be placed with statues of the divinely beautiful gods. The diction in this section reflects the tension between divine and mortal, creator and created. Phryne speaks of "your Aphrodite and Eros," as if the gods belonged to Praxiteles, just as Phryne belongs to him (or he *thinks* she belongs to him).[28] In reality, of course, it is the statues of the gods, not the gods themselves, that the sculptor has created in the precinct with the statue of Phryne, and all these marble likenesses "belong" to their creator.[29] The phrase "your mistress" does not bother us, but "your Aphrodite and Eros" does, and it nudges us to rethink the possibility of anyone "owning" someone else. The wording here, rather than implying a similar distance between the gods and their statues and Phryne and her statue, instead invites us to question which object the artist really controls: his live model or the resulting "better than lifelike" marble artifact.

So far I have made no distinction between Phryne and her statue. But this is a crucial point for the narrative, and needs clarification. Who is this "I" who stands in the sanctuary, gazed upon by spectators, a product of the

---

[27] See Havelock 1995: 22–27. Note that both Phryne and Aphrodite locate their statue but give no further ekphrastic details: no references to individual features, coloring, size, etc.

[28] This may have been the customary way in antiquity to refer to a work of art; but in this context of erotic and artistic ownership, I think we are meant to question the appropriateness of the possessive pronoun.

[29] See the Lucian passage quoted above.

artist's skill? It can be none other than the statue; in fact, the living woman herself is one of the gazers, as we saw in the opening lines. Phryne shifts from her own voice, using a third-person objectivity ("a statue of your mistress") to the imagined voice of the statue, using the first person to speak of her marble-imaged self. Alciphron here plays with the convention of the speaking statue, the funeral monument that calls out to the passerby to explain her identity and the occasion of her death.[30] Phryne leaves behind the model of the silent Galatea, silent even once she has been brought to life, and lends her voice to her representation, giving it the opportunity to be its own speaking subject. But a further complication arises when we recall the fiction of the epistolary mode: is the *statue* now meant to be imagined writing the letter (of praise, comfort, and invitation) to Praxiteles? The letter form is, of course, particularly suited to dealing with issues of presence and absence, disembodied voices, and an epistolary "self" constructed for the occasion. But what does it mean for a statue to write a letter? Do we imagine the letter as a realistic decoration of papyrus, like gold earrings or enameled eyeballs on otherwise pale marble statues, or is the letter itself also cold marble, inscribed with these very words? Whose voice is the "writing" voice?

A curious instability within the first-person voice emerges in this section and will control the rest of the letter. When Phryne-the-statue speaks of the people who gaze at her, she actually represents herself in the first-person plural: not, as Benner and Fobes translate it, those who "have gazed at me," but rather "those who have gazed at *us*" (οἱ γὰρ ἡμᾶς θεασάμενοι). The pronoun could have many referents. It could refer to the whole group of Praxiteles' marvelous marble works: Phryne, Eros, and Aphrodite; or the statue could proleptically refer to her (marble or flesh?) self and Praxiteles, if he accepts her invitation to come to the sanctuary and be with her. But I would suggest a slightly more complex interpretation here. While Greek grammar is notoriously loose with its royal "we," in this passage, the plural pronoun is surrounded by four instances of the singular "I" or "me": "I stand," "don't begrudge me," "I am a product," "they praise me." By using the plural "us," and returning to the plural verbal and pronomial forms in her last two sentences, Phryne begins to blur the boundary between herself and the statue, between the artist's living inspiration and the artistic representation. She is neither wholly flesh nor wholly stone, confused by the experience of seeing herself standing in the sanctuary, and seeing others see her and praise her as a statue.

Maude Gleason discusses a similar situation in Favorinus, where the orator cultivates grammatical ambiguity around the word "statue" by avoid-

---

[30] On this convention, see Svenbro 1988. On the statue in general, see Hunter 1992: 9–34.

ing the feminine noun εἰκών and choosing the masculine alternative ἀν-δριάς.[31] Thus it is often unclear whether the referent is the sophist or his statue, in whose voice he speaks as he maintains the illusion of the person-ification of an inanimate object.[32] Similarly with Alciphron's Phryne, we observe a certain redundancy, a vacillation between reference to the seeing subject and object seen, and a permeability between art and life that dis-ables conventional interpretive frameworks. Phryne's blurred language of vision and mixed-person markers reflects an attempt to deal with an image of herself that does not represent but replicates.[33] Favorinus' linguistic playfulness occurs in the context of epideictic rhetoric; his sophisticated au-dience would presumably have been attuned to such verbal nuance. Alci-phron has the added benefit of a self-consciously written medium, a read-ing public that was invited to peer over Praxiteles' shoulder as he tried to interpret Phryne's letter, inevitably "reading between the lines."

I am making two points here: first, that Alciphron, through Phryne's voice, explores the issue of a doubled self (person and representation), and second, that this exploration is reflected in the narrative on the level of syn-tax by an unusually marked use of pronouns. To bolster my arguments, let me turn to a series of poems in the *Greek Anthology*, mostly on the subject of Praxiteles' Knidian Aphrodite (modeled, we recall, on Phryne).[34] One brief epigram focuses on the question already raised of Praxiteles viewing Aphrodite naked.[35] Here Lucian (*Anth. Pal.* 16.163) presents an unnamed narrator observing the statue:

> Τὴν Παφίην γυμνὴν οὐδεὶς ἴδεν· εἰ δέ τις εἶδεν,
> οὗτος ὁ τὴν γυμνὴν στησάμενος Παφίην.

> Nobody ever saw the Paphian naked. But if anybody ever did,
> it was this man, who set up the naked Paphian.

The epigram plays with the lack of linguistic differentiation between the goddess and her statue. It relies on the written nature of its medium for added punch, namely the ability to position words in a specific spot in the line, the page, or the slab of stone, the very physicality of the text imagined (again) as an inscription. Lucian plays the game in chiasmus: "the Paphian naked" in

---

[31] Gleason 1995: 14–15.

[32] See also Elsner 1996b: 251 on *ekphrasis*, which "effaces the ontological difference be-tween artists' imitations and their objects"; here the multiplicity of Phrynes challenges the on-tological difference between self and statue.

[33] But cf. Stewart (1997: 44), who, in a different context, argues that stories such as Pyg-malion's do not elide the distance between image and subject but rather indicate the opposite: "while defining the image as a remedy for absence, they explicitly thematize difference, defin-ing it in terms of facture."

[34] See Figure 6 in this volume, p. 244.

[35] See also *Anth. Pal.* 16.162 Anon.

line 1 is Aphrodite herself, "the naked Paphian" her statue. The two Paphi-
ans neatly frame the couplet, further downplaying their "difference."

The same book of the *Greek Anthology* (16) provides me with further justification for reading the pronouns in the Alciphron passage "seriously."
Here we find texts not about Aphrodite, but specifically about Praxiteles,
Phryne, and Eros, caught up in the same fascination with the potential ambiguity of name and pronoun referents. Tullius Geminus (*Anth. Pal.*
16.205.1–2) starts his six-line verse with an abundance of Loves:

> Ἀντί μ' ἔρωτος Ἔρωτα βροτῷ θεὸν ὤπασε Φρυνῇ
> Πραξιτέλης, μισθὸν καὶ θεὸν εὑρόμενος. . . .

> In return for love, Praxiteles gave me, Love, a god, to mortal Phryne,
>   creating both a means of payment and a god. . . .

These two lines go wild with syntactical flourishes.[36] Mortal Phryne and
divine Eros stand entwined in an "*a-b-a-b*" pattern; Praxiteles' name is de-
ferred until the beginning of the following line; eros (love) and Eros (statue)
are neatly juxtaposed; the "god" in line 1 and that in line 2 vacillate between
the meanings "divinity" and "statue of the god"; the preposition ἀντί is separated from its noun ἔρως by the tiny pronoun "me," which works grammatically with "Eros . . . the god," yet sinks further into ambiguity through
elision. In this jungle of referents, the ultimate question hangs on the pronoun μ': Is it Eros the god, Eros the statue of the god, eros the emotion of
passion that surrounds it in the line and elides its vowel? If the latter, is it
Praxiteles' or Phryne's passion, and passion for what: the lover or the statue
itself? The possibilities expressed in these two lines are suggestively abundant, although "common sense" tells us to read the "me" as a reference to
the statue of Eros that we know, from other sources, Praxiteles gave to
Phryne as a gift. Tullius Geminus' epigram ends on an intriguing note:
Phryne, we are told, no longer is afraid of Eros the offspring of Kypris, but
rather of Praxiteles' offspring, since she knows that Art (τέχνη) is his
mother (*Anth. Pal.* 16.205.5–6). Art (the statue) replaces nature (the god)
as the ultimate authority.[37]

One final example, collected under the name of the artist himself:
Athenaeus (13.590f–91a) reports that an Eros by Praxiteles stood in the
theater at Athens,[38] and bore the following inscription (= *Anth. Pal.* 16.204
Praxiteles):

---

[36] A parallel for the opening of this epigram is the close of Julianus' (*Anth. Pal.* 16.203.5–
6), where Praxiteles' Eros appears in all his guises.

[37] See also Tullus Geminus (*Anth. Pal.* 6.620) on Praxiteles' statue of Eros.

[38] It is unclear whether we should take this as the same statue given later as a gift to Phryne.
Klein (*Prax.* 219f.), quoted by Raubitschek (1950: 899), seems to identify this piece with the
Thespian one.

Πραξιτέλης ὃν ἔπασχε διηκρίβωσεν Ἔρωτα
  ἐξ ἰδίης ἕλκων ἀρχέτυπον κραδίης,
Φρύνῃ μισθὸν ἐμεῖο διδοὺς ἐμέ. φίλτρα δὲ βάλλω
  οὐκέτ' οἰστεύων, ἀλλ' ἀτενιζόμενος.

Praxiteles accurately portrayed the love he suffered,
  drawing his model from the depths of his own heart,
dedicating me to Phryne as the price of me. I cast a spell of love
  no longer by shooting arrows, but by being gazed upon.

In line 3, we witness the telltale confusion of pronouns: the statue speaks in the first person, and says that "Praxiteles gave me [the statue, Eros] to Phryne as the price of me [love, eros]." One "me" refers to the statue itself, the marble object placed on display, while the other refers more abstractly to that which it represents, namely love, sex, the relationship between the dedicator and the dedicatee.

The pronouns here and in the Alciphron passage become destabilized around the figure of eros/Eros. Indeed, that is precisely the point, that eros blurs boundaries, confuses categories, and generally makes mischief.[39] But whereas in a less complex erotic relationship the confusion centers around lover and beloved, self and "other," in the case of Praxiteles and Phryne, the relationship is triangulated by the figure of the statue of Phryne, the symbol of Praxiteles' passion and Phryne's status. Or, in a dizzying expansion of the erotic exchange, looking to each side of Phryne's statue, their dyad/triad is further bisected by the statues of Eros and Aphrodite.

In the last example quoted above, Eros moves from his symbolic lodging in the lover's heart to a corporeal manifestation on a pedestal, a visible presence in the public eye. Not only is he represented in solid marble, but he even stands inscribed, making his "meaning" explicit to all who walk by. He casts a love spell no longer from his arrows, now immobilized, but simply from being gazed upon; and where better to be gazed upon than in the public forum of the theater? We imagine a constant flow of spectators glimpsing Praxiteles' Eros and immediately falling in love with . . . whom?[40] Pronoun confusion continues even as the epigram leaves it unspoken: there is no named referent, no direct object of "casting a spell of love." The statue commemorates Praxiteles' love for Phryne, so will this spell affect all men (and women?) in the same fashion? Here Phryne is just as public an object of the erotic gaze as she was when playing the part of Aphrodite in the sanctuary at Thespiae—in fact, even more so, given the context of the theater. If this is the same statue of Eros as the one later given to Phryne, we could

---

[39] On this topic in general, see Zeitlin 1996: ch. 6.
[40] Athenaeus (13.585–86) reports Phryne mockingly being called "Praxiteles' Aphrodite," but she could also be imagined as his "Eros."

imagine her displeasure at being displayed publicly for all to see, since, after all, her name is spelled out on the epigram. Surely she would rather take the image and place it in the more controlled environment of a sanctuary, where she could orchestrate her own visual narrative, placing the Eros beside the Praxitelean Aphrodite and Phryne, each member of the tableau commenting on the other.

In that sanctuary, Phryne herself becomes the main spectator, the audience for the statues. What are the implications of a woman acting as a spectator of art, especially if the art object is a female nude? Could some of her pronomial confusion stem from her gender? The gaze that she brings to the sculptures is compromised on many levels: she is subject and object, viewer and viewed; but this remains a same-sex, effectively narcissistic relationship of viewing. Andrew Stewart argues that Praxiteles is the first sculptor in the West to "get beyond the supposition that the (male) spectator necessarily plays active subject to the female body's passive object, which is simply taken over and possessed by his desire."[41] Praxiteles thus constructs his (male?) spectator as both seeing and being seen, voyeur and object of the statue's glance.[42] But how does this relationship between statue and spectator change if the erotics shift from across gender lines to within the same gender? This question is a critical one since, as Eva Stehle and Amy Day point out, "sexual representations engage any viewer according to his or her social identity and place in the sex-gender system and elicit readings that are at least in part based on bodily identification between sculpted figures and the viewer."[43]

So how do women look at themselves objectified in the nude? Robin Osborne poses this question with reference to the Knidian Aphrodite, but comes up with the rather disappointing conclusion that "classical statues of goddesses address themselves most powerfully and most richly to men and have little directly to say to women."[44] While acknowledging that women did look at sculpture, as we know from textual evidence (e.g., Eur. *Ion* 184ff.; Theoc. 15.76ff; Ov. *Tr.* 2.309–12), he implies that they did not get much out of their experience. I would argue tentatively here that Phryne is a good example of a woman looking at sculpture of nude women (one a goddess, one herself) and revealing the complexities of her reaction, inviting us to question how she will keep the categories of self and representation distinct.

---

[41] Stewart 1997: 104. On this question, see further Petersen 1997: 35–74; Frontisi-Ducroux 1996: 81–100; Stehle and Day 1996: 101–16; Stewart 1996: 136–54; Sutton 1992: 3–35; Zweig 1992: 73–89; Elsner 1996b: 247–61.

[42] See Osborne 1994: 81–96, esp. 84, on a spectator of the Aphrodite at Knidos: "The viewer finds himself and his male appetite framed"; he becomes self-conscious as he discovers that he is as much the object of Aphrodite's gaze as the reverse.

[43] Stehle and Day 1996: 101.

[44] Osborne 1994: 87.

John Berger claims that this curious situation of female viewing defines a woman's role in society in general:

> To be born a woman has been to be born, within an allotted and confined space, into the keeping of men. The social presence of women has developed as a result of their ingenuity in living under such tutelage within such a limited space. But this has been at the cost of a woman's self being split into two. A woman must continually watch herself. She is almost continually accompanied by her own image of herself . . . and so she comes to consider the *surveyor* and the *surveyed* within her as the two constituent yet always distinct elements of her identity as a woman.[45]

Although Berger does not refer specifically to Greco-Roman antiquity here, his description of the experience of a woman "watching herself," and the resulting inner tension between observer and observed, correspond closely to Stewart's assessment of Praxiteles' innovations in art mentioned above, and also to my interpretation of Phryne's confusion about her identity. Phryne's letter concludes as follows:

> One thing only is still lacking to your gift: that you come to me so that we may lie together in the precinct. Surely we shall bring no defilement on the gods that we ourselves have created. Farewell.

Phryne's response to the visual challenge is to merge her two selves. The vision of herself immortalized as an erotic object has an erotic effect on herself as viewing subject. She calls her lover, the "you" of the text, to come πρὸς ἡμᾶς, not "to me," as in Benner and Fobes, but to both of us, so that they, now redefined as her lover and her multiple selves, can make love together in the precinct, beside the gods that they have created.

Phryne usurps the creative power previously attributed to Praxiteles alone, and claims that they both have "created" the gods. Does she mean Aphrodite and Eros, the latter the "gift" she dedicated to the shrine and thus somehow "created" along with Praxiteles, or does she refer also to herself, the divinely beautiful statue? She seems to imply that acting as a model counts for more in the act of artistic creation than the craftsman's skill, as if she were the all-important Muse and he merely the obedient assistant. If Phryne includes the representation of herself in her private pantheon of gods, will Praxiteles also be affected by her muddling of mortal and divine, life and art? Will he make love with the real person, his mistress Phryne, underneath the gaze of the statue, or with the statue itself? If the statue itself, he would reenact the wonderful but presumably apocryphal story, re-

[45] Berger 1972: 46.

ported by Pliny and Pseudo-Lucian, of the unfortunate man who was so besotted with a statue of Aphrodite that he crept into the sanctuary at night and left an incriminating stain on her marble thigh.[46] Phryne seems to hint at this encounter when she chooses the verb μιαίνειν—denoting a moral or physical stain—to describe their actions. The word resonates with the threat of defilement of the sanctuary by sexual intercourse, whether involving the statue or its human representative, Phryne, and her mortal lover.[47]

The story of the rape of the statue mentioned above takes us back to our original paradigm, that of Ovid's Pygmalion. In his *Metamorphoses*, Ovid apparently transformed an earlier Greek version of the myth, itself transmitted by Philostephanos, a student or friend of Callimachus.[48] In the earlier version, Pygmalion was a king of Cyprus who fell madly in love with a cult statue of Aphrodite and slept with it. By shifting the focus to Pygmalion as sculptor rather than king, Ovid substitutes artistic force for political. But I wonder if Alciphron is trying to resuscitate that earlier Greek model, to remind us that art is always also political, and in this case, the politics is that of eros, power, voice, authority. When Phryne claims for herself as physical model a role in the creation of one or more of the statues ("the gods whom we ourselves have made"), she may also be claiming similar credit for the letters and anecdotes modeled on her life more generally. If she claims credit for this particular epistolary narrative (Alciphron *Letters* 4.1), then even if Alciphron is in one sense the author, the intertextual relations between his letter and her life, or at least the traditions of her "life," mean that there can be no single final authority.

Let me restate this from a slightly different angle: critics move easily from the authority of Pygmalion to that of Ovid. One artist represents the larger enterprise of the other, and the female body (Galatea) acts as a metaphor for the text (*Met.*). The male artist (Ovid, Pygmalion) introduces the female to speak about artistic creativity, and designs his own "muse." But when we turn to Alciphron's inversion, we find that Alciphron, through his ventriloquization and focalization, slyly invites us to consider the eloquent Phryne, rather than Praxiteles, as his alter ego. The use of Phryne's voice parallels his choice of epistolary form: both challenge the reader's assumptions about the fixity of subject and object. The external reader aligns himself with the internal addressee, the famous artist, only to discover that Alciphron has put his model firmly in charge, that Phryne's (doubled) voice

---

[46] See Elsner and Sharrock 1991; the ancient sources are in Pliny *HN* 36.20–21; Ps.-Lucian *Amores* 13–16; Lucian *Imagines*.

[47] Having sex on temple grounds constitutes a *miasma*; see Parker 1983: 74.

[48] The sources are discussed in Solodow 1988: 215–16; Philostephanos' version is reported in Clem. Al. *Protr.* 4.57.3 (Mondésert and Plassart 1976: 121); Arn. *Adv. nat.* 6.22.

controls the narrative. So to cap it all, this authoritative voice is that of a courtesan, a type of woman both visible in the male world by the very nature of her profession, and one closely associated in literary tradition with verbal deceit.

Alciphron offers us the Pygmalion theme inverted and gone wild: here the woman makes an erotic request of the man, a woman who is already very much alive in one manifestation, and there seems to be no sense that one manifestation will replace the other, but both will remain. Phryne existed before her statue, but her letter hints that Praxiteles can bring the statue to life by making love with it, just as Pygmalion slept with his ivory maiden and watched her become flesh before his eyes. This is precisely where Phryne, or Alciphron, stops the narrative. The artist, "letter" in hand, stands poised to make his choice, frozen at the moment of indecision. We might asks ourselves whether he even *wants* to bring her statue to life. The point of Pygmalion's experiment was to make the perfect woman, the object of his erotic fantasy; but Phryne has already gone beyond Praxiteles' expectations, giving her statue voice and characterizing it, like herself, as far from a submissive object of male desire. Her letter tries to seduce him into giving her that final "gift"—giving life to her statue, making it subject rather than object of the gaze.

In the picture I have just painted, I imagine Praxiteles standing at the edge of the sanctuary, gazing at Phryne. But I have, of course, let myself be seduced by the fiction of the narrative. In fact, we are asked to imagine Praxiteles gazing not on a person or a statue, but on a written text, a letter that he holds in his hands. Alciphron presents Phryne writing him a letter detailing the scene, inviting his participation in it. As a final tease, Phryne's letter ends with the conventional formula of "farewell": ἔρρωσο. What will Praxiteles find if and when he arrives in the sanctuary? Is the "farewell" from the mortal Phryne who accepts a temporary separation in the hopes of seeing her lover soon enter the temple grounds, or does the statue utter the final words, hinting that it could easily bring itself to life, and already have walked away by the time Praxiteles arrives?

Let me conclude with a few words on the unique nature of an epistolary narrative. A letter is both text, including a written message, and artifact, at least in its own fictional world. As such, it is an eminently gazeable object, a piece of writing that is also a piece of material culture. But just as Phryne's words lure us into an imaginary world of live bodies and marble reproductions, so letters trick us into believing their authenticity by drawing attention to their very physicality: "Do you recognize my handwriting?" says Ovid's Sappho to Phaon (*Her.* 15.1–4), or "Forgive the tears blurring my words on the page," says Cicero to his wife (*Fam.* passim). Yet the page we read is in a standard typefont, and no tears appear in the critical apparatus. Whenever we read such a letter, we are invited to play the same game as

Praxiteles. We can take for granted that this letter is a reproduction, but an "honest" reproduction of an original, and we can "bring the text to life" by adding to it our own imagination, providing our own visual imagery, breathing life into its lines.[49]

[49] I am grateful to audiences at SUNY Buffalo, University of Wisconsin-Madison, Indiana University, and Northwestern University for their attention and suggestions. I also have benefited from the advice of M. Buchan, K. Eldred, S. Goldhill, R. L. Hunter, A. Lardinois, S. Lindheim, J. J. Pollitt, D. T. Steiner, and F. I. Zeitlin. Thanks go to A. Lardinois and L. McClure for the invitation to include this piece in their volume.

Bibliography

Abu-Lughod, L. 1986. *Veiled Sentiments: Honor and Poetry in a Bedouin Society.* Berkeley.

Adams, J. N. 1984. "Female Speech in Latin Comedy." *Antichthon* 18: 43–77.

Adrados, F. R. [1972] 1975. *Festival, Comedy and Tragedy: The Greek Origins of Theatre.* Translated from the Spanish by C. Holme. Leiden.

Alexiou, M. 1974. *The Ritual Lament in Greek Tradition.* Cambridge.

Alexiou, M., and P. Dronke. 1971. "The Lament of Jephtha's Daughter: Themes, Traditions, Originality." *Studi medievali* 12: 816–63.

Allen, T., W. Halliday, and E. Sikes, eds. 1936. *The Homeric Hymns.* 2d ed. Oxford.

Aloni, A. 1989. *L'aedo e i tiranni: Ricerche sull'Inno omerico a Apollo.* Rome.

———. 1997. *Sappho. Framenti.* Florence.

Amandry, P. 1950. *La mantique Apollinienne à Delphes: Essai sur le fonctionnement de l'Oracle.* Paris.

Andersen, L. 1987. *Studies in Oracular Verses: Concordance to Delphic Responses in Hexameter.* Copenhagen.

Anderson, G. 1993. *The Second Sophistic: A Cultural Phenomenon in the Roman Empire.* London.

Anderson, W. B. 1966. *Ethos and Education in Greek Music.* Cambridge, Mass.

Andrewes, A. 1956. *The Greek Tyrants.* London.

Appleby, J., L. Hunt, and M. Jacob. 1994. *Telling the Truth about History.* New York.

Arthur [Katz], M. B. 1980. "The Tortoise and the Mirror: Erinna *PSI* 1090." *Classical World* 74: 53–65.

Austin, C. 1973. *Comicorum Graecorum fragmenta in papyris reperta.* Berlin.

Austin, N. 1975. *Archery at the Dark of the Moon: Poetic Problems in Homer's* Odyssey. Berkeley.

———. 1994. *Helen of Troy and Her Shameless Phantom.* Ithaca, N.Y.

Bader, F. 1989. *La langue des dieux, ou, L'hermétisme des poètes indo-européens.* Pisa.

Bagnasco, M. B. 1990. "Nuovi documenti sul culto di Afrodite a locri epizefiri." *Parola del passato* 45: 42–61.

Bain, D. 1984. "Female Speech in Menander." *Antichthon* 18: 24–42.

Bakhtin, M. 1968. *Rabelais and His World.* Translated by J. Leclercq. Cambridge, Mass.

———. 1986. "The Problem of Speech Genres." In *Speech Genres and Other Late Essays,* translated by V. McGee, 60–102. Austin.

Barnard, S. 1991. "Anyte: Poet of Children and Animals." In Martino 1991b: 165–76.

Barron, D. 1986. *Grammar and Gender.* New Haven.

Bassi, K. 1993. "Helen and the Discourse of Denial in Stesichorus' Palinode." *Arethusa* 26: 51–75.

Benner, A. R., and F. H. Fobes, eds. [1949] 1979. *The Letters of Alciphron, Aelian and Philostratus.* 2d ed. Cambridge, Mass.

Bentley, R. 1869. *Q. Horatius Flaccus, ex recensione et cum notis atque emendationibus.* 3d ed. Berlin.

Bergemann, J. 1997. *Demos und Thanatos: Untersuchungen zum Wertesystem der Polis im Spiegel der attischen Grabreliefs des 5. und 4. Jhs. v. Chr. und zur Funktion der gleichzeitigen Grabbauten.* Munich.

Berger, J. 1972. *Ways of Seeing.* London.

Bergk, T. 1915. *Poetae elegiaci et iambographi.* Leipzig.

Bergren, A. L. T. 1980. "Helen's Web: Time and Tableau in the *Iliad*." *Helios* 7: 19–34.

———. 1981. "Helen's 'Good Drug': *Odyssey* IV.1–305." In *Contemporary Literary Hermeneutics and the Interpretation of Classical Texts*, edited by S. Kresic, 517–30. Ottawa.

———. 1983. "Language and the Female in Early Greek Thought." *Arethusa* 16: 69–95.

Bernabò-Brea, L., and M. Cavalier. 1965. *Meligunìs-Lipára.* Vol. 2, *La Necropoli Greca e Romana nella Contrada Diana.* Palermo.

Bernardini, P. 1984. "La *Penia* nella vicenda storico-politica di Alceo." In *Lirica greca da Archiloco a Elitis: Studi in onore di Filippo Maria Pontani*, edited by B. Gentili et al., 93–104. Padua.

Bers, V. 1997. *Speech in Speech: Studies in Incorporated Oratio Recta in Attic Drama and Oratory.* Lanham, Md.

Berve, H. 1967. *Die Tyrannis bei den Greichen.* 2 vols. Munich.

Bielohlawek, K. 1940. *Hypotheke und Gnome: Untersuchungen über die griechische Weisheitsdichtung der vorhellenistischen Zeit. Philologus* suppl. 32, fasc. 3. Leipzig.

Bloch, H. R. 1983. *Etymologies and Genealogies: A Literary Anthropology of the French Middle Ages.* Chicago.

Blok, J. 1987. "Sexual Asymmetry: A Historiographical Essay." In Blok and Mason 1987: 1–57.

Blok, J., and P. Mason, eds. 1987. *Sexual Asymmetry: Studies in Ancient Society.* Amsterdam.

Blundell, S. 1995. *Women in Ancient Greece.* Cambridge, Mass.

Blundell, S., and M. Williamson, eds. 1998. *The Sacred and the Feminine in Ancient Greece.* London.

Boedeker, D. 1974. *Aphrodite's Entry into Greek Epic.* Leiden.

———. 1991. "Euripides' *Medea* and the Vanity of ΛΟΓΟΙ." *Classical Philology* 86: 95–112.

Boedecker, D., and K. A. Raaflaub, eds. 1998. *Democracy, Empire and the Arts in Fifth-Century Athens.* Cambridge, Mass.

Bonanno, M. G. 1973–74. "Note a Saffo." *Museum criticum* 8/9: 111–20.

Bongie, E. B. 1977. "Heroic Elements in the *Medea* of Euripides." *Transactions of the American Philological Association* 107: 27–56.

Bookides, N., and R. Stroud. 1997. *The Sanctuary of Demeter and Kore: Topography and Architecture, Corinth.* Princeton.

Bornstein, D. 1978. "As Meek as a Maid: A Historical Perspective on Language for Women in Courtesy Books from the Middle Ages to Seventeen Magazine." In *Women's Language and Style*, edited by D. Butturff and E. L. Epstein, 132–38. Akron.

Bourdieu, P. [1977–84] 1991. *Language and Symbolic Power.* Translated from the French by G. Raymond and M. Adamson. Cambridge, Mass.

. [1979] 1984. *Distinction: A Social Critique of the Judgement of Taste*. Translated from the French by R. Nice. Cambridge, Mass.

———. [1980] 1990. *The Logic of Practice*. Translated from the French by R. Nice. Stanford.

Bowie, E. 1997. "The *Theognidea*: A Step towards a Collection of Fragments?" In *Collecting Fragments. Fragmente sammeln*, edited by G. Most, 53–66. Göttingen.

Bowman, L. 1998. "Nossis, Sappho and Hellenistic Poetry." *Ramus* 27: 39–59.

Bowra, C. M. [1936] 1953. "Erinna's Lament for Baucis." In *Problems in Greek Poetry*, 151–68. Oxford. [First published in *Greek Poetry and Life*, 325–42. Oxford.]

———. 1961. *Greek Lyric Poetry from Alcman to Simonides*. 2d rev. ed. Oxford.

Bremmer, J. N. 1994. *Greek Religion. Greece and Rome*, New Surveys in the Classics 24. Oxford.

Briggs, C. 1988. *Competence in Performance: The Creativity of Tradition in Mexicano Verbal Art*. Philadelphia.

Brock, R. 1994. "The Labour of Women in Classical Athens." *Classical Quarterly* 44: 336–46.

Brown, C. 1989. "Anactoria and the Χαρίτων ἀμαρύγματα: Sappho fr. 16.18 Voigt." *Quaderni Urbinati di cultura classica* 61: 7–15.

Brulé, P. 1987. *La fille d'Athènes: La religion des filles à Athènes à l'époque classique: Mythes, cultes et société*. Paris.

Brumfield, A. 1981. *The Attic Festivals of Demeter and Their Relation to the Agricultural Year*. New York.

———. 1996. "Aporreta: Verbal and Ritual Obscenity in the Cults of Ancient Women." In *Opuscula Atheniensa*, Proceedings of the Third International Seminar on Ancient Greek Cult, organized by the Swedish Institute at Athens, 16–18 October 1992, edited by R. Hägg, 67–74. Stockholm.

Bundy, E. L. [1962] 1986. *Studia Pindarica*. Berkeley. [First published as vol. 18 nos. 1 and 2 of the University of California Publications in Classical Philology.]

Bunzl, M. 1997. *Real History: Reflections on Historical Practice*. London.

Burkert, W. 1965. "ΓΟΗΣ: Zum griechischen 'Shamanismus.'" *Rheinisches Museum für Philologie* 105: 36–55.

———. [1972] 1983. *Homo Necans: The Anthropology of Ancient Greek Sacrificial Ritual and Myth*. Translated from the German by P. Bing. Berkeley.

———. [1977] 1985. *Greek Religion*. Translated from the German by J. Raffan. Cambridge, Mass.

———. 1979. "Kynaithos, Polycrates, and the *Homeric Hymn to Apollo*." In *Arktouros : Hellenic Studies Presented to B.M.W. Knox*, edited by G. Bowersock et al., 53–62. Berlin.

———. 1987. "The Making of Homer in the Sixth Century B.C.: Rhapsodes versus Stesichorus." In *Papers on the Amasis Painter and His World*, edited by A. P. A. Bellioli, 43–62. Malibu.

Burnett, A. P. 1979. "Desire and Memory." *Classical Philology* 74: 16–27.

———. 1983. *Three Archaic Poets: Archilochus, Alcaeus, Sappho*. Cambridge, Mass.

Burns, T. 1976. "Riddling: Occasion to Act." *Journal of American Folklore* 89: 139–65.

Burton, J. 1995. *Theocritus's Urban Mimes: Mobility, Gender, Patronage*. Berkeley.

Butler, J. P. 1993. *Bodies That Matter*. New York.

———. 2000. *Antigone's Claim: Kinship between Life and Death*. New York.

Cairns, D. L. 1993. *Aidos: The Psychology and Ethics of Honour and Shame in Ancient Greek Literature*. Oxford.

Calame, C. 1977. *Les choeurs de jeunes filles en Grèce archaïque II: Alcman*. Rome.

———. [1977] 1997. *Choruses of Young Women in Ancient Greece: Their Morphology, Religious Role, and Social Functions*. Translated from the French by J. Orion and D. Collins. Lanham, Md.

———. 1987. "Sappho et Hélène: Le mythe comme argumentation narrative et parabolique." In *Parole-Figure-Parabole: Recherches autour du discours parabolique*, edited by J. Delormé, 209–29. Lyon.

———. 1989. "Entre rapports de parenté et relations civiques: Aphrodite l'hétaïre au banquet politique des *hetaîroi*." In *Aux sources de la puissance: Sociabilité et parenté*, edited by F. Thélamon, 101–11. Rouen.

———. [1992] 1999. *The Poetics of Eros in Ancient Greece*. Translated from the French by J. Lloyd. Princeton. [First published in Italian.]

———. 1996. "Sappho's Group: An Initiation into Womanhood." In Greene 1996a: 113–24.

Cameron, Al. 1995. *Callimachus and His Critics*. Princeton.

Cameron, Av., and Al. Cameron. 1969. "Erinna's Distaff." *Classical Quarterly* 19: 285–88.

Cameron, D. 1985. *Feminism and Linguistic Theory*. London.

Campbell, D. A. 1967. *Greek Lyric Poetry: A Selection of Early Greek Lyric, Elegiac and Iambic Poetry*. London.

———. 1982–93. *Greek Lyric*. 5 vols. Loeb Classical Library. Cambridge, Mass.

———. [1982] 1990. *Greek Lyric*. Vol. 1. Loeb Classical Library 142. 2d corr. ed. Cambridge, Mass.

———. 1983. *The Golden Lyre: The Themes of Greek Lyric Poetry*. London.

———. 1988. *Greek Lyric*. Vol. 2. Loeb Classical Library 143. Cambridge, Mass.

Campbell, J. K. 1964. *Honour, Family and Patronage: A Study of Institutions and Moral Values in a Greek Mountain Community*. Oxford.

Caraveli, A. 1980. "Bridge between Worlds: The Greek Women's Lament as Communicative Event." *Journal of American Folklore* 93: 129–57.

———. 1986. "The Bitter Wounding: The Lament as Social Protest in Rural Greece." In Dubisch 1986: 169–94.

Carey, C. 1978. "Sappho fr. 96 LP." *Classical Quarterly* 28: 366–71.

———. 1980. "Homeric *Hymn to Apollo*, 171." *Classical Quarterly* 30: 288–90.

———, ed. 1989. *Lysias: Selected Speeches*. Cambridge.

———, ed. and trans. 1992. *Greek Orators VI: Apollodoros, Against Neaira [Demosthenes] 59*. Warminster.

Carlson, M. 1996. *Performance: A Critical Introduction*. New York.

Carradine, D., and S. Price, eds. 1987. *Rituals of Royalty: Power and Ceremonial in Traditional Societies*. Cambridge.

Carrière, J. 1975. *Théognis: Poèmes élégiaques*. Paris.

Carson, A. [1980] 1996. "The Justice of Aphrodite in Sappho 1." In Greene 1996a: 226–32. [First published in *Transactions of the American Philological Association* 110: 135–42.]

———. 1990. "Putting Her in Her Place: Woman, Dirt, and Desire." In Halperin, Winkler and Zeitlin 1990: 135–69.

Càccolo, F. 1975. *Inni Omerici.* Verona.

Cavallini, E. 1986. *Presenza di Saffo e Alceo nella poesia greca fino ad Aristofane.* Ferrara.

———. 1994. "Eros 'Divoratore' (Sapph. fr. 19.15 ss. V. ≈Theocr. 30.21 s.)." *Sileno* 20: 353–55.

Cawkwell, G. L. 1992. "Early Colonisation." *Classical Quarterly* 42: 289–303.

Chamberlain, L. 1988. "Gender and the Metaphorics of Translation." *Signs* 13: 454–72.

Cixous, H. 1976. "The Laugh of the Medusa." *Signs* 1: 875–93.

Clader, L. L. 1976. *Helen: The Evolution from Divine to Heroic in Greek Epic Tradition.* Leiden.

Clark, K. 1956. *The Nude: A Study in Ideal Form.* Princeton.

Clay, J. S. 1989. *The Politics of Olympus: Form and Meaning in the Major Homeric Hymns.* Princeton.

Clinton, K. 1992. *Myth and Cult: The Iconography of the Eleusinian Mysteries.* Stockholm.

Coates, J. [1986] 1993. *Women, Men and Language: A Sociolinguistic Account of Gender Differences in Language.* 2d ed. London.

———. 1995. "Language, Gender and Career." In Mills 1995: 13–30.

Cohen, B., ed. 1995. *The Distaff Side: Representing the Female in Homer's* Odyssey. Oxford.

Cohen, D. 1989. "Seclusion, Separation, and the Status of Women in Classical Athens." *Greece and Rome* 36: 3–15.

———. 1991. *Law, Sexuality, and Society: The Enforcement of Morals in Classical Athens.* Cambridge.

———. 1995. *Law, Violence, and Community in Classical Athens.* Cambridge.

Cole, S. G. 1992. "*Gynaiki ou themis:* Gender Difference in the Greek *leges sacrae.*" *Helios* 19: 104–22.

Collins, B. J. 1995. "Greek ὀλολύζω and Hittite *palwai-:* Exultation in the Ritual Slaughter of Animals." *Greek, Roman, and Byzantine Studies* 36: 319–39.

Consbruch, M. B. [1906] 1971. *Hephaistion, Enchiridion, cum commentariis veteribus.* 2d ed. Stuttgart.

Contiades-Tsitsoni, E. 1990. *Hymenaios und Epithalamion: Das Hochzeitslied in der frühgriechischen Lyrik.* Beiträge zur Altertumskunde Bd. 16. Stuttgart.

Cook, A. B. 1895. "The Bee in Greek Mythology." *Journal of Hellenic Studies* 15: 1–23.

Coray, M. 1993. *Wissen und Erkennen bei Sophokles.* Basel.

Cosi, D. 1987. "Jammed Communication: Battos, the Founder of Cyrene, Stammering and Castrated." In *Regions of Silence: Studies on the Difficulty of Communicating,* edited by M. G. Ciani, 115–45. Amsterdam.

Cowan, J. K. 1991. "Going Out for Coffee? Contesting the Grounds of Gendered Pleasures in Everyday Sociability." In Loizos and Papataxiarchis 1991: 180–202.

Cox, C. A. 1998. *Household Interests: Property, Marriage Strategies, and Family Dynamics in Ancient Athens.* Princeton.

Crahay, R. 1956. *La littérature oraculaire chez Hérodote.* Paris.

Crane, G. 1988. *Calypso: Backgrounds and Conventions of the* Odyssey. Beiträge zur klassischen Philologie 191. Frankfurt am Main.

Cribiore, R. 1996. *Writing, Teachers and Students in Graeco-Roman Egypt.* Atlanta.

Cropp, M. 1997. "Antigone's Final Speech (Sophocles, *Antigone* 891–928)." *Greece and Rome* 44: 137–60.

Csapo, E., and M. Miller. 1998. "Democracy, Empire and Art: Towards a Politics of Time and Narrative." In Boedeker and Raaflaub 1998: 87–125.

Csapo, E., and W. J. Slater. 1995. *The Context of Ancient Drama*. Ann Arbor.

Cunningham, I. C. 1966. "Herodas 4." *Classical Quarterly* 16: 113–25.

———, ed. 1971. *Herodas: Mimiambi*. Oxford.

Danforth, L. M. 1982. *The Death Rituals of Rural Greece*. Princeton.

Davidson, J. N. 1997. *Courtesans and Fishcakes: The Consuming Passions of Classical Athens*. London.

Davies, M. 1995. "Theocritus' *Adoniazusae*." *Greece and Rome* 42: 152–58.

de Certeau, M. [1975] 1988. "Language Altered: The Sorcerer's Speech." In *The Writing of History*, translated from the French by T. Conley, 244–68. New York.

———. [1986] 1993. "Mystic Speech." In *Heterologies: Discourse on the Other*, translated from the French by B. Massumi, 80–100. Minneapolis.

Degani, E., and G. Burzacchini. 1977. *Lirici Greci*. Florence.

Degani, H. 1983. *Hipponactis testimonia et fragmenta*. Leipzig.

de Klerk, V. 1997. "The Role of Expletives in the Construction of Masculinity." In Johnson and Meinhof 1997: 144–58.

Delatte, A. 1955. *Le Cycéon, breuvage rituel des Mystères d'Eleusis*. Paris.

Des Bouvrie, S. 1990. *Women in Greek Tragedy: An Anthropological Approach*. Oslo.

Detienne, M. [1967] 1996. *The Masters of Truth in Archaic Greece*. Translated from the French by J. Lloyd. New York.

———. [1974] 1981. "The Myth of 'Honeyed Orpheus.'" Translated from the French by R. L. Gordon. In *Myth, Religion and Society: Structuralist Essays*, edited by R. L. Gordon, 95–109. Cambridge.

———. [1979] 1989. "The Violence of Wellborn Ladies: Women in the Thesmophoria." In *The Cuisine of Sacrifice among the Greeks*, edited by M. Detienne and J.-P. Vernant, translated from the French by P. Wissing, 129–47. Chicago.

Deubner, L. 1932. *Attische Feste*. Berlin

Devereux, G. 1983. *Baubo: La vulve mythique*. Paris.

Dickey, E. 1995. "Forms of Address and Conversational Language in Aristophanes and Menander." *Mnemosyne* 48: 257–71.

———. 1996. *Greek Forms of Address: From Herodotus to Lucian*. Oxford.

Dickson, K. 1995. *Nestor: Poetic Memory in Greek Epic*. New York.

Diehl, E. 1949. *Anthologia Lyrica Graeca*. Vol. 1. 3d ed. Leipzig.

Diels, H., ed. [1912] 1951. *Die Fragmente der Vorsokratiker*. 3 vols. 6th ed., revised by W. Kranz. Berlin.

Diggle, J. 1998. *Tragicorum Graecorum fragmenta selecta*. Oxford.

Di Nola, A. M. 1974. *Antropologia religiosa*. Florence.

Dobrov, G. W. 1994. "A Dialogue with Death: Ritual Lament and the θρῆνος θεοτόκου of Romanos Melodos." *Greek, Roman and Byzantine Studies* 35: 229–54.

Dobson, M. 1979. "Herodotus 1.47 and the *Hymn to Hermes*: A Solution to the Test Oracle." *American Journal of Philology* 100: 349–59.

Doherty, L. 1995a. *Siren Songs: Gender, Audiences, and Narrators in the* Odyssey. Ann Arbor.

————. 1995b. "Sirens, Muses, and Female Narrators in the *Odyssey*." In Cohen 1995: 81–92.

Dougherty, C. 1993. *The Poetics of Colonization: From City to Text in Archaic Greece.* Oxford.

Dover, K. J., ed. [1971] 1985. *Theocritus: Select Poems.* Bristol.

————. 1974. *Greek Popular Morality in the Time of Plato and Aristotle.* Oxford.

————. 1978. *Greek Homosexuality.* Oxford.

Dowden, K. 1989. *Death and the Maiden: Girls' Initiation Rites in Greek Mythology.* London.

Drachmann, A. B. 1910. *Scholia vetera in Pindari Carmina.* 3 vols. Leipzig.

Dubisch, J., ed. 1986. *Gender and Power in Modern Greece.* Princeton.

————. 1991. "Gender, Kinship, and Religion: 'Reconstructing' the Anthropology of Greece." In Loizos and Papataxiarchis 1991: 29–46.

duBois, P. [1978] 1996. "Sappho and Helen." In Greene 1996a: 79–88. [First published in *Arethusa* 11: 89–99.]

————. 1995. *Sappho Is Burning.* Chicago.

Du Boulay, J. 1986. "Women—Images of Their Nature and Destiny in Rural Greece." In Dubisch 1986: 139–68.

————. 1991. "Cosmos and Gender in Village Greece." In Loizos and Papataxiarchis 1991: 47–78.

Dyer, R. 1975. "The Blind Bard of Chios (*Hymn. Hom. Ap.* 171–76)." *Classical Philology* 70: 119–21.

Easterling, P. E. 1988. "Women in Tragic Space." *Bulletin of the Institute of Classical Studies* 34: 15–26.

————, ed. 1997. *The Cambridge Companion to Greek Tragedy.* Cambridge.

Edmonds, J. 1931. *Elegy and Iambus.* Vol. 1. London.

Edmunds, L. 1985. "The Genre of Theognidean Poetry." In Figueira and Nagy 1985: 96–111.

————. 1987. "Theognis 815–18 and the Banquet of Attaginus." *Classical Philology* 82: 323–25.

————. 1997. "The Seal of Theognis." In *Poet, Public, and Performance in Ancient Greece*, edited by L. Edmunds and R. Wallace, 29–48. Baltimore.

Edwards, A. T. 1991. "Aristophanes' Comic Poetics: Τρύξ, Scatology, Σκῶμμα." *Transactions of the American Philological Association* 121: 157–79.

Edwards, M. 1987. *Homer: Poet of the* Iliad. Baltimore.

Edwards, M., and S. Usher. 1985. *Greek Orators I: Antiphon and Lysias.* Warminster.

Elsner, J., ed. 1996a. *Art and Text in Roman Culture.* Cambridge, Mass.

————. 1996b. "Naturalism and the Erotics of the Gaze." In Kampen 1996: 247–61.

Elsner, J., and A. Sharrock. 1991. "Re-viewing Pygmalion." *Ramus* 20: 149–82.

Fabbro, E. 1995. *Carmina convivalia attica.* Rome.

Farnell, L. R. 1907. *The Cults of the Greek States.* 5 vols. Oxford.

Fehr, B. 1990. "Entertainers at the Symposion: The Akletoi in the Archaic Period." In Murray 1990: 185–95.

Felson-Rubin, N. 1994. *Regarding Penelope: From Character to Poetics.* Princeton.

Fernández, C. 1997. "Las voces del personaje cómico: A propósito del verso 600 de *Plutos* de Aristófanes." *Synthesis* 4: 127–40.

Fernandez, J. 1986. *Persuasions and Performances: The Play of Tropes in Culture*. Bloomington, Ind.

Fernández Delgado, J. A. 1986. *Los Oráculoas y Hesíodo: Poesía Oral Mántica y Gnómica Griegas*. Salamanca.

Ferrari, F. 1989. *Theognis: Elegie*. Milan.

Festugière, A. J. 1952. "Arnobiana." *Vigiliae Christianae* 6: 208–54.

Figueira, T., and G. Nagy, eds. 1985. *Theognis of Megara: Poetry and the Polis*. Baltimore.

Fluck, H. 1931. *Skurrile Riten in griechischen Kulten*. Endingen.

Foley, H. P., ed. 1981a. *Reflections of Women in Antiquity*. New York.

———. 1981b. "The Conception of Women in Athenian Drama." In Foley 1981a: 127–67.

———. 1982. "The 'Female Intruder' Reconsidered: Woman in Aristophanes' *Lysistrata* and *Ecclesiazusae*." *Classical Philology* 77: 1–21.

———. 1985. *Ritual Irony: Poetry and Sacrifice in Euripides*. Ithaca, N.Y.

———. 1988. "Women in Greece." In *Civilization of the Ancient Mediterranean: Greece and Rome*, edited by M. Grant and R. Kitzinger, 1301–17. New York.

———. 1989. "Medea's Divided Self." *Classical Antiquity* 8: 61–85.

———. 1993. "The Politics of Tragic Lamentation." In *Tragedy, Comedy and the Polis*, edited by A. Sommerstein, S. Halliwell, and B. Zimmerman, 101–43. Bari.

———. 1994. *The Homeric Hymn to Demeter*. Princeton.

———. 1995. "Tragedy and Democratic Ideology." In *History, Tragedy, Theory*, edited by B. Goff, 131–50. Austin.

———. 1996. "Antigone as a Moral Agent." In *Tragedy and the Tragic*, edited by M. S. Silk, 49–73. Oxford.

Fontenrose, J. 1978. *The Delphic Oracle: Its Responses and Operations with a Catalogue of Responses*. Berkeley.

Ford, A. 1992. *Homer: Poet of the Past*. Ithaca, N.Y.

Forrest, W. G. 1957. "Colonization and the Rise of Delphi." *Historia* 6: 160–75.

Fowler, B. H. 1989. *The Hellenistic Aesthetic*. Madison, Wis.

Fowler, D. P. 1991. "Narrate and Describe: The Problem of Ekphrasis." *Journal of Roman Studies* 81: 25–35.

Foxhall, L. 1989. "Household, Gender and Property in Classical Athens." *Classical Quarterly* 39: 22–44.

———. 1992. "The Control of the Attic Landscape." In *Agriculture in Ancient Greece: Proceedings of the Seventh International Symposium at the Swedish Institute at Athens, 16–17 May 1990*, edited by B. Wells, 155–59. Stockholm.

———. 1995. "Women's Ritual and Men's Work in Ancient Athens." In Hawley and Levick 1995: 97–110.

———. 1996. "The Law and the Lady: Women and Legal Proceedings in Classical Athens." In *Greek Law in Its Political Setting: Justifications Not Justice*, edited by L. Foxhall and A. D. E. Lewis, 133–52. Oxford.

Fränkel, H. [1924] 1968. "Eine Stileigenheit der frühgriechischen Literatur." Reprinted in *Wege und Forme frühgriechischen Denkens*, 40–96. 3d ed. Munich.

———. [1962] 1973. *Early Greek Poetry and Philosophy*. Translated from the German by M. Hadas and J. Willis. New York.

Friedl, E. 1962. *Vasilika: A Village in Modern Greece*. New York.

———. 1986. "The Position of Women. Appearance and Reality." In Dubisch 1986: 42–52.

Friedrich, P. 1978. *The Meaning of Aphrodite*. Chicago.

Frontisi-Ducroux, F. 1996. "Eros, Desire, and the Gaze." In Kampen 1996: 81–100.

Gagarin, M. 1974. "*Dike* in Archaic Greek Thought." *Classical Philology* 69: 186–97.

———, ed. 1997. *Antiphon, the Speeches*. Cambridge.

———. 1998. "Women in Athenian Courts." *Dike* 1: 39–51.

Gager, J. G. 1992. *Curse Tablets and Binding Spells from the Ancient World*. Oxford.

Gaisford, T. 1822. *Joannis Stobaei Florilegium*. Vol. 3. Oxford.

Gal, S. 1991. "Between Speech and Silence: The Problematics of Research on Gender and Language." In *Gender at the Crossroads of Knowledge*, edited by M. di Leonardo, 175–203. Berkeley.

———. 1995. "Language, Gender and Power: An Anthropological Review." In *Gender Articulated*, edited by M. Bucholtz and K. Hall, 169–82. New York and London.

Garland, B. J. 1981. "Gynaikonomai: An Investigation of Greek Censors of Women." Diss., The Johns Hopkins University, Baltimore, Md.

Garland, R. 1989. "The Well-Ordered Corpse: An Investigation into the Motives behind Greek Funerary Legislation." *Bulletin of the Institute of Classical Studies* 36: 1–15.

Garvie, A. F. 1986. *Aeschylus. Choephori*. Oxford.

Garzya, A. 1958. *Teognide: Elegie Libri I–II*. Florence.

Gelzer, T. 1985. "Mimus und Kunsttheorie bei Herondas, Mimiambus 4." In *Catalepton: Festschrift für Bernhard Wyss zum 80. Geburtstag*, edited by C. Schaeublin, 96–116. Basel.

Geoghegan, D. 1979. *Anyte: The Epigrams*. Testi e Commenti 4. Rome.

Gerber, D. E., ed. and trans. 1999. *Greek Elegiac Poetry*. Loeb Classical Library 258. Cambridge, Mass.

Gernet, L., and A. Boulanger. 1932. *Le Génie Grec dans la religion*. Paris.

Gigante, M. 1974. "Nosside." *Parola del passato* 29: 22–39.

Gilhus, I. S. 1997. *Laughing Gods, Weeping Virgins: Laughter in the History of Religion*. New York.

Gilleland, M. 1980. "Female Speech in Greek and Latin." *American Journal of Philology* 101: 180–83.

Gilligan, C. 1982. *In a Different Voice*. Cambridge.

Gilmore, D. 1987. *Aggression and Community: Paradoxes of Andalusian Culture*. New Haven.

Gisler, J.-R. 1994. "Prometheus." In *Lexicon iconographicum mythologiae classicae*, Vol. 7, edited by J. C. Balty et al., 1.531–52 (text), 2.420–30 (pictures). Zürich.

Gleason, M. W. 1990. "The Semiotics of Gender: Physiognomy and Self-Fashioning in the Second Century C.E." In Halperin, Winkler and Zeitlin 1990: 389–416.

———. 1995. *Making Men*. Princeton.

Goff, B. 1990. *The Noose of Words: Readings of Desire, Violence and Language in Euripides' Hippolytus*. Cambridge.

———. 1995. "Aithra at Eleusis." *Helios* 22: 65–78.

————. 1997. "Apollodorus' Imaginary Citizens." Paper delivered at the American Philological Association Meeting, Chicago. [A one-page summary of this paper is printed in *APA Abstracts* (1997): 173.]

Goffman, E. 1959. *The Presentation of Self in Everyday Life.* New York.

Goheen, R. F. 1951. *The Imagery of Sophocles' Antigone.* Princeton.

Goldberg, S. M. 1986. *Understanding Terence.* Princeton.

Goldhill, S. 1984. *Language, Sexuality and Narrative: The Oresteia.* Cambridge.

————. 1986. *Reading Greek Tragedy.* Cambridge.

————. 1990. "The Great Dionysia and Civic Ideology." In Winkler and Zeitlin 1990: 97–129.

————. 1994a. "The Naive and Knowing Eye: Ekphrasis and the Culture of Viewing in the Hellenistic World." In Goldhill and Osborne 1994: 197–223.

————. 1994b. "Representing Democracy: Women at the Great Dionysia." In *Ritual, Finance, Politics: Athenian Democratic Accounts Presented to David Lewis,* edited by R. Osborne and S. Hornblower, 347–69. Oxford.

————. 1997. "The Audience of Athenian Tragedy." In Easterling 1997: 54–68.

————. 1998. "The Seduction of the Gaze: Socrates and His Girlfriends." In *Kosmos: Essays in Order, Conflict and Community in Classical Athens,* edited by P. Cartledge and S. van Reden, 105–24. Cambridge, Mass.

————. Forthcoming. "The Erotic Eye: Visual Stimulation and Cultural Conflict." In *Everything's Greece to the Wise,* edited by S. Goldhill. Cambridge, Mass.

Goldhill, S., and R. Osborne, eds. 1994. *Art and Text in Ancient Greek Culture.* Cambridge.

————, eds. 1999. *Performance Culture and Athenian Democracy.* Cambridge.

Gomme, A. W. [1925] 1937. "The Position of Women in Athens in the Fifth and Fourth Centuries B.C." In *Essays in Greek History and Literature,* 89–115. Oxford. [First published in *Classical Philology* 20: 1–25.]

————. 1957. "Interpretations of Some Poems of Alkaios and Sappho." *Journal of Hellenic Studies* 77: 255–66.

Gomme, A. W., and F. H. Sandbach. 1973. *Menander: A Commentary.* Oxford.

Goold, G. P. 1988. *Catullus, Tibullus, Pervigilium Veneris.* Loeb Classical Library 6. 2d ed., revised by G. P. Goold. Cambridge, Mass.

Gould, J. P. 1973. "Hiketeia." *Journal of Hellenic Studies* 93: 74–103.

————. 1980. "Law, Custom and Myth: Aspects of the Social Position of Women in Classical Athens." *Journal of Hellenic Studies* 100: 38–59.

Gow, A. S. F. 1952. *Theocritus.* 2 vols. 2d ed. Cambridge.

Gow, A. S. F., and D. L. Page, eds. 1965. *The Greek Anthology: Hellenistic Epigrams.* 2 vols. Cambridge.

Graf, F. 1974. *Eleusis und die orphische Dichtung Athens in vorhellenistischer Zeit.* Berlin.

Grant, M. A. 1924. *The Ancient Rhetorical Theories of the Laughable: The Greek Rhetoricians and Cicero.* Madison, Wis.

Graver, M. 1995. "Dog-Helen and Homeric Insult." *Classical Antiquity* 14: 41–61.

Greene, E. [1994] 1996. "Apostrophe and Women's Erotics in the Poetry of Sappho." In Greene 1996a: 233–47. [First published in *Transactions of the American Philological Association* 124: 41–56.]

————, ed. 1996a. *Reading Sappho: Contemporary Approaches.* Berkeley.

———, ed. 1996b. *Re-Reading Sappho: Reception and Transmission.* Berkeley.

———. 2000. "Playing with Tradition: Gender and Innovation in the Epigrams of Anyte." *Helios* 27: 15–32.

Griffin, A. 1982. *Sikyon.* Oxford.

Griffith, M. 1998. "The King and Eye: The Rule of the Father in Greek Tragedy." *Proceedings of the Cambridge Philological Society* 41: 20–84.

———. 1999. *Sophocles. Antigone.* Cambridge.

Griffith, R. D. 1989. "In Praise of the Bride: Sappho Fr. 105 (A) L.-P., Voigt." *Transactions of the American Philological Association* 119: 55–66.

Griffith, R. D., and G. D'A. Griffith. 1991. "Il Gioco della 'Chilichelone.'" *Maia* 1: 83–87.

Griffiths, A. 1972. "Alcman's Partheneion: The Morning After the Night Before." *Quaderni Urbinati di cultura classica* 14: 1–30.

Griffiths, F. T. 1981. "Home before Lunch: The Emancipated Woman in Theocritus." In Foley 1981a: 247–73.

Groningen, B. van. 1960. *Pindare au banquet.* Leiden.

———. 1966. *Theognis. Le premier livre.* Amsterdam.

Gutzwiller, K. J. 1997. "Genre Development and Gendered Voices in Erinna and Nossis." In *Dwelling in Possibility: Women Poets and Critics on Poetry,* edited by Y. Prins and M. Shreiber, 202–22. Ithaca, N.Y.

———. 1998. *Poetic Garlands: Hellenistic Epigrams in Context.* Berkeley.

Hague, R. 1983. "Ancient Greek Wedding Songs: The Tradition of Praise." *Journal of Folklore Research* 20: 131–43.

———. 1984. "Sappho's Consolation for Atthis, fr. 96 LP." *American Journal of Philology* 105: 29–36.

Hall, E. 1989. *Inventing the Barbarian.* Oxford.

———. 1993. "Asia Unmanned: Images of Victory in Classical Athens." In *War and Society in the Greek World,* edited by J. Rich and G. Shipley, 107–33. London.

———. 1997. "The Sociology of Athenian Tragedy." In Easterling 1997: 93–126.

———. 1999. "Actor's Song in Tragedy." In Goldhill and Osborne 1999: 96–124.

Halperin, D. 1990a. *One Hundred Years of Homosexuality and Other Essays on Greek Love.* London.

———. 1990b. "Why Is Diotima a Woman? Platonic *Erōs* and the Figuration of Gender." In Halperin, Winkler and Zeitlin 1990: 257–309.

Halperin, D., J. Winkler, and F. Zeitlin, eds. 1990. *Before Sexuality: The Construction of Erotic Experience in the Ancient Greek World.* Princeton.

Hansen, P. 1983–89. *Carmina epigraphica Graeca.* Vol. 1, *Saeculorum VIII–V A.Chr.N.* Vol. 2, *Saeculi IV A.Chr.N.* Berlin.

Harding, S. 1975. "Women and Words in a Spanish Village." In Reiter 1975a: 283–308.

Harrison, E. 1902. *Studies in Theognis.* Cambridge.

Hart, L. K. 1993. *Time, Religion and Social Experience in Rural Greece.* Lanham, Md.

Havelock, C. M. 1995. *The Aphrodite of Knidos and Her Successors.* Ann Arbor.

Hawley, R., and B. Levick, eds. 1995. *Women in Antiquity: New Assessments.* London.

Henderson, J. W. 1975. *The Maculate Muse: Obscene Language in Attic Comedy.* New Haven.

———. 1987. *Aristophanes. Lysistrata.* Oxford.

———. 1991. "Women and the Athenian Dramatic Festivals." *Transactions of the American Philological Association* 121: 133–47.

———. 1996. *Three Plays by Aristophanes: Staging Women.* London.

Henley, N., and B. Thorne, eds. 1975. *Language and Sex: Difference and Dominance.* Rowley, Mass.

Henley, N., C. Kramarae, and B. Thorne, eds. 1983. *Language, Gender and Society.* Rowley, Mass.

Henry, M. 1995. *Prisoner of History: Aspasia of Miletus and Her Biographical Tradition.* Oxford.

Herfst, P. [1922] 1979. *Le travail de la femme dans la Grèce ancienne.* New York.

Herington, C. J. 1985. *Poetry into Tragedy.* Berkeley.

Herzfeld, M. 1986. "Within and Without: The Category of 'Female' in the Ethnography of Modern Greece." In Dubisch 1986: 215–33.

———. 1991. "Silence, Submission, and Subversion: Towards a Poetics of Womanhood." In Loizos and Papataxiarchis 1991: 79–97.

Heubeck, A., S. West, and J. B. Hainsworth. 1988. *The Odyssey: A Commentary.* Vol. 1. Oxford.

Heubeck, A., and A. Hoekstra. 1989. *The Odyssey: A Commentary.* Vol. 2. Oxford.

Hirschon, R. 1978. "Open Body/Closed Space: The Transformation of Female Sexuality." In *Defining Females: The Nature of Women in Society*, edited by S. Ardener, 66–88. London.

Høibye, A. B. 1995. "A Joke with the Inevitable: Men as Women and Women as Men in Aristophanes' *Thesmophoriazusae* and *Ekklesiasuzae.*" In *Greece and Gender*, edited by B. Berggren and N. Marinatos, 43–54. Athens

Holst-Warhaft, G. 1992. *Dangerous Voices: Women's Lament in Greek Literature.* New York.

———. 1995. "The Fun in the Funeral." Paper delivered at the American Philological Association Annual Meeting, San Diego. [A one-page summary of this paper is printed in *APA Abstracts* (1995): 69.]

Hooker, J. T. 1979. *Iliad III.* Bristol.

Howie, J. G. 1977. "Sappho Fr. 16 (LP): Self-Consolation and Encomium." In *Papers of the Liverpool Latin Seminar, Vol. 1*, edited by F. Cairns, 207–35. Liverpool.

Hubbard, T. 1994. "Elemental Psychology and the Date of Semonides of Amorgos." *American Journal of Philology* 115: 175–97.

Humphreys, S. C. [1983] 1993. *The Family, Women and Death: Comparative Studies.* 2d ed. Ann Arbor.

Hunter, R. L. 1992. "Writing the God: Form and Meaning in Callimachus' *Hymn to Athena.*" *Materiali e discussioni* 29: 9–34.

———. 1996. *Theocritus and the Archaeology of Greek Poetry.* Cambridge.

Hunter, V. J. 1994. *Policing Athens: Social Control in the Attic Lawsuits, 420–320 B.C.* Princeton.

Hurwit, J. 1990. "The Words in the Image: Orality, Literacy, and Early Greek Art." *Word and Image* 6: 180–97.

Husson, G. 1983. *Oikia: le vocabulaire de la maison privée en Égypte d'après les papyrus grecs.* Paris.

Hutchinson, G. O. 1988. *Hellenistic Poetry.* Oxford.

Jacoby, F. 1923–58. *Die Fragmente der griechischen Historiker.* 15 vols. Berlin.

Jameson, M. 1990a. "Private Space and the Greek City." In *The Greek City from Homer to Alexander*, edited by O. Murray and S. Price, 171–95. Oxford.

———. 1990b. "Domestic Space in the Greek City-State." In *Domestic Architecture and the Use of Space*, edited by S. Kent, 92–113. Cambridge.

Janko, R. 1982. *Homer, Hesiod and the Hymns: Diachronic Development in Epic Diction*. Cambridge.

———. 1982b. "Sappho fr. 96, 8 L-P: A Textual Note." *Mnemosyne*, ser. 4, vol. 35: 322–24.

Jenkins, I. 1983. "Is There Life after Marriage? A Study in the Abduction Motif in Vase Paintings of the Athenian Wedding Ceremony." *Bulletin of the Institute of Classical Studies* 30: 137–45.

Jenkins, K. 1997. *The Postmodern Reader*. London.

Jens, W., ed. 1971. *Die Bauformen der griechischen Tragödie*. Poetika Beiheft 6. Munich.

Jesperson, O. 1922. *Language, Its Nature, Development and Origin*. London.

Jiménez, M. 1987. "Algunos aspectos de los *Aenigmata symphosii*." *Emerita* 55: 307–12.

Johnson, P. J. 1997. "Woman's Third Face: A Psycho-Social Reconsideration of Sophocles' Antigone." *Arethusa* 30: 369–98.

Johnson, S., and U. Meinhof, eds. 1997. *Language and Masculinity*. Oxford.

Johnston, S. I. 1989. *Hekate Soteira: A Study of Hekate's Role in the Chaldean Oracles and Related Literature*. American Classical Studies 21. Atlanta.

———. 1994. "Penelope and the Erinyes: *Odyssey* 20.61–82." *Helios* 21: 137–59.

———. 1999. *Restless Dead: Encounters between the Living and the Dead in Ancient Greece*. Berkeley.

Joplin, P. K. 1991. "The Voice of the Shuttle Is Ours." In *Rape and Representation*, edited by L. A. Higgins and B. R. Silver, 35–64. New York.

Just, R. 1989. *Women in Athenian Law and Life*. London.

Kaibel, G. 1899. *Comicorum Graecorum fragmenta*. Vol. 1. Berlin.

Kamerbeek, J. C. 1956. "Sapphica." *Mnemosyne*, ser. 4, vol. 9: 97–102.

Kampen, N. B., ed. 1996. *Sexuality in Ancient Art*. Cambridge, Mass.

Karaghiorga-Stathacopoulou, T. 1986. "Baubo." In *Lexicon iconographicum mythologiae classicae*, Vol. 3, edited by J. C. Balty et al., 1.87–90 (text), 2.67–68 (pictures). Zürich.

Kassel, R. 1991. *Quomodo . . . infantes atque parvuli pueri inducantur describantur commemorentur*. Berlin.

Kassel, R., and C. Austin. 1983–96. *Poetae comici Graeci*. 8 vols. Berlin.

Kassis, K. 1980. *Mirologhia tis Mesa Manis*. Vol. 2. Athens.

Katz, M. A. 1991. *Penelope's Renown: Meaning and Indeterminancy in the* Odyssey. Princeton.

———. 1994. "The Character of Tragedy: Women and the Greek Imagination." *Arethusa* 27: 81–103.

Keenan, E. 1974. "Norm-Makers, Norm-Breakers: Uses of Speech by Men and Women in a Malagasy Community." In *Explorations in the Ethnography of Speaking*, edited by R. Bauman and J. Sherzer, 125–43. Cambridge.

Kennedy, G. A. 1986. "Helen's Web Unraveled." *Arethusa* 19: 5–14.

Kenyon, F. G. 1893. *Greek Papyri in the British Museum*. London.

Kern, O. 1900. *Die Inschriften von Magnesia am Menander.* Berlin.

———. [1922] 1963. *Orphicorum fragmenta.* 2d ed. Berlin.

King, H. 1986. "Agnodike and the Profession of Medicine." *Proceedings of the Cambridge Philological Society* 32: 53–77.

Kingsley, P. 1994. *Ancient Philosophy, Mystery, and Magic.* Oxford.

Kirk, G. S. 1985. *The Iliad: A Commentary.* Vol. 1: *Books 1–4.* Cambridge.

Kirkwood, G. M. 1974. *Early Greek Monody: The History of a Poetic Type.* Ithaca, N.Y.

Kitzinger, R. 1976. "Stylistic Methods of Characterization in Sophocles' Antigone." Diss., Stanford University.

Knox, B. M. W. 1964. *The Heroic Temper.* Berkeley.

———. 1979. *Word and Action.* Baltimore.

Kock, T. 1880–88. *Comicorum Atticorum fragmenta.* 3 vols. Leipzig.

Koloski-Ostrow, A. O., and C. L. Lyons, eds. 1997. *Naked Truths: Women, Sexuality and Gender in Classical Art and Archeology.* London.

Konstan, D. 1995. *Greek Comedy and Ideology.* New York.

Körte, A. 1957–59. *Menandri quae supersunt.* 2 vols. 3d ed., revised by A. Thierfelder. Leipzig.

Kranz, W. 1933. *Stasimon.* Berlin.

Kris, E., and O. Kurz. 1979. *Legend, Myth, and Magic in the Image of the Artist.* New Haven.

Kron, U. 1996. "Priesthoods, Dedications and Euergetism: What Part Did Religion Play in the Political and Social Status of Women?" In *Religion and Power in the Ancient Greek World: Proceedings of the Uppsala Symposium of 1993. Boreas,* vol. 24, edited by P. Hellström and B. Alroth, 139–82. Uppsala.

Labarbe, J. 1992. "Identification d'une noctambule (Théognis, 861–864)." In *Serta Leodiensia Secunda,* 237–45. Liège.

Lacan, J. [1986] 1992. *The Ethics of Psychoanalysis, 1959–1960: The Seminar of Jacques Lacan, Book VII.* Edited by J. A. Miller. Translated from the French by D. Porter. New York.

Lacey, W. K. 1968. *The Family in Classical Greece.* London.

Lada-Richards, I. 1999. *Initiating Dionysus: Ritual and Theatre in Aristophanes'* Frogs. Oxford.

Lakoff, R. 1973. "Language and Woman's Place." *Language in Society* 2: 45–81.

———. 1975. *Language and Woman's Place.* New York.

Lambert, S. D. [1993] 1998. *The Phratries of Attica.* 2d ed. Ann Arbor.

Lanata, G. [1966] 1996. "Sappho's Amatory Language." Translated from the Italian by W. Robins. In Greene 1996a: 11–25.

Lardinois, A. 1989. "Lesbian Sappho and Sappho of Lesbos." In *From Sappho to de Sade: Moments in the History of Sexuality,* edited by J. N. Bremmer, 15–35. London.

———. 1994. "Subject and Circumstance in Sappho's Poetry." *TAPA* 124: 57–84.

———. 1995. "Wisdom in Context: The Use of Gnomic Statements in Archaic Greek Poetry." Diss., Princeton University.

———. 1996. "Who Sang Sappho's Songs?" In Greene 1996a: 150–72.

———. 1998a. Review of Calame [1977] 1997. *Bryn Mawr Classical Review* 9.2: 116–25.

———. 1998b. Review of Wilson 1996. *Bryn Mawr Classical Review* 1998=07=03.

———. 1998c. Review of Stehle 1997. *American Journal of Philology* 119: 633–36.

Lasserre, F. 1974. "Ornements érotiques dans la poésie lyrique archaïque." In *Serta Turyniana: Studies in Greek Literature and Palaeography in Honor of Alexander Turyn*, edited by J. L. Heller and J. K. Newman, 1–33. Urbana, Ill.

———. 1989. *Sappho: Une autre lecture*. Padua.

Latacz, J. 1985. "Realität und Imagination: Eine neue Lyrik-Theorie und Sapphos φαίνεταί μοι κῆνος—Lied." *Museum Helveticum* 42: 67–94.

Latte, K. 1940. "The Coming of the Pythia?" *Harvard Theological Review* 33: 9–18.

———. 1953. "Erinna." *Nachrichten der Akademie—Göttingen (phil-hist. kl.)* 3: 81–94.

Lausberg, M. 1982. *Das Einzeldistichon: Studien zum antiken Epigramm*. Munich.

Lawler, L. B. 1964. *The Dance in Ancient Greece*. Middletown, Conn.

———. 1964. *The dance of the ancient Greek theatre*. Iowa City.

Lefkowitz, M. 1981. *The Lives of the Greek Poets*. Baltimore.

Levin, D. N. 1962. "Quaestiones Erinneanae." *Harvard Studies in Classical Philology* 66: 193–204.

Lévi-Strauss, C. [1958] 1963. "Language and the Analysis of Social Laws." *Structural Anthropology*. Vol. 1. Translated from the French by C. Jacobson and B. G. Schoepf. New York.

Lewis, D. M., and L. H. Jeffery, eds. 1981. *Inscriptiones Graecae* 1.2. 3d ed. Berlin.

Lissarrague, F. [1987] 1990. *The Aesthetics of the Greek Banquet*. Translated from the French by A. Szegedy-Maszale. Princeton.

———. 1992. "Figures of Women." In Pantel 1992: 139–229.

———. 1995. "Women, Boxes, Containers: Some Signs and Metaphors." Translated from the French by E. Brulotte. In Reeder 1995: 91–101.

Lloyd-Jones, H. 1975. *Females of the Species: Semonides on Women*. London.

———. 1979. *Aeschylus: The Oresteia*. Berkeley.

Lloyd-Jones, H., and P. Parsons. 1983. *Supplementum Hellenisticum*. Berlin.

Lohmann, D. 1988. *Die Andromache-Szenen der Ilias: Ansätze und Methoden der Homer-Interpretation*. Hildesheim.

Loizos, P., and E. Papataxiarchis, eds. 1991. *Contested Identities: Gender and Kinship in Modern Greece*. Princeton.

Lonsdale, S. H. 1993. *Dance and Ritual Play in Greek Religion*. Baltimore.

———. 1995. "Homeric Hymn to Apollo: Prototype and Paradigm of Choral Performance." *Arion* 3: 25–40.

Loomba, A. 1993. "Dead Women Tell No Tales: Issues of Female Subjectivity, Subaltern Agency and Tradition in Colonial and Post-Colonial Writings on Widow Immolation in India." *History Workshop Journal* 36: 209–27.

Loraux, N. [1978] 1993. "Of the Race of Women and Some of Its Tribes: Hesiod and Semonides." In Loraux 1993: 72–110. [First published in *Arethusa* 11: 43–87.]

———. [1981] 1986. *The Invention of Athens: The Funeral Oration in the Classical City*. Translated from the French by A. Sheridan. Cambridge, Mass.

———. 1986. "La main d' Antigone." *Métis* 1: 165–96.

———. [1990] 1998. *Mothers in Mourning*. Translated from the French by C. Pache. Ithaca, N.Y.

———. 1993. *The Children of Athena: Athenian Ideas about Citizenship and the Division between the Sexes*. Translated from the French by C. Levine. Princeton.

Lowe, N. J. 1998. "Thesmophoria and Haloa: myth, physics and mysteries." In Blundell, S. and Williamson, M., *The Sacred and the Feminine in Ancient Greece*, London and New York 1998, 149–73.

Luck, G. 1954. "Die Dichterinnen der Griechischen Anthologie." *Museum Helveticum* 11: 170–87.

Lyghounis, M. G. 1991. "Elementi tradizionali nella poesia nuziale greca." *Materiali e discussioni* 27: 159–98.

Lynn-George, M. 1988. Epos: *Word, Narrative, and the* Iliad. Atlantic Highlands, N.J.

Lyons, D. 1997. *Gender and Immortality: Heroines in Ancient Greek Myth and Cult.* Princeton.

Maas, P. 1914. "Hymenaios." In *Real-Encyclopädie der classischen Altertumswissenschaft*, Vol. 9, edited by W. Kroll, 130–34. Stuttgart.

MacDowell, D. M. 1995. *Aristophanes and Athens: An Introduction to the Plays.* Oxford.

Mackie, H. 1995. *Talking Trojan: Speech and Community in the* Iliad. Lanham, Md.

Macleod, C. W. 1974. "Two Comparisons in Sappho." *Zeitschrift für papyrologie und epigraphik* 15: 217–20.

Maehler, H. 1989. *Pindari carmina cum fragmentis, Pars II: Fragmenta, Indices.* Leipzig.

Malkin, I. 1987. *Religion and Colonization in Ancient Greece.* Leiden.

———. 1989. "Delphoi and the Founding of Social Order in Archaic Greece." *Métis* 4: 129–53.

Mangelsdorff, E. A. 1913. *Das lyrische Hochzeitsgedicht bei den Griechen und Römern.* Hamburg.

Mankidou, E. 1992–93. "Äthenerinnen in schwarzfigurigen Brunnenhausszenen." *Hephaistos* 11–12: 51–91.

Marcovich, M. [1986] 1988. "Demeter, Baubo, Iacchus—and a Redactor." Reprinted in *Studies in Graeco-Roman Religions and Gnosticism*, 20–27. Leiden. [First published in *Vigiliae Christianae* 40: 294–301.]

Martin, R. P. 1983. *Healing, Sacrifice and Battle: Amēchania and Related Concepts in Early Greek Poetry.* Innsbruck.

———. 1984. "Hesiod, Odysseus, and the Instruction of Princes." *Transactions of the American Philological Association* 114: 29–48.

———. 1989. *The Language of Heroes: Speech and Performance in the* Iliad. Ithaca, N.Y.

———. 1992. "Hesiod's Metanastic Poetics." *Ramus* 21: 111–33.

———. 1993. "The Seven Sages as Performers of Wisdom." In *Cultural Poetics in Archaic Greece: Cult, Performance, Politics*, edited by C. Dougherty and L. Kurke, 108–28. Cambridge.

———. 1995. "Keening Helen." Paper delivered at the 1995 Corhali conference. Lausanne.

———. 1997. "Similes and Performance." In *Written Voices, Spoken Signs: Tradition, Performance, and the Epic Text*, edited by E. Bakker and A. Kahane, 138–66, 249–52. Cambridge, Mass.

———. Forthcoming. "Synchronic Aspects of Homeric Performance: The Evidence of *The Hymn to Apollo.*" Proceedings of the First International Conference on Hellenism at the End of the Millennium. LaPlata, Argentina.

Martino, F. de. 1982. *Omero agonista in Delo.* Brescia.

———. 1991a. "Appunti sulla scrittura al femminile nel mondo antico." In Martino 1991b: 19–75.

———. ed. 1991b. *Rose di Pieria.* "Le Rane" Collana di Studi e Testi 9. Bari.

Martino, F. de, and A. H. Sommerstein, eds. 1995. *Lo Spettacolo delle Voci.* Naples.

Masson, O. 1974. "Deux ouvrages récents concernant Hérondas." *Revue de philologie de littérature et d'histoire anciennes* 48: 81–91.

Mastronarde, D. J., ed. 1994. *Euripides, Phoenissae.* Cambridge.

Maurizio, L. 1993. "Delphic Narratives: Recontextualizing the Pythia and Her Prophecies." Diss., Princeton University.

———. 1995. "Anthropology and Spirit Possession: A Reconsideration of the Pythia's Role at Delphi." *Journal of Hellenic Studies* 115: 69–86.

———. 1997. "Delphic Oracles as Oral Performances: Authenticity and Historical Evidence." *Classical Antiquity* 16: 308–34.

McClure, L. K. 1993. "On Knowing Greek: George Eliot and the Classical Tradition." *Classical and Modern Literature* 13: 139–56.

———. 1995. "Female Speech and Characterization in Euripides." In Martino and Sommerstein 1995, part 2: 35–60.

———. 1997. "*Logos Gunaikos:* Speech, Gender, and Spectatorship in the *Oresteia.*" *Helios* 24: 112–35.

———. 1999. *Spoken Like a Woman: Speech and Gender in Athenian Drama.* Princeton.

McDonnell, M. 1996. "Writing, Copying, and Autograph Manuscripts in Ancient Rome." *Classical Quarterly* 46: 469–91.

McEvilley, T. 1971. "Sappho, Fragment 94." *Phoenix* 25: 1–11.

———. 1972. "Sappho, Fragment Two." *Phoenix* 26: 323–33.

———. 1973. "Sapphic Imagery and Fragment 96." *Hermes* 101: 257–78.

———. 1978. "Sappho, Fragment Thirty One: The Face behind the Mask." *Phoenix* 32: 1–18.

McGlew, J. F. 1993. *Tyranny and Political Culture in Ancient Greece.* Ithaca, N.Y.

McLeod, W. E. 1961. "Oral Bards at Delphi." *Transactions of the American Philological Association* 92: 317–25.

Merkelbach, R. 1957. "Sappho und ihre Kreis." *Philologus* 101: 1–29.

Merkelbach, R., and M. L. West. 1967. *Fragmenta Hesiodea.* Oxford.

Mezzadri, B. 1987. "La pierre et le foyers." *Métis* 2: 215–20.

Michelazzo Magrini, M. 1975. "Una nuova linea interpretativa della 'Conocchia' di Erinna." *Prometheus* 1: 225–36.

Mikalson, J. D. 1975. *The Sacred and Civil Calendar of the Athenian Year.* Princeton.

Mills, S., ed. 1995. *Language and Gender: Interdisciplinary Perspectives.* New York.

Modrzejewski, J. M. 1995. *The Jews of Egypt: From Rameses II to Emperor Hadrian.* Philadelphia

Mondésert, C., and A. Plassart, eds. 1976. *Clément d' Alexandrie: Le Protreptique.* 3d ed., revised with a Greek text by A. Plassart. Paris.

Monsacré, H. 1984. *Les larmes d'Achille: Le héros, la femme et la souffrance dans la poésie d'Homère.* Paris.

Montrose, L. 1980. "The Purpose of Playing: Reflexions on a Shakespearean Anthropology." *Helios* 7: 51–74.

Morgan, C. 1990. *Athletes and Oracles: The Transformation of Olympia and Delphi in the Eighth Century B.C.* Cambridge.

Morris, S. P. 1992. *Daidalos and the Origins of Greek Art.* Princeton.

Mosse, C. 1969. *La tyrannie dans la Grèce antique.* Paris.

Most, G. W. 1982. "Greek Lyric Poets." In *Ancient Writers: Greece and Rome,* vol. 1, *Homer to Caesar,* edited by T. J. Luce, 75–98. New York.

———. [1995] 1996. "Reflecting Sappho." In Greene 1996b: 11–35. Berkeley. [First published in *Bulletin of the Institute of Classical Studies* 40: 15–38.]

Munroe, D. B., and T. W. Allen. 1912–20. *Homeri Opera I–V.* Oxford.

Murnaghan, S. 1986. *"Antigone 904–920* and the Institution of Marriage." *American Journal of Philology* 107: 192–207.

———. 1999. "The Poetics of Loss in the Greek Epic." In *Epic Traditions in the Contemporary World: The Poetics of Community,* edited by M. Beissinger, J. Tylus, and S. Wofford, 203–20. Berkeley.

Murray, O. 1980. *Early Greece.* Stanford.

———, ed. 1990. *Sympotica: A Symposium on the Symposion.* Oxford.

Murray, P. 1981. "Poetic Inspiration in Early Greece." *Journal of Hellenic Studies* 101: 87–100.

Murru, F. 1980. *"Aenigmata symphosii* ou *aenigmata symposii."* *Eos* 68: 155–58.

Muth, R. 1954. "'Hymenaios' und 'Epithalamion.'" *Wiener Studien* 67: 5–45.

Nagy, G. [1977] 1990. "Phaethon, Sappho's Phaon, and the White Rocks of Leukas: 'Reading' the Symbols of Greek Lyric." In *Greek Mythology and Poetics,* 223–62. Ithaca, N.Y. [First published in *Harvard Studies in Classical Philology* 77: 137–77.]

———. 1979. *The Best of the Achaeans.* Baltimore.

———. 1985. "Theognis and Megara: A Poet's Vision of His City." In Figueira and Nagy 1985: 22–81.

———. 1990. *Pindar's Homer: The Lyric Possession of an Epic Past.* Baltimore.

———. 1996. *Poetry as Performance: Homer and Beyond.* Cambridge.

Nauck, A. 1964. *Tragicorum graecorum fragmenta: Euripidea et adespota.* 2d ed., revised by B. Snell. Hildesheim.

Neri, C. 1994. "Erinna in Eronda." *Eikasmos* 5: 221–32.

———. 1996. *Studi sulle testimonianze di Erinna.* Bologna.

———. 1997. "Erinna a Ossirinco." *Zeitschrift für Papyrologie und Epigraphik* 115: 57–72.

Neuburg, M. 1990. "How Like a Woman: Antigone's 'Inconsistency.'" *Classical Quarterly* 40: 54–76.

Nikolaidis, A. 1997. "Plutarch on Women and Marriage." *Wiener Studien* 110: 27–88.

Nilsson, M. 1906. *Griechische Feste von religiöser Bedeutung mit Ausschluss der Attischen.* Leipzig.

Nixon, L. 1995. "The Cults of Demeter and Kore." In Hawley and Levick 1995: 75–96.

North, H. 1966. *Sophrosyne: Self-Knowledge and Self-Restraint in Greek Literature.* Ithaca, N.Y.

Nussbaum, M. C. 1986. *The Fragility of Goodness.* Cambridge.

Oakley, J. H., and R. H. Sinos. 1993. *The Wedding in Ancient Athens.* Madison, Wis.

Ober, J. 1989. *Mass and Elite in Democratic Athens: Rhetoric, Ideology, and the Power of the People.* Princeton.

Olender, M. 1990. "Aspects of Baubo: Ancient Texts and Contexts." In Halperin, Winkler, and Zeitlin 1990: 83–113.

Olson, S. D. 1989. "The Stories of Helen and Menelaus (*Odyssey* 4.240–89) and the Return of Odysseus." *American Journal of Philology* 110: 387–94.

Onians, J. 1979. *Art and Thought in the Hellenistic Age.* London.

O'Rahilly, C. 1970. *Táin Bó Cúalnge: From the Book of Leinster.* Dublin.

Orlandini, P. 1967. "Lo Scavo del Thesmophorion di Bitalemi e il culto delle divinità Ctonie a Gela." *Kokalos* 12: 8–35.

Osborne, R. 1985. *Demos: The Discovery of Classical Attika.* Cambridge.

———. 1993. "Women and Sacrifice in Classical Greece." *Classical Quarterly* 43, 2: 392–405.

———. 1994. "Looking on—Greek Style: Does the Sculpted Girl Speak to Women Too?" In *Classical Greece: Ancient Histories and Modern Archaeologies,* edited by I. Morris, 81–96. Cambridge, Mass.

Oudemans, T. C. W., and A. P. M. H. Lardinois. 1987. *Tragic Ambiguity: Anthropology, Philosophy, and Sophocles' Antigone.* Leiden.

Overbeck, J. 1868. *Die antiken Schriftquellen zur Geschichte der bildenden Künste bei den Griechen.* Leipzig.

Padel, R. 1983. "Women: Model for Possession by Greek Daemons." In *Images of Women in Antiquity,* edited by A. Cameron and A. Kuhrt, 3–19. London.

———. 1992. *In and Out of Mind: Greek Images of the Tragic Self.* Princeton.

Padgug, R. A. 1972. "Eleusis and the Union of Attica." *Greek, Roman and Byzantine Studies* 13: 135–50.

Page, D. L. 1941. *Select Papyri.* London.

———. 1955. *Sappho and Alcaeus: An Introduction to the Study of Ancient Lesbian Poetry.* Oxford.

———. 1962a. *Poetae Melici Graeci.* Oxford.

———. 1962b. *Select Papyri III: Literary Papyri, Poetry.* Cambridge, Mass.

———. 1975. *Epigrammata Graeca.* Oxford.

———. 1981. *Further Greek Epigrams.* Cambridge.

Pantel, P., ed. 1992. *A History of Women in the West.* Vol. 1, *From Ancient Goddesses to Christian Saints.* Cambridge, Mass.

Papadopoulou-Belmehdi, I. 1994. *Le chant de Pénélope: Poétique du tissage féminin dans l'Odyssée.* Paris.

Papataxiarchis, E. 1991. "Friends of the Heart: Male Commensal Solidarity, Gender and Kinship in Aegean Greece." In Loizos and Papataxiarchis 1991: 156–79.

Parke, H. W. 1977. *Festivals of the Athenians.* Ithaca, N.Y.

Parke, H. W., and D. E. W. Wormell. 1956. *The Delphic Oracle.* 2 vols. Oxford.

Parker, A., and E. K. Sedgwick, eds. 1995. *Performance and Performativity.* New York.

Parker, H. 1993. "Sappho Schoolmistress." *Transactions of the American Philological Association* 123: 309–51.

Parker, R. C. T. 1983. *Miasma.* Oxford.

———. 1987. "Festivals of the Attic Demes." In *Gifts to the Gods: Proceedings of the Uppsala Symposium 1985. Boreas* vol. 15, edited by T. Linders and G. Nordquist, 137–47. Uppsala.

———. 1996a. *Athenian Religion: A History.* Oxford.

———. 1996b. "Keres." In *The Oxford Classical Dictionary,* edited by S. Hornblower and A. Spawforth, 3d ed., 806. Oxford.

Parks, W. 1990. *Verbal Dueling in Heroic Narrative.* Princeton.

Patterson, C. B. 1998. *The Family in Greek History.* Cambridge, Mass.

Pelling, C. R., ed. 1990. *Characterization and Individuality in Greek Literature.* Oxford.

Pellizer, E. 1990. "Outlines of a Morphology of Sympotic Entertainment." In Murray 1990: 177–84.

Peponi, A.-E. Forthcoming. *Mousikōs Erōn: On Lyric Pleasure.*

Peredolskaya, A. A. 1964. *Attische Tonfiguren aus einem südrussischen Grab.* Antike Kunst Beiheft 2. Basel.

Perry, B. E. 1952. *Aesopica.* Vol. 1. Urbana, Ill.

Peschel, I. 1987. *Die Hetäre bei Symposion und Komos in der attisch-rotfigurigen Vasenmalerei des 6.–4. Jahrh. v. Chr.* Frankfurt am Main.

Petersen, L. H. 1997. "Divided Consciousness and Female Companionship: Reconstructing Female Subjectivity on Greek Vases." *Arethusa* 30: 35–74.

Philips, S., S. Steele, and C. Tanz, eds. 1987. *Language, Gender and Sex in Comparative Perspective.* Cambridge.

Pickard-Cambridge, A. W. 1962. *Dithyramb, Tragedy and Comedy.* 2d ed., revised by T.B.L. Webster. Oxford.

———. 1986. *Art in the Hellenistic Age.* Cambridge.

———. 1988. *The Dramatic Festivals of Athens.* 2d ed., revised by J. Gould and D. M. Lewis. Oxford.

Pircher, J. 1979. *Das Lob der Frau im vorchristlichen Grabepigramm der Griechen.* Innsbruck.

Pleket, H. W. 1969. "The Archaic Tyrannis." *Talanta* 1: 19–61.

Podlecki, A. 1990. "Could Women Attend the Theater in Ancient Athens?" *The Ancient World* 21: 27–43.

Pollitt, J. J. 1974. *The Ancient View of Greek Art: Criticism, History, and Terminology.* Yale Publications in the History of Art 26. New Haven.

———. 1986. *Art in the Hellenistic Age.* Cambridge.

———. 1990. *The Art of Ancient Greece: Sources and Documents.* Cambridge, Mass.

Pomeroy, S. B. 1973. "Selected Bibliography on Women in Antiquity." *Arethusa* 6: 125–57.

———. 1977. "*Technikai kai Mousikai:* The Education of Women in the Fourth Century and in the Hellenistic Period." *American Journal of Ancient History* 2: 51–68.

———. 1978. "Supplementary Notes on Erinna." *Zeitschrift für Papyrologie und Epigraphik* 32: 17–21.

———. 1981. "Women in Roman Egypt." In Foley 1981a: 303–22.

———, ed. 1991. *Women's History and Ancient History.* Chapel Hill.

———. 1994. *Xenophon, Oeconomicus: A Social and Historical Commentary.* Oxford.

Potter, C. [1949] 1984. "Riddles." In *Funk and Wagnalls Standard Dictionary of Folklore, Mythology, and Legend,* edited by M. Leach and J. Fried, 938–44. New York. [First published in two volumes, New York.]

Price, S. 1985. "Delphi and Divination." In *Greek Religion and Society,* edited by P. Easterling and J. V. Muir, 128–54. Cambridge.

Prytz-Johansen, J. 1975. "The Thesmophoria as a Women's Festival." *Temenos* 11: 78–87.

Pucci, P. [1979] 1998. "The Song of the Sirens." In *The Song of the Sirens: Essays on Homer,* 1–9. Lanham, Md. [First published in *Arethusa* 12: 121–32.]

———. 1987. *Odysseus Polutropos: Intertextual Readings in the* Odyssey *and the* Iliad. Ithaca, N.Y.

Rabe, H. 1906. *Scholia in Lucianium.* Leipzig.

Rabinowitz, N., and A. Richlin, eds. 1993. *Feminist Theory and the Classics.* New York.

Radt, S. 1985. *Tragicorum Graecorum fragmenta.* Vol 3: *Aeschylus.* Göttingen.

Raheja, G. 1996. "The Limits of Patriarchy: Kinship, Gender and Women's Speech

Practices in Rural North India." In *Gender, Kinship, Power; A Comparative and Interdisciplinary Approach*, edited by M. J. Maynes, A. Waltner, B. Soland, and U. Strasser, 149–74. New York.

Raubitschek, A. 1950. "Phryne." In *Paulys Real-Encyclopädie der classischen Altertumswissenschaft*, Vol. 20, edited by K. Ziegler, 893–907. Stuttgart.

Rauk, J. 1989. "Erinna's *Distaff* and Sappho Fr. 94." *Greek, Roman and Byzantine Studies* 30: 101–16.

Rayor, D. 1991. *Sappho's Lyre: Archaic Lyric and Women Poets of Ancient Greece*. Berkeley.

———. 1993. "Korinna: Gender and the Narrative Tradition." *Arethusa* 26: 219–31.

Redfield, J. [1975] 1991. *Nature and Culture in the* Iliad: *The Tragedy of Hector*. Expanded edition. Chicago.

———. 1982. "Notes on the Greek Wedding." *Arethusa* 15: 181–201.

Reeder, E. D., ed. 1995. *Pandora: Women in Classical Greece*. Princeton.

Rehm, R. 1994. *Marriage to Death: The Conflation of Wedding and Funeral Rituals in Greek Tragedy*. Princeton.

Reinach, S. 1912. "Le Rire rituel." In *Cultes, Mythes et Religions*, Tome 4, 109–29. Paris.

Reiner, E. 1938. *Die rituelle Totenklage der Griechen*. Stuttgart.

Reinhardt, K. [1947] 1979. *Sophocles*. Translated by H. and D. Harvey. Oxford.

Reiter, R., ed. 1975a. *Toward an Anthropology of Women*. London.

———. 1975b. "Men and Women in the South of France: Public and Private Domains." In Reiter 1975a: 251–83.

Reynolds, D. 1995. *Heroic Poets, Poetic Heroes: The Ethnography of Performance in an Arabic Oral Epic Tradition*. Ithaca, N.Y.

Richardson, N. J. 1974. *The Homeric Hymn to Demeter*. Oxford.

———. 1993. *The Iliad: A Commentary*. Vol. 6. Oxford.

Richlin, A., ed. 1992. *Pornography and Representation in Ancient Greece and Rome*. Oxford.

———. 1993. "The Ethnographer's Dilemma and the Dream of a Lost Golden Age." In Rabinowitz and Richlin 1993: 272–303.

Rissman, L. 1983. *Love as War: Homeric Allusions in the Poetry of Sappho*. Beiträge zur klassischen Philologie 157. Königstein.

Robb, K. 1994. *Literacy and Paideia in Ancient Greece* Oxford.

Robbins, E. 1990. "Who's Dying in Sappho fr. 94?" *Phoenix* 44: 111–21.

Rogers, B., ed. 1907. *The Comedies of Aristophanes*. Vol. 6: *The Plutus*. London.

Roscher, W. H. 1913. *Omphalos*. Leipzig.

Rosen, R. M. 1988. "A Poetic Initiation Scene in Hipponax?" *American Journal of Philology* 109: 174–79.

———. 1992. "Mixing of Genres and Literary Program in *Herodas* 8." *Harvard Studies in Classical Philology* 94: 205–16.

———. 1997. "The Gendered Polis in Eupolis' *Cities*." In *The City as Comedy: Society and Representation in Athenian Drama*, edited by G. Dobrov, 149–76. Chapel Hill.

Rosenmeyer, P. 1991. "Simonides' Danaë Fragment Reconsidered." *Arethusa* 24: 5–29.

Rosivach, V. J. 1998. *When a Young Man Falls in Love: The Sexual Exploitation of Women in New Comedy* London.

Rösler, W. 1975. "Ein Gedicht und sein Publikum: Überlegungen zu Sappho Fr. 44 Lobel-Page." *Hermes* 103: 275–85.

Roth, P. A. 1982. "Mantis: The Nature, Function and Status of a Greek Prophetic Type." Diss., Bryn Mawr College.

Rouveret, A. 1989. *Histoire et imaginaire de la peinture ancienne.* Rome.

Roux, G. 1976. *Delphes: Son oracle et ses dieux.* Paris.

Rowlandson, J., ed. 1998. *Women and Society in Greek and Roman Egypt.* Cambridge.

Saake, H. 1971. *Zur Kunst Sapphos: Motiv-analytische und kompositionstechnische Interpretationen.* Munich.

——. 1972. *Sapphostudien: Forschungsgeschichtliche, biographische und literarästhetische Untersuchungen.* Munich.

Saïd, S. 1987. "Travestis et travestissements dans les comedies d'Aristophane." In *Anthropologie et theatre antique. Actes du colloque international Montpellier 6–8 Mars 1986*, Cahiers du GITA 3, edited by P. Ghiron-Bistagne, 217–46. Montpellier.

Salamone, S. D., and J. B. Stanton. 1986. "Introducing the *Nikokyra:* Ideality and Reality in Social Process." In Dubisch 1986: 97–120.

Salomon, N. 1997. "Making a World of Difference." In Koloski-Ostrow and Lyons 1997: 197–219.

Sandbach, F. H. 1990. *Menandri reliquiae selectae.* Rev. ed. Oxford.

Schadewaldt, W. 1950. *Sappho: Welt und Dichtung. Dasein in der Liebe.* Potsdam.

Schaps, D. 1977. "The Woman Least Mentioned: Etiquette and Women's Names." *Classical Quarterly* 27: 323–30.

Scheid, J., and J. Svenbro. [1994] 1996. *Myths of Weaving and Fabric.* Translated from the French by C. Volk. Cambridge, Mass.

Scheidel, W. 1995. "The Most Silent Women of Greece and Rome: Rural Labour and Women's Life in the Ancient World (I)." *Greece and Rome* 42: 202–17.

——. 1996. *Measuring Sex, Age and Death in the Roman Empire. Journal of Roman Studies* suppl. ser. 21. Ann Arbor.

Scheidweiler, F. 1956. "Erinnas Klage um Baukis." *Philologus* 100: 40–51.

Schmitt-Pantel, P. 1977. "Athéna Apatouria et la ceinture: Les aspects féminins des Apatouries à Athènes." *Annales ESC* 32: 1059–73.

Scholz, U. W. 1973. "Erinna." *Antike und Abendland* 18: 15–40.

Schwartz, J. 1962. "En marge du dossier d'Apollonios le stratège." *Cronique d'Égypte* 37: 348–58.

Schwyzer, E., and A. Debrunner. 1950. *Griechische Grammatik.* Vol. 2. Munich.

Scott, J. C. 1990. *Domination and the Arts of Resistance: Hidden Transcripts.* New Haven.

Scullion, S. 1998. "Three Notes on Attic Sacrificial Calendars." *Zeitschrift für Papyrologie und Epigraphik* 121: 116–22.

Seaford, R. 1987. "The Tragic Wedding." *Journal of Hellenic Studies* 107: 106–30.

——. 1990. "The Imprisonment of Women in Greek Tragedy." *Journal of Hellenic Studies* 110: 76–90.

——. 1994. *Reciprocity and Ritual: Homer and Tragedy in the Developing City-State.* Oxford.

Searle, J. R. 1995. *The Construction of Social Reality.* New York.

Segal, C. 1993. *Euripides and the Poetics of Sorrow.* Durham, N.C.

——. 1998. "Beauty, Desire, and Absence: Helen in Sappho, Alcaeus, and Ibycus." In *Aglaia: The Poetry of Alcman, Sappho, Pindar, Bacchylides and Corinna*, 63–03. Lanham, Md.

Seidensticker, B. 1982. *Palintonos Harmonia: Studien zu komischen Elementen in der griechischen Tragödie.* Göttingen.

———. 1995. "Women on the Tragic Stage." In *History, Tragedy, Theory: Dialogues on Athenian Drama*, edited by B. Goff, 151–73. Austin.

Sellew, P. Forthcoming. "Delphi A: Temenos of Apollo and Its Oracle." In *Archaeological Resources for New Testament Study*, vol. 3, edited by H. Koester. Philadelphia.

Seremetakis, C. N. 1991. *The Last Word: Women, Death, and Divination in Inner Mani.* Chicago.

Servais, J. 1981. "La date des Adonies d'Athènes et l'Expedition de Sicile (à propos d'Aristophane, *Lysistrate* 387–98)." In *L'Adonis: Aspetti orientali di un mito greco*, edited by S. Ribichini, 83–93. Rome.

Sfyroeras, P. 1995. "What Wealth Has to Do with Dionysus: From Economy to Poetics in Aristophanes' *Plutus.*" *Greek, Roman and Byzantine Studies* 36: 231–61.

Sharrock, A. 1991. "Womanufacture." *Journal of Roman Studies* 81: 36–49.

Sherzer, J. 1987. "A Diversity of Voices: Men's and Women's Speech in Ethnographic Perspective." In Philips, Steele, and Tanz 1987: 95–120.

Simms, R. 1998. "Mourning and Community at the Athenian Adonia." *Classical Journal* 93: 121–41.

Simon, E. 1983. *Festivals of Attica: An Archaeological Commentary.* London.

Sissa, G. [1987] 1990. *Greek Virginity.* Translated from the French by A. Goldhammer. Cambridge, Mass.

Skinner, M. B. 1982. "Briseis, the Trojan Women, and Erinna." *Classical World* 75: 265–69.

———. 1987. "Greek Women and the Metronymic: A Note on an Epigram by Nossis." *Ancient History Bulletin* 19: 39–42.

———. 1989. "Sapphic Nossis." *Arethusa* 22: 5–18.

———. 1991a. "Aphrodite Garlanded: *Erōs* and Poetic Creativity in Sappho and Nossis." In Martino 1991b: 77–96.

———. 1991b. "Nossis Thēlyglōssos: The Private Text and the Public Book." In Pomeroy 1991: 20–47.

———. 1993. "Woman and Language in Archaic Greece, or, Why Is Sappho a Woman?" In Rabinowitz and Richlin 1993: 125–44.

Skutsch, O. 1987. "Helen, Her Name and Nature." *Journal of Hellenic Studies* 107: 188–93.

Slater, W. 1990. "Sympotic Ethics in the *Odyssey.*" In Murray 1990: 213–20.

Slings, S. R. 1994. "Sappho, fr. 94, 10." *Zeitschrift für Papyrologie und Epigraphik* 102: 8.

Snell, B. [1931] 1966. "Sapphos Gedicht φαίνεταί μοι κῆνος." In *Gesammelte Schriften*, 82–97. Göttingen. [First published in *Hermes* 66: 71–90.]

Snell, B., and H. Maehler, eds. 1987. *Pindari carmina cum fragmentis.* Vol. 1: *Epinicia.* 8th ed. Leipzig.

Snell, B., and H.-J. Mette, eds. 1955. *Lexikon des frühgriechischen Epos.* Göttingen.

Snodgrass, A. 1980. *Archaic Greece: The Age of Experiment.* Berkeley.

Snyder, J. M. 1981. "The Web of Song: Weaving Imagery in Homer and the Lyric Poets." *Classical Journal* 76: 193–96.

————. 1989. *The Woman and the Lyre: Women Writers in Classical Greece and Rome.* Carbondale, Ill.

————. 1991. "Public Occasion and Private Passion in the Lyrics of Sappho of Lesbos." In Pomeroy 1991: 1–19.

————. 1997a. *Lesbian Desire in the Lyrics of Sappho.* New York.

————. 1997b. "Sappho in Attic Vase Painting." In Koloski-Ostrow and Lyons 1997: 108–19.

Sokolowski, F. 1962. *Lois sacrées des cités grecques: Supplément.* Paris.

Solodow, J. B. 1988. *The World of Ovid's Metamorphoses.* Chapel Hill.

Sommerstein, A. H. 1995. "The Language of Athenian Women." In Martino and Sommerstein 1995, part 2: 61–85.

Sourvinou-Inwood, C. 1995. *"Reading" Greek Death to the End of the Classical Period.* Oxford.

Spariosu, M. I. 1991. *God of Many Faces: Play, Poetry and Power in Hellenic Thought from Homer to Aristotle.* Durham, N.C.

Stanford, W. B. 1939. *Ambiguity in Greek Literature.* Oxford.

Stanley, K. 1976. "The Rôle of Aphrodite in Sappho fr. 1." *Greek, Roman and Byzantine Studies* 17: 305–21.

Stears, K. 1998. "Death Becomes Her: Gender and Athenian Death Ritual." In Blundell and Williamson 1998: 113–27.

Stehle, E. [1990] 1996. "Sappho's Gaze: Fantasies of a Goddess and Young Man." In Greene 1996a: 193–225. [First published in *differences* 2: 88–125.]

————. 1997. *Performance and Gender in Ancient Greece: Nondramatic Poetry in Its Setting.* Princeton.

Stehle, E., and A. Day. 1996. "Women Looking at Women: Women's Ritual and Temple Sculpture." In Kampen 1996: 101–16.

Steiner, G. 1984. *Antigones.* Oxford.

Stephens, S. 1981. "Aristophanes, *Poiēsis.*" In *Papyri, Greek and Egyptian*, edited by various hands (in honor of E. G. Turner), 23–25. London.

Stern, J. 1979. "Herodas' *Mimiamb* 6." *Greek, Roman and Byzantine Studies* 20: 247–54.

Stewart, A. 1996. "Reflections." In Kampen 1996: 136–54.

————. 1997. *Art, Desire, and the Body in Ancient Greece.* Cambridge, Mass.

Stieber, M. 1994. "Aeschylus' *Theoroi* and Realism in Greek Art." *Transactions of the American Philological Association* 124: 85–119.

Stigers [Stehle], E. 1981. "Sappho's Private World." In Foley 1981a: 45–61.

Straten, F. T. van. 1995. *Hiera kala: Images of Animal Sacrifice in Archaic and Classical Greece.* Leiden.

Stroud, R. 1968. "The Sanctuary of Demeter and Kore on Acrocorinth: Preliminary Report II; 1964–1965." *Hesperia* 37: 299–333.

Sultan, N. 1993. "Private Speech, Public Pain: The Power of Women's Laments in Ancient Greek Poetry and Tragedy." In *Rediscovering the Muses*, edited by K. Marshall, 92–110. Boston.

Suter, A. 1987. "Aphrodite/Paris/Helen: A Vedic Myth in the *Iliad.*" *Transactions of the American Philological Association* 117: 51–58.

————. 1993. "Paris and Dionysos: *Iambos* in the *Iliad.*" *Arethusa* 26: 1–18.

Sutton, D. F. 1980. *The Greek Satyr Play.* Meisenheim am Glan.

Sutton, R. F. 1992. "Pornography and Persuasion on Attic Pottery." In Richlin 1992: 3–35.

Suzuki, M. 1989. *Metamorphoses of Helen*. Ithaca, N.Y.

Svenbro, J. 1988. *Phrasikleia: Anthropologie de la lecture en Grèce ancienne*. [An English translation was published by Cornell University Press in 1993.]

Taaffe, L. 1993. *Aristophanes and Women*. London.

Tandy, D. W. 1997. *Warriors into Traders: The Powers of the Market in Early Greece*. Berkeley.

Tannen, D. 1986. *That's Not What I Meant! How Conversational Style Makes or Breaks Your Relations with Others*. New York.

———. 1996. *Gender and Discourse*. Oxford.

Taplin, O. 1993. *Comic Angels and Other Approaches to Greek Drama through Vase-Paintings*. Oxford.

Thierfelder, A. 1968. *Philogelos der Lachfreund*. Munich.

Tigerstedt, E. N. 1970. "*Furor Poeticus*: Poetic Inspiration in Greek Literature before Democritus and Plato." *Journal of the History of Ideas* 31.2: 163–78.

Todd, S. C. 1997. "Status and Gender in Athenian Public Records." In *Symposion 1995: Vorträge zur griechischen und hellenistischen Rechtsgeschichte*, edited by G. Thür and J. Vélissaropoulos-Karakostas, 113–24. Cologne.

Todorov, T. [1975] 1990. "The Origin of Genres." In *Genres of Discourse*, translated from the French by C. Porter, 13–26. Cambridge, Mass.

———. 1978. *Les genres du discours*. Paris.

Too, Y. L. 1996. "Statues, Mirrors, Gods: Controlling Images in Apuleius." In Elsner 1996a: 133–52.

Tsouderou, Y. E. 1976. *Kritika Mirologhia*. Athens.

Turyn, A. 1929. *Studia Sapphica*. *Eos* suppl. 6. Paris.

Usher, S. 1965. "Individual Characterization in Lysias." *Eranos* 63: 99–119.

———. 1976. "Lysias and His Clients." *Greek, Roman and Byzantine Studies* 17: 31–40.

Vermeule, E. 1974. *Götterkult*. Göttingen.

———. 1979. *Aspects of Death in Early Greek Art and Poetry*. Berkeley.

Vernant, J.-P. [1965] 1983. "Hestia-Hermes: The Religious Expression of Space and Movement in Ancient Greece." In *Myth and Thought among the Greeks*, 127–75. [First published in French in *L'Homme* 3:12–50.]

———. [1974] 1991. "Speech and Mute Signs." Translated from the French by F. I. Zeitlin. In Vernant 1991: 303–17.

———. [1977] 1981. "Sacrifical and Alimentary Codes in Hesiod's Myth of Prometheus." In *Myth, Religion, and Society*, edited and translated from the French by R. Gordon, 57–79. Cambridge. [First published in *Annali della Schola Normale di Pisa* 7: 905–40.]

———. [1985] 1991a. "Death in the Eyes: Gorgo, Figure of the Other." Translated from the French by F. I. Zeitlin. In Vernant 1991: 111–38. [First published in *La Mort dans les yeux: Figures de l'Autre en Grèce ancienne*, 31–89 (Paris).]

———. [1985] 1991b. "Feminine Figures of Death in Greece." In Vernant 1991: 95–110. Translated from the French by A. Doueihi, revised and corrected by F. I. Zeitlin. [The first, short version of this text was published in *Lettre internationale* 6: 45–48.]

————. 1991. *Mortals and Immortals: Collected Essays.* Edited by F. I. Zeitlin. Princeton.

Versnel, H. S. 1987. "Wife and Helpmate: Women of Ancient Athens in Anthropological Perspective." In Blok and Mason 1987: 59–88.

————. 1990. *Inconsistencies in Greek and Roman Religion.* Vol. 1: *Ter Unus: Isis, Dionysos, Hermes. Three Studies in Henotheism.* Leiden.

————. [1992] 1993. "The Roman Festival for Bona Dea and the Greek Thesmophoria." In *Inconsistencies in Greek and Roman Religion.* Vol. 2: *Transition and Reversal in Myth and Ritual,* 228–88. Leiden. [An earlier version was published in *Greece and Rome* 39: 31–55.]

————. 1998. "An Essay on Anatomical Curses." In *Ansichten griechischer Rituale. Geburtstags-Symposium für Walter Burkert, 15–18. März 1996,* edited by F. Graf, 217–67. Stuttgart.

Vial, C. 1985. "La femme Athénienne vue par les orateurs." In *La femme dans le monde Méditerranéen,* vol. 1: *Antiquité,* edited by A.-M. Vérilhac, 47–60. Lyon.

Voigt. E.-M. 1971. *Sappho et Alcaeus.* Amsterdam.

Waern, I. 1960. "Greek Lullabyes." *Eranos* 58: 1–8.

Walcot, P. 1994. "Separatism and the Alleged Conversation of Women." *Classica et mediaevalia* 45: 27–50.

————. 1996. "Continuity and Tradition: The Persistence of Greek Values." *Greece and Rome* 43: 169–77.

Walker, A. D. 1993. "*Enargeia* and the Spectator in Greek Historiography." *Transactions of the American Philological Association* 123: 353–77.

Walters, K. R. 1993. "Women and Power in Classical Athens." In *Woman's Power, Man's Game: Essays on Classical Antiquity in Honor of Joy K. King,* edited by M. DeForrest, 194–214. Chicago.

Watkins, C., ed. 1985. *The American Heritage Dictionary of Indo-European Roots.* Boston.

Webster, T. B. L. 1972. *Potter and Patron in Classical Athens.* London.

————. [1978] 1995. *Monuments Illustrating New Comedy.* 3d ed., revised by J. R. Green and A. Seeburg. London.

Wehrli, F. 1969. *Die Schule des Aristoteles.* Vol. 3: *Klearchos.* Basel.

Welcker, F. G. 1826. *Theognidis reliquiae.* Frankfurt am Main.

————. [1857] 1861. "Über die beiden Oden der Sappho." Reprinted in *Kleine Schriften,* vol. 4, 68–99. Bonn. [First published in *Rheinisches Museum für Philologie* 11: 226–59.]

Wendel, C. 1914. *Scholia in Theocritum vetera.* Leipzig.

West, C., and D. Zimmerman. 1983. "Small Insults: A Study of Interruptions in Cross-Sex Conversations between Unacquainted Persons." In Henley, Kramarae, and Thorne 1983: 102–17.

West, M. L. 1966. *Hesiod, Theogony.* Oxford.

————. 1970. "Burning Sappho." *Maia* 22: 307–30.

————. 1974. *Studies in Greek Elegy and Iambus.* Berlin.

————. 1977. "Erinna." *Zeitschrift für Papyrologie und Epigraphik* 25: 95–119.

————. 1989–92. *Iambi et elegi Graeci ante Alexandrum cantati.* 2 vols. 2d ed. Oxford.

————. 1992. *Ancient Greek Music.* Oxford.

Whitehorne, J. 1994. "Religious Expressions in the Correspondence of the Strategus Apollonius." *Analecta papyrologica* 6: 21–36.

——. 1995. "Women's Work in Theocritus, Idyll 15." *Hermes* 123: 63–75.

Whitman, C. H. 1951. *Sophocles*. Cambridge, Mass.

Wickert-Micknat, G. 1982. *Die Frau*. Archeologica Homerica 3. Göttingen.

Wilamowitz-Moellendorff, U. von. 1913. *Sappho und Simonides: Untersuchungen über griechische Lyriker*. Berlin.

——. 1916. *Die Ilias und Homer*. Berlin.

Williamson, M. 1995. *Sappho's Immortal Daughters*. Cambridge, Mass.

——. [1995] 1996. "Sappho and the Other Woman." In Greene 1996a: 248–64. [First published in Mills 1995: 76–94.]

Wilson, L. H. 1996. *Sappho's Sweetbitter Songs: Configurations of Female and Male in Ancient Greek Lyric*. London.

Wilson, N. J. 1999. *History in Crisis? Recent Directions in Historiography*. Cambridge.

Wilson, P. 1999. "The *aulos* in Athens." In Goldhill and Osborne 1999: 58–95.

Winkler, J. J. [1981] 1996. "Gardens of Nymphs: Public and Private in Sappho's Lyrics." In Greene 1996a: 89–109. [First published in Foley 1981a: 63–90.]

——. 1990a. *The Constraints of Desire: The Anthropology of Sex and Gender*. London.

——. 1990b. "The Laughter of the Oppressed: Demeter and the Gardens of Adonis." In Winkler 1990a: 188–209.

——. 1990c. "The Ephebes' Song." In Winkler and Zeitlin 1990: 20–62.

Winkler, J. J., and Zeitlin, F. I., eds. 1990. *Nothing to Do with Dionysos?* Princeton.

Wohl, V. J. 1993. "Standing by the Stathmos: The Creation of Sexual Ideology in the *Odyssey*." *Arethusa* 26: 19–50.

——. 1998. *Intimate Commerce*. Austin, Tex.

Woodhead, A. G., ed. 1971. *Supplementum epigraphicum Graecum* 25.

Worman, N. 1997. "The Body as Argument: Helen in Four Greek Texts." *Classical Antiquity* 16: 151–203.

Yatromanolakis, D. 1998. "Simonides Fr. Eleg. 22W^2: To Sing or to Mourn?" *Zeitschrift für Philologie und Epigraphik* 120: 1–11.

Young, D. 1971. *Theognis*. Leipzig.

Zagagi, N. 1995. *The Comedy of Menander*. Bloomington, Ind.

Zaidman, L. B., and P. Schmitt-Pantel. [1989] 1992. *Religion in the Ancient Greek City*. Translated from the French by P. Cartledge. Cambridge.

Zanker, G. 1981. "*Enargeia* in the Ancient Criticism of Poetry." *Rheinisches Museum für Philologie* 124: 297–311.

——. 1987. *Realism in Alexandrian Poetry*. London.

Zeitlin, F. I. [1978] 1996. "The Dynamics of Misogyny: Myth and Mythmaking in the *Oresteia*." In Zeitlin 1996: 87–119. [First published in *Arethusa* 11: 149–84.]

——. [1981] 1996. "Travesties of Gender and Genre in Aristophanes' *Thesmophoriazousae*." In Zeitlin 1996: 375–416. [First published in Foley 1981a: 169–217.]

——. 1982a. "Cultic Models of the Female: Rites of Dionysus and Demeter." *Arethusa* 15: 129–57.

——. 1982b. *Under the Sign of the Shield: Semiotics and Aeschylus' Seven against Thebes*. Rome.

——. [1985] 1996. "Playing the Other: Theater, Theatricality, and the Feminine in Greek Drama." In Zeitlin 1996: 341–74. [First published in *Representations* 11: 63–94.]

———. 1986. "Thebes: Theater of Self and Society in Athenian Drama." In *Greek Tragedy and Political Theory*, edited by J. P. Euben, 101–41. Berkeley.

———. 1994. "The Artful Eye: Vision, Ekphrasis and Spectacle in Euripidean Theatre." In Goldhill and Osborne 1994: 138–96.

———. 1995a. "The Economics of Hesiod's Pandora." In *Pandora: Women in Classical Greece*, edited by E. Reeder, 49–56. Princeton.

———. 1995b. Review of Rehm 1994. In *Bryn Mawr Classical Review* 1995–02–05.

———. 1996. *Playing the Other: Gender and Society in Classical Greek Literature.* Chicago.

Ziegler, H. 1891. *Cleomedis De motu circulari corporum caelestium libri duo.* Leipzig.

Zuntz, G. 1939. "De Sapphus carminibus e3, e4, e5." *Mnemosyne* ser. 3, 7: 81–114.

Zweig, B. 1992. "The Mute Nude Female Characters in Aristophanes' Plays." In Richlin 1992: 73–89.

———. 1999. "Euripides' *Helen* and Female Rites of Passage." In *Rites of Passage in Ancient Greece: Literature, Religion, Society*, edited by M. Padilla, 158–80. Cranbury, N.J.

Contributors

JOSINE H. BLOK is Associate Professor of Ancient History and Classical Culture at the University of Utrecht. She studied History at the University of Groningen and took her doctorate degree at the University of Leiden. She edited, with Peter Mason, *Sexual Asymmetry: Studies in Ancient Society* (Amsterdam, 1987) and published *The Early Amazons: Modern and Ancient Perspectives on a Persistent Myth* (Leiden, 1995), in addition to many articles. Her primary fields of interest are the social, cultural, and political history of ancient Greece and the history of classical scholarship.

RAFFAELLA CRIBIORE obtained a Ph.D. in Classics from Columbia University in 1993. Her dissertation on school texts from Hellenistic and Roman Egypt was published with the title *Writing, Teachers and Students in Graeco-Roman Egypt* (Atlanta, 1996). She is currently the associate curator of the papyrus collection in the Rare Book and Manuscript Library of Columbia University, where she teaches courses on education in antiquity. She has published extensively on ancient literacy and education and is currently working on a book on education in the Greek East for Princeton University Press.

MICHAEL GAGARIN is James R. Daughtery Jr. Centennial Professor of Classics at the University of Texas. His main areas of research are ancient Greek law and oratory. Among his publications are *Early Greek Law* (Berkeley, 1986) and an edition with commentary of the speeches of Antiphon (Cambridge, 1997). He is currently the general editor of a series of new translations of the Attic orators being published by the University of Texas Press.

MARK GRIFFITH is Professor of Classics and Theater Arts at the University of California at Berkeley. He has published commentaries on *Prometheus Bound* (1983) and *Antigone* (1999) in the Cambridge Greek and Latin Classics series, and a number of articles on Greek tragedy and culture.

ANDRÉ LARDINOIS is Assistant Professor of Classics at the University of Minnesota. His interests center on early Greek poetry, Greek religion, genre, and gender studies. He has co-authored a book, with T.C.W. Oudemans, entitled *Tragic Ambiguity: Anthropology, Philosophy, and Sophocles' Antigone* (Leiden, 1987), and has published several articles on Sappho, Greek epic, and tragedy.

RICHARD P. MARTIN is the Antony and Isabelle Raubitschek Professor of Classics at Stanford University. His interests are Greek poetry, especially Homer and lyric; Greek religion and myth; Old Irish literature; and comparative studies of oral-traditional performance. He is the author of *Healing, Sacrifice and Battle* (Innsbruck, 1983) and *The Language of Heroes: Speech and Performance in the Iliad* (Ithaca, N.Y., 1989), and of articles on Greek comedy, philosophy, and wisdom traditions. He is currently completing *The Last Hero Song: Telemakhos and the Generation of the Odyssey.*

LISA MAURIZIO is an Assistant Professor of Classics at Bates College. She has published articles on Delphi, the Pythia, and most recently the Panathenaia. She is currently working on the relationship between politics (men's public service) and religion (women's public service) in classical Athens.

LAURA McCLURE is Associate Professor of Classics at the University of Wisconsin at Madison. Her primary areas of research are Athenian drama and ancient gender studies. She is the author of *Spoken Like a Woman: Speech and Gender in Athenian Drama* (Princeton, 1999), as well as of articles on Greek tragedy, pedagogy, and the classical tradition.

D. M. O'HIGGINS trained at Trinity College, Dublin, and Cornell University, where she received her Ph.D. She has published articles on Greek epic, lyric, and tragedy and Latin epic. She is currently working on a book on women's cultic joking in ancient Greece. Laurie is an Associate Professor in the program of Classical and Medieval Studies at Bates College.

PATRICIA A. ROSENMEYER is Associate Professor of Classics at the University of Wisconsin at Madison. She received undergraduate degrees in Classics from Harvard University and King's College, Cambridge, and her Ph.D. in Comparative Literature and Classics from Princeton. She is author of *The Poetics of Imitation: Anacreon and the Anacreontic Tradition* (Cambridge, 1992) and *Epistolary Fictions: The Letter in Ancient Greek Literature* (forthcoming), as well as articles on Greek and Latin poetry.

MARILYN B. SKINNER is Professor of Classics at the University of Arizona. She is the author of *Catullus' Passer: The Arrangement of the Book of Polymetric Poems* (New York, 1981), and co-editor, with Judith Hallett, of *Roman Sexualities* (Princeton, 1998). In addition to research on Latin poetry, she has published numerous articles on Sappho and the Hellenistic women poets.

EVA STEHLE teaches classics at the University of Maryland at College Park. Her recent publications on women and gender in ancient Greece include *Performance and Gender in Ancient Greece: Nondramatic Poetry in Its Setting* (Princeton, 1997) and "Sappho's Gaze: Fantasies of a Goddess and Young Man," reprinted in *Reading Sappho: Contemporary Approaches,* edited by Ellen Greene (Berkeley, 1996). She is currently working on women's religious practice at Athens and its reflection in Attic drama.

NANCY WORMAN is an Assistant Professor of Classics at Barnard College, Columbia University. She has published articles on Greek poetry and rhetorical theory, and is currently working on a book-length project about notions of style and character type in Greek literature before Aristotle.